EUROPEAN SURVEY 1979/80

Fewest conceded	Most drawn	Average goals per game	Top scorer	Cup final result or winners	
Dinamo 23	Labinoti 12	2.33	Kovaci (Tomori) 18	Partizan	**Albania**
Linz ASK 34	Linz ASK 17	2.74	Schachner (Austria Vienna) 34	Austria Vienna v Austria Salzburg 0–1, 2–0	**Austria**
RWD Molenbeek, Lokeren 28	Berchem 13	2.83	Van den Bergh (Lierse) 39	Waterschei 2 Beveren 1	**Belgium**
Slavia 27	Chernomore 13	2.64	**	Slavia 3 Beroe 1	**Bulgaria**
				Omonia	**Cyprus**
Banik Ostrava, Inter Bratislava 23	Spartak Trnava, Sparta Prague, RH Cheb 10	2.58	Licka (Banik) 18	Sparta 2 ZTS Kosice 0	**Czechoslovakia**
Esbjerg, Kastrup 30	Kastrup, Skovbakken 11	2.98	Eriksen (Odense) 20	B 1903 1 Koge 0 (Div. 2)	**Denmark**
Liverpool 30	West Bromwich A 19	2.51	Boyer (Southampton) 23	West Ham U 1 Arsenal 0	**England**
OPS Oulu 15	OPS Oulu 10	2.89	Linnusmaki (Ilves) 13	Ilves 2 HJK 0	**Finland**
Nantes, Monaco 30	Valenciennes 12	2.82	Onnis (Monaco) Kostedde (Laval) 21	Monaco 3 US Orleans 1 (Div. 2)	**France**
Dynamo Berlin 16	Stahl Riesa 10	2.89	Kuhn (Lok. Leipzig) 20	Carl Zeiss Jena 3 Rot-Weiss Erfurt 1	**East Germany**
Bayern Munich 33	Moenchengladbach 12	3.34	Rummenigge (Bayern) 26	Fortuna Dusseldorf 2 Cologne 1	**West Germany**
Aris Salonika 20	Panathinaikos 15	2.31	Bajevic (AEK) 25	Kastoria 5 Iraklis 2	**Greece**
Honved 38	Debrecen 14	3.16	Fazekas (Ujpest) 36	Diosgyor 3 Vasas 1	**Hungary**
IBV Westmann 13	Fram 9	2.82	Thorleifsson (Vikingur) 10	Fram 1 Valur 0	**Iceland**
Cliftonville 16	Glentoran 7	3.02	Dickson (Coleraine) 19	Linfield 2 Crusaders 0	**N. Ireland**
Dundalk 13	Drogheda 16	2.78		1 s	**Rep. of Ireland**

** Details not available at the time of going to press.

THE GUINNESS BOOK OF
SOCCER
FACTS & FEATS

THE GUINNESS BOOK OF
SOCCER
FACTS & FEATS
3rd Edition

By Jack Rollin

GUINNESS SUPERLATIVES LIMITED
2 Cecil Court, London Road, Enfield, Middlesex

ACKNOWLEDGEMENTS
The author wishes to acknowledge the follow-
ing sources: Maurice Golesworthy, The Encyclo-
paedia of Association Football; C. R. Williamson;
Rothmans Football Yearbooks; FIFA News;
World Soccer; also the following assistance:
Lionel Francis and Margaret Millership.

First published in 1978
Second edition 1979
Third edition 1980

© **Jack Rollin and Guinness Superlatives
Ltd 1978, 1979, 1980**

Editorial: Beatrice Frei, Stan Greenberg
and David Roberts
Artwork: Eddie Botchway, Don Roberts,
Pat Gibbon, Mick Hooker and David Roberts
Design and layout: David Roberts
Picture research: Beverley Waites

Published in Great Britain by
Guinness Superlatives Ltd
2 Cecil Court London Road Enfield Middlesex

British Library Cataloguing in Publication Data
Rollin, Jack
    Guinness book of soccer facts and feats.
    3rd ed.—(Facts and feats).
    1. Soccer
    I. Title   II. Series
    796.33'4   GV943

    ISBN 0–85112–213–2

ISBN 0 85112 213 2

'Guinness' is a registered trade mark of
Guinness Superlatives Ltd

Colour separation by
Newsele Litho Ltd, London and Milan

Printed and bound in Great Britain by
Hazell Watson & Viney Ltd
Aylesbury, Bucks

Contents

Introduction

The third edition of the *Guinness Book of Soccer Facts and Feats* is a continuation of the ideas originally established in the first edition and carried on in the second book, to increase the content of completely new material, add to the hitherto different aspects of familiar subjects and further update the basic facts and figures as before.

One of the most popular features in the second edition was the A to Z section of all Football League and Scottish League clubs with one main story for each. This has again been included with entirely new entries for each of the 130 clubs.

Also the Miscellany of odd facts and feats has had similar treatment with many innovations from the past of long ago as well as that of just a few years' vintage.

Indeed another trend in this third edition is to prove that not all the most interesting stories have to be discovered in the earlier days of the game, and many of a more contemporary nature are included.

The North London rivalry of Tottenham Hotspur and Arsenal is featured, as is the Sheffield derby between United and Wednesday which in the 1979–80 season succeeded in producing a record attendance for a match in Division Three.

There is an emphasis on the European Championship which was played during the summer months in Italy, a more detailed look at the equivalent competition in the New World for the South American Championship and other leading tournaments around the world.

The two other features are Around the World stories and an appreciation of the role played by British footballers and managers in spreading their talents and abilities on foreign shores.

The pictorial section includes team photographs representing the eight finalists in the 1980 European Championship, badges of the various winners of the European Cup and photos recalling one of the most famous of all giant-killing FA Cup teams since the last war.

MILESTONES

1848 The first rules drawn up at Cambridge University.

1855* Sheffield, the oldest soccer club still in existence, founded.

1862 Notts County, the oldest Football League club, founded.

1863 Football Association formed in London on 26 October.

1865 Tape to be stretched across the goals 8 ft (2·4 m) from the ground.

1866 Offside rule altered to allow a player to be onside when three of opposing team are nearer their own goal-line.
Fair catch rule omitted.

1867 Queen's Park, the oldest Scottish club, founded.

1869 Kick-out rule altered and goal-kicks introduced.

1871 Start of the FA Cup. Goalkeepers first mentioned in laws.

1872 First official international, between Scotland and England at Glasgow.
The Wanderers win the FA Cup final.
Corner kick introduced.

1873 Scottish FA formed and the start of the Scottish Cup.

1874 Umpires first mentioned in laws.
Shinguards introduced.

1875 The cross-bar replaces tape on the goal-posts.

1876 FA of Wales formed.
The first international between Scotland and Wales.

1877 The London Association and the Sheffield Association agree to use the same rules.
A player may be charged by an opponent if he is facing his own goal.

1878 Referees use a whistle for the first time.

1879 First international between England and Wales.
Cliftonville, the oldest Irish club, founded.

1880 Irish FA formed and the start of the Irish Cup.

1882 Ireland's first internationals with Wales and England.
International Football Association Board set up.
Two-handed throw-in introduced.

1883 First international between Scotland and Ireland.
The first British International Championship.

1885 Professionalism legalised in England.
Arbroath beat Bon Accord 36–0 in Scottish Cup; still a record score for an official first-class match.

1886 International caps first awarded.

1888 Football League formed.

1889 Preston North End achieve the League and FA Cup 'double'.

1890 Irish League formed.
First hat-trick in the FA Cup Final, by Blackburn's William Townley.
Goal nets invented.
Scottish League formed.

1891 Referees and linesmen replace umpires.
Introduction of the penalty kick.

1892 Penalty taker must not play the ball twice.
Extra time allowed for taking a penalty.
Goal nets used in FA Cup Final for the first time.
Division Two of the Football League formed.

1893 Scotland adopts professionalism.

1894 First FA Amateur Cup final.
Division Two of Scottish League formed.
Referee given complete control of the game. Unnecessary for players in future to appeal to him for a decision.
Goalkeeper can only be charged when playing the ball or obstructing an opponent.

1895 FA Cup stolen from a Birmingham shop window. It was never recovered.
Goalposts and cross-bars must not exceed 5 in (127 mm) in width.
Player taking throw-in must stand on touch-line.

1897 Aston Villa win both the League and the FA Cup.
The Corinthians tour South America.
The word 'intentional' introduced into the law on handling.

1898 Players' Union first formed.

1899 Promotion and relegation first used in the Football League, replacing Test Matches.

---

* The date of Sheffield's foundation was given as 1855 in the Sheffield City Almanack (1902). And in the issue of the *Sheffield Telegraph* dated 29 September 1954 an article quoted H B Willey, a previous Secretary of the club, as follows: 'I used to have the Minute Book for 1855 but it was borrowed and never returned.'

1901   Tottenham Hotspur win the FA Cup while members of the Southern League.

1902   Terracing collapses during the Scotland–England match at Ibrox Park, killing 25.

1904   FIFA formed in Paris, on 21 May.

1905   First £1000 transfer. Alf Common moves from Sunderland to Middlesbrough.
First international in South America, between Argentina and Uruguay.
England joins FIFA.

1907   Amateur FA formed. Players' Union (now Professional Footballers' Association (PFA) re-formed.

1908   England play in Vienna, their first international against a foreign side.
The first Olympic soccer tournament in London, won by the United Kingdom.

1910   Scotland, Wales and Ireland join FIFA.

1912   Goalkeeper not permitted to handle ball outside his own penalty area.

1913   Defending players not to approach within ten yards of ball at a free-kick.

1914   Defending players not to approach within ten yards of ball at corner kick.

1916   The South American Championship first held.

1920   Division Three (Southern Section) of the Football League formed.
Players cannot be offside at a throw-in.

1921   Division Three (Northern Section) formed.

1922   Promotion and relegation introduced in the Scottish League.

1923   First FA Cup final at Wembley: Bolton beat West Ham before a record crowd.

1924   A goal may be scored direct from a corner kick.

1925   Offside law changed to require two instead of three defenders between attacker and goal.
Player taking throw-in must have both feet on touch-line.

1926   Huddersfield Town achieve the first hat-trick of League Championships.

1927   Cardiff City take the FA Cup out of England for the first time.
Mitropa Cup begins.
J C Clegg, President of the FA, knighted.

1928   British associations leave FIFA over broken-time payments to amateurs.
First £10 000 transfer: David Jack goes from Bolton to Arsenal.
Dixie Dean scores 60 goals for Everton in Division One, a Football League record.

1929   England lose 4–3 to Spain in Madrid, their first defeat on the continent.
Goalkeeper compelled to stand still on his goal-line at penalty-kick.

1930   Uruguay win the first World Cup, in Montevideo, Uruguay.
F J Wall, secretary of the FA, knighted.

1931   Goalkeeper permitted to carry ball four steps instead of two.
Instead of free-kick after a foul throw-in it reverts to opposing side.
Scotland lose 5–0 to Austria in Vienna, their first defeat on the continent.

1933   Numbers worn for the first time in the FA Cup Final.

1934   Italy win the second World Cup, in Rome, Italy.

1935   Arsenal equal Huddersfield's hat-trick of League Championships.
Arsenal centre-forward Ted Drake scores seven goals against Aston Villa at Villa Park, a Division One record.

1936   Defending players not permitted to tap the ball into goalkeeper's hands from a goal-kick.
Luton centre-forward Joe Payne scores ten goals against Bristol Rovers, a Football League record.
Dixie Dean overhauls Steve Bloomer's 352 goals in the Football League.

1937   A record crowd of 149,547 watch the Scotland v England match at Hampden Park.
Defending players not permitted to tap the ball into goalkeeper's hands from free-kick inside penalty area.
Weight of ball increased from 13–15 oz (368–425 g) to 14–16 oz (397–454 g).
Arc of circle 10 yd (9 m) radius from penalty spot to be drawn outside penalty area.

1938   Italy retain the World Cup, in Paris, France.
Laws of the game rewritten.
Scotland's Jimmy McGrory retires, having scored 550 goals in first-class football, a British record.

1946   British associations rejoin FIFA.
The Burnden Park tragedy: 33 killed and over 400 injured during an FA Cup tie between Bolton and Stoke.

1949   Aircraft carrying Italian champions Torino crashes at Superga near Turin, killing all on board.
England are beaten 2–0 by Republic of Ireland at Goodison Park, so losing their unbeaten home record against sides outside the home countries.
Rangers win the first 'treble' – Scottish League, Scottish Cup and League Cup.
S F Rous, secretary of the FA, knighted.

1950   Uruguay win the fourth World Cup, in Rio de Janeiro, Brazil.

England, entering for the first time, lose 1–0 to USA.

Scotland's unbeaten home record against foreign opposition ends in a 1–0 defeat by Austria at Hampden Park.

1951 Obstruction included as an offence punishable by indirect free-kick.

Studs must project $\frac{3}{4}$ in (19 mm) instead of $\frac{1}{2}$ in (13 mm).

1952 Billy Wright overhauls Bob Crompton's record of 42 caps.

Newcastle United retain the FA Cup, the first club to do so in the 20th century.

England lose their unbeaten home record against continental opposition, going down 6–3 to Hungary at Wembley.

1954 West Germany win the fifth World Cup in Berne, Switzerland.

England suffer their heaviest international defeat, beaten 7–1 by Hungary at Budapest.

The Union of European Football Associations (UEFA) formed.

Ball not to be changed during the game unless authorised by the referee.

1955 European Cup of the Champions and Inter-Cities Fairs Cup started.

1956 Real Madrid win the European Cup.

First floodlit match in the Football League: Portsmouth v Newcastle United on 22 February.

1957 George Young retires with a record 53 Scottish caps.

John Charles of Leeds United becomes the first British player to be transferred to a foreign club (Juventus, Italy).

1958 Manchester United lose eight players in the Munich air disaster on 6 February.

Brazil win the sixth World Cup, in Stockholm, Sweden.

Sunderland, continuously in Division One, relegated.

Football League re-organisation: Division Three and Division Four started.

1959 Billy Wright plays his 100th game for England, against Scotland, and retires at the end of the season with a world record 105 appearances.

1960 USSR win the first European Nations Cup, in Paris, France.

Real Madrid win the European Cup for the fifth consecutive time.

1961 Sir Stanley Rous becomes President of FIFA.

Tottenham Hotspur win the League and Cup, the first 'double' of the 20th century.

The Professional Football Association (PFA) succeed in achieving the abolition of the maximum wage.

Fiorentina win the first European Cup-Winners Cup.

1962 Brazil retain the seventh World Cup in Santiago, Chile.

Denis Law is transferred from Torino to Manchester United, the first transfer over £100 000 paid by a British club.

1963 The centenary of the FA. England beat the Rest of the World 2–1, at Wembley.

The Football League's 'retain and transfer' system declared illegal.

Tottenham Hotspur win the European Cup-Winners Cup, the first British success in Europe.

1964 Spain win the European Nations' Cup, in Madrid, Spain.

More than 300 killed and 500 injured in rioting during an Olympic qualifying game between Peru and Argentina at Lima, Peru.

Jimmy Dickinson (Portsmouth) becomes the first player to make 700 Football League appearances.

1965 Stanley Matthews becomes the first footballer to be knighted.

Arthur Rowley retires having scored a record 434 Football League goals.

The Football League agree to substitutes for one injured player.

1966 England win the eighth World Cup, at Wembley.

The Football League allow substitutes for any reason.

1967 Alf Ramsey, England's team manager, knighted.

Celtic become the first Scottish club to win the European Cup.

1968 Italy win the European Football Championship, in Rome, Italy.

A world record transfer: Pietro Anastasi moves from Varese to Juventus for £440,000. Manchester United win the European Cup: Matt Busby knighted.

Leeds United become the first British club to win the Fairs Cup.

1969 Leeds win the Football League Championship with a record 67 points.

1970 Brazil win the ninth World Cup, in Mexico City and win the Jules Rimet Trophy outright.

Bobby Charlton wins his 106th England cap in the quarter-finals to overhaul Billy Wright's record.

The first £200 000 transfer in Britain: Martin Peters moves from West Ham to Tottenham Hotspur.

1971 Britain's worst-ever crowd disaster: 66

killed at a match between Rangers and Celtic and Ibrox Park.

Arsenal achieve the League and Cup 'double'.

Barcelona win the Fairs Cup outright (to be replaced by the UEFA Cup) after beating the holders Leeds United 2–1.

1972   Tottenham Hotspur defeat Wolverhampton Wanderers in the first all-British European final, the UEFA Cup.

West Germany win the European Football Championship, in Brussels, Belgium.

1973   Ajax win the European Cup for the third consecutive time.

Bobby Moore makes his 108th appearance for England, a new record.

Johan Cruyff becomes the first £1 million transfer, moving from Ajax to Barcelona for £922 300.

1974   Joao Havelange of Brazil replaces Sir Stanley Rous as President of FIFA.

West Germany win the tenth World Cup in Munich, West Germany.

Denis Law makes his 55th appearance for Scotland, a new record.

1975   Leeds United banned from competing in Europe for any of two seasons in the next four, after their fans rioted at the European Cup final in Paris.

Terry Paine overhauls Jimmy Dickinson's record of 764 League games.

1976   Bayern Munich win the European Cup for the third consecutive time.

Czechoslovakia win the European Football Championship in Belgrade, Yugoslavia, beating West Germany.

Pat Jennings makes his 60th appearance for Northern Ireland, a new record.

The Football League abandon 'goal average', introducing 'goal difference'.

Liverpool win their ninth League title, overhauling Arsenal's record.

1977   Liverpool win their 10th League title as well as the European Cup.

Kevin Keegan transferred from Liverpool to SV Hamburg for £500 000, the highest fee involving a British club.

Kenny Dalglish transferred from Celtic to Liverpool for £440 000, a record fee between British clubs.

First World Youth Cup, held in Tunisia and won by USSR.

1978   Liverpool retain the European Cup.

Nottingham Forest the only Football League club not a limited company win their first Championship title. Forest also win the League Cup.

Ipswich Town become the 40th different team to win the FA Cup.

Kenny Dalglish makes his 56th appearance for Scotland to overhaul Denis Law's record.

Argentina win the eleventh World Cup in Buenos Aires, Argentina.

1979   David Mills transferred from Middlesbrough to West Bromwich Albion for £516 000, a record fee between British clubs.

Trevor Francis, transferred from Birmingham City to Nottingham Forest for £1 million, breaks the record for a single transfer involving British clubs.

Phil Parkes transferred from Queen's Park Rangers to West Ham United for £565 000 establishes a new record fee for a goalkeeper.

Manchester City pay £750,000 for Mick Robinson the Preston North End striker.

Laurie Cunningham, the West Bromwich Albion and England winger, signs for Real Madrid in a £900 000 move.

Liverpool win their eleventh League title.

Nottingham Forest become the third English club to win the European Cup.

Andy Gray, transferred from Aston Villa to Wolverhampton Wanderers, breaks the record for a single transfer involving British clubs at £1 469 000.

Steve Daley joins Manchester City from Wolves for £1 437 500.

Argentina win the Second World Youth Cup in Japan.

1980   Manchester City are involved in the fourth £1 million transfer in England when they sign Norwich City striker Kevin Reeves.

Liverpool retain the championship for their 12th League honour.

Nottingham Forest retain the European Cup.

Steve Archibald joins Tottenham Hotspur from Aberdeen in a £800 000 deal which makes him the most expensive transfer from a Scottish club.

West Germany regain their European championship title, beating Belgium in Rome, Italy.

**Ray Wilkins, England's goalscorer against Belgium in the European Championship.
(Syndication International)**

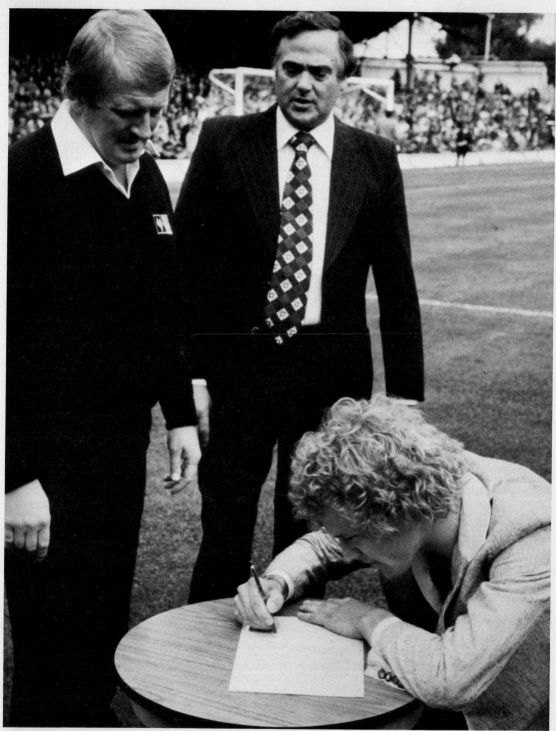

Andy Gray puts the most expensive signature in football to paper by signing for Wolverhampton Wanderers, watched by his new manager John Barnwell *(left)* and a rather apprehensive-looking club secretary, Phil Shaw. (Syndication International)

BRITISH SOCCER

League Club Stories

Aberdeen, pioneers of the first all-seated stadium in the British Isles at Pittodrie, and about to become the first to provide seating under complete cover, had a different innovation in the 1967-68 season. They introduced numbers on the front of their players' shirts in the same manner as American 'Gridiron' Footballers uniforms.

The first penalty kick act undertaken in Scotland is believed to have taken place on the ground of **Airdrieonians** on 6 January 1891, three days after the rule was adopted by the Scottish Football Association.

Albion Rovers and East Stirling drew their Scottish League Cup first round first leg match on the latter's ground 1-1 on 15 August 1979. At the end of the second leg at Coatbridge on 21 August the teams were scoreless. East Stirling won the subsequent penalty kick competition 9-8 but the Scottish League ruled that as no extra time had been played the match would have to be replayed. Albion duly won the replay on 27 August by 4-1.

On 19 August 1950 Harry Woodhouse made his debut for **Aldershot** in their 'A' team against Eastleigh Spartans and had scored a hat-trick before having the misfortune to break his leg. Aldershot won 4-1. Signed by the club the previous month Woodhouse had had twin careers, his other vocation being that of a musician.

His first honours came for Mossley Boys and he also represented Manchester at the same level. He was soon noticed by Ashton United and he signed for them before war service took him to Dover where he specialised in radar and reached the rank of sergeant.

Throughout his boyhood Woodhouse had also studied music and learned to play the violin, eventually reaching a standard whereby he was able to attend the Royal College of Music at Manchester. He progressed so well that he completed a season's engagement with the Halle Orchestra under the baton of Sir John Barbirolli.

What exactly was expected of the first penalty kick taken in Scotland is not clear, but the locals obviously decided to prepare for the worst.

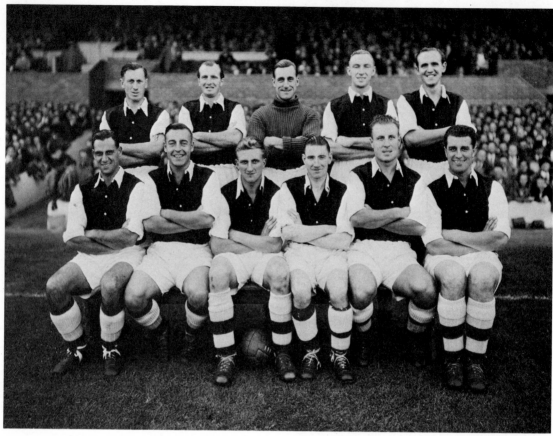

Looking particularly spry, the 1949–50 Arsenal team poses for the photographer, making light of the advanced age which necessarily put them into the FA Cup veteran category. (Colorsport)

His fortune on the football field was much less successful and it was February 1951 before he was able to even resume training. Almost immediately he was called up for his 'Z' training as an army reservist and at the end of the season was given a free transfer.

In one episode of the BBC TV series Dr Finlay's Casebook which ran from 1959 to 1966, **Alloa Athletic** players took part in a football story involving Tannochbrae, the fictional local team.

When **Arbroath** manager Albert Henderson parted company with the club by mutual agreement in January 1980 it ended the longest contemporary reign for a manager with one club in Britain. He had taken over as secretary-manager in September 1962 after a playing career with St Mirren and Dundee.

At the end of the 1949–50 season, **Arsenal** retained all of the 59 professional players on their staff. It is believed to have been the largest number recorded in Football League history. The club had finished sixth in Division One and won the FA Cup by beating Liverpool 2–0 in the final with the oldest side to win the trophy. Its average age was 31.

Aston Villa spent £35 500 on seven new players in the 1935–36 season in an effort to avoid relegation to Division Two. Some £23 500 of this was paid out on five men between 6 November and 6 December, but it did not prevent them going down from Division One.

Ayr United won the championship of Division Two of the Scottish League in the 1936–37 season, winning all their home matches with the exception of one. This ended in a 1–1 draw against Morton who finished as runners-up three points away.

Although Lol Chappell scored four goals for **Barnsley** against Bristol City in a Division Two match on 27 August 1958 he managed to finish on the losing side at home as the opposition scored seven times.

Two seasons before they were elected to the Scottish League, Division Two **Berwick Rangers** had an impressive run in the Scottish Cup during 1953–54. It culminated in a 3–0 win against Dundee who were to finish seventh in Division One that season. Berwick lost in the fourth round 4–0 away to Rangers.

Gil Merrick was in charge of **Birmingham City** when they won the League Cup in the 1962–63 season, the only post-war occasion that a former goalkeeper has been manager of a Football League club which has achieved such an honour. Merrick had made a record 486 league appearances for City between 1946 and 1960.

On Christmas Day 1890 **Blackburn Rovers** attempted to field their reserve side against Nelson. The crowd was annoyed as they had paid 8d (3½p) admission, and the visitors were themselves insulted. A compromise of trying to persuade Nelson to play their second team failed as the crowd ran riot preventing the game from starting. They did some damage to the ground before receiving free tickets for the next game.

Blackpool had the unusual experience of achieving more points away than at home in the 1966–67 season. They won only one match at Bloomfield Road, but that was 6–0 against Newcastle United, and drew another five. Away they had five wins and four draws, but, finishing bottom of Division One, were relegated.

In the 1902–03 season **Bolton Wanderers** played 23 Division One matches without a win and only three of them were drawn. Their first success was on 17 January 1903 when they won 3–1 at Notts County. At the end of the season they had managed to win eight matches, but still finished bottom six points away from Grimsby Town and were relegated.

Bournemouth changed their name for the fourth time in 1971 when they became known as AFC Bournemouth. The idea came from Dickie Dowsett, the club's commercial manager and a former professional footballer himself. It was intended to put the club first in an alphabetical list of members of the Football League.

Jimmy Conlin was the first **Bradford City** player to receive international honours when

It is unlikely that many other footballers in Football League history have had the same need to adhere to the words of 'Get Me to the Church on time' as Lee Holmes of Brentford.

Though there have been one or two unfortunate accidents with dogs on the football field, the canine intrusion often comes as welcome and light relief, but not so at Bristol.

he was selected to play at outside-left for England against Scotland on 7 April 1906. He was subsequently transferred to Manchester City where he became known as 'Will of the Wisp'.

When Willie Lawson a **Brechin City** forward and part-time window cleaner was transferred to Sheffield Wednesday on 2 October 1969 the fee involved of £4000 was enough to enable the Glebe Park club to make a modest profit that season of £2000. A proviso that Brechin would receive a further £1000 when he had played 12 first team matches for Wednesday was not forthcoming as he made only nine League appearances and in February 1971 was released to join St Mirren.

After playing centre-forward in the **Brentford** team which beat Southend United 2–0 at Griffin Park on 29 September 1979 in a Division Three match, Lee Holmes put his tracksuit over his playing kit and climbed on the back of a friend's motorcycle at 4.45pm. Then he was off on his way to get married at a church in Barking on the other side of London with the ceremony due to start at 5.30pm. The pair arrived at 5.25pm, but he did not have time to remove all his gear before putting on the bridegroom's suit. A part-timer he combined football with employment for the GLC in their civil engineering department.

Jack Doran an Irish international centre-forward achieved a unique scoring feat of its kind with **Brighton and Hove Albion** in the 1921–22 season. He collected all their first 15 Division Three (Southern Section) goals. His two appearances for Ireland came in the same season, as centre-forward against England and then Wales in 1–1 draws. Doran scored 23 goals for Brighton that season, two more than in 1920–21 when he had previously been their leading scorer. Once he scored five goals out of seven against Northampton. In the First World War he had earned the DCM and MM. After leaving Brighton he played for Manchester City and Crewe Alexandra.

Bristol City were formerly known as Bristol South End and their first match was on 1 September 1894 against Swindon Town who were billed as the 'Champions of the West'. The admission fee was 3d (1¼p), enclosure 3d extra with no dogs admitted.

Bristol Rovers were founded in 1883 as the Black Arabs wearing black shirts with yellow sashes. Though they were later seen in Badminton hoops of light blue and white and then black and white stripes, they have retained their distinctive royal blue and white quarters with white shorts until the present day.

After beating Blackburn Rovers 2–1 away on 14 April 1979, **Burnley** had a run of 24 League games without a win. On 24 November 1979 at home to Cambridge United they ended the sequence with a 5–3 win, but only after their opponents had had two players sent off just before the interval and five booked by the referee. The half-time score was 2–2 and Burnley went ahead after the break with an own goal. Cambridge drew level again, but Burnley scored twice in the last four minutes.

Peter Swan scored on his first appearance for **Bury** on 25 August 1973 in a Division Four match against Torquay United. It was something that he had never been able to do during any of the 272 Football League matches in which he had played for Sheffield Wednesday in a career which also earned him 19 full international appearances for England.

Cambridge United are the only club in current membership of the Football League to have recorded their highest attendance figure in a friendly match. A crowd of 14 000 watched them play Chelsea at the Abbey Stadium on 1 May 1970 before they were elected to the Football League the following month.

In a fourth round FA cup tie against Aston Villa on 26 January 1980 their present capacity of 12 000 was filled for the first time. Four days later in the replay at Villa Park which they lost 4–1 their share of the gate receipts was £22 000, the club's highest single financial return from one match.

Cardiff City experienced a dramatic ten years after just failing to win the League championship due to an inferior goal average in the 1923–24 season. At the end of 1933–34 they were forced to seek re-election to Division Three (Southern Section) having twice been relegated in 1929 and 1931. In between they had reached the FA Cup final in 1925 and 1927, winning the trophy on the latter occasion.

The record number of League games for **Carlisle United** was established by goalkeeper Allan Ross between 1963 and 1979 when he made a total of 466 League appearances, one of which was as an outfield

It took long enough for Peter Swan to register his first goal in Football League company, but it came through a change of clubs and a traversal of the Pennines. (Colorsport)

player. On 28 February 1970 the club was hard hit by injuries and Ross was named as substitute at Portsmouth. He came on for defender Peter Garbutt who was himself injured in the match which Carlisle lost 4–0.

Ross finished his playing career at the end of the 1978–79 season in which he had combined duties as reserve goalkeeper with organising the club's lottery. His last first team match was against Swindon on 28 October 1978 in a 2–0 win. At the start of the 1979–80 season he was appointed the club's commercial manager, but left in February 1980 to become a car salesman.

On 21 May 1979 **Celtic** needed to beat Rangers to win the Scottish League championship, otherwise their opponents with matches in hand would have taken the title for themselves. A crowd of 52 000 at Parkhead watched Celtic go a goal down after only nine minutes. Then Celtic were reduced to ten men when Johnny Doyle was sent off early in the second half. Celtic managed to equalise after 67 minutes, and then took the lead, only for Rangers to draw level at 2–2. But two further goals gave Celtic a 4–2 win and their 31st championship success.

Charlton Athletic were 5–1 down to

Huddersfield Town on 21 December 1957 with 20 minutes of the match remaining when Johnny Summers scored five times to enable Charlton to win 7–6. Summers achieved another five goals from the wing against Portsmouth on 1 October 1960 in a 7–4 win.

Chelsea won an FA Cup fourth round replay at home against Preston North End in January 1969 by 2–1 despite being a goal down after 90 minutes. But they scored twice in the two minutes of injury time added on by the referee.

In the 1964–65 season four **Chester** players scored 20 or more League goals, the only occasion that so many have reached this figure for one team. Gary Talbot scored 28, Mike Metcalf 27, Elfed Morris 24 and Hugh Ryden 20. Chester scored a club record 119 goals that season in Division Four and only four other players shared the remaining 20. Of these Jimmy Humes scored 17 goals himself.

When **Chesterfield** were reorganised after the First World War they were known as Chesterfield Municipal FC, as the corporation had taken a hand in the organisation of the club.

On 8 December 1979 **Clyde** beat Airdrieonians 2–1 in a Scottish Division One match at Shawfield. Neil Hood scored both Clyde goals, conceded the penalty from which Airdrie obtained theirs and was sent off the field before the end of the game.

Blair Miller set up a new individual scoring record for **Clydebank** in the 1978–79 season overtaking Tony Moy's 24 League goals achieved in 1967–68. Miller established a new figure on 24 March 1979 against Airdrie, with two goals in a 4–1 win taking his total to 26. Miller added two more goals in the remaining eight games in which he played until the end of the season. Frank McDougall who had scored the other two against Airdrie then made it ten goals in the last ten matches and actually overhauled Moy's total himself, finishing the season with 25 League goals. McDougall was then transferred to St Mirren for a club record fee of £150 000.

Colchester United were the first Football League club to stage a commercially sponsored League match in September 1973. It was against Crewe Alexandra and sponsored by a local newspaper which provided the money for pre-match entertainment.

Coventry City used three different goalkeepers in three successive matches in 1979 and not one of them conceded a goal. On 28 August Jim Blyth kept goal in the League Cup second round first leg match at Portman Road against Ipswich Town which Coventry won

The circumstances of a club using three different goalkeepers in successive matches is not a unique one. However, for Coventry City a special set of events brought about the unique treble in which they were involved during 1979–80, happily all of them resulting in matches which produced satisfactory endings. *Left* Jim Blyth and *right* Les Sealey are in action. (Keystone)

1–0. On 1 September, during the warm up before the start of the Division One game with Norwich City also at Coventry, Blyth injured his back during the kick-in and was unable to take any part in the match. He was replaced just before the kick-off by Steve Murcott who on the same morning had played in goal for the club's youth team. It was Murcott's debut and he was able to keep his charge intact in a 2–0 win. For the return League Cup game with Ipswich on 4 September at Highfield Road, Coventry had Les Sealey on duty between the posts in a goalless draw.

In 1909 the finances of **Cowdenbeath** had reached such a low state that only the staging of whippet racing at their ground saved them from extinction. At that time an away tie in the Scottish Cup proved an embarrassment through lack of funds, but the local station master turned a blind eye to them travelling without railway tickets to fulfil the fixture.

Bruce Grobbelaar, a Rhodesian-born goalkeeper signed from North American Soccer League club Vancouver Whitecaps, made his debut for **Crewe Alexandra** against Wigan Athletic on 21 December 1979, the day his country was officially recognised by Great Britain after the period of UDI.

In eight FA Cup matches, from the third round of the 1928–29 season until the second round in 1930–31, **Crystal Palace** played eight games which produced a total of 44 goals, though two of the matches ended as goalless draws. The sequence began with a 0–0 draw away to Luton Town whom they beat 7–0 in the replay. In the fourth round they again drew scoreless away to Millwall before beating them 5–3. In the fifth round Palace, lost 5–3 at Huddersfield Town. In the third round in 1929–30 Palace were beaten 8–1 at Leeds, but in the first two rounds of the following season they had 6–0 home wins against non-league teams Taunton and Newark Town.

Kevin Cane was unemployed at the time he was offered six months' work experience as a footballer with **Darlington** under the Manpower Services Commission's youth opportunities scheme. After successfully completing the trial period the 18-year-old midfield player was signed as a professional by the club on 13 January 1980.

In only their second season after being formed. **Derby County** were able to beat Aston Villa 2–0 in the second round of the FA Cup in 1885–86, the season before their victims won the first of a record seven cup finals. Derby were founded as an offshoot of the Derbyshire County Cricket Club.

One day in September 1879 one of the masters of the Yorkshire Institute for the Deaf asked Albert Jenkins, a local sportsman, to organise a team to play his boys. After the match the two men walked home, stopped at the bottom of Hall Cross Hill and after a discussion decided to form a club, calling it **Doncaster Rovers**.

George Dewar was a local discovery of **Dumbarton** prior to the turn of the century. He made two appearances for Scotland, the first against Ireland on 24 March 1888 in Belfast when the Scots won 10–2. Not all the goalscorers were reported, though Dewar himself certainly had one of the goals. His second appearance was against England on 13 April 1889 when the Scots won 3–2. That year he was transferred to Blackburn Rovers, winning FA Cup medals in 1890 and 1891 at centre-half before finishing his career with New Brighton and Southampton.

Two of the most successful seasons enjoyed by **Dundee** came in the years before the First World War when they were captained from outside-left by Jack Fraser. In the 1908–09 season they were runners-up in the Scottish League championship finishing only a point behind Celtic. The following season they won the Scottish Cup for the first time, beating Clyde 2–1 after extra time in a second replay after which Fraser was carried off with the trophy.

Dundee United achieved their first major honour when they won the Scottish League Cup in 1979 beating Aberdeen after a replay. The original game on 8 December ended in a goalless draw at Hampden Park before a disappointing crowd of 27173; but the replay four days later at Dens Park, home of their rivals Dundee, produced an attendance of 28933, the gates having been closed. United won 3–0 with goals by Willie Pettigrew (2) and Paul Sturrock.

Dunfermline Athletic entered the last match of the 1957–58 season, needing a draw

When is a 9 not a nine? From this example it would appear to be when it is a 6. No lasting ill-effects were suffered by Exeter City after this game because, though they slipped to 20th position in Division Three by the end of November, they picked up noticeably in the second half of the season to finish the term a respectable eighth in the table.

with Rangers to be safe on goal average from relegation to the Scottish Division Two. With half a minute remaining they were drawing 3–3 when Billy Simpson scored for Rangers which clinched the League championship for them and doomed Dunfermline to the lower division.

East Fife transferred their 18-year-old midfield player John Lumsden to Stoke City for £40 000 in January 1980, only seven months after they had signed him from Melbourne Thistle, an Edinburgh juvenile team.

East Stirlingshire have had only one player awarded full international honours while on their staff. He was David Alexander who made two appearances for Scotland in 1894 before the club had entered the Scottish League. He scored once on his debut at centre-forward in a 5–2 success against Wales on 24 March and also appeared in the next match won 2–1 against Ireland in Belfast a week later.

In the 1930–31 season **Everton** not only made a quick return to Division One after their first experience in the lower division, but were able to revenge themselves on Crystal Palace for the humiliation of a 6–0 FA Cup defeat they had suffered at Goodison Park in 1921–22. Everton themselves won by six clear goals at Selhurst Park with Dixie Dean scoring four of them.

Exeter City were losing their Division Three match at Reading 2–0 on 20 October 1979 with 25 minutes remaining. Manager Brian Godfrey signalled to trainer Alan Beer to make a substitution, indicating that City's No. 6 Dick Forbes should be replaced. Beer held up the number board only for the club's leading scorer Keith Bowker to start walking towards the touchline. Godfrey realised that Beer had held the board upside down showing '9' and was just in time to prevent the wrong substitution. Ian Pearson then took over from Forbes, managed to score a goal, but Exeter still lost 2–1.

Falkirk achieved a record number of drawn matches in successive seasons. They drew 17 of 42 Scottish Division One games in the 1921–22 season and 17 of 38 in the same division the following term.

Forfar Athletic had to pay out £8.6s.4d (£8.32p) for their away fixture against Partick Thistle on 9 March 1912. The balance sheet for the day read:

	Wages	Fares	Teas	Lost time	Total
Paterson	3/-	6d	2/-		5/6
Skene	3/-	9/3	1/6	6d	14/3
Gibb	3/-	9/3	1/11	1/-	15/2
Fairley				6/6	6/6
Chapman	3/-	11/3	1/11	1/-	17/2
Bruce	6/-	9/3	1/11	1/-	18/2
Milne				6/6	6/6
Wilson				6/6	6/6
D. Anderson	3/-	9/3	1/11		14/2
Boyle	3/-	9/3	1/11		14/2
Petrie	3/-	9/3	1/11	6d	14/8
Trainer	3/-	9/3	1/6		13/9
Committees rail fare and car					9/5
Committees dinner and tea					2/11
Cab fare for hamper					3/6
Refreshments					2/-
Drive home to Chapman					1/-
Tip to waitress					1/-
Grand total					£8.6.4.

Ernie Beecham, who had learned the art of goalkeeping in a fairground, was signed by **Fulham** as an amateur from Hertford Town in the 1923–24 season. He began 1925–26 as third choice, but made his senior debut against Blackpool in December 1925, turning out on 120 consecutive occasions before breaking a bone in his neck in a match against Exeter City in November 1928 after diving at the feet of an opposing forward. For a time he was paralysed, but recovered to regain his place before moving to Queen's Park Rangers where he broke an arm. Later he assisted Brighton and Swindon before retiring in October 1935. He once won a cup for kicking a dead ball 127 yards (116m) at an athletics meeting held at Craven Cottage.

When **Gillingham** were known as New Brompton they defeated Woolwich Arsenal 1–0 at Gravesend in an FA Cup tie during the 1899–1900 season after drawing 1–1 at Plumstead, 0–0 at New Brompton, 2–2 at Millwall and 1–1 at Tottenham. The games involved nine hours playing time. In 1924–25 Gillingham met Barrow five times in the sixth qualifying round before Barrow won 2–1 at New Cross after nine hours, 30 minutes of play.

In 1968 **Grimsby Town** completed association with all six divisions that have existed in the Football League, including both sections of the former Division Three, despite failing to gain re-election in 1910. They came back the following year and were founder members of Division Three in 1920, then composed entirely of southern based clubs apart from themselves and known as the Southern Section when the Northern Section was added the following year.

Halifax Town, having been unable to play a home match since the previous 14 December because of frost and snow, made football history on 2 March 1963 when they opened their Shay ground to a paying public as an ice rink.

Although **Hamilton Academical** were beaten on both of their appearances in the Scottish Cup final they emerged with credit on each occasion. In 1911 they held Celtic to a goalless draw before losing the replay 2–0 and in 1935 lost by the odd goal in three to Rangers in a memorable match.

During the 1971–72 season **Hartlepool United** used four different goalkeepers in four successive matches: Barry Noble, Mick Gadsby, Eddie Nisbett and Ron Hillyard, conceding respectively 2, 2, 1 and three goals in the process. At the end of the season the club had no professional goalkeepers on their staff, Hillyard having been on loan, Noble and Nisbett signed as amateurs and Gadsby granted a free transfer.

Heart of Midlothian were indirectly responsible for the introduction of the penalty kick in Scotland following an incident in the 1890–91 Scottish Cup. Hearts full-back Jimmy Adams fisted out a shot from an East Stirling player which was entering the goal. Hearts went on to win 3–1 and subsequently the cup itself.

Hereford United are the only club to have lost at home in both national cup competitions to lower grade opponents, and to have been relegated in the same season. In the 1977–78 season they were beaten by Wealdstone (Southern League) 3–2 on their own ground in an FA Cup first round replay having already lost to Bournemouth from Division Four in a League Cup first round replay after extra time. At the end of the season they finished 23rd in Division Three and went down.

In 1938 **Hibernian** decided to copy the Arsenal style of shirt though not their colours.

They added white sleeves to their green shirts and discarded their black stockings in favour of green with white tops, colours which have been retained to the present.

In the 1919–20 season **Huddersfield Town** faced a financial crisis due to liabilities to two influential sponsors who wanted their money returned. Sanction was sought from the Football League to remove the club 'lock, stock and barrel' to Leeds. But stirred by the possible loss of first-class football the few faithful supporters were able to fire the imagination of the whole town against the idea. Aided by the team's playing effort, which resulted in promotion to Division One and becoming runners-up in the FA Cup, the problems were overcome.

Twelve weeks before the start of the 1946–47 season **Hull City** had no ground suitable for Football League matches. The site at Boothferry Park was being completely renovated and was virtually bare lacking even dressing-room accommodation. But it was ready in time for the opening and within three seasons attendances of 50 000 were not uncommon at the ground.

Safe handling is a pre-requisite of any goalkeeper worth pulling the jersey over. Peter Shilton has demonstrated it on more than one occasion and even off the field as well as on it. But scoring goals is not one of essential requirements in the make-up of any last line of defence—or is it? (Syndication International)

Ipswich Town produced the widest margin between a club's points total in successive seasons in the same division of the Football League. In the 1961–62 season they won the championship of Division One with 56 points, but finished bottom the following season with 25 points.

Kilmarnock ended Celtic's unbeaten sequence of 63 matches on 21 April 1977 when they won 2–0 at Parkhead. They also became the only club to win at East Fife in the 1947–48 season, winning 3–1 at Methil.

Leeds United had a team of experienced finalists including several who had made more than two appearances when they won the FA Cup in 1972. Allan Clarke was making his third appearance having played in the beaten Leicester City side in 1969 and United's in 1970. Johnny Giles was appearing in his fourth final having been with Leeds in 1965 and 1970 and previously with Manchester United in 1963. Manager Don Revie was centre-forward in Manchester City's beaten side in 1955 and their successful one in 1956.

Playing in goal for **Leicester City** at Southampton in a Division One match on 14 October 1967, Peter Shilton made a long clearance which was helped by the wind and bounced over the head of Southampton goalkeeper Campbell Forsyth and into the net. Leicester won 5–1.

Lincoln City became champions of Division Three (Northern Section) in the 1947–48 season with a team of part-time players. Only four of them actually went to the Sincil Bank ground for training. However, at the end of the following season they were relegated from Division Two.

The only occasion that **Liverpool** have achieved a century of League goals was in the 1895–96 season when they scored 106 in 30 Division Two matches to win the championship on goal average from Manchester City. Their centre-forward George Allan was involved in an incident with Billy Foulke of Sheffield United during one game. Allan charged the 19-stone (120-kg) goalkeeper who promptly picked him up by his ankles and bumped him up and down on his head in the muddy goal area. Allan was capped for England against Scotland the following year but twelve months later died aged 24.

The aspirations of many a team have gone up in smoke throughout the history of the game. But having pipe dreams might have had a different meaning in the years before the present century at Luton.

When **Luton Town** were formed in 1885 the colours adopted were navy blue and pink halves for shirts and caps. It was recorded in the club minutes that 'both cap and shirt be worn by each player on the field'. The head-gear in fact was in the shape of a smoking cap.

Manchester City needed two points to make sure of the championship of the Football League in the 1936–37 season when they met Sheffield Wednesday at Maine Road. Eric Brook and Fred Tilson put City two in front before one of the most memorable goals seen on the ground was scored. Goalkeeper Frank Swift cleared downfield and Peter Doherty gained possession in the centre of the field. Doherty and Tilson then ran through the Wednesday defence with a rapid interchange of passes which carried them over 40 yards (36m) and well into their opponents' penalty area before Doherty applied the finishing touch. City eventually won 4–1 in what was their 21st League game without defeat. Their last match at Birmingham was drawn 2–2.

In the 1901–02 season, their last under the title of Newton Heath, **Manchester United** were in the middle of a financial crisis which eventually led to the re-forming of the club

under its present name. On 18 January 1902 a Division Two fixture was due to be under-taken away to Bristol City, but before railway tickets could be purchased a house-to-house collection had to be made to raise the necessary cash. During the course of the sub-sequent match Caesar Augustus Llewellyn Jenkyns, a Newton heath stalwart, was injured and as he was about to leave the field, a direc-tor called out: 'Go back, Caeser, and I'll stand you a fish and chips supper.' Jenkyns returned and duly received his sustenance despite a 4–0 defeat.

Glasgow born Alexander Montgomery Pate, known as 'Sandy', made 314 consecutive League appearances as a full-back for **Mansfield Town** between 1968 and 1975. He made his 413th appearance against Millwall on 2 May 1978 before being granted a free trans-fer. He had failed by five matches to establish a new club record as Don Bradley had reached 417 League games between 1949 and 1962, though Pate actually appeared in more matches as he originally made 14 with his first senior club, Watford.

On 22 December 1979 the attendance for the visit of Stenhousemuir to **Meadowbank Thistle** was given as 80. Across the city of Edinburgh at Easter Road, Hibernian with the attraction of George Best in their side were

BOOK EM!

Below: **Andy Ritchie has proved himself a goalscoring success in recent seasons with Morton, but what might have happened to his career had his father not insisted upon a certain course of action?**

Above: **Nowadays the worst thing that can happen to a coach is that he suffers some kind of nervous breakdown when results are not to his liking. Alas, in a former age the motorised charabanc often took on more lethal disaster.**

entertaining Rangers before 18 740. When Meadowbank were drawn against Hibs in the third round of the Scottish Cup on 26 January 1980 the tie was switched to Hearts ground at Tynecastle on police advice. Hibs won 1–0 before a crowd of 8 415.

In the second round of the 1906–07 FA Cup first Division **Middlesbrough** were drawn away at Brentford, members of the Southern League. Middlesbrough had five international players in their team including Steve Bloomer and Alf Common who was then the most expensively transferred player at £1 000. A record crowd of 21 296 filed into the ground and after ten minutes spilled onto the pitch when fencing collapsed on one side. Brentford scored the only goal after 62 minutes. After the match, as the Middlesbrough charabanc wended its way down Brentford High Street, one of the wheels came off. Fortunately nobody was injured, but jubilant Brentford supporters could scarcely contain themselves.

In the 1961–62 season **Millwall** half-back Dave Harper sustained an injury which was not officially registered. Playing against Accrington Stanley he was so badly injured that he could not play again that season. But the Lancashire side resigned from the competition shortly afterwards and their record was expunged.

In the 1929–30 season **Montrose** established their highest win and also had their longest run in the Scottish Cup. In the first round they beat Solway Star 8–0 on 18 January 1930 and eventually reached the last eight where they lost 3–0 to Rangers at Ibrox Park.

Andy Ritchie who was the leading scorer in the Scottish League Division One during the 1978–79 season with 29 League and Cup goals for **Morton** owed his first serious recognition as a player to the insistence of his father. As a 15-year-old he lived in Bellshill and played for the local YMCA. Middlesbrough were holding trials at Cumbernauld United's ground, but it turned out to be a wet day and Ritchie was not keen to attend until his father intervened.

Fortunately Ritchie impressed at the trial and was approached by Middlesbrough manager Stan Anderson. Other clubs showed interest and after playing for Kirkintilloch Rob Roy, Ritchie joined Celtic before moving to Morton in an exchange deal. When he was elected Scotland's Footballer of the Year in 1978–79 he was still a part-timer occupying himself outside the game as the club's pools agent.

Ben Ellis joined **Motherwell** in 1930 from Bangor in his native Wales. As a left-back he made six appearances for Wales in international matches and became something of a penalty expert for his club. On one occasion against Kilmarnock on 27 August 1938 he scored three from the spot in a 4–2 win. On hanging up his boots he became groundsman and coach at Fir Park before retiring in 1955 to become a masseur in the town.

Newcastle United played under their present title for the first time on the last Saturday in 1892 in a match against the formidable Corinthians. A contemporary report on the match read: 'The Corinthians were represented by a strong team but Newcastle United simply played with them. The correct score was eight goals, two offside goals and twenty smacks at the crossbar, to one goal.'

Ray Wilcox set up the **Newport County** record of 530 League appearances between 1946 and 1960. This centre-half had joined the club in 1939 from his local club Treharris

The seven-year-itch is usually something of a nature far removed from activities on the football arena, yet that was the time lapse before Ray Wilcox could start on his 'marriage' to Newport.

having been discovered in his youth playing for Merthyr schools. Because of the Second World War his senior debut was delayed seven years, though he had become an experienced player in wartime on military service. He guested for Lovell's Athletic and East Fife and after going to India he played for Tommy Walker's celebrated touring team which entertained troops in the Far East and other theatres of war.

Northampton Town right-winger Jack English scored a club record 135 League goals, including 28 in the 1953–54 season, which made him the leading marksman in Division Three (Southern Section) that term. He signed for the club in November 1946 and remained until 1960. His father, also called Jack, had been manager of the club in the pre-war era. In the 1979–80 season Northampton Town striker Keith Bowen was the son of the club's secretary/general manager Dave Bowen, a former Town half-back.

In the 1908–09 season **Norwich City**, then members of the Southern League, had an eventful run in the FA Cup, having first to meet Reading at Stamford Bridge because of an objection to the size of their home playing area at The Nest. The match ended in a goalless draw and in the replay at Reading it finished level at 1–1. A further replay at Villa Park ended in a 3–2 win for Norwich who were drawn to play Liverpool, then members of Division Two. City won 3–2 at Anfield before losing to the eventual beaten finalists Bristol City who defeated them 2–0 in the third round.

After only 21 matches in European competition, **Nottingham Forest** could claim to have won two major honours: The European Cup on their 15th appearance and the Super Cup after 21.

Notts County are not only the oldest club in the Football League, but can claim to have had a player in the first official England team against Scotland on 30 November 1872. Ernest Greenhalgh was at right-back and also figured in the corresponding fixture the following year. His career with Notts County spanned 16 years.

Tony Smyth was appointed secretary of **Oldham Athletic** on 1 March 1973 and resigned two days later because of ill-health. He had collapsed with a duodenal ulcer.

Orient are the oldest current inhabitants of Division Two having been associated with the division since winning the championship of Division Three in the 1969–70 season.

When **Oxford United** achieved promotion to Division Two by winning the championship of Division Three in the 1967–68 season, their highest scoring victories were only by 4–0 at home to Walsall and away to Stockport County. Although it was their highest finishing position in any division since they had been elected to the Football League in 1962, it was the first season in which they had failed to score more than four goals in at least one League game.

When Alan Rough, the **Partick Thistle** goalkeeper, played for Scotland against Belgium on 21 November 1979 it was his 29th appearance in a full international, a record for a goalkeeper in Scotland's history. He was four days short of his 28th birthday.

Jim Hall and Peter Price both scored hat-tricks for **Peterborough United** against Oldham Athletic on 26 November 1969. Peterborough won 8–1 and Hall actually scored four times. The next occasion two players each scored a hat-trick for the same team in a Football League match was on 9 October 1971 when Peterborough beat Barrow 7–0 with a trio each for Hall and Price.

Pat Jones made 425 League appearances for **Plymouth Argyle** between 1947 and 1958, including a run of 279 consecutive matches from April 1947 to 7 November 1953 when he was forced to miss a game with an ankle injury. A local discovery, this left-back eventually joined St Austell.

Portsmouth came into being after a meeting held in the offices of Alderman J E Pink, a local solicitor. The club's first colours were pink shirts with maroon collars and cuffs.

Port Vale had an outstanding season in 1953–54, not only winning the championship of Division Three (Northern Section) but reaching the semi-finals of the FA Cup beating Darlington (A) 3–1, Southport (H) 2–0 after a 1–1 draw (A), Queen's Park Rangers (A) 1–0, Cardiff City (A) 2–0, Blackpool (H) 2–0 and Leyton Orient (A) 1–0 before losing 2–1 to West Bromwich Albion, the eventual winners and League championship runners-up.

Preston North End were unchanged during their FA Cup run in the 1953–54 season when they fielded five Englishmen, five Scots and an Australian-born centre-half in Joe Marston. In the final they lost 3–2 to West Bromwich Albion, but centre-forward Charlie Wayman kept his record of scoring in every round.

Queen of the South goalkeeper Alan Ball celebrated his 37th birthday in February 1980, having the same month received £100 and a giant bottle of whisky as MacKinlay personality of the month for January. The following day he was booked in the 3–1 win at Montrose, his 747th game for the club. He had returned to the side in December 1979 after eleven and a half months out of action with a broken forearm. His first match had been against Partick Thistle reserves in October 1962 and in December 1967 he had made his 200th appearance for the Dumfries club.

Queen's Park undertook their first official

tour in 1898 when they went to Denmark to take part in a Carnival of Sports and Gymnastics in Copenhagen. They beat a Danish representative team on two occasions by seven and three clear goals.

Queen's Park Rangers, with many changes of venue in their history, had to suffer the indignity of local tenants in Notting Hill organising a petition against them because the presence of a football club apparently lowered the tone of the neighbourhood. It was when they occupied the Latimer Road ground from 1901 to 1904 before moving to the Agricultural Society ground at Park Royal.

Before their election to the Scottish League **Raith Rovers** had the distinction of winning five cups in one season. In 1897–98 they won the East of Scotland Qualifying Cup, the East of Scotland Consolation Cup, the Nairn Charity Cup, the Fife Challenge Cup and the Wemyss Cup.

Rangers have played more matches in European competition than any other club in the British Isles. At the end of the 1979–80 season they had appeared in 111 games in the European Cup, Cup Winners Cup, Fairs Cup and Super Cup.

Reading goalkeeper Steve Death established a Football League record by keeping the opposition from scoring for 1103 consecutive minutes. After Bobby Hoy scored against him for Rochdale in the sixth minute of their Division Four match at Spotland on 24 March 1979, Death did not concede a goal until the 29th minute of the match against Brentford on 18 August 1979. The sequence included eleven complete League matches. Death had originally joined Reading on loan from West Ham United in November 1969, making his debut in a 1–0 win over Brighton. Reading signed him on a permanent basis in August 1970, after paying a then club record fee of £20000.

Rochdale are the only club from Division Four to have reached the final of the Football League Cup. In the 1961–62 season they beat Southampton (H) 2–1 after a 0–0 draw (A), Doncaster Rovers (H) 4–0, Charlton Athletic (H) 1–0, received a bye in the fourth round, York City (H) 2–1 and then Blackburn Rovers 4–3 on aggregate in the semi-final. At home they beat Blackburn 3–1 and lost 2–1 at Ewood

Many forwards must have had cause to remember the name of **Steve Death** during the period when he meant nothing but the end of their hopes for goalscoring in match after match.

Goalkeepers are not often allowed the luxury of getting excited about goals being scored, especially if they are concerned with shots finishing in the net behind them. Ray Clemence celebrates a score at the other end. (Syndication International)

Park. In the final Norwich City won 3–0 at Rochdale on 26 April 1962 before a crowd of 11 123 and in the second leg at Carrow Road on 1 May 1962 Norwich won 1–0 before an attendance of 19 708.

Rotherham United is the only current Football League club to have suffered two defeats in one season conceding ten or more goals. They were beaten 11–1 at Bradford City and 10–1 at South Shields in the 1928–29 season. Despite this they conceded only 77 goals in their 42 Division Three (Northern Section) matches and had six clubs underneath them in the final table.

St Johnstone winger Jimmy Caskie was only 5ft 2½in (2.59m), but created a fine impression in the mid-1930s. The intervention of the Second World War robbed him of full international honours, though he did appear in nine wartime games for Scotland. He also represented the Scottish League against the Football League. He joined Everton in March 1939, but finished his career in his native Scotland with Rangers.

Although **St Mirren** have never finished higher than third in the Scottish League championship; they had spent only two seasons outside the then Division One between 1890 and 1971. In 1935–36 they were runners-up in Division Two and won pro-

motion and finished as champions of the same division in 1967–68.

Scunthorpe United have not had a full international honour awarded to any of their players, but they can claim to have started two of England's most consistent contemporary players in Ray Clemence (Liverpool) and Kevin Keegan (Southampton) in League football. Clemence made his League debut in 1965–66 for Scunthorpe, while Keegan followed him in their colours in 1968–69.

In the 1905–06 season **Sheffield United** were drawn away in the second round of the FA Cup to Blackpool, but persuaded their opponents to switch the tie for £250. Blackpool then won 2–1 at Bramall Lane.

On the morning of Good Friday 1928, **Sheffield Wednesday** were bottom of Division One with 25 points from 34 matches and with little prospect of escaping relegation as they were four points below Manchester United, their closest rivals. But they began the long haul up by beating Tottenham Hotspur 3–1 at White Hart Lane, captained by ex-Spurs player Jimmy Seed. Spurs were tenth with 35 points from 36 games before the match. Wednesday went on to win four and draw the other four of their remaining fixtures to avoid the drop while Middlesbrough and Tottenham were the two teams relegated.

Jimmy Seed *(right)* had good cause to recall the day he skippered Sheffield Wednesday against his former club Tottenham Hotspur which started a short, but sharp recovery.

Goalkeeper Ken Mulhearn established a new record of League appearances for **Shrewsbury Town** during the 1978–79 season, overhauling Joe Wallace's figure of 329. He started his career with Everton, but did not make any senior appearances until moving to Stockport County where he had exactly 100 in the League before adding another 50 at Manchester City. He made his Shrewsbury debut on 24 March 1971 against Brighton, in goal for the remaining 12 matches that season. The following term he missed only three League games and, beginning with the match against Chesterfield on 27 October 1972, he started a run of 236 consecutive League games, finishing on Boxing Day 1977 against Chester. In just over seven seasons up to the end of the 1977–78 season he had missed only eight League appearances.

On 19 January 1980 Mike Channon scored his 200th League and Cup goal for **Southampton**, against his former club Manchester City. It was also his 161st in League matches alone and set up a new club record overhauling the previous total achieved by Terry Paine. Southampton won 4–1, Alan Ball scoring his first goal of the season, Dave Watson also managing to register against his old club and 18-year-old Steve Moran coming on as substitute and adding the fourth with his second touch and first kick of the ball on his debut.

In January 1980 **Southend United** employed the services of Lennie Hepple, 60, former professional ballroom dancing champion and father-in-law of Sunderland forward Bryan Robson. He had improved the play of his son-in-law and others including Bobby Moore, Alan Ball and Peter Shilton. Hepple showed that he could beat the players over ten yards (9m) and in a two-day clinic at Southend he was able to make the players aware of balance and upper body mechanics.

Although **Stenhousemuir** did not enter the Scottish League until gaining admission to Division Two in 1921 they earned something of a reputation as a cup fighting team in the early years after the turn of the century. They reached the semi-final of the Scottish Cup in the 1902–03 season before losing to the eventual winners, Rangers 4–1 on 7 March 1903. In the two previous seasons they had won the Scottish Qualifying Cup.

Stirling Albion were formed from the ashes of King's Park whose Forth Bank ground was destroyed by enemy action in a 1940 air raid. From their foundation in 1945 Stirling rose to Scottish League status in two years. Their first chairman coal merchant Tom Fergusson had held a similar position with King's Park. Albion's ground at Annfield Park had a mansion as its dressing-rooms.

Stockport County signed centre-forward Joe Smith from Bolton Wanderers in 1927. He made his first appearance on 19 March against Stoke City and a record crowd of 22500 packed into Edgeley Park to see him. But a few minutes before kick-off a telegram arrived at the ground from the Football League which read: 'Don't play Smith. Registration not in order.' The County chairman Ernest Barlow received the telegram and was faced with a dilemma: to withdraw Smith and break faith with the capacity crowd or risk the wrath of the League and suffer the consequences. He put the telegram in his pocket and said nothing until after the match. County drew 2–2 with Stoke. In the subsequent inquiry County were fined £100 and had to forfeit two points. Worse still Smith was only allowed to play

When Mike Channon returned to his former club Southampton from Manchester City he was able to begin just where he had left off in the business of record goalscoring. (Syndication International)

that season in matches where the League management committee granted permission.

Stockport's case had been that they signed Smith on the last day of the transfer deadline. The letter was posted and it was thought that the date on the postmark would be sufficient proof of the signing and registration.

Stoke City outside-right Neville Coleman established an individual scoring record for a winger when he scored seven times against Lincoln City on 23 February 1957 in an 8–0 win at the Victoria Ground.

John McCutcheon known as 'Lolly' scored 329 goals for **Stranraer** in a career which ended in 1958. He had played one game prewar when only 14 years of age and during the Second World War he guested for Bletchley and Bradford Park Avenue as an inside-left. Even so he rejoined Stranraer as a left-back in the 1946–47 season after scoring nine goals for Railway Swifts in a Junior League match. After a short spell with Tarff Rovers he returned and eventually switched to the left-wing where his goalscoring brought him 238 goals in one spell of 239 games. He had another short period away with East Stirling, but came back a third time and at the start of the 1957–58 season he was presented with a statuette and £100. A broken arm restricted his final tally that term, but even in his official farewell game against Morton in which he was given the captaincy he scored twice. And he was even recalled later in an emergency and added to his tally.

Sunderland broke their transfer fee record three times during the 1979–80 season. In October they paid Leeds United £200000 for centre-forward John Hawley, £300000 for Middlesbrough's midfield player Stan Cummins a month later and then bought the Argentine forward Claudio Marangoni for £320000 in December 1979.

Robbie James of **Swansea City** who had become the youngest player to complete 100 Football League appearances when he played against Torquay United on 14 February 1976, a month short of his 19th birthday, reached his 250th on 21 August 1979 against Watford.

The youngest full-back partnership seen in a Football League match occurred when **Swindon Town** fielded Terry Wollen and John Trollope together at the start of the

Quickness off the mark was one of the traits in the goalscoring career of Sammy Collins, but he received an unexpected bonus to this from one particular penalty kick for Torquay United.

1960–61 season. Wollen was 17 in August, one month after Trollope's 17th birthday.

In August 1956 Sammy Collins scored the quickest Football League penalty for **Torquay United** in a Division Three (Southern Section) match against Walsall after only ten seconds. The previous season Collins had established a club record 40 League goals and between 1948 and 1958 this former Bristol City player set an aggregate of 204 League goals for United.

Tottenham Hotspur owes its origin to a group of grammar school boys who had formed a cricket club in 1880, naming it after Sir Henry Percy (1364–1403) called 'Hotspur' because of his valour in battle. Two years later they started a football team, Hotspur FC. The following year it was reorganised and played matches on Tottenham Marshes. By 1886 it had become Tottenham Hotspur Athletic Club.

Tranmere Rovers playing at home against Hereford United on 20 January 1978 made their first team change of the season in their 29th match for a post-war record sequence for an unaltered line-up.

The 1979–80 season was a particularly satisfying one for Alan Buckley in his new role of player-manager with Walsall. He was able to guide them to promotion from Division Four. (Bill Goulden)

On the morning of 5 January 1980 Alan Buckley, the **Walsall** player-manager, was named as manager of the month for Division Four in the Bell's Scotch Whisky Awards. In the afternoon against second placed Huddersfield Town at Fellows Park he took a 12th minute penalty, but merely managed to hit the left-hand post with his kick. However, he was able to make amends after 77 minutes with a volley to put Walsall ahead only for Huddersfield to equalise in the last minute.

Two years earlier, in February 1978, Buckley had signed a nine-year contract with Walsall, but in October the same year he was transferred to Birmingham City for £175 000. He returned to Walsall in June 1979 as player-manager at exactly the same transfer fee, which made him the most expensive player to sign for a club in Division Four.

Watford adopted professionalism in 1897 and in the early part of the 20th century they employed 21 professionals paying them at rates varying between 30s (£1.50) and £3. Committee minutes reveal that they had many troubles among the players; there were several instances of men being penalised for drunkenness and absence from training according to the club's official handbook. One persistent offender was asked to sign a total abstinence pledge, but apparently it did little good, for eventually the club bought him a railway ticket and sent him back to his home in the north.

Dixie McNeil will doubtless remember the visit of Charlton Athletic to the Racecourse Ground, Wrexham in January 1980. It ended with him literally paying the penalty. (Syndication International)

West Bromwich Albion needed one point from their last Division Two match against Huddersfield Town in the 1910–11 season to be sure of winning promotion. After ten minutes the ball burst, but the arrival of the new one almost immediately resulted in an incident that produced a penalty from which Albion scored the only goal. Albion's team was the youngest in the club's history with an average age of 23. Even so the combined ages of three of the players totalled 93, but this was offset by one of 18 and two aged 20.

West Ham United centre-half Jim Barrett had the shortest full international career of any player starting a match for England, when he was carried off injured in the eighth minute of his debut against Ireland on 22 October 1928. But Barrett made 442 League appearances for his club between 1924 and 1939 and scored 45 goals.

In only their second season as a Football League club, **Wigan Athletic** reached the fourth round of the FA Cup for the first time in their history. In the third round they won 1–0 at Chelsea, then leaders of Division Two before losing 3–0 at Everton. The entire Wigan team cost £17 000, of which all but £2 000 had been spent on one player, the remainder on another.

Wimbledon beat Orient in their League Cup second round second leg match at Plough Lane on 4 September 1979 on penalty kicks. The first leg the previous week had ended in a 2–2 draw at Brisbane Road and that was the score after extra time had been played in the second leg. Wimbledon won 5–4 on spot kicks one of which was successfully converted by Ray Goddard, Wimbledon's former Orient goalkeeper.

On 19 January 1980 Dixie McNeil was sent off as he was waiting to take a penalty kick for **Wrexham** against Charlton Athletic. With the scores level at 2–2 on the Racecourse Ground, Wrexham were awarded a penalty in the closing minutes and visiting players first protested and then indulged in some gamesmanship tactics while McNeil was waiting to take the kick. Eventually McNeil's patience evaporated and he kicked the ball into the crowd and was promptly sent off by the referee who had booked him earlier in the match. It was left to Mick Vinter to score from the spot and give Wrexham a 3–2 win. Two weeks previously Charlton had lost 6–0 on the same ground in the FA Cup.

Wolverhampton Wanderers received £110658 in transfer fees for players in four years from May 1935 to May 1939. Over the same period they paid out £42330 for players for a credit balance on moves amounting to £68328. In the 1979–80 season they spent £1930000 and recouped £1785000 in a similar way.

On 29 December 1979 Stewart Ferebee, aged 19 and in his first season with **York City**, came on as a second half substitute away to Lincoln City for his League debut in Division Four before a crowd of 3492. He had been discovered playing for St John Fisher in the Harrogate League, but could claim a previously more impressive background. Playing in West German schoolboy football, while his father was serving in the armed forces in Rheindahlen, he had joined one of the youth teams organised by Borussia Moenchengladbach. Several times he played in warm-up games before the first team Bundesliga fixtures and on one occasion, prior to a match against Bayern Munich, some 30000 spectators had filed into the ground before the youths had finished their game.

LEAGUE INFORMATION

When the wartime regional competitions ended and a full resumption to pre-war divisions was made for the 1946–47 season, there was nearly one notable absentee from Division Three (Northern) in the form of New Brighton who had not competed at all during the later war period.

The club's Sandheys Park ground had been damaged by enemy action in an air raid and in 1944 Wallasey Corporation requisitioned the site for housing. The club was left without ground or players and had little money.

At the Football League's AGM in June 1946 there were 14 applicants for possible vacancies in the competition as there was talk of the formation of a fourth division. The clubs concerned were: Chelmsford City, Colchester United, Gillingham, Hyde United, Merthyr Tydfil, North Shields, Scunthorpe and Lindsey United, Shrewsbury Town, South Liverpool, Wellington Town, Wigan Athletic, Worcester City, Workington and Yeovil and Petters United.

New Brighton were anxious to resume, but the League wanted to keep them under observation for a further month and then decide whether to admit them or run the Northern Section as a 21 club competition.

Dr Tom Martlew, founder chairman of New Brighton and a local GP, agreed to abide by these conditions and the meeting gave the Management Committee authority to make the final selection. Eventually the club secured a lease on the Tower Ground in time for the season.

The Northern Section had been extended to 22 clubs in May 1923 and New Brighton were one of the new entrants. They had been formed in 1921 and occupied the Sandheys Park ground in Rakes Lane, Wallasey—hence their nickname of the Rakers. They were not connected with the New Brighton Tower club who were members of the Football League, Division Two from 1898 to 1901.

New Brighton were 18th in the 1923–24 season and third the following term, only failing to gain runners-up position on goal average. They remained a consistent middle of the table team until 1930–31 when they were 19th, and finished 20th the next season in which Wigan Borough resigned.

They were 21st in 1932–33 and after picking up noticeably in the following two terms, were bottom in 1935–36 with 24 points, seven fewer than Southport, their closest rivals.

During the 1920s and 1930s they had at various times the assistance of five players with international honours and one of them, Bill Lacey, an inside-forward formerly of Everton and Liverpool, had won his 24th cap for Northern Ireland against England in 1924 while on the club's books, even though he had achieved his first such international recognition in 1909.

New Brighton were able to take their place in 1946–47 to finish 18th, but were bottom again the following season. They climbed to 17th in 1948–49 and 14th the next term when their ill-fortune included losing three promising players with fractured legs.

At the start of the 1950–51 season they won their first four League matches without conceding a goal and were top of the table. Yet they slumped to bottom by the end of the programme and obtained only 30 points. They were not re-elected.

Since leaving the League they have played in

When this photograph was taken of Burslem Port Vale before the turn of the century, they had little difficulty in identifying themselves. It was less easy to fathom them out later on.

the Lancashire Combination and from 1963 in the Cheshire County League. In 1956–57 they enjoyed some modest FA Cup giant-killing success against Division Three opposition when they beat Stockport County (A) 3–2 in the first round, Derby County (A) 3–1 in the second and Torquay United (H) 2–1 in the third before losing to Burnley (A) 9–0 in the fourth in front of a crowd of 42 000. Derby were Northern Section champions that season, Stockport finished fifth in the same section and Torquay were runners-up in the Southern. Burnley were placed seventh in Division One.

But it was the turning point for New Brighton's financial fortunes after some traumatic experiences which culminated in 1954–55 when as members of the Lancashire Combination they had lost the tenancy of the Tower Ground for non-payment of rent and moved to a Corporation-owned open field at Leasowe. It was half a mile away from their dressing room accommodation supplied by the New Brighton Rugby Union club.

That indignity lasted only a year when they secured a joint tenancy of the Tower Ground with the now defunct Wallasey Borough FC.

Among the 80 Football League clubs which are located outside London there are only two that do not carry the name of the city, town or locality in which they belong. They are Port Vale and Tranmere Rovers, though Grimsby Town's ground is actually in Cleethorpes.

However, Port Vale cannot geographically speaking be found on the map, for although this North Staffordshire club is based in the mother town of the Potteries, Burslem, and was for a spell known as Burslem Port Vale, the name was shortened in 1913 leaving a curious one which has remained to this day.

The name Port Vale is believed to have been taken from a house near to where the inaugural meeting of the club took place in 1876 at Middleport near Burslem.

Though the origins of Tranmere Rovers, now situated in Birkenhead, are as obscure, it is believed that they came into existence around the early 1880s. Certainly cricketers played a leading role in the formation of 'the club. Some were attached to the 'Scotch Kirk' in Tranmere.

Two Birkenhead cricket clubs, Belmont CC and Lyndhurst Wanderers CC, met and decided to form a football team to be known as Belmont FC. They ran for one season in 1881–82 before gathering in Sainty's Cocoa Rooms, behind the old Market Hall, and forming Tranmere Rovers FC; the name Tranmere is the oldest of the several townships that made up the burgh of Birkenhead.

But the club's Jubilee celebration held on 11 April 1933 seemed a further indication that 1883 was the year it was constituted.

LEAGUE RECORDS

The fewest number of points achieved by a League Championship winning team in a 42-match programme is 52. It has happened on three occasions: Sheffield Wednesday in 1928–29, Arsenal in 1937–38 and Chelsea in 1954–55.

The fewest number of points to separate the top and bottom teams in any division is 16. It happened in Division One in 1901–02, 1927–28 and 1937–38.

Only five teams have gone through a season without gaining at least one away point. Four of them did so in Division Two: Northwich Victoria in 1893–94, Crewe Alexandra in 1894–95, Loughborough Town in 1899–1900 and Doncaster Rovers in 1904–05. Nelson, the fifth team, equalled the record when they were members of Division Three (Northern) in 1930–31.

Rochdale suffered 13 consecutive home defeats in one season. After beating New Brighton 3–2 on 7 November 1931 they lost their remaining home games. They also lost the first match in 1932–33 to make it 14 defeats, but then drew 0–0 with Barrow who themselves had lost a total of 15 home Division Three (Northern) matches in 1925–26.

Newport County completed 25 Division Four matches in 1970–71 before their first win. The sequence ended on 15 January 1971 when they beat Southend United 3–0 at home following 21 defeats and four draws. Yet they had beaten Reading 2–1 in a Football League Cup tie on 19 August.

Coventry City played eight consecutive away matches in Division One between home fixtures against Middlesborough on 29 January 1977 and Tottenham Hotspur on 2 April.

Only once since the Second World War have there been more away than home wins in a full day's programme. On 2 February 1957 the 46 matches produced 16 home victories, 18 away and 12 draws.

Of the 32 matches played on 4 February 1954 the only draw in the Football League was recorded between York City and Workington in a Division Three (Northern) match which ended 1–1.

Since the First World War all eleven matches in a single division have resulted in home wins on four occasions: 13 February 1926 in Division One; 3 April 1926 in Division Three (Northern), 14 March 1931 in Division Three (Northern) and 10 December 1955 in Division One.

On Christmas Day 1936, ten of the eleven Division One matches resulted in home wins. The other was drawn. A similar situation occurred on 1 September 1956 and again on 12 September 1964.

On 18 September 1948 there were nine drawn matches in Division One and the entire Football League programme on 13 October 1962 produced 22 draws.

Seven clubs have gone through an entire season without a drawn match in the Football League and they did so in a period of six seasons before the turn of the century: Aston Villa and Sunderland in Division One 1891–92 (26 matches), Small Heath, Division Two 1893–94 (28), Lincoln City and Walsall Town Swifts, Division Two 1894–95 (30), Stoke, Division One 1895–96 (30) and Darwen, Division Two 1896–97 (30).

Torquay United drew eight consecutive Division Three matches between 25 October and 13 December 1969.

The highest number of away wins in any division is eight. This has occurred on three occasions: 27 September 1958 in Division Three; 12 September 1959 in Division Two and 25 November 1967 in Division Two.

The Division One programme on 28 April 1923 comprised ten matches and not a solitary goal was scored by an away team in any of them.

Believed to have been the only Football League match without a corner kick was the Division One game between Newcastle United and Portsmouth on 5 December 1931. It also failed to produce a goal as it ended in a 0–0 draw.

Crewe Alexandra and Hartlepool United have met in the Football League more times than any other pair of clubs since the First World War. They were founder members of Division Three (Northern) in 1921 and apart from 1963–64 when Crewe were in Division Three, they have been in the same division together ever since.

A common denominator among the seven clubs to have forfeited Football League status for one reason or another since the Second World War— Accrington Stanley, Barrow, Bradford Park

Avenue, Gateshead, New Brighton, Southport and Workington—is that they have all come from the north.

The eleven clubs to have been admitted to the Football League since the Second World War have been: Colchester United, Gillingham (who had previously been members), Scunthorpe United, Shrewsbury Town, Workington, Peterborough United, Oxford United, Cambridge United, Hereford United, Wimbledon and Wigan Athletic. Apart from Wigan who have completed only two seasons in the League all of them won promotion at least once, although Workington subsequently lost their place in the competition.

LEAGUE POINTS

Most points in a single season
Liverpool achieved 68 points in 42 Division One matches in 1978–79. They lost only four games and conceded 16 goals, the lowest for League Champions in a 42-match programme. Unbeaten at home, they dropped only two points to Leeds United and Everton. Liverpool were eight points ahead and achieved their 30th and last win at Elland Road in their 11th title on 17 May 1979, by 3–0 against Leeds who had held the previous record of 67 points in 1968–69.

Tottenham Hotspur achieved 70 points in 42 Division Two matches in 1919–20. They won their first seven matches and only suffered their initial defeat in the thirteenth at Bury on 8 November. They were also unbeaten at home where only two visitors escaped with a point. Tottenham failed to score in only two matches from a total of 102 goals.

Aston Villa achieved 70 points in 46 Division Three matches in 1971–72. Their most successful spell came from mid-January to mid-March when an unbeaten run produced 19 points out of a possible 22. Their 32 wins was also a record for the division, with 20 of these coming at home.

Nottingham Forest achieved 70 points in 46 Division Three (Southern) matches in 1950–51. Their 110 goals established a club record, while the 30 wins was also a record for the division. Wally Ardron set up a club record with 36 goals.

Bristol City also achieved 70 points in 46 Division Three (Southern) matches in 1954–55. They were champions, nine points ahead of Leyton Orient. Of their 101 goals, John Atyeo scored 28 and Jimmy Rogers 25. City also set up a record of 30 wins for the division. Yet Orient had led the division in mid-season.

Doncaster Rovers achieved 72 points in 42 Division Three (Northern) matches in 1946–47. They completed the double of home and away wins over twelve of their rivals. Five players between them collected 109 of the club's 123 League goals, with Clarrie Jordan top scorer with 42. Two other division records were achieved with 33 wins and only three defeats.

Lincoln City achieved 74 points in 46 Division Four matches in 1975–76. They also set up a record of 32 wins and only four defeats. They had two unbeaten runs of 14 matches; the first from mid-October to the end of the season. Their 111 goals was the first three-figure total in the League since 1966–67. Only once however did the side reach as many as six goals.

Most home points in a single season
Six clubs have achieved maximum points from home matches in the Football League: Sunderland, Division One in 1891–92 (13 games); Liverpool, Division Two in 1893–94 (15); Bury, Division Two in 1894–95 (16); Sheffield Wednesday, Division Two in 1899–1900 (18); Small Heath, Division Two in 1902–03 (18) and Brentford, Division Three (Southern) in 1929–30 (21).

Most away points in a single season
Arsenal achieved 33 points in 21 away Division One matches in 1930–31. They won 14 and drew five of their games. Tottenham Hotspur equalled their performance in 1960–61 obtaining their record with 16 wins and one draw.

Bristol City achieved 31 points in 19 away Division Two matches in 1905–06. They won 13 and drew five of their games.

Oldham Athletic achieved 30 points in 23 away Division Three matches in 1973–74. They won 12 and drew six of their games.

Walsall achieved 32 points in 23 away Division Four matches in 1959–60. They won 14 and drew four of their games.

Nottingham Forest achieved 32 points in 23 away Division Three (Southern) matches in 1950–51. They won 14 and drew four of their games.

Doncaster Rovers achieved 37 points in 21 away

Division Three (Northern) matches in 1946–47. They won 18 and drew one of their games.

Fewest points in a single season
Leeds United achieved only 18 points in 42 Division One matches 1946–47. Six matches were won, all at home, and only one draw was achieved away and that to Brentford, the side who were relegated with Leeds but had achieved seven more points than United.

Queen's Park Rangers achieved only 18 points in 42 Division One matches in 1968–69. They had won promotion from Division Two for the first time the previous season. During the 1968–69 term they equalled their heaviest defeat when beaten 8–1 by Manchester United on 19 March 1969. Their four wins all came at home and only three points were derived away. They finished 12 points beneath the second from bottom club Leicester City.

Glossop only achieved 18 points in 34 Division One matches in 1899–1900. It was their only season in the division and they won just four matches. The club resigned from the League in 1919.

Notts County achieved only 18 points in 34 Division One matches in 1904–05. They won only five matches but despite finishing bottom were re-elected to Division One on its extension to 20 clubs.

Woolwich Arsenal achieved only 18 points in 38 Division One matches in 1912–13. They won only three matches. They did not win promotion to Division One but were elected to it on the extension to 22 clubs in 1919.

Doncaster Rovers achieved only eight points in 34 matches in Division Two in 1904–05. Their nearest rivals were 12 points away. They were not re-elected. Originally they gained admission in 1901 but dropped out two years later only to be re-elected in 1904. Subsequently they returned to the League as members of Division Three (Northern) in 1923.

Loughborough Town achieved only eight points in 34 Division Two matches in 1899–1900. They won only one match and were not re-elected. They conceded 100 goals. Yet the previous season they had beaten Darwen 10–0 for their highest scoring victory.

Rochdale achieved only 21 points in 46 Division Three matches in 1973-74. They won only twice, including once away in September. In February a home match with Cambridge United attracted only 450 spectators.

Merthyr Town achieved only 21 points in 42 Division Three (Southern) matches in 1924–25 and equalled this figure in 1929–30. They won eight matches in the former season suffering 29 defeats but only six in the latter when they conceded a record 135 goals and were not re-elected.

Queen's Park Rangers achieved only 21 points in 42 matches in Division Three (Southern) in 1925–26. They had to apply for re-election for the second time in three years. Their nearest rivals were Charlton Athletic and Exeter City, 14 points above them.

Rochdale achieved only 11 points in 40 matches in Division Three (Northern) in 1931–32. They suffered 33 defeats, including 17 in succession. They also suffered a record 13 consecutive home defeats after beating New Brighton 3–2 on 7 November 1931. Wigan Borough's withdrawal from the League meant only 40 matches were played that season.

Workington achieved only 19 points in 46 matches in Division Four in 1976–77. Only two points came from their last 13 games and 102 goals were conceded. They finished bottom six points behind their nearest rivals and were not re-elected.

LEAGUE WINS

Most wins in single season
Tottenham Hotspur won 31 of their 42 Division One matches in 1960–61. They finished eight points ahead of Sheffield Wednesday to win the championship with 66 points. Of their 115 goals all but 14 were from their most regularly called upon five forwards. The same season they achieved the League and Cup double, the third team to accomplish the feat. Only four other sides have scored more goals in the history of Division One.

Tottenham Hotspur also won 32 of their 42 Division Two matches in 1919–20. Nineteen of these came from home wins but it was a 3–1 win at Stoke on 10 April that ensured the club of winning the championship.

Plymouth Argyle won 30 of their 42 Division

Three (Southern) matches in 1929–30. They had finished as runners-up six times in succession during the previous eight seasons. But not until the 19th match did they lose and their total of 68 points was a club record. Yet they had started the season £6000 in debt.

Millwall won 30 of their 42 Division Three (Southern) matches in 1927–28. Nineteen of these came from home wins where only two points were dropped in drawn matches.

Cardiff City won 30 of their 42 Division Three (Southern) matches in 1946–47. Eighteen of these came from home wins where just three points were dropped in drawn matches. Only eleven goals were conceded at home.

Nottingham Forest won 30 of their 46 Division Three (Southern) matches in 1950–51. Sixteen of these came from home wins. Only six matches were lost overall and ten drawn. The club also achieved a record 70 points and a record total of 110 goals. Thirty-two points were contributed from away matches.

Bristol City also won 30 of their 46 Division Three (Southern) matches in 1954–55. Thirteen came from away wins. The club also achieved a record 70 points.

Doncaster Rovers won 33 of their 42 Division Three (Northern) matches in 1946–47. They won 18 away matches, taking 37 points, lost only three times overall and established a record 72 points.

Aston Villa won 32 of their 46 Division Three matches in 1971–72. Twenty matches were won at home including eleven consecutively between October and March.

Lincoln City won 32 of their 46 Division Four matches in 1975–76. Twenty-one of these came from home wins. Only two points were dropped in drawn games on their own ground. The club also set records for most wins, most points and fewest defeats in a season in the division.

Record home wins in single season
Brentford won all 21 games in Division Three (Southern) in 1929–30.

Record away wins in single season
Doncaster won 18 of 21 games in Division Three (Northern) in 1946–47.

Most drawn games in single season
Norwich City drew 23 of their 42 Division One matches in 1978–79. They finished 16th in the division, drawing 10 times at home and 13 away in gaining 37 points. In 1978–79 Carlisle United had equalled the previous record of 22 drawn games in Division Three which had been held by three clubs: Tranmere Rovers in Division Three in 1970–71; Aldershot in Division Four in 1971–72 and Chester in Division Three in 1977–78. Carlisle had finished sixth, compared with Tranmere (18th), Aldershot (17th) and Chester (fifth).

LEAGUE DEFEATS

Most defeats in single season
Leeds United suffered 30 defeats in 42 Division One matches in 1946–47. Ten came from home matches and 20 away. Only six matches were won all at home.

Blackburn Rovers suffered 30 defeats in 42 Division One matches in 1965–66. Fourteen came from home matches and 16 away. Eight matches were won and they included 6–1 and 5–0 wins at home and 4–1 and 3–0 successes away.

Tranmere Rovers suffered 31 defeats in 42 Division Two matches in 1938–39. They finished 14 points beneath their nearest rivals and picked up only one point from away games.

Newport County suffered 31 defeats in 46 Division Three matches in 1961–62. Twelve of these came from home matches. Their heaviest defeat was 8–1 at Notts County.

Merthyr Town suffered 29 defeats in 42 Division Three (Southern) matches in 1924–25. Their 21 points was a record low for the division.

Rochdale suffered 33 defeats in 40 Division Three (Northern) matches in 1931–32. Only eleven points were taken, including just one away from home. 135 goals were conceded and their nearest rivals were 13 points above them.

Workington suffered 32 defeats in 46 Division Four matches in 1975–76. Fourteen of these came from home matches and only 21 points were achieved. The record would have been worse but for the club recording their only two away wins in the last two games of the season.

Fewest defeats in single season

Preston North End went through 22 Division One matches in 1888–89 without a defeat. Only four points were dropped, including just one at home to Aston Villa on 10 November, the runners-up who finished eleven points behind them.

Leeds United suffered only two defeats in 42 Division One matches in 1968–69. These occurred on 28 September at Manchester City when they lost 3–1 and at Burnley on 19 October when they were beaten 5–1. After this defeat Leeds had a run of 28 undefeated matches until the end of the season.

Liverpool went through 28 Division Two matches without defeat in 1893–94. They won 22 and drew six of their matches. They then won their test match for promotion and drew the first two games of the following season to establish a run of 31 matches without defeat.

Burnley suffered only two defeats in 30 Division Two matches in 1897–98. They won 20 and drew eight of their games. Included among the 80 goals they scored was a 9–3 victory over Loughborough Town.

Bristol City suffered only two defeats in 38 Division Two matches in 1905–06. They won 30 and drew six of their matches. Thirty-one of their points came from away matches which produced 13 wins and five draws. They also won 14 consecutive League matches.

Leeds United suffered only three defeats in 42 Division Two matches in 1963–64. They won 24 matches which was one fewer than runners-up Sunderland who finished two points below them.

Queen's Park Rangers suffered five defeats in 46 Division Three matches in 1966–67. They won 26 and drew 15 of their matches. They finished 12 points ahead of runners-up Middlesbrough and scored 103 goals while conceding only 38. The same season they won the League Cup.

Southampton suffered only four defeats in 42 Division Three (Southern) matches in 1921–22. They conceded just 21 goals, a record for the division. Their 61 points was also a club record. Among their wins was an 8–0 success over Northampton Town. However they won 23 matches, two fewer than Plymouth Argyle who finished as runners-up on goal average behind them.

Plymouth Argyle suffered only four defeats in 42 Division Three (Southern) matches in 1929–30. Their 68 points was a club record. They conceded only 38 goals and won 30 of their matches.

Port Vale suffered only three defeats in 46 Division Three (Northern) matches in 1953–54. They won 26 matches and drew 17. Both figures were better than those of any of their rivals and they finished eleven points ahead of Barnsley, the runners-up.

Doncaster Rovers suffered only three defeats in 42 Division Three (Northern) matches in 1946–47. Of their record 33 wins, 18 came away and they established a record of 72 points as well.

Wolverhampton Wanderers suffered only three defeats in 42 Division Three (Northern) matches in 1923–24. Twenty-four matches were won, one fewer than achieved by the runners-up Rochdale who finished a point behind. Fifteen matches were drawn by Wolves and only 27 goals conceded, one more than Rochdale.

Lincoln City suffered only four defeats in 46 Division Four matches in 1975–76. They won 32 matches, achieved a record 74 points and scored 111 goals.

Fewest wins in single season

Stoke achieved only three wins in 22 Division One matches in 1889–90. They finished bottom with ten points, only two fewer than the previous season when they had won only four matches. They failed to gain re-election but subsequently returned to the League in 1891 when it was extended to 14 clubs.

Woolwich Arsenal achieved only three wins in 38 Division One matches in 1912–13. They also amassed just 18 points. They scored only 26 goals, finished bottom and were relegated to the Second Division.

Loughborough Town achieved only one win in 34 Division Two matches in 1899–1900. They drew six games but finished bottom, ten points beneath their nearest rivals Luton Town. They scored only 18 goals and conceded 100. They failed to gain re-election.

Merthyr Town achieved six wins in 42 Division Three (Northern) matches in 1929–30. They drew nine but finished bottom nine points behind Gillingham.

Rochdale achieved four wins in 40 Division Three (Northern) matches in 1931–32. They suffered 33 defeats, including 17 in succession, as well as a record 13 consecutive home defeats.

Rochdale achieved only two wins in 46 Division Three matches in 1973–74. They played the last 22 matches without a win and achieved only nine points from them in drawn games.

Southport achieved only three wins in 46 matches in Division Four in 1976–77. But they managed to finish six points above the bottom club Workington.

SEQUENCES

After losing 1–0 at Leeds United's Elland Road ground on 19 November 1977, Nottingham Forest completed 42 Division One matches without defeat until losing 2–0 at Anfield against Liverpool on 9 December 1978. They drew 21 and won the other 21 matches. On 30 September 1978 their 2–1 win at Aston Villa had equalled Leeds United's record of 34 matches without defeat, established in the 1968–69 and 1969–70 seasons.

Leeds United were undefeated in the first 29 matches of the 1973–74 season before losing 3–2 at Stoke City on 23 February 1974. This is a Football League record from the start of the season.

Liverpool were unbeaten in all 28 matches (winning 22, drawing 6) in Division Two during the 1893–94 season. They also won their 29th match, the extra 'Test Match' (used to decide promotion and relegation between the top two divisions) and the first two matches of the 1894–95 season in Division One before losing 2–1 to Aston Villa on 8 September 1894. In all there had been 31 games without defeat. They were the first club to win the Division Two championship without losing.

Millwall were undefeated in the first 19 matches of the 1959–60 season in Division Four. They also hold the Football League record for the longest home run without defeat. After losing their last match of 1963–64 season at The Den they were unbeaten in 59 consecutive League games on their own ground before losing 2–1 to Plymouth Argyle on 14 January 1967.

Winning Sequences
Manchester United won 14 successive Division Two matches in the 1904–05 season, an achieve-ment which was equalled by Bristol City in 1905–06 and Preston North End in 1950–51.

Tottenham Hotspur won eleven successive Division One matches from the start of 1960–61. They also achieved eight consecutive away wins and a total of 16 throughout the season.

Huddersfield Town completed 18 Division One matches without defeat between 15 November 1924 and 14 November 1925, winning 12 and drawing six.

Losing Sequences
Crewe Alexandra went 30 Division Three (Northern) matches in the 1956–57 season without a win. After defeating Scunthorpe United 2–1 on 19 September they did not achieve victory again until 13 April when they beat Bradford City 1–0. Crewe finished bottom with 21 points and were forced to seek re-election.

Manchester United lost their first 12 matches in Division One during the 1930–31 season. The first win was 2–0 against Birmingham at Old Trafford on 1 November 1930. They did not recover from this disastrous start and finished bottom with 22 points, nine points behind their nearest rivals.

Rochdale lost 17 successive Division Three (Northern) matches in 1931–32. After defeating New Brighton 3–2 on 7 November 1931 they had to wait until drawing 1–1 with the same opposition on 9 March 1932. Rochdale finished bottom with only eleven points from 40 matches, as Wigan Borough had resigned.

Nelson played 24 away matches in Division Three (Northern) without achieving a point. Their 1–1 draw with Halifax Town on 29 March 1930 had been their last away from home because they failed to gain re-election at the end of the 1930–31 season.

Merthyr played 61 away matches in Division Three (Southern) without a win between September 1922 and September 1925. In the 1922–23 season they still finished 17th, were 11th the following season and 13th in 1923–24. But in 1924–25 they were bottom with 21 points.

LEAGUE GOALS

Fewest goals conceded in single season
Liverpool conceded only 16 goals in 42 Division

One matches in 1978–79. Goalkeeper Ray Clemence, who played in every match, was beaten three times on one occasion away to Aston Villa on 16th April 1979 in a 3–1 defeat, but did not let more than one goal past him in any other game. On 28 occasions he kept a clean sheet, including 17 times at home where just four goals were conceded. Liverpool were champions eight points ahead of Nottingham Forest who had shared with them the previous lowest-goals total of 24. Liverpool achieved 85 goals themselves, the highest by the League champions since 1967–68. They conceded only seven goals in the last 21 games.

Manchester United conceded only 23 goals in 42 Division Two matches in 1924–25. Only a late revival in which they took as many points in their last six matches as they had achieved in the previous 11, enabled them to gain promotion in second place. Significantly they drew their last match at Barnsley 0–0.

Southampton conceded 21 goals in 42 Division Three (Southern) matches in 1921–22. They were champions and were promoted, but with two matches remaining Plymouth Argyle had led them by four points. However, while Southampton won twice, Plymouth lost their last two games and were edged out on goal average.

Port Vale conceded 21 goals in 46 Division Three (Northern) matches in 1953–54. The three games they lost also established a record for fewest defeats. Only five goals were conceded at home in four matches. Port Vale kept a clean sheet in 30 games overall. And in winning the championship they had an 11 point lead over runners-up Barnsley.

Bristol Rovers conceded 33 goals in 46 Division Three matches in 1973–74. Though they were top after completing their programme, Oldham Athletic overtook them and York City were level on 61 points with an inferior goal average. Rovers had managed only 12 points from their last 12 matches after 42 from the first 27 games.

Peterborough United conceded 33 goals in 46 Division Three matches in 1977–78. Seven of these came in two matches at the end of the season and cost them promotion as they finished fourth, with an inferior goal difference to Preston North End.

Gillingham conceded 30 goals in 46 Division Four matches in 1963–64. They were champions on goal average despite the fact that they scored only 59 goals, one more than Carlisle United had actually conceded. Carlisle scored 113 themselves but Gillingham were divisional champions by .018 of a goal.

Fewest goals scored in single season

Leicester City scored only 26 goals in 42 Division One matches in 1977–78. Three goals on one occasion was their highest total. They failed to score at all in 23 matches. They finished bottom, with an inferior goal difference to Newcastle United and ten points beneath the third relegated club West Ham United.

Watford scored only 24 goals in 42 Division Two matches in 1971–72. They also failed to score more than two goals in any one match and did not score at all in 23. In the second half of the season they achieved only six goals in 21 matches.

Crystal Palace scored only 33 goals in 42 Division Three (Southern) matches in 1950–51. Though they reached four goals on two occasions, they failed to score at all in 24 games.

Crewe Alexandra scored only 32 goals in 42 Division Three (Northern) matches in 1923–24. They did however manage to achieve 27 points, two more than the bottom two clubs.

Stockport County scored only 27 goals in 46 Division Three matches in 1969–70. Three goals on one occasion was their highest total. They failed to score at all in 25 matches. They finished bottom, seven points beneath their nearest rivals Barrow.

Bradford (Park Avenue) scored only 30 goals in 46 Division Four matches in 1967–68. They did not score more than two goals in any one match and failed to score at all in 22. They won four matches and drew 15 but finished bottom, eight points beneath their nearest rivals Workington.

Workington scored only 30 goals in 46 Division Four matches in 1975–76. Three goals on one occasion was their highest score. In fact five goals came in their last two matches, their only two away wins of the season. They failed to score at all in 23 matches and finished bottom.

Most goals scored in single season (Team)

Aston Villa scored 128 goals in 42 Division One matches during 1930–31. They scored in every home match and failed in only three away. Eighty-six goals came at home and in 20 games four goals or more were recorded. At Villa Park, Middlesbrough were beaten 8–1; Manchester United 7–0; Huddersfield Town 6–1 and Arsenal 5–1. Villa also won 6–1 at Huddersfield and 4–0 at Birmingham. Top scorer was Pongo Waring with 49 goals, while Eric Houghton had 30. Yet Villa could only finish runners-up, seven points behind Arsenal.

Middlesbrough scored 122 goals in 42 Division Two matches during 1926–27. On three occasions they scored seven goals: against Portsmouth and Swansea at home and also at Grimsby, while they managed six on two other occasions. Portsmouth in fact finished eight points behind them but were also promoted. Yet Middlesbrough took only one point and scored just one goal in their first four League matches. In the fourth they brought in George Camsell who ended the season as their top scorer with 59 goals. His total included eight hat-tricks.

Millwall scored 127 goals in 42 Division Three (Southern) matches in 1927–28. Unbeaten at home where they dropped only two points, Millwall also won 11 times away and finished ten points ahead of second placed Northampton Town. Millwall achieved 9–1 wins against Torquay United and Coventry City as well as scoring seven goals once and six on four occasions including once away. However, they themselves were also beaten 5–0 and 6–1 away.

Bradford City scored 128 goals in 42 Division Three (Northern) matches in 1928–29. They managed double figures in their opening League game at home to Rotherham United whom they defeated 11–1, in what proved to be the club's record victory. Promotion was not decided until the last match of the season, however, with Stockport County finishing one point behind them. Top scorer Albert Whitehurst, secured during the season, was leading scorer with 24 goals in only 15 matches, including seven in succession against Tranmere Rovers on 6 March 1929 in an 8–0 win.

City not only habitually scored more goals than the opposition but they were so often in total command that they prevented their opponents from scoring. In one run of five League games during March that season they reached a total of 29 goals without reply in this sequence: 8–0, 8–0, 5–0, 5–0 and 3–0. Indeed, around this period this astonishing team netted 43 goals in 12 games during which they conceded only two goals and not more than one in a particular game. Yet the club had faced liquidation at the end of the previous season and was almost wound up.

Queen's Park Rangers scored 111 goals in 46 Division Three matches in 1961–62. But they could finish no higher than fourth and Bournemouth who were third edged them out on goal average despite scoring 42 fewer goals.

Peterborough United scored 134 goals in 46 Division Four matches in 1960–61. Seven goals were reached twice, six on four occasions including once away at Stockport, who were ironically the only side to prevent Peterborough from scoring at home during the season. Terry Bly was top scorer with 52 league goals, a record for the division. The second best supported team in the division at home with an average of 14 222, Peterborough produced the highest support away with 12 182 on average in their first season in the Football League.

Most goals against in single season (Team)
Blackpool conceded 125 goals in 42 Division One matches during 1930–31. Their heaviest defeat, 10–1, a club record, was against Huddersfield Town on 13 December 1930. Seven goals were conceded on three occasions, including at home to Leeds United in a 7–3 defeat. But Blackpool escaped relegation by one point, finishing above Leeds. The previous season they had won promotion as Division Two champions with record points and goals.

Darwen conceded 141 goals in 34 Division Two matches during 1898–99. It proved the last season in the club's eventful eight season League history and they suffered three 10–0 defeats away, gathering only nine points from a possible 68 and were not re-elected.

Merthyr Town conceded 135 goals in 42 Division Three (Southern) matches in 1929–30. They were bottom, nine points beneath their nearest rivals. Coventry City still have the cheque they received as their share of the receipts from a midweek match at Merthyr's Penydarren Park in April 1930 which amounted to 18s 4d (92p). Merthyr were not re-elected in what was their third plea for re-admission. Between September 1922 and September 1925 they had created a Football League record with a run of 61 away games without a win. And in 1924–25 they suffered 29 defeats overall in 42 matches, a record for the division.

Nelson conceded 136 goals in 42 Division Three (Northern) matches in 1927–28. These included conceding nine goals in one match, eight in another and seven in a third. But they had had their own scoring successes earlier. In 1924–25 they scored seven on two occasions, while in their most prolific season 1926–27 a total of 104 goals included two more scores of seven. In 1925–26 they also scored seven goals in successive games.

Accrington Stanley conceded 123 goals in 46 Division Three matches in 1959–60. But only once did they concede as many as six goals. And they took more points (14) from away matches than at home.

Hartlepool United conceded 109 goals in 46 Division Four matches in 1959–60. Seven goals were conceded once and six on two occasions.

Managers

The most extensive Soccer family in the history of club management was that of the **Maleys.** Tom Maley, born in Scotland, managed Manchester City and Bradford Park Avenue; Willie Maley, his brother, born in Ireland, managed Celtic, and Alec Maley, born in England, managed Hibernian. Charlie Maley, son of Tom, was secretary of both Bradford clubs and also of Leicester City.

Sir Alf Ramsey (before he was knighted) is the only man since the Second World War to have been manager of championship teams from Divisions One, Two and Three. He led Ipswich Town to the Division Three title in the 1956–57 season, Division Two in 1960–61 and the League Championship itself in 1961–62.

The following **ten** players all appeared for England in **full internationals** in the 1948–49 season: Laurie Scott, Alf Ramsey, Tim Ward, Neil Franklin, Billy Wright, Stanley Matthews, Stan Mortensen, Jackie Milburn, Roy Bentley and Stan Pearson. All ten later became Football League club managers. The only one who still had any administrative position with a Football League club during the 1979–80 season was Bentley as Reading's secretary.

Former managers Geoff Twentyman (Hartlepool), Tim Ward (Derby County), Pat Saward (Brighton and Hove Albion), Don Revie (Leeds United) and Allan Brown (Nottingham Forest) shared a kindred experience. They left the clubs mentioned for a variety of reasons and were succeeded in each instance by **Brian Clough.**

Exeter City manager **Brian Godfrey** ranks as the only player who ever went to Wembley for cup finals with teams from Divisions Two and Three in turn. He was Preston North End's (Division Two) twelfth man when they lost to West Ham United in the 1964 FA Cup final and he captained Aston Villa (Division Three) against Tottenham Hotspur in the 1971 League Cup final.

Jimmy McGuigan was made Stockport County's manager 30 years after he had been a player with them. He was an outside-right at Edgeley Park in the 1949–50 season after service with Sunderland and Hamilton Academical, then was player or manager with Crewe Alexandra, Rochdale, Grimsby Town, Chesterfield and Rotherham United before being appointed manager at Stockport in November 1979.

Former Scottish international **Billy Bremner** must view himself as one of the most severely dealt with players of all time in the matter of FA fines. As a Leeds United player he was fined a

Jimmy McGuigan seen here during his playing days probably had no idea that his association with one club would be renewed many years later in the role of manager.

total of £1125 between 1964 and 1974—and, as Doncaster Rovers manager, received another fine of £200 in January 1980.

Ian Greaves was a Manchester United back when they were Division One champions in the 1955–56 season and again in 1956–57, with Lincoln City when relegated from Division Two in 1960–61 and Oldham Athletic when promoted from Division Four in 1962–63. He managed Huddersfield Town when they rose from Division Two in 1969–70 and dropped from Division One (1971–72) and Division Two (1972–73). He was also in charge of Bolton Wanderers when they were promoted from Division Two (1977–78) and was dismissed by them in January 1980 when they were at the bottom of Division One.

Of the managers in charge of clubs in the Football League competition at the end of the 1979–80

The vagaries of managerial life reached a climax for Ian Greaves in the 1979–80 season when he parted company with Bolton Wanderers. But he had known many ups and downs in his career.

season, Lawrie McMenemy (Southampton), Mike Smith (Hull City) and Colin Murphy (Lincoln City) were the only ones who had **never played in a Football League match** themselves during their own playing careers.

Bobby Smith, manager of Swindon Town in the 1979–80 season, can claim to have been the youngest club chief who ever led his team to promotion. He was only two months past his 30th birthday when he managed Bury's promotion from Division Four in 1973–74.

Middlesbrough, Southampton, West Ham United, Gillingham and Sheffield Wednesday are the only clubs in current membership of the Football League which have never been managed by other than an **Englishman** throughout the post-war period. West Ham have never had a non-English manager in all their 80 years' existence.

Recruitment of **managers direct from Scotland** by clubs in England has been one of the rarest phases of the Soccer scene ever since the war. Those who have been engaged by Football League clubs in this way take in Scot Symon and Bobby Seith (both Preston North End), Ian McColl (Sunderland) and Willie Reid (Norwich City).

Cardiff City have had post-war managers from all five countries of the British Isles—Cyril Spiers and George Swindin (English), Jimmy Scoular and Jimmy Andrews (Scottish), Trevor Morris, Bill Jones and Richie Morgan (Welsh), Billy McCandless (Northern Ireland) and Frank O'Farrell (Republic of Ireland).

Not one Football League club has had more than **five Scottish managers** since the war. But there have been two with that number: Rotherham United and Leicester City. United have had: Tom Johnston, Tommy Docherty, Jimmy McAnearney, Jimmy McGuigan and Ian Porterfield; City: Johnny Duncan, David Halliday, Matt Gillies, Frank McLintock and Jock Wallace.

There has been only one instance of **father and son becoming English full internationals** and later, Football League club managers. George Eastham played once for England when with Bolton Wanderers and later managed Accrington Stanley. George junior, like father, was an England inside-forward playing for his country on 19 occasions before he managed Stoke City.

Giant-killing acts provide tremendous excitement for those who are the victors. But as Jock Wallace can prove, it is a different matter when you are one of its victims.

Jimmy Hill, Tommy Cummings, Malcolm Musgrove, Noel Cantwell, Terry Neill, Derek Dougan and Gordon Taylor in that order have been the last seven Players Union (or Professional Footballers' Association) chairmen. All the first six later turned to club management. Taylor was still a registered player with Bury in the 1979–80 season having previously played for Blackburn Rovers, Birmingham City and Bolton Wanderers.

In June 1952 the **Taylor brothers,** who had been Wolverhampton Wanderers full-back partners, both became managers within eight days of each other—Frank with Stoke City and Jack with Queen's Park Rangers. But in May 1973 the **Charlton brothers** both became managers within a day of each other, Bobby with Preston North End and Jack with Middlesbrough.

Players who made 300 Football League appearances with each of two clubs are rare enough.

It was third time lucky in Lancashire for Bob Stokoe with Rochdale in 1979–80. They were re-elected at the League's AGM by one vote more than Altrincham, the Alliance Premier League champions. (Syndication International)

Current Brighton and Hove Albion manager **Alan Mullery** did so making 364 appearances in two spells with Fulham and 312 with Tottenham Hotspur. He was appointed Brighton manager in July 1976.

A distinction unique in Football League history has been experienced by **Bob Stokoe** in having put in two separate managerial spells with three Lancastrian clubs in turn: Bury, Blackpool and Rochdale whom he rejoined in the 1979–80 season. He also managed Charlton Athletic, Carlisle United and Sunderland.

The first three Football League goals scored by current Tranmere Rovers manager **John King** were collected with different clubs in different divisions in different seasons: Everton (Division One in 1958–59), Bournemouth (Division Three in 1960–61) and Tranmere Rovers (Division Four in 1961–62). He became manager of Tranmere in May 1975.

Yorkshire born **Keith Burkinshaw** has had the unique experience of being made manager of three clubs after they had originally engaged him in a different capacity. He signed for Workington and Scunthorpe United as a player and both clubs promoted him to be their manager while Tottenham Hotspur appointed him coach in May 1975 and made him manager in July 1976.

Tommy Docherty had the unusual experience as a manager of taking his team to the same ground for FA Cup away ties in four successive seasons when he visited Villa Park with Chelsea in 1964–65, 1965–66 and 1966–67 and with Rotherham United in 1967–68.

Cambridge United manager and a former inside-forward with other clubs **John Docherty** is the only man in any sphere of Football League activity who has had four separate spells with one club. Brentford recruited him from his native Glasgow junior circles in 1959, sold him to Sheffield United and Reading in turn and later bought him back twice. He left again to become a Queen's Park Rangers coach, but then returned to Brentford as manager.

There have been only three **Division One club player-managers** in Football League history: the late Andy Cunningham (Newcastle United) before the Second World War and Les Allen (Queen's Park Rangers) and Johnny Giles (West Bromwich Albion) since it. Cunningham was signed as an inside-right from Glasgow Rangers in January 1929. At the beginning of 1930 he was appointed player-manager and then manager for the 1930–31 season. He had played twelve times for Scotland.

Manchester United manager **Dave Sexton** was formerly with seven London clubs. He played for West Ham United and Crystal Palace, filled administrative posts with Chelsea, Orient, Fulham and Arsenal and managed Queen's Park Rangers. But the late **Ned Liddell**, a Sunderland native claimed the record with eight. He played for Orient and Arsenal, managed QPR and Fulham and was chief scout of West Ham, Chelsea, Brentford and Tottenham Hotspur.

No one man since the Second World War has managed both Scottish Cup winning and FA Cup winning teams, but Johnny Cochrane (St Mirren in 1926 and Sunderland in 1937) did so before it. Cochrane, often called Jimmy, had been appointed as Sunderland's manager in 1928 and shortly afterwards he brought down to Roker Park Andy Reid who had been his trainer with St Mirren. Cochrane resigned in March 1939.

Leicester City manager **Jock Wallace** is more familiar than most with quests for honours. When with Glasgow Rangers he achieved a 'double' treble. In the 1975–76 season he led them to the Scottish League championship, the Scottish Cup and the League Cup and repeated that hat-trick

Bob Jack, the Plymouth Argyle manager, is pictured here in a team group taken in the 1905–06 season. He is in the middle of the back row. And it was before his days as a 'family' transfer man.

two years later. Wallace had been player-manager of Berwick Rangers when they defeated Glasgow Rangers 1–0 in the Scottish Cup in 1966–67, but found himself on the receiving end of a giant-killing act in 1979–80. It happened when Harlow Town beat Leicester 1–0 in a third round FA Cup replay after a 1–1 draw at Leicester.

Current Stoke City manager **Alan Durban,** when Shrewsbury Town's player-manager, led their scoring list in the 1973–74 season with nine goals. Unfortunately, they scored only 41 in 46 League games and were relegated to Division Four. It was also the first time that any player-manager had finished first among the scorers of any club in the Football League since 1962–63 when it was achieved by Arthur Rowley also for Shrewsbury.

Stan Anderson, the only player during the last 50 years to have turned out in the Football League with the north-east's three leading clubs, had a variety of experience with them. He was relegated with Sunderland in the 1957–58 season, promoted with Newcastle United in 1964–65 and relegated as manager with Middlesbrough in 1965–66, only to be promoted a year later. At the end of the 1979–80 season he was relegated again as Bolton Wanderers manager.

Liverpool's manager **Bob Paisley** and his opposite number at Bournemouth, **Alec Stock**

are in good company in both remaining in League club control when over the age of 60. Others since the Second World War who did so included Sir Matt Busby, Bill Shankly, Major Frank Buckley and Charlie Paynter.

Alan Ball taking on the Blackpool post in the 1979–80 season after his father used to be in charge at Halifax and Preston, completes the fourth post-war instance of father and son having managed Football League clubs. The others: Bill Dodgin senior and junior, George Eastham senior and junior and Jimmy and Gordon Milne.

When **John Mitten** made his Football League debut on 5 April 1958 as Mansfield Town's outside-left against Southport he appeared in the position which his father Charlie, the club's player-manager, had been filling regularly in the side during the season.

In September 1946 former England goalkeeper **Jack Hacking,** as Accrington Stanley's manager, transferred his own son Jack Hacking junior, also a goalkeeper, to Stockport County. In the early 1920s Plymouth Argyle manager Bob Jack sold his three sons: David, Robert and Rollo, all forwards, to Bolton Wanderers.

F.A. Cup

The highest attendance for an FA Cup Final is 126 047 in 1923. Nearer 200 000 actually gained entry to the ground, although official receipts were £27 776. However, the FA later had to return £2797 to ticket holders who had been unable to claim their seats. From 1950 onwards the attendance at the Empire Stadium, Wembley has been fixed at 100 000, but before the game moved there in 1923 there were three other crowds of six figures, all at Crystal Palace, in 1901 when it was 110 820, in 1905 when it was 101 117 and in 1913 when 120 081 attended.

The highest score in an FA Cup Final is six goals achieved on two occasions. Blackburn Rovers beat Sheffield Wednesday 6–1 in 1890, and Bury defeated Derby County 6–0 in 1903 for the biggest margin of victory recorded in a final.
No team has ever scored five goals in a final. The highest score of a defeated side is three goals achieved by Bolton Wanderers in 1953. They were beaten by Blackpool on that occasion 4–3 which equalled the highest aggregate of goals achieved in the 1890 final.
Six clear goals is also the biggest margin in the semi-finals and occurred in 1890 when Newcastle United beat Fulham 6–0. The only other semi-final to produce six goals for one team was in 1892 when West Bromwich Albion beat Nottingham Forest 6–2.

The first entrants for the FA Cup in the 1871–72 season were: Barnes, Civil Service, Crystal Palace, Clapham Rovers, Donington Grammar School (Spalding), Hampstead Heathens, Harrow Chequers, Hitchin, Maidenhead, Marlow, Queen's Park (Glasgow), Reigate Priory, Royal Engineers, Upton Park and Wanderers. Only Queen's Park and Donington came from north of Hertfordshire. The Harrow, Reigate and Donington teams all scratched before playing.

Extra time was first played in the Cup Final in 1877. Wanderers and Oxford University were drawing 0–0 at full-time, but Wanderers scored twice in the extra period.

There have been three different trophies in the FA Cup competition. The original was stolen in 1895 and the replacement was withdrawn by the FA in 1910 and presented to Lord Kinnaird as a mark of respect on his completion of 21 years as the organisation's President.

The first recorded penalty kick was taken and scored by Albert Shepherd for Newcastle United in the 1910 replay against Barnsley. The first decisive penalty was in 1922 when Billy Smith scored for Huddersfield Town to beat Preston North End 1–0. All four penalties awarded at Wembley have been converted by: George Mutch for Preston v Huddersfield Town in 1938; Eddie Shimwell for Blackpool v Manchester United in 1948; Ronnie Allen for West Bromwich Albion v Preston in 1954; and Danny Blanchflower for Tottenham Hotspur v Burnley in 1962. Shimwell was the first full-back to score in an FA Cup Final at Wembley and was the only penalty taker to finish on the losing side there.

Only two clubs have won the cup three times in succession: Wanderers from 1876 to 1878 and Blackburn Rovers from 1884 to 1886. Blackburn played 24 FA Cup matches without defeat from December 1883 to December 1886. Huddersfield Town were unbeaten at home in 26 FA Cup games between 1913 and 1932, but Leeds United went 16 without a win anywhere from 1952 to 1963.

Nine different players have scored in every round, but only three others have recorded hat-tricks in finals. Alex Brown (Tottenham Hotspur) established a record number of FA Cup goals in 1900–01 when he scored 15.

Six clubs from Division One have been knocked-out by non-league sides in the period since the First World War:

1919–20 Sheffield Wednesday 0 Darlington (North-Eastern League) 2 after a 0–0 draw in the first round.
1923–24 Corinthians 1 Blackburn Rovers 0 (first round).
1947–48 Colchester United (Southern League) 1 Huddersfield Town 0 (third round).
1948–49 Yeovil Town (Southern League) 2 Sunderland 1 (fourth round).
1971–72 Hereford United (Southern League) 2 Newcastle United 1 after 2–2 draw (third round).
1974–75 Burnley 0 Wimbledon 1 (Southern League) (third round).

Aston Villa have become the most famous name in the history of the FA Cup. In the 1920 final they beat Huddersfield Town by the only goal. Here Andy Ducat clears a corner kick for them.

The oldest players in an FA Cup final have been: Walter Hampson for Newcastle United in 1924 at 41 years 8 months and John Oakes for Charlton Athletic in 1946 at 40 years 7 months.

The oldest player to appear in the FA Cup proper was Billy Meredith at 49 years 8 months for Manchester City against Newcastle on 29 March 1924.

Paul Allen at 17 years 256 days became the youngest finalist in the history of the competition when he played for the winners West Ham United, against Arsenal in 1980. The youngest scorer in a final was John Sissons also for West Ham v Preston North End in 1964 when 18 years 215 days.

After creating some FA Cup final history of his own, Walter Hampson graduated to the exacting task of becoming a Football League club manager and is pictured here with Leeds United in 1938. (Keystone)

John Sissons was the youngest player to score a goal in the FA Cup Final at Wembley in 1964. And he had the satisfaction of finishing on the winning side against Preston North End. (Syndication International)

The youngest player to appear in the FA Cup proper was Scott Endersby for Kettering v Tilbury on 26 November 1977 at 15 years 288 days.

Clubs from Northern Ireland and Scotland have competed in the FA Cup. Those from Wales, which is the only country to have taken the trophy outside England when Cardiff City won it in 1927, still compete though their number is restricted to 14 and entries have to be submitted by 1 March each year not 1 May as for other teams.

Three Irish clubs appeared in it, Cliftonville reaching the third round in the 1886–87 season before being beaten 11–1 by the Scottish club Partick Thistle; Linfield Athletic who scratched after drawing 2–2 with Nottingham Forest in 1888–89 and Belfast Distillery who lost 10–2 to Bolton Wanderers in the first round in 1889–90.

Scottish clubs last competed in 1886–87. After that season the Scottish FA introduced a rule preventing them from entering any national competition other than their own. Heart of Midlothian, Cowlairs, Renton, Queen's Park, Rangers, Partick Thistle and Third Lanark had all competed with Queen's Park the most successful, twice reaching the final in 1884 and 1885.

Stan Crowther was granted special permission to play for Manchester United after the Munich air disaster in 1958 though he had already turned out for Aston Villa in the FA Cup earlier that season.

The highest score by any team in the FA Cup was achieved by Preston North End when they beat Hyde United 26–0 on 15 October 1887. The highest individual score was nine goals by Ted MacDougall for Bournemouth v Margate on 20 November 1971. Nottingham Forest scored three goals within five minutes of the kick-off against Clapton on 17 January 1895 in a first round tie away. Forest went on to win 14–0 that day for the record away score in the competition.

The highest number of FA Cup final appearances is nine made by the Hon Sir Arthur Fitzgerald Kinnaird. He won five medals in 1873, 1877 and 1878 with Wanderers and 1879 and 1882 with Old Etonians.

Major, later Sir Francis Marindin, the Brigade Major at Chatham from 1866 to 1874, played in the 1872 and 1874 finals for Royal Engineers and refereed eight finals between 1880 and 1890. He was President of the FA from 1874 to 1890.

There have been 40 different winning teams of the FA Cup and since the formation of the Football League in 1888 all but eight have been drawn from clubs in Division One. The exceptions were Notts County (1894), Wolverhampton Wanderers (1908), Barnsley (1912), West Bromwich Albion (1931), Sunderland (1973), Southampton (1976) and West Ham United (1980) all from Division Two. Tottenham Hotspur (1901) were members of the Southern League when they won it.

Only one replay has been necessary for a Wembley final. In 1970 Chelsea beat Leeds United 2–1 at Old Trafford after a 2–2 draw at Wembley after extra time. The attendance of 62 078 was the lowest crowd for a final since 1922.

Dennis Clarke (West Bromwich Albion) was the first substitute called upon to participate in an FA Cup Final against Everton in 1968. Eddie Kelly was the first substitute to score a goal when he did so for Arsenal against Liverpool in 1971.

Eight different venues, excluding replays, have been used for the FA Cup final.

Aston Villa have won the FA Cup a record seven times. Newcastle United and Arsenal share the highest number of wins at Wembley, each having achieved five successes there. Arsenal made three successive appearances at Wembley from 1978 to 1980, winning once in 1979.

The 1980 FA Cup semi-final between Arsenal and Liverpool was the longest in the history of the competition. It needed three replays to decide the winner.

There have been 99 finals with replays adding another nine matches. A total of 281 goals have been scored, 224 by the winning teams and 57 by the defeated ones.

Billy Minter scored seven goals for St Albans City against Dulwich Hamlet in a replayed fourth qualifying round FA Cup tie on 22 November 1922 but Dulwich won 8–7.

Five replays were needed before Alvechurch beat Oxford City 1–0 in a fourth qualifying round tie in the 1971–72 season. The six matches produced a total playing time of eleven hours.

In 1887 Old Carthusians lost 2–1 after extra time to Preston North End. It was the last occasion that an Old Boys team reached as far. Included in their side was C Aubrey Smith (1863–1948), later a captain of an England cricket team and a Hollywood film actor, while in goal was C Wreford Brown who in three seasons played as a forward, centre-half and goalkeeper.

Brian Kidd (Everton) became only the third player in FA Cup history to be sent off in a semi-final when he was dismissed against West Ham United in 1980. The others were: Arthur Childs (Hull City) in 1930 and Mick Martin (West Bromwich Albion) in 1978. Kidd was the first to be sent off three times in the competition, having previously suffered this fate with Manchester United in 1968 v Tottenham Hotspur, and with Everton in 1980 v Wigan Athletic.

Brian Kidd spent the early part of the 1980 close season deciding to join Bolton Wanderers from Everton and looking forward to creating more positive records for his new club. (Syndication International)

Charles Wreford Brown was an Oxford Soccer Blue who missed a similar award at cricket through injury. A centre-half, he was capped four times by England before the turn of the century.

Football League Club directory

Ground	Capacity & Record	League career		Honours (domestic) League	Cup

ALDERSHOT (1926) Red, blue, white trim/white

Ground	Capacity & Record	League career		Honours (domestic) League	Cup
Recreation Ground High Street Aldershot GU11 1TW 117×76 yd	16,000 19,138 v Carlisle FA Cup 4th Rd replay, 28 January 1970	1932–58 Div. 3(S) 1958–73 Div. 4 1973–76 Div. 3	1976– Div. 4	Highest placing 8th Div. 3 1974	FA Cup never past 5th Rd League Cup never past 2nd Rd

ARSENAL (1886) Red, white sleeves/white

Ground	Capacity & Record	League career		Honours (domestic) League	Cup
Arsenal Stadium Highbury London N5 110×71 yd	60,000 73,295 v Sunderland Div. 1 9 March 1935	1893–1904 Div. 2 1904–13 Div. 1 1913–15 Div. 2 1919– Div. 1		Div. 1 Champions 1931, 1933, 1934, 1935, 1938, 1948, 1953, 1971 Runners-up 1926, 1932, 1973, Div. 2 runners-up 1904	FA Cup winners 1930, 1936, 1950, 1971, 1979 Runners-up 1927, 1932, 1952, 1972, 1978, 1980 League Cup runners-up 1968, 1969

ASTON VILLA (1874) Claret, blue sleeves/white

Ground	Capacity & Record	League career		Honours (domestic) League	Cup
Villa Park Trinity Road Birmingham B6 6HE 115×75 yd	48,000 76,588 v Derby Co FA Cup 6th Rd 2 March 1946	1888 (founder member of League) 1936–38 Div. 2 1938–59 Div. 1 1959–60 Div. 2 1960–67 Div. 1	1967–70 Div. 2 1970–72 Div. 3 1972–75 Div. 2 1975– Div. 1	Div. 1 Champions 1894, 1896, 1897, 1899, 1900, 1910, Runners-up 1889, 1903, 1908, 1911, 1913, 1914, 1931, 1933 Div. 2 Champions 1938, 1960 Runners-up 1975 Div. 3 Champions 1972	FA Cup winners 1887, 1895, 1897, 1905, 1913, 1920, 1957 (a record) Runners-up 1892, 1924 League Cup winners 1961, 1975, 1977 Runners-up 1963, 1971

BARNSLEY (1887) Red/white

Ground	Capacity & Record	League career		Honours (domestic) League	Cup
Oakwell Ground Grove Street Barnsley 111×75 yd	38,500 40,255 v Stoke City FA Cup 5th Rd 15 February 1936	1898 elected to Div. 2 1932–34 Div. 3(N) 1934–38 Div. 2 1938–39 Div. 3(N) 1946–53 Div. 2 1953–55 Div. 3(N)	1955–59 Div. 2 1959–65 Div. 3 1965–68 Div. 4 1968–72 Div. 3 1972–79 Div. 4 1979– Div. 3	Div. 3(N) Champions 1934, 1939, 1955 Runners-up 1954 Div. 4 runners-up 1968	FA Cup winners 1912 Runners-up 1910 League Cup never past 3rd Rd

BIRMINGHAM CITY (1875) Blue, white trim/white, blue trim

Ground	Capacity & Record	League career		Honours (domestic) League	Cup
St Andrews Birmingham B9 4NH 115×75 yd	41,000 66,844 v Everton FA Cup 5th Rd 11 February 1939	1892–94 Div. 2 1894–96 Div. 1 1896–1901 Div. 2 1901–02 Div. 1 1902–03 Div. 2 1903–08 Div. 1 1908–21 Div. 2 1921–39 Div. 1	1946–48 Div. 2 1948–50 Div. 1 1950–55 Div. 2 1955–65 Div. 1 1965–72 Div. 2 1972–79 Div. 1 1979–80 Div. 2 1980– Div. 1	Div. 2 Champions 1893, 1921, 1948, 1955 Runners-up 1894, 1901, 1903, 1972	FA Cup runners-up 1931, 1956 League Cup winners 1963

Most League Points	Goals	Record win	Player highest number of goals		Most League appearances	Most capped player
			Aggregate	Individual		
						ALDERSHOT
57, Div. 4 1978–79	83, Div. 4 1963–64	8–1 v Gateshead Div. 4 13 September 1958	Jack Howarth 171, 1965–71, 1972–77	John Dungworth 26 Div. 4 1978–79	Len Walker 450, 1964—76	Peter Scott, 1, N. Ireland 1979
						ARSENAL
66, Div. 1 1930–31	127, Div. 1 1930–31	12–0 v Loughborough T. Div. 2 12 March 1900	Cliff Bastin 150, 1930–47	Ted Drake 42 Div. 1 1934–35	George Armstrong 500, 1960–77	Pat Rice 49, N. Ireland 1968–80
						ASTON VILLA
70, Div. 3 1971–72	128, Div. 1 1930–31	13–0 v Wednesbury Old Athletic FA Cup 1st Rd 1886	Harry Hampton 213, 1904–20 Billy Walker 213, 1919–34	Pongo Waring 49 Div. 1 1930–31	Charlie Aitken 560, 1961–76	Peter McParland 33, N. Ireland 1954–61
						BARNSLEY
67, Div. 3(N) 1938–39	118, Div. 3(N) 1933–34	9–0 v Loughborough T Div. 2 28 January 1899 Accrington Stanley Div. 3(N) 3 February 1934	Ernest Hine 123, 1921–26, 1934–38	Cecil McCormack 33 Div. 2 1950–51	Barry Murphy 514, 1962–78	Eddie McMorran 9, N. Ireland 1950–52
						BIRMINGHAM CITY
59, Div. 2 1947–48	103, Div. 2 1893–94	12–0 v Walsall Town Swifts Div. 2 17 December 1892 Doncaster Rovers Div. 2 11 April 1903	Joe Bradford 249, 1920–35	Joe Bradford 29 Div. 1 1927–28	Gil Merrick 486, 1946–60	Malcolm Page 28, Wales 1971–79

Ground	Capacity & Record	League career	Honours (domestic) League	Cup

BLACKBURN ROVERS (1875) Blue-white halves/white

Ground	Capacity & Record	League career	League	Cup
Ewood Park Blackburn BB2 4JF 116 × 72 yd	30,000 61,783 v Bolton W FA Cup 6th Rd 2 March 1929	1888 (founder member of League) 1936–39 Div. 2 1946–47 Div. 1 1947–57 Div. 2 1957–66 Div. 1	1966–71 Div. 2 1971–75 Div. 3 1975–79 Div. 2 1979–80 Div. 3 1980– Div. 2	Div. 1 Champions 1912, 1914 Div. 2 Champions 1939 Runners-up 1958 Div. 3 Champions 1975 Runners-up 1980	FA Cup winners 1884, 1885, 1886, 1890, 1891, 1928 Runners-up 1882, 1960 League Cup semi-finalists 1962

BLACKPOOL (1887) Tangerine, white trim/white

Ground	Capacity & Record	League career	League	Cup
Bloomfield Road Blackpool FY1 6JJ 111 × 73 yd	29,540 39,118 v Manchester U Div. 1 19 April 1952	1896 elected to Div. 2 1899 failed re-election 1900 re-elected 1900–30 Div. 2 1930–33 Div. 1	1933–37 Div. 2 1937–67 Div. 1 1967–70 Div. 2 1970–71 Div. 1 1971–78 Div. 2 1978– Div. 3	Div. 1 runners-up 1956 Div. 2 Champions 1930 Runners-up 1937, 1970	FA Cup winners 1953 Runners-up 1948, 1951 League Cup semi-finalists 1962

BOLTON WANDERERS (1874) White/navy blue

Ground	Capacity & Record	League career	League	Cup
Burnden Park Bolton BL3 2QR 113 × 76 yd	43,000 69,912 v Manchester C FA Cup 5th Rd 18 February 1933	1888 (founder member of League) 1899–1900 Div. 2 1900–03 Div. 1 1903–05 Div. 2 1905–08 Div. 1 1908–09 Div. 2 1909–10 Div. 1	1910–11 Div. 2 1911–33 Div. 1 1933–35 Div. 2 1935–64 Div. 1 1964–71 Div. 2 1971–73 Div. 3 1973–78 Div. 2 1978–80 Div. 1 1980– Div. 2	Div. 2 Champions 1909, 1978 Runners-up 1900, 1905, 1911, 1935 Div. 3 Champions 1973	FA Cup winners 1923, 1926, 1929, 1958 Runners-up 1894, 1904, 1953 League Cup semi-finalists 1977

AFC BOURNEMOUTH (1899) Red /white

Ground	Capacity & Record	League career	League	Cup
Dean Court Ground Bournemouth Dorset 118 × 75 yd	19,175 28,799 v Manchester U FA Cup 6th Rd 2 March 1957	1923 elected to Div. 3(S) 1970–71 Div. 4 1971–75 Div. 3 1975– Div. 4		Div. 3(S) runners-up 1948 Div. 4 runners-up 1971	FA Cup never past 6th Rd League Cup never past 4th Rd

BRADFORD CITY (1903) White with maroon and amber trim/white

Ground	Capacity & Record	League career	League	Cup
Valley Parade Ground Bradford BD8 7DY 110 × 76 yd	23,469 39,146 v Burnley FA Cup 4th Rd 11 March 1911	1903 elected to Div. 2 1908–22 Div. 1 1922–27 Div. 2 1927–29 Div. 3(N) 1929–37 Div. 2	1937–61 Div. 3 1961–69 Div. 4 1969–72 Div. 3 1972–77 Div. 4 1977–78 Div. 3 1978– Div. 4	Div. 2 Champions 1908 Div. 3(N) Champions 1929	FA Cup winners 1911 League Cup never past 5th Rd

BRENTFORD (1889) Red-white stripes/black

Ground	Capacity & Record	League career	League	Cup
Griffin Park Braemar Road Brentford Middlesex TW8 0NT 114 × 75 yd	37,000 39,626 v Preston NE FA Cup 6th Rd 5 March 1938	1920 (founder member of Div. 3) 1921–33 Div. 3(S) 1933–35 Div. 2 1935–47 Div. 1 1947–54 Div. 2 1954–58 Div. 3 (S) 1958–62 Div. 3	1962–63 Div. 4 1963–66 Div. 3 1966–72 Div. 4 1972–73 Div. 3 1973–78 Div. 4 1978– Div. 3	Div. 2 Champions 1935 Div. 3(S) Champions 1933 Runners-up 1930, 1958 Div. 4 Champions 1963	FA Cup never past 6th Rd League Cup never past 3rd Rd

Most League Points	Goals	Record win	Player highest number of goals Aggregate	Individual	Most League appearances	Most capped player

BLACKBURN ROVERS

| 60, Div. 3 1974–75 | 114, Div. 2 1954–55 | 11–0 v Rossendale United FA Cup 1884–85 | Tommy Briggs 140, 1952–58 | Ted Harper 43 Div. 1 1925–26 | Ronnie Clayton 580, 1950–69 | Bob Crompton 41, England 1902–14 |

BLACKPOOL

| 58, Div. 2 1929–30 & 1967–68 | 98, Div. 2 1929–30 | 10–0 v Lanerossi Vicenza Anglo-Italian tournament 10 June 1972 | Jimmy Hampson 247, 1927–38 | Jimmy Hampson 45 Div. 2 1929–30 | Jimmy Armfield 568, 1952–71 | Jimmy Armfield 43, England 1959–66 |

BOLTON WANDERERS

| 61, Div. 3 1972–73 | 96, Div. 2 1934–35 | 13–0 v Sheffield United FA Cup 2nd Rd 1 February 1890 | Nat Lofthouse 255, 1946–61 | Joe Smith 38 Div. 1 1920–21 | Eddie Hopkinson 519, 1956–70 | Nat Lofthouse 33 England 1951–58 |

AFC BOURNEMOUTH

| 62, Div. 3 1971–72 | 88, Div. 3(S) 1956–57 | 11–0 v Margate FA Cup 1st Rd 20 November 1971 | Ron Eyre 202, 1924–33 | Ted MacDougall 42 Div. 4 1970–71 | Ray Bumstead 412, 1958–70 | Tommy Godwin 4, Eire 1956–58 |

BRADFORD CITY

| 63, Div. 3(N) 1928–29 | 128, Div. 3(N) 1928–29 | 11–1 v Rotherham United Div. 3(N) 25 August 1928 | Frank O'Rourke 88, 1906–13 | David Layne 34 Div. 4 1961–62 | Ian Cooper 443, 1965–77 | Harry Hampton 9, N. Ireland 1911–14 |

BRENTFORD

| 62, Div. 3(S) 1932–33 Div. 4 1962–63 | 98, Div. 4 1962–63 | 9–0 v Wrexham Div. 3 15 October 1963 | Jim Towers 153, 1954–61 | Jack Holliday 38 Div. 3(S) 1932–33 | Ken Coote 514, 1949–64 | Idris Hopkins 12, Wales 1934–39 |

Ground	Capacity & Record	League career		Honours (domestic) League	Cup

BRIGHTON & HOVE ALBION (1900) All blue

The Goldstone Ground	32,500	1920 (founder	1965–72 Div. 3	Div. 2 Runners-up	FA Cup never
Old Shoreham Road	36,747 v	member of Div. 3)	1972–73 Div. 2	1979	past 5th Rd
Hove, Sussex	Fulham Div. 2	1921–58 Div. 3(S)	1973–77 Div. 3	Div. 3(S)	League Cup
BN3 7DE	27 December 1958	1958–62 Div. 2	1977–79 Div. 2	Champions 1958	never past
112 × 75 yd		1962–63 Div. 3	1979– Div. 1	Runners-up	5th Rd
		1963–65 Div. 4		1954, 1956	
				Div. 3 runners-up	
				1972, 1977	
				Div. 4 Champions	
				1965	

BRISTOL CITY (1894) Red/white

Ashton Gate	30,868	1901 elected	1927–32 Div. 2	Div. 1 runners-up	FA Cup
Bristol	43,335 v	to Div. 2	1932–55 Div.3(S)	1907	runners-up
BS3 2EJ	Preston NE	1906–11 Div. 1	1955–60 Div. 2	Div. 2 champions	1909
115 × 75 yd	FA Cup 5th Rd	1911–22 Div. 2	1960–65 Div. 3	1906	League Cup
	16 February 1935	1922–23 Div. 3(S)	1965–76 Div. 2	Runners-up 1976	semi-finalists
		1923–24 Div. 2	1976–80 Div. 1	Div. 3(S)	1971
		1924–27 Div. 3(S)	1980– Div. 2	Champions 1923,	
				1927, 1955	
				Runners-up 1938	
				Div. 3 runners-up	
				1965	

BRISTOL ROVERS (1883) Blue-white quarters/white

Bristol Stadium	32,000	1920 (founder	1962–74 Div. 3	Div. 3(S)	FA Cup never
Eastville	38,472 v	member of Div. 3)	1974– Div. 2	Champions 1953	past 6th Rd
Bristol BS5 6NN	Preston NE	1921–53 Div. 3(S)		Div. 3 runners-up	League Cup
110 × 70 yd	FA Cup 4th Rd	1953–62 Div. 2		1974	never past
	30 January 1960				5th Rd

BURNLEY (1882) Claret/Blue

Turf Moor	38,000	1888 (founder	1930–47 Div. 2	Div. 1 Champions	FA Cup winners
Burnley	54,775 v	member of	1947–71 Div. 1	1921, 1960	1914
BB10 4BX	Huddersfield T	League)	1971–73 Div. 1	Runners-up	Runners-up
115 × 73 yd	FA Cup 3rd Rd	1897–98 Div. 2	1973–76 Div. 1	1920, 1962	1947, 1962
	23 February 1924	1898–1900 Div. 1	1976–80 Div. 2	Div. 2 Champions	League Cup
		1900–13 Div. 2	1980– Div. 3	1898, 1973	semi-finalists
		1913–30 Div. 1		Runners-up	1961, 1969
				1913, 1947	

BURY (1885) White/royal blue

Gigg Lane	35,000	1894 elected	1961–67 Div. 2	Div. 2 Champions	FA Cup winners
Bury	35,000 v	to Div. 2	1967–68 Div. 3	1895	1900, 1903
BL9 9HR	Bolton W	1895–1912 Div. 1	1968–69 Div. 2	Runners-up	League Cup
112 × 72 yd	FA Cup 3rd Rd	1912–24 Div. 2	1969–71 Div. 3	1924	semi-finalists
	9 January 1960	1924–29 Div. 1	1971–74 Div. 4	Div. 3 Champions	1963
		1929–57 Div. 2	1974– Div. 3	1961	
		1957–61 Div. 3		Runners-up	
				1968	

CAMBRIDGE UNITED (1919) Amber/black

Abbey Stadium	12,000	1970 elected	1977–78 Div. 3	Div. 4 Champions	FA Cup never
Newmarket Road	14,000 v	to Div. 4	1978– Div. 2	1977	past 4th Rd
Cambridge	Chelsea	1973–74 Div. 3		Div. 3 runners-up	League Cup
115 × 75 yd	Friendly	1974–77 Div. 4		1978	never past
	1 May 1970				2nd Rd

Most League Points	Goals	Record win	Player highest number of goals Aggregate	Individual	Most League appearances	Most capped player
						BRIGHTON & HOVE ALBION
65, Div. 3(S) 1955–56 Div. 3 1971–72	112, Div. 3(S) 1955–56	10–1 v Wisbech FA Cup 1st Rd 13 November 1965	Tommy Cook 113, 1922–29	Peter Ward 32 Div. 3 1976–77	Tug Wilson 509, 1922–36	Jack Jenkins 8, Wales 1924–26
						BRISTOL CITY
70, Div. 3(S) 1954–55	104, Div. 3(S) 1926–27	11–0 v Chichester FA Cup 1st Rd 5 November 1960	John Atyeo 315, 1951–66	Don Clark 36 Div. 3(S) 1946–47	John Atyeo 597, 1951–66	Billy Wedlock 26, England 1907–14
						BRISTOL ROVERS
64, Div. 3(S) 1952–53	92, Div. 3(S) 1952–53	7–0 Swansea T Div. 2 2 Oct. 1954 Brighton & HA Div. 3(S) 29 Nov. 1952 Shrewsbury T Div. 3, 21 Mar. 1964	Geoff Bradford 245, 1949–64	Geoff Bradford 33 Div. 3(S) 1952–53	Stuart Taylor 545, 1966–79	Matt O'Mahoney 6, Eire ; 1, N Ireland 1938–39
						BURNLEY
62, Div. 2 1972–73	102, Div. 1 1960–61	9–0 v Darwen Div. 1 9 January 1892 Crystal Palace FA Cup 2nd Rd replay 1908–09 New Brighton FA Cup 4th Rd 26 January 1957	George Beel 178, 1923–32	George Beel 35 Div. 1 1927–28	Jerry Dawson 530, 1906–29	Jimmy McIlroy 52, N. Ireland 1951–63
						BURY
68, Div. 3 1960–61	108, Div. 3 1960–61	12–1 v Stockton FA Cup 1st Rd replay 1896–97	Norman Bullock 124, 1920–35	Norman Bullock 31 Div. 1 1925–26	Norman Bullock 506, 1920–35	Bill Gorman 11, Eire 1936–38
						CAMBRIDGE UNITED
65, Div. 4 1976–77	87, Div. 4 1976–77	6–0 v Darlington Div. 4 18 September 1971	Alan Biley 75, 1975–79	Alan Biley 21 Div. 3 1977–78	Terry Eades 248, 1970–77	Tom Finney 7, N. Ireland 1979–80

Ground	Capacity & Record	League career		Honours (domestic) League	Cup

CARDIFF CITY (1899) Blue with yellow and white trim/blue

Ninian Park	43,000	1920 elected	1957–60 Div. 2	Div. 1 runners-up	FA Cup winners
Cardiff	57,800 v	to Div. 2	1960–62 Div. 1	1924	1927
CF1 8SX	Arsenal Div. 1	1921–29 Div. 1	1962–75 Div. 2	Div. 2 runners-up	Runners-up
112 × 76 yd	22 April 1953	1929–31 Div. 2	1975–76 Div. 3	1921, 1952, 1960	1925
		1931–47 Div. 3(S)	1976– Div. 2	Div. 3(S)	League Cup
		1947–52 Div. 2		Champions 1947	semi-finalists
		1952–57 Div. 1		Div. 3 runners-up	1966
				1976	

CARLISLE UNITED (1904) Blue/white

Brunton Park	25,000	1928 elected	1965–74 Div. 2	Promoted to	FA Cup never
Carlisle	27,500 v	to Div. 3(N)	1974–75 Div. 1	Div. 1 1974	past 6th Rd
CA1 1LL	Birmingham C	1958–62 Div. 4	1975–77 Div. 2	Div. 3 Champions	League Cup
117 × 78 yd	FA Cup 3rd Rd	1962–63 Div. 3	1977– Div. 3	1965	semi-finalists
	5 January 1957	1963–64 Div. 4		Div. 4 runners-up	1970
	and Middlesbrough	1964–65 Div. 3		1964	
	FA Cup 5th Rd				
	7 February 1970				

CHARLTON ATHLETIC (1905) Red/white

The Valley	66,000	1921 elected	1936–57 Div. 1	Div. 1 runners-up	FA Cup winners
Floyd Road	75,031 v	to Div. 3(S)	1957–72 Div. 2	1937	1947
Charlton	Aston Villa	1929–33 Div. 2	1972–75 Div. 3	Div. 2 runners-up	Runners-up
London SE7 8AW	FA Cup 5th Rd	1933–35 Div. 3(S)	1975–80 Div. 2	1936	1946
114 × 78 yd	12 February 1938	1935–36 Div. 2	1980– Div. 3	Div. 3(S)	League Cup
				Champions 1929,	never past
				1935	4th Rd

CHELSEA (1905) Blue/blue

Stamford Bridge	41,000	1905 elected	1930–62 Div. 1	Div. 1 Champions	FA Cup winners
London SW6	82,905 v	to Div. 2	1962–63 Div. 2	1955	1970
114 × 71 yd	Arsenal Div. 1	1907–10 Div. 1	1963–75 Div. 1	Div. 2 runners-up	Runners-up
	12 October 1935	1910–12 Div. 2	1975–77 Div. 2	1907, 1912, 1930,	1915, 1967
		1912–24 Div. 1	1977–79 Div. 1	1963, 1977	League Cup
		1924–30 Div. 2	1979– Div. 2		winners 1965
					Runners-up
					1972

CHESTER (1884) Blue-white stripes/blue

The Stadium	20,000	1931 elected		Div. 3(N)	FA Cup never
Sealand Road	20,500 v	to Div. 3(N)		runners-up 1936	past 5th Rd
Chester CH1 4LW	Chelsea	1958–75 Div. 4			League Cup
114 × 76 yd	FA Cup 3rd Rd	1975– Div. 3			semi-finalists
	replay				1975
	16 January 1952				

CHESTERFIELD (1866) Blue/white

Recreation Ground	28,500	1899 elected	1933–36 Div. 3(N)	Div. 3(N)	FA Cup never
Chesterfield	30,968 v	to Div. 2	1936–51 Div. 2	Champions	past 5th Rd
114 × 72 yd	Newcastle U	1909 failed	1951–58 Div. 3(N)	1931, 1936	League Cup
	Div. 2	re-election	1958–61 Div. 3	Runners-up 1934	never past
	7 April 1939	1921 elected	1961–70 Div. 4	Div. 4 Champions	4th Rd
		to Div. 3(N)	1970– Div. 3	1970	
		1931–33 Div. 2			

Most League Points	Goals	Record win	Player highest number of goals Aggregate	Individual	Most League appearances	Most capped player
						CARDIFF CITY
66, Div. 3(S) 1946–47	93, Div. 3(S) 1946–47	9–2 v Thames Div. 3(S) 6 February 1932	Len Davies 127, 1921–29	Stan Richards 31 Div. 3(S) 1946–47	Tom Farquharson 445, 1922–35	Alf Sherwood 39, Wales 1946–56
						CARLISLE UNITED
62, Div. 3(N) 1950–51	113, Div. 4 1963–64	8–0 v Hartlepool United Div. 3(N) 1 September 1928 Scunthorpe United Div. 3(N) 25 December 1952	Jimmy McConnell 126, 1928–32	Jimmy McConnell 42 Div. 3(N) 1928–29	Alan Ross 466, 1963–79	Eric Welsh 4, N Ireland 1966–67
						CHARLTON ATHLETIC
61, Div. 3(S) 1934–35	107, Div. 2 1957–58	8–1 Middlesbrough Div. 1 12 September 1953	Stuart Leary 153, 1953–62	Ralph Allen 32 Div. 3(S) 1934–35	Sam Bartram 583, 1934–56	John Hewie 19, Scotland 1956–60
						CHELSEA
57, Div. 2 1906–07	98, Div. 1 1960–61	13–0 v Jeunesse Hautcharage Cup-Winners' Cup 1st Rd 29 September 1971	Bobby Tambling 164, 1958–70	Jimmy Greaves 41 Div. 1 1960–61	Ron Harris 655, 1962–80	Ray Wilkins 24, England 1976–79
						CHESTER
56, Div. 3(N) 1946–47 Div. 4 1964–65	119, Div. 4 1964–65	12–0 v York City Div. 3(N) 1 February 1936	Gary Talbot 83, 1963–67 1968–70	Dick Yates 36 Div. 3(N) 1946–47	Ray Gill 408, 1951–62	Bill Lewis 9, Wales 1894–96
						CHESTERFIELD
64, Div. 4 1969–70	102, Div. 3(N) 1930–31	10–0 v Glossop North End Div. 2 17 January 1903	Ernie Moss 113, 1969–76, 1979–80	Jimmy Cookson 44 Div. 3(N) 1925–26	Dave Blakey 613, 1948–67	Walter McMillen 4, N Ireland 1937–38

Ground	Capacity & Record	League career		Honours (domestic) League	Cup

COLCHESTER UNITED (1937) Blue-white stripes/blue

Ground	Capacity & Record	League career		Honours (domestic) League	Cup
Layer Road Ground Colchester 110 × 71 yd	16,150 19,072 v Reading FA Cup 1st Rd 27 November 1948	1950 elected to Div. 3(S) 1958–61 Div. 3 1961–62 Div. 4 1962–65 Div. 3 1965–66 Div. 4	1966–68 Div. 3 1968–74 Div. 4 1974–76 Div. 3 1976–77 Div. 4 1977– Div. 3	Div. 4 runners-up 1962	FA Cup never past 6th Rd League Cup never past 5th Rd

COVENTRY CITY (1883) Sky blue/sky blue

Ground	Capacity & Record	League career		Honours (domestic) League	Cup
Highfield Road Coventry 110 × 75 yd	48,000 51,457 v Wolverhampton W Div. 2 29 April 1967	1919 elected to Div. 2 1925–26 Div. 3(N) 1926–36 Div. 3(S) 1936–52 Div. 2 1952–58 Div. 3(S)	1958–59 Div. 4 1959–64 Div. 3 1964–67 Div. 2 1967– Div. 1	Div. 2 Champions 1967 Div. 3 Champions 1964 Div. 3(S) Champions 1936 Runners-up 1934 Div. 4 runners-up 1959	FA Cup never past 6th Rd League Cup never past 5th Rd

CREWE ALEXANDRA (1877) Red/white

Ground	Capacity & Record	League career		Honours (domestic) League	Cup
Football Ground Gresty Road Crewe 112 × 74 yd	17,000 20,000 v Tottenham H FA Cup 4th Rd 30 January 1960	1892 (founder member of Div. 2) 1896 failed re-election 1921 re-elected to Div. 3(N)	1958–63 Div. 4 1963–64 Div. 3 1964–68 Div. 4 1968–69 Div. 3 1969– Div. 4	Highest placing 10th Div. 2 1893	FA Cup semi-finalists 1888 League Cup never past 3rd Rd

CRYSTAL PALACE (1905) White with red diagonal band/white

Ground	Capacity & Record	League career		Honours (domestic) League	Cup
Selhurst Park London SE25 6PU 110 × 75 yd	51,000 51,801 v Burnley Div. 2 11 May 1979	1920 (founder member of Div. 3) 1921–25 Div. 2 1925–58 Div. 3(S) 1958–61 Div. 4 1961–64 Div. 3	1964–69 Div. 2 1969–73 Div. 1 1973–74 Div. 2 1974–77 Div. 3 1977–79 Div. 2 1979– Div. 1	Div. 2 Champions 1979 runners-up 1969 Div. 3 runners-up 1964 Div. 3(S) Champions 1921 Runners-up 1929, 1931, 1939 Div. 4 Runners-up 1961	FA Cup semi-finalists 1976 League Cup never past 5th Rd

DARLINGTON (1883) White with black trim/black

Ground	Capacity & Record	League career		Honours (domestic) League	Cup
Feethams Ground Darlington 110 × 74 yd	20,000 21,023 v Bolton W League Cup 3rd Rd 14 November 1960	1921 (founder member of Div. 3(N)) 1925–27 Div. 2 1927–58 Div. 3(N)	1958–66 Div. 4 1966–67 Div. 3 1967– Div. 4	Div. 3(N) Champions 1925 Runners-up 1922 Div. 4 runners-up 1966	FA Cup never past 5th Rd League Cup never past 5th Rd

DERBY COUNTY (1884) White/blue

Ground	Capacity & Record	League career		Honours (domestic) League	Cup
Baseball Ground Shaftesbury Crescent Derby DE3 8NB 110 × 71 yd	35,000 41,826 v Tottenham H Div. 1 20 September 1969	1888 (founder member of League) 1907–12 Div. 2 1912–14 Div. 1 1914–15 Div. 2 1915–21 Div. 1	1921–26 Div. 2 1926–53 Div. 1 1953–55 Div. 2 1955–57 Div. 3(N) 1957–69 Div. 2 1969–80 Div. 1 1980– Div. 2	Div. 1 Champions 1972, 1975 Runners-up 1896, 1930, 1936 Div. 2 Champions 1912, 1915, 1969 Runners-up 1926 Div. 3(N) Champions 1957 Runners-up 1956	FA Cup winners 1946 Runners-up 1898, 1899, 1903 League Cup semi-finalists 1968

Most League Points	Goals	Record win	Player highest number of goals		Most League appearances	Most capped player
			Aggregate	Individual		
COLCHESTER UNITED						
60, Div. 4 1973–74	104, Div. 4 1961–62	9–1 v Bradford City Div. 4 30 December 1961	Martyn King 131, 1959–65	Bobby Hunt 37 Div. 4 1961–62	Micky Cook 445, 1969–80	None
COVENTRY CITY						
60, Div. 4 1958–59 Div. 3 1963–64	108, Div. 3(S) 1931–32	9–0 v Bristol City Div. 3(S) 28 April 1934	Clarrie Bourton 171, 1931–37	Clarrie Bourton 49 Div. 3(S) 1931–32	George Curtis 486, 1956–70	Dave Clements 21, N Ireland 1965–71
CREWE ALEXANDRA						
59, Div. 4 1962–63	95, Div. 3(N) 1931–32	8–0 v Rotherham United Div. 3(N) 1 October 1932	Bert Swindells 126, 1928–37	Terry Harkin 34 Div. 4 1964–65	Tommy Lowry 436, 1966–78	Bill Lewis 12, Wales 1890–92
CRYSTAL PALACE						
64, Div. 4 1960–61	110, Div. 4 1960–61	9–0 v Barrow Div. 4 10 October 1959	Peter Simpson 154, 1930–36	Peter Simpson 46 Div. 3(S) 1930–31	Terry Long 432, 1956–69	Ian Evans 13, Wales 1975–77
DARLINGTON						
59, Div. 4 1965–66	108, Div. 3(N) 1929–30	9–2 v Lincoln City Div. 3(N) 7 January 1928	David Brown 74, 1923–26	David Brown 39 Div. 3(N) 1924–25	Ron Greener 442, 1955–68	None
DERBY COUNTY						
63, Div. 2 1968–69 Div. 3(N) 1955–56, 1956–57	111, Div. 3(N) 1956–57	12–0 v Finn Harps UEFA Cup 3rd Rd First leg 15 September 1976	Steve Bloomer 291, 1892–1906 1910–14	Jack Bowers 37 Div. 1 1930–31 Ray Straw 37 Div. 3(N) 1956–57	Jack Parry 478, 1949–66	Roy McFarland 28, England 1971–76

Ground	Capacity & Record	League career		Honours (domestic) League	Cup

DONCASTER ROVERS (1879) Red/white

| Belle Vue Ground Doncaster 110×77 yd | 21,150 37,149 v Hull City Div. 3(N) 2 October 1948 | 1901 elected to Div. 2 1903 failed re-election 1904 re-elected 1905 failed re-election 1923 re-elected to Div. 3(N) 1935–37 Div. 2 | 1937–47 Div. 3(N) 1947–48 Div. 2 1948–50 Div. 3(N) 1950–58 Div. 2 1958–59 Div. 3 1959–66 Div. 3 1966–67 Div. 3 1967–69 Div. 4 1969–71 Div. 3 1971– Div. 4 | Div. 3(N) Champions 1935, 1947, 1950 Runners-up 1938, 1939 Div. 4 Champions 1966, 1969 | FA Cup never past 5th Rd League Cup never past 5th Rd |

EVERTON (1878) Blue/white

| Goodison Park Liverpool L4 4EL 112×78 yd | 55,000 78,299 v Liverpool Div. 1 18 September 1948 | 1888 (founder member of League) 1930–31 Div. 2 1931–51 Div. 1 1951–54 Div. 2 1954– Div. 1 | | Div. 1 Champions 1891, 1915, 1928, 1932, 1939, 1963, 1970 Runners-up 1890, 1895, 1902, 1905, 1909, 1912 Div. 2 Champions 1931 Runners-up 1954 | FA Cup winners 1906, 1933, 1966 Runners-up 1893 1897, 1907, 1968 League Cup runners-up 1977 |

EXETER CITY (1904) Red-white stripes/black

| St James Park Exeter 114×73 yd | 17,500 20,984 v Sunderland FA Cup 6th Rd replay 4 March 1931 | 1920 elected to Div. 3 1921–58 Div. 3(S) 1958–64 Div. 4 1964–66 Div. 3 | 1966–77 Div. 4 1977– Div. 3 | Div. 3(S) runners-up 1933 Div. 4 runners-up 1977 | FA Cup never past 6th Rd League Cup never past 4th Rd |

FULHAM (1879) White/black

| Craven Cottage Stevenage Road Fulham London SW6 110×75 yd | 42,000 49,335 v Millwall Div. 2 8 October 1938 | 1907 elected to Div. 2 1928–32 Div. 3(S) 1932–49 Div. 2 1949–52 Div. 1 1952–59 Div. 2 | 1959–68 Div. 1 1968–69 Div. 2 1969–71 Div. 3 1971–80 Div. 2 1980– Div. 3 | Div. 2 Champions 1949 Runners-up 1959 Div. 3(S) Champions 1932 Div. 3 runners-up 1971 | FA Cup runners-up 1975 League Cup never past 5th Rd |

GILLINGHAM (1893) Blue/white

| Prestfield Stadium Gillingham 114×75 yd | 22,000 23,002 v QPR FA Cup 3rd Rd 10 January 1948 | 1920 (founder member of Div. 3) 1921 Div. 3(S) 1938 failed re-election 1950 re-elected to Div. 3(S) | 1958–64 Div. 4 1964–71 Div. 3 1971–74 Div. 4 1974– Div. 3 | Div. 4 Champions 1964 Runners-up 1974 | FA Cup never past 5th Rd League Cup never past 4th Rd |

Most League Points	Goals	Record win	Player highest number of goals Aggregate	Individual	Most League appearances	Most capped player
						DONCASTER ROVERS
72, Div. 3(N) 1946–47	123, Div. 3(N) 1946–47	10–0 v Darlington Div. 4 25 January 1964	Tom Keetley 180, 1923–29	Clarrie Jordan 42 Div. 3(N) 1946–47	Fred Emery 406, 1925–36	Len Graham 14, N Ireland 1951–58
						EVERTON
66, Div. 1 1969–70	121, Div. 2 1930–31	11–2 v Derby County FA Cup 1st Rd 1889–90	Dixie Dean 349, 1925–37	Dixie Dean 60 Div. 1 1927–28	Ted Sagar 465, 1929–53	Alan Ball 39, England 1966–71
						EXETER CITY
62, Div. 4 1976–77	88, Div. 3(S) 1932–33	8–1 v Coventry City Div. 3(S) 4 December 1926 Aldershot Div. 3(S) 4 May 1935	Alan Banks 105, 1963–66, 1967–73	Fred Whitlow 34 Div. 3(S) 1932–33	Arnold Mitchell 495, 1952–66	Dermot Curtis 1, Eire 1963
						FULHAM
60, Div. 2 1958–59 Div. 3 1970–71	111, Div. 3(S) 1931–32	10–1 v Ipswich Town Div. 1 26 December 1963	Bedford Jezzard 154, 1948–56	Frank Newton 41 Div. 3(S) 1931–32	Johnny Haynes 594, 1952–70	Johnny Haynes 56, England 1954–62
						GILLINGHAM
62, Div. 4 1973–74	90, Div. 4 1973–74	10–1 v Gorleston FA Cup 1st Rd 16 November 1957	Brian Yeo 135, 1963–75	Ernie Morgan 31 Div. 3(S) 1954–55 Brian Yeo 31 Div. 4 1973–74	John Simpson 571, 1957–72	Damien Richardson 2, Eire 1973–79

Ground	Capacity & Record	League career	Honours (domestic) League	Cup

GRIMSBY TOWN (1878) Black-white stripes/black

| Blundell Park Cleethorpes South Humberside DN35 7PY 111 × 74 yd | 24,000 31,657 v Wolverhampton W FA Cup 5th Rd 20 February 1937 | 1892 (founder member of Div. 2) 1901–03 Div. 1 1903–10 Div. 2 1910 failed re-election 1911 re-elected to Div. 2 1920–21 Div. 3 1921–26 Div. 3(N) 1926–29 Div. 2 1929–32 Div. 1 | 1932–34 Div. 2 1934–48 Div. 1 1948–51 Div. 2 1951–56 Div. 3(N) 1956–59 Div. 2 1959–62 Div. 3 1962–64 Div. 2 1964–68 Div. 3 1968–72 Div. 4 1972–77 Div. 3 1977–79 Div. 4 1979–80 Div. 3 1980–   Div. 2 | Div. 2 Champions 1901, 1934 Runners-up 1929 Div. 3(N) Champions 1926, 1956 Runners-up 1952 Div. 3 Champions 1980 Div. 3 runners-up 1962 Div. 4 Champions 1972 Runners-up 1979 | FA Cup semi-finalists 1936, 1939 League Cup never past 5th Rd |

HALIFAX TOWN (1911) Royal blue with white trim/white

| Shay Ground Halifax HX1 2YS 110 × 70 yd | 23,000 36,885 v Tottenham H FA Cup 5th Rd 14 February 1953 | 1921 (founder member of Div. 3(N)) 1958–63 Div. 3 1963–69 Div. 4 | 1969–76 Div. 3 1976–   Div. 4 | Div. 3(N) runners-up 1935 Div. 4 runners-up 1969 | FA Cup never past 5th Rd League Cup never past 4th Rd |

HARTLEPOOL UNITED (1908) Blue/white

| The Victoria Ground Hartlepool 113 × 77 yd | 16,000 17,426 v Manchester U FA Cup 3rd Rd 5 January 1957 | 1921 (founder member of Div. 3(N)) 1958–68 Div. 4 | 1968–69 Div. 3 1969–   Div. 4 | Div. 3 (N) runners-up 1957 | FA Cup never past 4th Rd League Cup never past 4th Rd |

HEREFORD UNITED (1924) White with black and red trim/black

| Edgar Street Hereford 111 × 80 yd | 17,500 18,114 v Sheffield W FA Cup 3rd Rd 4 January 1958 | 1972 elected to Div. 4 1973–76 Div. 3 1976–77 Div. 2 | 1977–78 Div. 3 1978–   Div. 4 | Div. 3 Champions 1976 Div. 4 runners-up 1973 | FA Cup never past 4th Rd League Cup never past 3rd Rd |

HUDDERSFIELD TOWN (1908) Blue-white stripes/white

| Leeds Road Huddersfield HD1 6PE 115 × 75 yd | 48,000 67,037 v Arsenal FA Cup 6th Rd 27 February 1932 | 1910 elected to Div. 2 1920–52 Div. 1 1952–53 Div. 2 1953–56 Div. 1 1956–70 Div. 2 | 1970–72 Div. 1 1972–73 Div. 2 1973–75 Div. 3 1975–80 Div. 4 1980–   Div. 3 | Div. 1 Champions 1924, 1925, 1926 Runners-up 1927, 1928, 1934 Div. 2 Champions 1970 Runners-up 1920, 1953 Div. 4 Champions 1980 | FA Cup winners 1922 Runners-up 1920, 1928, 1930, 1938 League Cup semi-finalists 1968 |

Most League Points	Goals	Record win	Player highest number of goals		Most League appearances	Most capped player
			Aggregate	Individual		
						GRIMSBY TOWN
68, Div. 3(N) 1955–56	103, Div. 2 1933–34	9–2 v Darwen Div. 2 15 April 1899	Pat Glover 182, 1930–39	Pat Glover 42 Div. 2 1933–34	Keith Jobling 448, 1953–69	Pat Glover 7, Wales 1931–39
						HALIFAX TOWN
57, Div. 4 1968–69	83, Div. 3(N) 1957–58	7–0 v Bishop Auckland FA Cup 2nd Rd replay 10 January 1967	Ernest Dixon 129, 1922–30	Albert Valentine 34 Div. 3(N) 1934–35	John Pickering 367, 1965–74	None
						HARTLEPOOL UNITED
60, Div. 4 1967–68	90, Div. 3(N) 1956–57	10–1 v Barrow Div. 4 4 April 1959	Ken Johnson 98, 1949–64	William Robinson 28 Div. 3(N) 1927–28	Wattie Moore 448, 1948–64	Ambrose Fogarty 1, Eire 1964
						HEREFORD UNITED
63, Div. 3 1975–76	86, Div. 3 1975–76	11–0 v Thynnes FA Cup 1947–48	Dixie McNeil 85, 1974–77	Dixie McNeil 35 Div. 3 1975–76	Tommy Hughes 222, 1973–80	Brian Evans 1, Wales 1973
						HUDDERSFIELD TOWN
66, Div. 4 1979–80	101, Div. 4 1979–80	10–1 v Blackpool Div. 1 13 December 1930	George Brown 142, 1921–29	Sam Taylor 35 Div. 2 1919–20 George Brown 35 Div. 1 1925–26	Billy Smith 520, 1914–34	Jimmy Nicholson 31, N Ireland 1965–71

Ground	Capacity & Record	League career		Honours (domestic) League	Cup

HULL CITY (1904) Black-amber stripes/black

Boothferry Park	42,000	1905 elected	1958–59 Div. 3	Div. 3(N)	FA Cup
Hull HU4 6EU	55,019 v	to Div. 2	1959–60 Div. 2	Champions	semi-finalists
112 × 75 yd	Manchester U	1930–33 Div. 3(N)	1960–66 Div. 3	1933, 1949	1930
	FA Cup 6th Rd	1933–36 Div. 2	1966–78 Div. 2	Div. 3 Champions	League Cup
	26 February 1949	1936–49 Div. 3(N)	1978– Div. 3	1966	never past
		1949–56 Div. 2		Runners-up 1959	4th Rd
		1956–58 Div. 3(N)			

IPSWICH TOWN (1887) Blue/white

Portman Road	32,000	1938 elected to	1961–64 Div. 1	Div. 1 Champions	FA Cup
Ipswich	38,010 v	Div. 3(S)	1964–68 Div. 2	1962	winners 1978
Suffolk	Leeds United	1954–55 Div. 2	1968– Div. 1	Div. 2 Champions	League Cup
IP1 2DA	FA Cup 6th Rd	1955–57 Div. 3(S)		1961, 1968	never past
112 × 72 yd	8 March 1975	1957–61 Div. 2		Div. 3(S)	5th Rd
				Champions	
				1954, 1957	

LEEDS UNITED (1919) White/white

Elland Road	43,900	1920 elected to	1932–47 Div. 1	Div. 1 Champions	FA Cup winners
Leeds LS11 0ES	57,892 v	Div. 2	1947–56 Div. 2	1969, 1974	1972
117 × 76 yd	Sunderland	1924–27 Div. 1	1956–60 Div. 1	Runners-up	Runners-up
	FA Cup 5th Rd	1927–28 Div. 2	1960–64 Div. 2	1965, 1966, 1970,	1965, 1970, 1973
	replay	1928–31 Div. 1	1964– Div. 1	1971, 1972	League Cup
	15 March 1967	1931–32 Div. 2		Div. 2 Champions	winners 1968
				1924, 1964	
				Runners-up	
				1928, 1932, 1956	

LEICESTER CITY (1884) Blue/white

City Stadium	32,000	1894 elected	1946–54 Div. 2	Div. 1 runners-up	FA Cup
Filbert Street	47,298 v	to Div. 2	1954–55 Div. 1	1929	runners-up 1949,
Leicester	Tottenham H	1908–09 Div. 1	1955–57 Div. 2	Div. 2 Champions	1961, 1963, 1969
112 × 75 yd	FA Cup 5th Rd	1909–25 Div. 2	1957–69 Div. 1	1925, 1937, 1954,	League Cup
	18 February 1928	1925–35 Div. 2	1969–71 Div. 2	1957, 1971, 1980	winners 1964
		1935–37 Div. 2	1971–78 Div. 1	Runners-up 1908	Runners-up
		1937–39 Div. 1	1978–80 Div. 2		1965
			1980– Div. 1		

LINCOLN CITY (1883) Red-white stripes/black

Sincil Bank	25,300	1892 (founder	1921–32 Div. 3(N)	Div. 3(N)	FA Cup never
Lincoln	23,196 v	member of Div. 2)	1932–34 Div. 2	Champions	past 5th Rd
110 × 75 yd	Derby Co	1908 failed	1934–48 Div. 3(N)	1932, 1948, 1952	(equivalent)
	League Cup 4th Rd	re-election	1948–49 Div. 2	Runners-up	League Cup
	15 November 1967	1909 re-elected	1949–52 Div. 3(N)	1928, 1931, 1937	never past
		1911 failed	1952–61 Div. 2	Div. 4 Champions	4th Rd
		re-election	1961–62 Div. 3	1976	
		1912 re-elected	1962–76 Div. 4		
		1920 failed	1976–79 Div. 3		
		re-election	1979– Div. 4		
		1921 re-elected			

Most League Points	Goals	Record win	Player highest number of goals Aggregate	Individual	Most League appearances	Most capped player

HULL CITY

| 69, Div. 3 1965–66 | 109, Div. 3 1965–66 | 11–1 v Carlisle United Div. 3(N) 14 January 1939 | Chris Chilton 195, 1960–71 | Bill McNaughton 39 Div. 3(N) 1932–33 | Andy Davidson 511, 1952–67 | Terry Neill 15, N Ireland 1970–73 |

IPSWICH TOWN

| 64, Div. 3(S) 1953–54 1955–56 | 106, Div. 3(S) 1955–65 | 10–0 v Floriana (Malta) Euro. Cup 1st Rd 25 September 1962 | Ray Crawford 203, 1958–63, 1966–69 | Ted Phillips 41 Div. 3(S) 1956–57 | Mick Mills 506, 1966–80 | Allan Hunter 47, N Ireland 1972–80 |

LEEDS UNITED

| 67, Div. 1 1968–69 | 98, Div. 2 1927–28 | 10–0 v Lyn Oslo (Norway) Euro. Cup 1st Rd First leg 17 September 1969 | John Charles 154, 1948–57, 1962 | John Charles 42 Div. 2 1953–54 | Jack Charlton 629, 1953–73 | Billy Bremner 54, Scotland 1965–75 |

LEICESTER CITY

| 61, Div. 2 1956–57 | 109, Div. 2 1956–57 | 10–0 v Portsmouth Div. 1 20 October 1928 | Arthur Chandler 262, 1923–35 | Arthur Rowley 44 Div. 2 1956–57 | Adam Black 530, 1919–35 | Gordon Banks 37, England 1963–66 |

LINCOLN CITY

| 74, Div. 4 1975–76 | 121, Div. 3(N) 1951–52 | 11–1 v Crewe Alexandra Div. 3(N) 29 September 1951 | Andy Graver 144, 1950–55, 1958–61 | Allan Hall 42 Div. 3(N) 1931–32 | Tony Emery 402, 1946–59 | David Pugh 3, Wales,1900–01 Con Moulson 3, Eire 1936–37 George Moulson 3, Eire 1948 |

Ground	Capacity & Record	League career	Honours (domestic) League	Cup

LIVERPOOL (1892) Red/red

Anfield Road Liverpool 4 110 × 75 yd	52,518 61,905 v Wolverhampton W FA Cup 4th Rd 2 February 1952	1893 elected to Div. 2 1894–95 Div. 1 1895–96 Div. 2 1896–1904 Div. 1	1904–05 Div. 2 1905–54 Div. 1 1954–62 Div. 2 1962– Div. 1	Div. 1 Champions 1901, 1906, 1922, 1923, 1947, 1964, 1966, 1973, 1976, 1977, 1979, 1980 (record) Runners-up 1899, 1910, 1969, 1974, 1975, 1978 Div. 2 Champions 1894, 1896, 1905, 1962	FA Cup winners 1965, 1974 Runners-up 1914, 1950, 1971, 1977 League Cup runners-up 1978

LUTON TOWN (1885) White with navy blue and orange trim/white

70-72 Kenilworth Road Luton 112 × 72 yd	22,741 30,069 v Blackpool FA Cup 6th Rd replay 4 March 1959	1897 elected to Div. 2 1900 failed re-election 1920 elected to Div. 3 1921–37 Div. 3(S) 1937–55 Div. 2 1955–60 Div. 1	1960–63 Div. 2 1963–65 Div. 3 1965–68 Div. 4 1968–70 Div. 3 1970–74 Div. 2 1974–75 Div. 1 1975– Div. 2	Div. 2 runners-up 1955, 1974 Div. 3 runners-up 1970 Div. 4 Champions 1968 Div. 3(S) Champions 1937 Runners-up 1936	FA Cup runners-up 1959 League Cup never past 5th Rd

MANCHESTER CITY (1887) Sky blue/sky blue

Maine Road Moss Side Manchester M14 7WN 119 × 79 yd	52,500 84,569 v Stoke City FA Cup 6th Rd 3 March 1934	1892 elected to Div. 2 as Ardwick FC 1894 elected to Div. 2 as Manchester C 1899–1902 Div. 1 1902–03 Div. 2 1903–09 Div. 1 1909–10 Div. 2	1910–26 Div. 1 1926–28 Div. 2 1928–38 Div. 1 1938–47 Div. 2 1947–50 Div. 1 1950–51 Div. 2 1951–63 Div. 1 1963–66 Div. 2 1966– Div. 1	Div. 1 Champions 1937, 1968 Runners-up 1904, 1921, 1977 Div. 2 Champions 1899, 1903, 1910, 1928, 1947, 1966 Runners-up 1896, 1951	FA Cup winners 1904, 1934, 1956, 1969 Runners-up 1926, 1933, 1955 League Cup winners 1970, 1976 Runners-up 1974

MANCHESTER UNITED (1878) Red/white

Old Trafford Manchester M16 0RA 116 × 76 yd	58,504 70,504 v Aston Villa Div. 1 27 December 1920	1892 elected to Div. 1 as Newton Heath. Changed name 1902 1894–1906 Div. 2 1906–22 Div. 1 1922–25 Div. 2 1925–31 Div. 1	1931–36 Div. 2 1936–37 Div. 1 1937–38 Div. 2 1938–74 Div. 1 1974–75 Div. 2 1975– Div. 1	Div. 1 Champions 1908, 1911, 1952, 1956, 1957, 1965, 1967 Runners-up 1947, 1948, 1949, 1951, 1959, 1964, 1968, 1980 Div. 2 Champions 1936, 1975 Runners-up 1897, 1906, 1925, 1938	FA Cup winners 1909, 1948, 1963, 1977 Runners-up 1957, 1958, 1976, 1979 League Cup semi-finalists 1970, 1971, 1975

Most League Points	Goals	Record win	Player highest number of goals		Most League appearances	Most capped player
			Aggregate	Individual		
						LIVERPOOL
68, Div. 1 1978–79	106, Div. 2 1895–96	11–0 v Stromsgodset (Norway) Cup-Winners' Cup 17 September 1974	Roger Hunt 245, 1959–69	Roger Hunt 41 Div. 2 1961–62	Ian Callaghan 640, 1960–78	Emlyn Hughes 59, England 1970–79
						LUTON TOWN
66, Div. 4 1967–68	103, Div. 3(S) 1936–37	12–0 v Bristol Rovers Div. 3(S) 13 April 1936	Gordon Turner 243, 1949–64	Joe Payne 55 Div. 3(S) 1936–37	Bob Morton 494, 1948–64	George Cummins 19, Eire 1953–61
						MANCHESTER CITY
62, Div. 2 1946–47	108, Div. 2 1926–27	11–3 v Lincoln City Div. 2 23 March 1895	Tommy Johnson 158, 1919–30	Tommy Johnson 38 Div. 1 1928–29	Alan Oakes 565, 1959–76	Colin Bell 48, England 1968–75
						MANCHESTER UNITED
64, Div. 1 1956–57	103, Div. 1 1956–57, 1958–59	10–0 v Anderlecht (Belgium) European Cup Prelim Rd 26 September 1956	Bobby Charlton 198, 1956–73	Dennis Viollet 32 Div. 1 1959–60	Bobby Charlton 606, 1956–73	Bobby Charlton 106, England 1958–70

Ground	Capacity & Record	League career	Honours (domestic) League	Cup

MANSFIELD TOWN (1905) Amber/blue

Field Mill Ground	23,500	1931 elected	1963–72 Div. 3	Div. 3 Champions	FA Cup never
Quarry Lane	24,467 v	to Div. 3(S)	1972–75 Div. 4	1977	past 6th Rd
Mansfield	Nottingham F	1932–37 Div. 3(N)	1975–77 Div. 3	Div. 4 Champions	League Cup
115 × 72 yd	FA Cup 3rd Rd	1937–47 Div. 3(S)	1977–78 Div. 2	1975	never past
	10 January 1953	1947–58 Div. 3(N)	1978–80 Div. 3	Div 3(N)	5th Rd
		1958–60 Div. 3	1980– Div. 4	Runners-up 1951	
		1960–63 Div. 4			

MIDDLESBROUGH (1876) Red with white trim/red

Ayresome Park	42,000	1899 elected to	1929–54 Div. 1	Div. 2 Champions	FA Cup never
Middlesbrough	53,596 v	Div. 2	1954–66 Div. 2	1927, 1929, 1974	past 6th Rd
Teesside	Newcastle U	1902–24 Div. 1	1966–67 Div. 3	Runners-up 1902	League Cup
115 × 75 yd	Div. 1	1924–27 Div. 2	1967–74 Div. 2	Div. 3 runners-up	semi-finalists
	27 December 1949	1927–28 Div. 1	1974– Div. 1	1967	1976
		1928–29 Div. 2			

MILLWALL (1885) Blue/white

The Den	32,000	1920 (founder	1962–64 Div. 3	Div. 3(S)	FA Cup
Cold Blow Lane	48,672 v	members of Div. 3)	1964–65 Div. 4	Champions	semi-finalists
London SE14 5RH	Derby Co	1921 Div. 3(S)	1965–66 Div. 3	1928, 1938	1900, 1903, 1937
112 × 74 yd	FA Cup 5th Rd	1928–34 Div. 2	1966–75 Div. 2	Div. 3 runners-up	League Cup
	20 February 1937	1934–38 Div. 3(S)	1975–76 Div. 3	1966	never past
		1938–48 Div. 2	1976– Div. 2	Div. 4 Champions	5th Rd
		1948–58 Div. 3(S)		1962	
		1958–62 Div. 4		Runners-up 1965	

NEWCASTLE UNITED (1882) Black-white stripes/black

St James' Park	40,480	1893 elected	1961–65 Div. 2	Div. 1 Champions	FA Cup winners
Newcastle-upon-Tyne	68,386 v	to Div. 2	1965–78 Div. 1	1905, 1907, 1909,	1910, 1924, 1932,
NE1 4ST	Chelsea Div. 1	1898–1934 Div. 1	1978– Div. 2	1927	1951, 1952, 1955
115 × 75 yd	3 September 1930	1934–48 Div. 2		Div. 2 Champions	Runners-up
		1948–61 Div. 1		1965	1905, 1906, 1908,
				Runners-up	1911, 1974
				1898, 1948	League Cup
					runners-up 1976

NEWPORT COUNTY (1912) Sky blue-white stripes/sky blue

Somerton Park	18,000	1920 (founder	1932–39 Div. 3(S)	Div. 3(S)	FA Cup never
Newport	24,268 v	member of Div. 3)	1946–47 Div. 2	Champions 1939	past 5th Rd
Mon	Cardiff City	1921 Div. 3(S)	1947–58 Div. 3(S)		League Cup
112 × 78 yd	Div. 3(S)	1931 dropped out	1958–62 Div. 3		never past
	16 October 1937	of League	1962–80 Div. 4		3rd Rd
		1932 re-elected	1980– Div. 3		

Most League Points	Goals	Record win	Player highest number of goals		Most League appearances	Most capped player
			Aggregate	Individual		
						MANSFIELD TOWN
68, Div. 4 1974–75	108, Div. 4 1962–63	9–2 v Rotherham United Div. 3(N) 27 December 1932 Hounslow Town replay 5 November 1962	Harry Johnson 104, 1931–36	Ted Harston 55 Div. 3(N) 1936–37	Don Bradley 417, 1949–62	John McClellend 4, N Ireland 1980
						MIDDLESBROUGH
65, Div. 2 1973–74	122, Div. 2 1926–27	9–0 v Brighton & HA Div. 2 23 August 1958	George Camsell 326, 1925–39	George Camsell 59 Div. 2 1926–27	Tim Williamson 563, 1902–23	Wilf Mannion 26, England 1946–51
						MILLWALL
65, Div. 3(S) 1927–28 Div. 3 1965–66	127, Div. 3(S) 1927–28	9–1 v Torquay United Div. 3(S) 29 August 1927 Coventry City Div. 3(S) 19 November 1927	Derek Possee 79, 1967–73	Richard Parker 37 Div. 3(S) 1926–27	Barry Kitchener 501, 1967–80	Eamonn Dunphy 22, Eire 1966–71
						NEWCASTLE UNITED
57, Div. 2 1964–65	98, Div. 1 1951–52	13–0 v Newport County Div. 2 5 October 1946	Jackie Milburn 178, 1946–57	Hughie Gallacher 36 Div. 1 1926–27	Jim Lawrence 432, 1904–22	Alf McMichael 40, N Ireland 1949–60
						NEWPORT COUNTY
61, Div. 4 1979–80	85, Div. 4 1964–65	10–0 v Merthyr Town Div. 3(S) 10 April 1930	Reg Parker 99, 1948–54	Tudor Martin 34 Div. 3(S) 1929–30	Ray Wilcox 530, 1946–60	(All for Wales) Fred Cook 2 1925 Jack Nicholls 2 1924 Alf Sherwood 2 1956 Bill Thomas 2 1930 Harold Williams 2 1949

Ground	Capacity & Record	League career		Honours (domestic) League	Cup

NORTHAMPTON TOWN (1897) White with claret trim/white

County Ground	20,000	1920 (founder	1966–67 Div. 2	Div. 2 runners-up	FA Cup never
Abington Avenue	24,523 v	member of Div. 3)	1967–68 Div. 3	1965	past 5th Rd
Northampton	Fulham Div. 1	1921 Div. 3(S)	1968–76 Div. 4	Div. 3 Champions	League Cup
NN1 4PS	23 April 1966	1958–61 Div. 4	1976–77 Div. 3	1963	never past
120 × 75 yd		1961–63 Div. 3	1977– Div. 4	Div. 3(S)	5th Rd
		1963–65 Div. 2		runners-up	
		1965–66 Div. 1		1928, 1950	
				Div. 4 runners-up	
				1976	

NORWICH CITY (1905) Yellow/green

Carrow Road	29,000	1920 (founder	1958–60 Div. 3	Div. 2 Champions	FA Cup
Norwich	43,984 v	member of Div. 3)	1960–72 Div. 2	1972	semi-finalists
NR1 1JE	Leicester City	1921 Div. 3(S)	1972–74 Div. 1	Div. 3(S)	1959
114 × 74 yd	FA Cup 6th Rd	1934–39 Div. 2	1974–75 Div. 2	Champions 1934	League Cup
	30 March 1963	1946–58 Div. 3(S)	1975– Div. 1	Div. 3 runners-up	winners 1962
				1960	Runners-up
					1973, 1975

NOTTINGHAM FOREST (1865) Red/white

City Ground	35,000	1892 elected to	1949–51 Div. 3(S)	Div. 1 Champions	FA Cup winners
Nottingham	49,945 v	Div. 1	1951–57 Div. 2	1978, Runners-up	1898, 1959
NG2 5FJ	Manchester U	1906 Div. 2	1957–72 Div. 1	1967, 1979	League Cup
115 × 78 yd	Div. 1	1907 Div. 1	1972–77 Div. 2	Div. 2 Champions	winners 1978,
	28 October 1967	1911–22 Div. 2	1977– Div. 1	1907, 1922	1979
		1922–25 Div. 1		Runners-up 1957	Runners-up 1980
		1925–49 Div. 2		Div. 3(S)	
				Champions 1951	

NOTTS COUNTY (1862) Black-white stripes/black

County Ground	40,000	1888 (founder	1930–31 Div. 3(S)	Div. 2 Champions	FA Cup winners
Meadow Lane	47,310 v	member of	1931–35 Div. 2	1897, 1914, 1923	1894
Nottingham	York City	League)	1935–50 Div. 3(S)	Runners-up 1895	Runners-up
NG2 3HJ	FA Cup 6th Rd	1893–97 Div. 2	1950–58 Div. 2	Div. 3(S)	1891
117 × 76 yd	12 March 1955	1897–1913 Div. 1	1958–59 Div. 3	Champions	League Cup
		1913–14 Div. 2	1959–60 Div. 4	1931, 1950	never past
		1914–20 Div. 1	1960–64 Div. 3	Runners-up 1937	5th Rd
		1920–23 Div. 2	1964–71 Div. 4	Div. 4 Champions	
		1923–26 Div. 1	1971–73 Div. 3	1971	
		1926–30 Div. 2	1973– Div. 2	Runners-up 1960	

OLDHAM ATHLETIC (1894) Blue/white

Boundary Park	30,000	1907 elected	1958–63 Div. 4	Div. 1 runners-up	FA Cup
Oldham	47,671 v	to Div. 2	1963–69 Div. 3	1915	semi-finalists
110 × 74 yd	Sheffield W	1910–23 Div. 1	1969–71 Div. 2	Div. 2 runners-up	1913
	FA Cup 4th Rd	1923–35 Div. 2	1971–74 Div. 3	1910	League Cup
	25 January 1930	1935–53 Div. 3(N)	1974– Div. 2	Div. 3(N)	never past
		1953–54 Div. 2		Champions 1953	3rd Rd
		1954–58 Div. 3(N)		Div. 3 Champions	
				1974	
				Div. 4 runners-up	
				1963	

Most League Points	Goals	Record win	Player highest number of goals Aggregate	Individual	Most League appearances	Most capped player
				NORTHAMPTON TOWN		
68, Div. 4 1975–76	109, Div. 3 1962–63 Div. 3(S) 1952–53	10–0 v Walsall Div. 3(S) 5 November 1927	Jack English 135, 1947–60	Cliff Holton 36 Div. 3 1961–62	Tommy Fowler 521, 1946–61	E Lloyd Davies 12, Wales 1908–14
				NORWICH CITY		
64, Div. 3(S) 1950–51	99 Div. 3(S) 1952–53	10–2 v Coventry City Div. 3(S) 15 March 1930	Johnny Gavin 122, 1945–54, 1955–58	Ralph Hunt 31 Div. 3(S) 1955–56	Ron Ashman 590, 1947–64	Ted MacDougall 7, Scotland 1975
				NOTTINGHAM FOREST		
70, Div. 3(S) 1950–51	110, Div. 3(S) 1950–51	14–0 v Clapton FA Cup 1st Rd 1890–91	Grenville Morris 199, 1898–1913	Wally Ardron 36 Div. 3(S) 1950–51	Bob McKinlay 614, 1951–70	Martin O'Neill 34, N Ireland 1972–80
				NOTTS COUNTY		
69, Div. 4 1970–71	107, Div. 4 1959–60	15–0 v Thornhill United FA Cup 1st Rd 24 October 1885	Les Bradd 125, 1967–78	Tom Keetley 39 Div. 3(S) 1930–31	Albert Iremonger 564, 1904–26	Bill Fallon 7, Eire 1934–38
				OLDHAM ATHLETIC		
62, Div. 3 1973–74	95, Div. 4 1962–63	11–0 v Southport Div. 4 26 December 1962	Eric Gemmell 110, 1947–54	Tom Davis 33 Div. 3(N) 1936–37	Ian Wood 525, 1966–80	Albert Gray 9, Wales 1924–27

Ground	Capacity & Record	League career		Honours (domestic) League	Cup

ORIENT (1881) White with two red stripes/white

Leyton Stadium	25,000	1905 elected	1963–66 Div. 2	Div. 2 runners-up	FA Cup
Brisbane Road	34,345 v	to Div. 2	1966–70 Div. 3	1962	semi-finalists
Leyton	West Ham U	1929–56 Div. 3(S)	1970– Div. 2	Div. 3 Champions	1978
London E10 5NE	FA Cup 4th Rd	1956–62 Div. 2		1970	League Cup
110×75 yd	25 January 1964	1962–63 Div. 1		Div. 3(S)	never past
				Champions 1956	5th Rd
				Runners-up 1955	

OXFORD UNITED (1896) Yellow/blue

Manor Ground	17,350	1962 elected	1968–76 Div. 2	Div. 3 Champions	FA Cup never
Beech Road	22,730 v	to Div. 4	1976– Div. 3	1968	past 6th Rd
Headington	Preston NE	1965–68 Div. 3			League Cup
Oxford	FA Cup 6th Rd				never past
112×78 yd	29 February 1964				5th Rd

PETERBOROUGH UNITED (1923) Blue-white stripes/blue

London Road Ground	30,000	1960 elected	1968–74 Div. 4	Div. 4 Champions	FA Cup never
Peterborough	30,096 v	to Div. 4	1974–79 Div. 3	1961, 1974	past 6th Rd
PE2 8AL	Swansea T	1961–68 Div. 3	1979– Div. 4		League Cup
112×76 yd	FA Cup 5th Rd	1968 demoted			semi-finalists
	20 February 1965	for financial			1966
		irregularities			

PLYMOUTH ARGYLE (1886) Green/white

Home Park	40,000	1920 (founder	1958–59 Div. 3	Div. 3(S)	FA Cup never
Plymouth	43,596 v	member of Div. 3)	1959–68 Div. 2	Champions	past 5th Rd
Devon	Aston Villa Div. 2	1921–30 Div. 3(S)	1968–75 Div. 3	1930, 1952	League Cup
112×75 yd	10 October 1936	1930–50 Div. 2	1975–77 Div. 2	Runners-up	semi-finalists
		1950–52 Div. 3(S)	1977– Div. 3	1922, 1923, 1924,	1965, 1974
		1952–56 Div. 2		1925, 1926, 1927	
		1956–58 Div. 3(S)		Div. 3 Champions	
				1959	
				Runners-up 1975	

PORTSMOUTH (1898) Blue/white

Fratton Park	46,000	1920 (founder	1961–62 Div. 3	Div. 1 Champions	FA Cup winners
Frogmore Road	51,385 v	member of Div. 3)	1962–76 Div. 2	1949, 1950	1939
Portsmouth	Derby Co	1921–24 Div. 3(S)	1976–78 Div. 3	Div. 2 runners-up	Runners-up
PO4 8RA	FA Cup 6th Rd	1924–27 Div. 2	1978– Div. 4	1927	1929, 1934
116×73 yd	26 February 1949	1927–59 Div. 1		Div. 3(S)	League Cup
		1959–61 Div. 2		Champions 1924	never past
				Div. 3 Champions	5th Rd
				1962	

Most League Points	Goals	Record win	Player highest number of goals		Most League appearances	Most capped player
			Aggregate	Individual		
						ORIENT
66, Div. 3(S) 1955–56	106, Div. 3(S) 1955–56	9–2 v Aldershot Div. 3(S) 10 February 1934 Chester League Cup 3rd Rd 15 October 1962	Tom Johnston 121, 1956–58, 1959–61	Tom Johnston 35 Div. 2 1957–58	Peter Allen 430, 1965–78	Tony Grealish 8, Eire 1976–79
						OXFORD UNITED
61, Div. 4 1964–65	87, Div. 4 1964–65	7–1 v Barrow Div. 4 19 December 1964	Graham Atkinson 73, 1962–73	Colin Booth 23 Div. 4 1964–65	John Shuker 480, 1962–77	David Roberts 6, Wales 1973–74
						PETERBOROUGH UNITED
66, Div. 4 1960–61	134, Div. 4 1960–61	8–1 v Oldham Athletic Div. 4 26 November 1969	Jim Hall 120, 1967–75	Terry Bly 52 Div. 4 1960–61	Tommy Robson 461, 1968–80	Ollie Conmy 5, Eire 1965–69
						PLYMOUTH ARGYLE
68, Div. 3(S) 1929–30	107, Div. 3(S) 1925–26, 1951–52	8–1 v Millwall Div. 2 16 January 1932	Sammy Black 180, 1924–38	Jack Cock 32 Div. 3(S) 1925–26	Sammy Black 470, 1924–38	Moses Russell 20, Wales 1920–28
						PORTSMOUTH
65, Div. 3 1961–62	91, Div. 4 1979–80	9–1 v Notts County Div. 2 9 April 1927	Peter Harris 194, 1946–60	Billy Haines 40 Div. 2 1926–27	Jimmy Dickinson 764, 1946–65	Jimmy Dickinson 48, England 1949–56

Ground	Capacity & Record	League career	Honours (domestic) League	Cup

PORT VALE (1876) White/black

Vale Park Burslem Stoke-on-Trent 116 × 76 yd	35,000 50,000 v Aston Villa FA Cup 5th Rd 20 February 1960	1892 (founder member of Div. 2) 1896 failed re-election 1898 re-elected 1907 resigned 1919 returned in October and took over the fixtures of Leeds City 1929–30 Div. 3(N)	1930–36 Div. 2 1936–38 Div. 3(N) 1938–52 Div. 3(S) 1952–54 Div. 3(N) 1954–57 Div. 2 1957–58 Div. 3(S) 1958–59 Div. 4 1959–65 Div. 3 1965–70 Div. 4 1970–78 Div. 3 1978– Div. 4	Div. 3(N) Champions 1930, 1954 Runners-up 1953 Div. 4 Champions 1959	FA Cup semi-finalists 1954 League Cup never past 2nd Rd

PRESTON NORTH END (1881) White/white

Deepdale Preston PR1 6RU 112 × 78 yd	25,000 42, 684 v Arsenal Div. 1 23 April 1938	1888 (founder member of League) 1901–04 Div. 2 1904–12 Div. 1 1912–13 Div. 2 1913–14 Div. 1 1914–15 Div. 2 1919–25 Div. 1 1925–34 Div. 2	1934–49 Div. 1 1949–51 Div. 2 1951–61 Div. 1 1961–70 Div. 2 1970–71 Div. 3 1971–74 Div. 2 1974–78 Div. 3 1978– Div. 2	Div. 1 Champions 1889, 1890 Runners-up 1891, 1892, 1893, 1906, 1953, 1958 Div. 2 Champions 1904, 1913, 1951 Runners-up 1915, 1934 Div. 3 Champions 1971	FA Cup winners 1889, 1938 Runners-up 1888, 1922, 1937, 1954, 1964 League Cup never past 4th Rd

QUEEN'S PARK RANGERS (1885) Blue-white hoops/white

South Africa Road London W12 7PA 112 × 72 yd	30,000 35,353 v Leeds U Div. 1 28 April 1974	1920 (founder member of Div. 3) 1921–48 Div. 3(S) 1948–52 Div. 2 1952–58 Div. 3(S) 1958–67 Div. 3	1967–68 Div. 2 1968–69 Div. 1 1969–73 Div. 2 1973–79 Div. 1 1979– Div. 2	Div. 1 runners-up 1976 Div. 2 runners-up 1968, 1973 Div. 3(S) Champions 1948 Runners-up 1947 Div. 3 Champions 1967	FA Cup never past 6th Rd or equivalent League Cup winners 1967

READING (1871) Blue-white hoops/white

Elm Park Norfolk Reading 112 × 77 yd	27,200 33,042 v Brentford FA Cup 5th Rd 19 February 1927	1920 (founder member of Div. 3) 1921–26 Div. 3(S) 1926–31 Div. 2 1931–58 Div. 3(S)	1958–71 Div. 3 1971–76 Div. 4 1976–77 Div. 3 1977–79 Div. 4 1979– Div. 3	Div. 3(S) Champions 1926 Runners-up 1932, 1935, 1949, 1952 Div. 4 Champions 1979	FA Cup semi-finalists 1927 League Cup never past 4th Rd

ROCHDALE (1907) Blue/white

Spotland Willbutts Lane Rochdale 113 × 75 yd	28,000 24,231 v Notts Co FA Cup 2nd Rd 10 December 1949	1921 elected to Div. 3(N) 1958–59 Div. 3 1959–69 Div. 4	1969–74 Div. 3 1974– Div. 4	Div. 3(N) runners-up 1924, 1927	FA Cup never past 4th Rd League Cup runners-up 1962

Most League Points	Goals	Record win	Player highest number of goals		Most League appearances	Most capped player
			Aggregate	Individual		

PORT VALE

Most League Points	Goals	Record win	Aggregate	Individual	Most League appearances	Most capped player
69, Div. 3(N) 1953–54	110, Div. 4 1958–59	9–1 v Chesterfield Div. 2 24 September 1932	Wilf Kirkham 154, 1923–29, 1931–33	Wilf Kirkham 38 Div. 2 1926–27	Roy Sproson 761, 1950–72	Sammy Morgan 7, N Ireland 1972–73

PRESTON NORTH END

| 61, Div. 3 1970–71 | 100, Div. 2 1927–28 Div. 1 1957–58 | 26–0 v Hyde FA Cup 1st series 1st Rd 15 October 1887 | Tom Finney 187, 1946–60 | Ted Harper 37 Div. 2 1932–33 | Alan Kelly 447, 1961–75 | Tom Finney 76, England 1946–58 |

QUEEN'S PARK RANGERS

| 67, Div. 3 1966–67 | 111, Div. 3 1961–62 | 9–2 v Tranmere Rovers Div. 3 3 December 1960 | George Goddard 172, 1926–34 | George Goddard 37 Div. 3(S) 1929–30 | Tony Ingham 519, 1950–63 | Don Givens 21, Eire 1973–78 |

READING

| 65, Div. 4 1978–79 | 112, Div. 3(S) 1951–52 | 10–2 v Crystal Palace Div. 3(S) 4 September 1946 | Ronnie Blackman 156, 1947–54 | Ronnie Blackman 39 Div. 3(S) 1951–52 | Dick Spiers 453, 1955–70 | Pat McConnell 8, N Ireland 1925–28 |

ROCHDALE

| 62, Div. 3(N) 1923–24 | 105, Div. 3(N) 1926–27 | 8–1 v Chesterfield Div. 3(N) 18 December 1926 | Albert Whitehurst 117, 1923–28 | Albert Whitehurst 44 Div. 3(N) 1926–27 | Graham Smith 317, 1966–74 | None |

Ground	Capacity & Record	League career		Honours (domestic) League	Cup

ROTHERHAM UNITED (1884) Red, white sleeves/white

Millmoor Ground	22,000	1893 elected	1923–51 Div. 3(N)	Div. 3(N)	FA Cup never
Rotherham	25,000 v	to Div. 2	1951–68 Div. 2	Champions 1951	past 5th Rd
115 × 76 yd	Sheffield U	1896 failed	1968–73 Div. 3	Runners-up	League Cup
	Div. 2	re-election	1973–75 Div. 4	1947, 1948, 1949	runners-up 1961
	13 December 1952	1919 re-elected	1975– Div. 3		
	and Sheffield W	to Div. 2			
	Div. 2				
	26 January 1952				

SCUNTHORPE UNITED (1904) Red/red

Old Show Ground	27,000	1950 elected to	1968–72 Div. 4	Div. 3(N)	FA Cup never
Scunthorpe	23,935 v	Div. 3(N)	1972–73 Div. 3	Champions 1958	past 5th Rd
South Humberside	Portsmouth	1958–64 Div. 2	1973– Div. 4		League Cup
112 × 78 yd	FA Cup 4th Rd	1964–68 Div. 3			never past
	30 January 1954				3rd Rd

SHEFFIELD UNITED (1889) White with red, black stripes/black

Bramall Lane Ground	49,000	1892 elected	1956–61 Div. 2	Div. 1 Champions	FA Cup winners
Sheffield	68,287 v	to Div. 2	1961–68 Div. 1	1898	1899, 1902, 1915,
S2 4SU	Leeds U	1893–1934 Div. 1	1968–71 Div. 2	Runners-up	1925
117 × 75 yd	FA Cup 5th Rd	1934–39 Div. 2	1971–76 Div. 1	1897, 1900	Runners-up
	15 February 1936	1946–49 Div. 1	1976–79 Div. 2	Div. 2 Champions	1901, 1936
		1949–53 Div. 2	1979– Div. 3	1953	League Cup
		1953–56 Div. 1		Runners-up 1893	never past
				1939, 1961, 1971	5th Rd

SHEFFIELD WEDNESDAY (1867) Blue-white stripes/blue

Hillsborough	50,174	1892 elected	1951–52 Div. 2	Div. 1 Champions	FA Cup winners
Sheffield	72,841 v	to Div. 1	1952–55 Div. 1	1903, 1904, 1929,	1896, 1907, 1935
S6 1SW	Manchester C	1899–1900 Div. 2	1955–56 Div. 2	1930	Runners-up
115 × 75 yd	FA Cup 5th Rd	1900–20 Div. 1	1956–58 Div. 1	Runners-up 1961	1890, 1966
	17 February 1934	1920–26 Div. 2	1958–59 Div. 2	Div. 2 Champions	League Cup
		1926–37 Div. 1	1959–70 Div. 1	1900, 1926, 1952,	never past
		1937–50 Div. 2	1970–75 Div. 2	1956, 1959	4th Rd
		1950–51 Div. 1	1975–80 Div. 3	Runners-up 1950	
			1980– Div. 2		

SHREWSBURY TOWN (1886) Blue/blue

Gay Meadow	18,000	1950 elected	1959–74 Div. 3	Div. 3 Champions	FA Cup never
Shrewsbury	18,917 v	to Div. 3(N)	1974–75 Div. 4	1979	past 6th Rd
116 × 76 yd	Walsall Div. 3	1951–58 Div. 3(S)	1975–79 Div. 3	Div. 4 runners-up	League Cup
	26 April 1961	1958–59 Div. 4	1979– Div. 2	1975	semi-finalists
					1961

SOUTHAMPTON (1885) Red-white stripes/black

The Dell	24,000	1920 (founder	1960–66 Div. 2	Div. 2 runners-up	FA Cup winners
Milton Road	31,044 v	member of Div. 3)	1966–74 Div. 1	1966, 1978	1976
Southampton	Manchester U	1921–22 Div. 3(S)	1974–78 Div. 2	Div. 3(S)	Runners-up
SO9 4XX	Div. 1	1922–53 Div. 2	1978– Div. 1	Champions 1922	1900, 1902
110 × 72 yd	8 October 1969	1953–58 Div. 3(S)		Runners-up 1921	League Cup
		1958–60 Div. 3		Div. 3 Champions	runners-up 1979
				1960	

Most League Points	Goals	Record win	Player highest number of goals		Most League appearances	Most capped player
			Aggregate	Individual		
ROTHERHAM UNITED						
71, Div. 3(N) 1950–51	114, Div. 3(N) 1946–47	8–0 v Oldham Athletic Div. 3(N) 26 May 1947	Gladstone Guest 130, 1946–56	Wally Ardron 38 Div. 3(N) 1946–47	Danny Williams 459, 1946–62	Harold Millership 6, Wales 1920–21
SCUNTHORPE UNITED						
66, Div. 3(N) 1957–58	88, Div. 3(N) 1957–58	9–0 v Boston United FA Cup 1st Rd 21 November 1953	Barrie Thomas 92, 1959–62, 1964–66	Barrie Thomas 31 Div. 2 1961–62	Jack Brownsword 600, 1950–65	None
SHEFFIELD UNITED						
60, Div. 2 1952–53	102, Div. 1 1925–26	11–2 v Cardiff City Div. 1 1 January 1926	Harry Johnson 205, 1919–30	Jimmy Dunne 41 Div. 1 1930–31	Joe Shaw 629, 1948–66	Billy Gillespie 25, N Ireland 1913–30
SHEFFIELD WEDNESDAY						
62, Div. 2 1958–59	106, Div. 2 1958–59	12–0 v Halliweil FA Cup 1st Rd 17 January 1891	Andy Wilson 200, 1900–20	Derek Dooley 46 Div. 2 1951–52	Andy Wilson 502, 1900–20	Ron Springett 33, England 1959–66
SHREWSBURY TOWN						
62, Div. 4 1974–75	101, Div. 4 1958–59	7–0 v Swindon Town Div. 3(S) 1954–55	Arthur Rowley 152, 1958–65	Arthur Rowley 38 Div. 4 1958–59	Ken Mulhearn 370, 1971–80	Jimmy McLaughlin 5, N Ireland 1961–63
SOUTHAMPTON						
61, Div. 3(S) 1921–22 Div. 3 1959–60	112, Div. 3(S) 1957–58	11–0 v Northampton Town Southern League 28 December 1901	Mike Channon 165, 1966–77 1979–80	Derek Reeves 39 Div. 3 1959–60	Terry Paine 713, 1956–74	Mike Channon 45, England 1972–77

Ground	Capacity & Record	League career		Honours (domestic) League	Cup

SOUTHEND UNITED (1906) Blue/white

Roots Hall Ground	32,000	1920 (founder	1966–72 Div. 4	Div. 4 runners-up	FA Cup never
Victoria Avenue	31,036 v	member of Div. 3)	1972–76 Div. 3	1972, 1978	past 5th Rd
Southend-on-Sea	Liverpool	1921–58 Div. 3(S)	1976–78 Div. 4		League Cup
SS2 6NQ	FA Cup 3rd Rd	1958–66 Div. 3	1978–80 Div. 3		never past
110 × 74 yd	10 January 1979		1980– Div. 4		3rd Rd

STOCKPORT COUNTY (1883) White/blue

Edgeley Park	16,500	1900 elected	1922–26 Div. 2	Div. 3(N)	FA Cup never
Stockport	27,833 v	to Div. 2	1926–37 Div. 3(N)	Champions	past 5th Rd
Cheshire	Liverpool	1904 failed	1937–38 Div. 2	1922, 1937	League Cup
SK3 9DD	FA Cup 5th Rd	re-election	1938–58 Div. 3(N)	Runners-up	never past
110 × 75 yd	11 February 1950	1905 re-elected	1958–59 Div. 3	1929, 1930	4th Rd
		to Div. 2	1959–67 Div. 4	Div. 4 Champions	
		1905–21 Div. 2	1967–70 Div. 3	1967	
		1921–22 Div. 3(N)	1970– Div. 4		

STOKE CITY (1863) Red-white stripes/white

Victoria Ground	35,000	1888 (founder	1922–23 Div. 1	Div. 2 Champions	FA Cup
Stoke-on-Trent	51,380 v	member of	1923–26 Div. 2	1933, 1963	semi-finalists
116 × 75 yd	Arsenal Div. 1	League) 1926–27 Div. 3(N)		Runners-up 1922	1899, 1971, 1972
	29 March 1937	1890 not re-elected	1927–33 Div. 2	Div. 3(N)	League Cup
		1891 re-elected	1933–53 Div. 1	Champions 1927	winners 1972
		1907–08 Div. 2	1953–63 Div. 2		
		1908 resigned for	1963–77 Div. 1		
		financial reasons	1977–79 Div. 2		
		1919 re-elected	1979– Div. 1		
		to Div. 2			

SUNDERLAND (1879) Red-white stripes/black

Roker Park	47,000	1890 elected	1970–76 Div. 2	Div. 1 Champions	FA Cup winners
Sunderland	75,118 v	to Div. 1	1976–77 Div. 1	1892, 1893, 1895,	1937, 1973
112 × 72 yd	Derby Co	1958–64 Div. 2	1977–80 Div. 2	1902, 1913, 1936	Runners-up 1913
	FA Cup 6th Rd	1964–70 Div. 1	1980– Div. 1	Runners-up	League Cup
	replay			1894, 1898, 1901,	semi-finalists
	8 March 1933			1923, 1935	1963
				Div. 2 Champions	
				1976, 1980	
				Runners-up 1964	

SWANSEA CITY (1900) White/white

Vetch Field	35,000	1920 (founder	1965–67 Div. 3	Div. 3 runners-up	FA Cup
Swansea	32,796 v	member of Div. 3)	1967–70 Div. 4	1979	semi-finalists
110 × 70 yd	Arsenal	1921–25 Div. 3(S)	1970–73 Div. 3	Div. 3(S)	1926, 1964
	FA Cup 4th Rd	1925–47 Div. 2	1973–78 Div. 4	Champions	League Cup
	17 February 1968	1947–49 Div. 3(S)	1978–79 Div. 3	1925, 1949	never past
		1949–65 Div. 2	1979– Div. 2		4th Rd

Most League Points	Goals	Record win	Player highest number of goals Aggregate	Individual	Most League appearances	Most capped player
				SOUTHEND UNITED		
60, Div. 4 1971–72 Div. 4 1977–78	92, Div. 3(S) 1950–51	10–1 v Golders Green FA Cup 1st Rd 24 November 1934 Brentwood FA Cup 2nd Rd 7 December 1968	Roy Hollis 122, 1953–60	Jim Shankly 31 Div. 3(S) 1928–29 Sammy McCrory 31 Div. 3(S) 1957–58	Sandy Anderson 451, 1950–63	George Mackenzie 9, Eire 1937–39
				STOCKPORT COUNTY		
64, Div. 4 1966–67	115, Div. 3(N) 1933–34	13–0 v Halifax Town Div. 3(N) 6 January 1934	Jackie Connor 132, 1951–56	Alf Lythgoe 46 Div. 3(N) 1933–34	Bob Murray 465, 1952–63	Harry Hardy 1, England 1924
				STOKE CITY		
63, Div. 3(N) 1926–27	92, Div. 3(N) 1926–27	10–3 v West Bromwich Albion Div. 1 4 February 1937	Freddie Steele 142, 1934–49	Freddie Steele 33 Div. 1 1936–37	Eric Skeels 506, 1958–76	Gordon Banks 36, England 1967–72
				SUNDERLAND		
61, Div. 2 1963–64	109, Div. 1 1935–36	11–1 v Fairfield FA Cup 1st Rd 1894–95	Charlie Buchan 209, 1911–25	Dave Halliday 43 Div. 1 1928–29	Jim Montgomery 537, 1962–77	Billy Bingham 33, N Ireland 1951–58 Martin Harvey 33, N Ireland 1961–71
				SWANSEA CITY		
62, Div. 3(S) 1948–49	90, Div. 2 1956–57	8–0 v Hartlepool United Div. 4 1 April 1978	Ivor Allchurch 166, 1949–58, 1965–68	Cyril Pearce 35 Div. 2 1931–32	Wilfred Milne 585, 1919–37	Ivor Allchurch 42, Wales 1950–58

Ground	Capacity & Record	League career		Honours (domestic) League	Cup

SWINDON TOWN (1881) Red/white

| County Ground Swindon Wiltshire 114 × 72 yd | 28,000 32,000 v Arsenal FA Cup 3rd Rd 15 January 1972 | 1920 (founder member of Div. 3) 1921–58 Div. 3(S) 1958–63 Div. 3 1963–65 Div. 2 | 1965–69 Div. 3 1969–74 Div. 2 1974–   Div. 3 | Div. 3 runners-up 1963, 1969 | FA Cup semi-finalists 1910, 1912 League Cup winners 1969 |

TORQUAY UNITED (1898) White with blue and yellow trim/white

| Plainmoor Ground Torquay Devon TQ1 3PS 112 × 74 yd | 22,000 21,908 v Huddersfield T FA Cup 4th Rd 29 January 1955 | 1927 elected to Div. 3(S) 1958–60 Div. 4 1960–62 Div. 3 | 1962–66 Div. 4 1966–72 Div. 3 1972–   Div. 4 | Div. 3(S) runners-up 1957 | FA Cup never past 4th Rd League Cup never past 3rd Rd |

TOTTENHAM HOTSPUR (1882) White/blue

| 748 High Road Tottenham London N17 110 × 73 yd | 52,000 75,038 v Sunderland FA Cup 6th Rd 5 March 1938 | 1908 elected to Div. 2 1909–15 Div. 1 1919–20 Div. 2 1920–28 Div. 1 1928–33 Div. 2 | 1933–35 Div. 1 1935–50 Div. 2 1950–77 Div. 1 1977–78 Div. 2 1978–   Div. 1 | Div. 1 Champions 1951, 1961 Runners-up 1922, 1952, 1957, 1963 Div. 2 Champions 1920, 1950 Runners-up 1909, 1933 | FA Cup winners 1901, 1921, 1961, 1962, 1967 League Cup winners 1971, 1973 |

TRANMERE ROVERS (1883) White with blue trim/white

| Prenton Park Prenton Road West Birkenhead 112 × 74 yd | 25,000 24,424 v Stoke City FA Cup 4th Rd 5 February 1972 | 1921 (founder member of Div. 3(N)) 1938–39 Div. 2 1946–58 Div. 3(N) 1958–61 Div. 3 | 1961–67 Div. 4 1967–75 Div. 3 1975–76 Div. 4 1976–79 Div. 3 1979–   Div. 4 | Div. 3(N) Champions 1938 | FA Cup never past 5th Rd League Cup never past 4th Rd |

WALSALL (1888) Red/white

| Fellows Park Walsall 113 × 73 yd | 24,100 25,453 v Newcastle U Div. 2 29 August 1961 | 1892 elected to Div. 2 1895 failed re-election 1896–1901 Div. 2 1901 failed re-election 1921 (founder member of Div. 3(N)) | 1927–31 Div. 3(S) 1931–36 Div. 3(N) 1936–58 Div. 3(S) 1958–60 Div. 4 1960–61 Div. 3 1961–63 Div. 2 1963–79 Div. 3 1979–80 Div. 4 1980–   Div. 3 | Div. 4 Champions 1960 Runners-up 1980 Div. 3 runners-up 1961 | FA Cup never past 5th Rd League Cup never past 4th Rd |

WATFORD (1891) Yellow/red

| Vicarage Road Watford WD1 8ER 113 × 73 yd | 32,000 34,099 v Manchester U FA Cup 4th Rd 3 February 1969 | 1920 (founder member of Div. 3) 1921–58 Div. 3(S) 1958–60 Div. 4 1960–69 Div. 3 | 1969–72 Div. 2 1972–75 Div. 3 1975–78 Div. 4 1978–79 Div. 3 1979–   Div. 2 | Div. 3 Champions 1969 Runners-up 1979 Div. 4 Champions 1978 | FA Cup semi-finalists 1970 League Cup semi-finalists 1979 |

Most League Points	Goals	Record win	Player highest number of goals		Most League appearances	Most capped player
			Aggregate	Individual		

SWINDON TOWN

| 64, Div. 3 1968–69 | 100, Div. 3(S) 1926–27 | 10–1 v Farnham United Breweries FA Cup 1st Rd 28 November 1925 | Harry Morris 216, 1926–33 | Harry Morris 47 Div. 3(S) 1926–27 | John Trollope 756, 1960–79 | Rod Thomas 30, Wales 1967–73 |

TORQUAY UNITED

| 60, Div. 4 1959–60 | 89, Div. 3(S) 1956–57 | 9–0 v Swindon Town Div. 3(S) 8 March 1952 | Sammy Collins 204, 1948–58 | Sammy Collins 40 Div. 3(S) 1955–56 | Dennis Lewis 443, 1947–59 | None |

TOTTENHAM HOTSPUR

| 70, Div. 2 1919–20 | 115, Div. 1 1960–61 | 13–2 v Crewe Alexandra FA Cup 4th Rd replay 3 February 1960 | Jimmy Greaves 220, 1961–70 | Jimmy Greaves 37 Div. 1 1962–63 | Pat Jennings 472, 1964–77 | Pat Jennings 66, N Ireland 1964–77 |

TRANMERE ROVERS

| 60, Div. 4 1964–65 | 111, Div. 3(N) 1930–31 | 13–4 v Oldham Athletic Div. 3(N) 26 December 1935 | Bunny Bell 104, 1931–36 | Bunny Bell 35 Div. 3(N) 1933–34 | Harold Bell 595, 1946–64 | Albert Gray 3, Wales 1931 |

WALSALL

| 65, Div. 4 1959–60 | 102, Div. 4 1959–60 | 10–0 v Darwen Div. 2 4 March 1899 | Tony Richards 184, 1954–63 Colin Taylor 184, 1958–73 | Gilbert Alsop 40 Div. 3(N) 1933–34, 1934–35 | Colin Taylor 459, 1958–63, 1964–68, 1969–73 | Mick Kearns 15, Eire 1973–79 |

WATFORD

| 71, Div. 4 1977–78 | 92, Div. 4 1959–60 | 10–1 v Lowestoft Town FA Cup 1st Rd 27 November 1926 | Tom Barnett 144. 1928–39 | Cliff Holton 42 Div. 4 1959–60 | Duncan Welbourne 411, 1963–74 | Frank Hoddinott 2, Wales 1921 Pat Jennings 2, N Ireland 1964 |

Ground	Capacity & Record	League career	Honours (domestic) League	Cup

WEST BROMWICH ALBION (1879) Blue-white stripes/white

The Hawthorns West Bromwich B71 4LF 115 × 75 yd	38,600 64,815 v Arsenal FA Cup 6th Rd 6 March 1937	1888 (founder member of League) 1901–02 Div. 2 1902–04 Div. 1 1904–11 Div. 2 1911–27 Div. 1	1927–31 Div. 2 1931–38 Div. 1 1938–49 Div. 2 1949–73 Div. 1 1973–76 Div. 2 1976– Div. 1	Div. 1 Champions 1920 Runners-up 1925, 1954 Div. 2 Champions 1902, 1911 Runners-up 1931, 1949	FA Cup winners 1888, 1892, 1931, 1954, 1968 Runners-up 1886, 1887, 1895, 1912, 1935 League Cup winners 1966 Runners-up 1967, 1970

WEST HAM UNITED (1900) Claret with blue sleeves/white

Boleyn Ground Green Street Upton Park London E13 110 × 72 yd	39.500 42,322 v Tottenham H Div. 1 17 October 1970	1919 elected to Div. 2 1923–32 Div. 1 1932–58 Div. 2	1958–78 Div. 1 1978– Div. 2	Div. 2 Champions 1958 Runners-up 1923	FA Cup winners 1964, 1975, 1980 Runners-up 1923 League Cup runners-up 1966

WIGAN ATHLETIC (1932) Blue-white stripes/blue

Springfield Park Wigan 117 × 73 yd	30,000 27,500 v Hereford U FA Cup 2nd Rd 12 December 1953	1978 elected to Div. 4		Highest placing 6th Div. 4 1979 1980	FA Cup never past 4th Rd League Cup never past 2nd Rd

WIMBLEDON (1889) Yellow and blue/blue

Plough Lane Ground Durnsford Wimbledon London SW19	15,000 18,000 v HMS Victory FA Amateur Cup 3rd Rd 1934–35	1977 elected to Div. 4 1979–80 Div. 3 1980– Div. 4		Promoted to Div. 3 1979	FA Cup never past 4th Rd League Cup never past 2nd Rd

WOLVERHAMPTON WANDERERS (1877) Gold/black

Molineux Grounds Wolverhampton WV1 4QR 115 × 72 yd	41,074 61,315 v Liverpool FA Cup 5th Rd 11 February 1939	1888 (founder member of League) 1906–23 Div. 2 1923–24 Div. 3(N) 1924–32 Div. 2	1932–65 Div. 1 1965–67 Div. 2 1967–76 Div. 1 1976–77 Div. 2 1977– Div. 1	Div. 1 Champions 1954, 1958, 1959 Runners-up 1938, 1939, 1950, 1955, 1960 Div. 2 Champions 1932, 1977 Runners-up 1967 Div. 3(N) Champions 1924	FA Cup winners 1893, 1908, 1949, 1960 Runners-up 1889, 1896, 1921, 1939 League Cup winners 1974, 1980

WREXHAM (1873) Red/white

Racecourse Ground Mold Road Wrexham 117 × 75 yd	28,000 34,445 v Manchester U FA Cup 4th Rd 26 January 1957	1921 (founder member of Div. 3(N)) 1958–60 Div. 3 1960–62 Div. 4	1962–64 Div. 3 1964–70 Div. 4 1970–78 Div. 3 1978– Div. 2	Div. 3 Champions 1978 Div. 3(N) runners-up 1933 Div. 4 runners-up 1970	FA Cup never past 6th Rd League Cup never past 5th Rd

YORK CITY (1922) Red/navy blue

Bootham Crescent York 115 × 75 yd	16,529 28,123 v Huddersfield T FA Cup 5th Rd 5 March 1938	1929 elected to Div. 3(N) 1958–59 Div. 4 1959–60 Div. 3 1960–65 Div. 4 1965–66 Div. 3	1966–71 Div. 4 1971–74 Div. 3 1974–76 Div. 2 1976–77 Div. 3 1977– Div. 4	Highest placing 15th Div. 2 1975	FA Cup semi-finalists 1955 League Cup never past 5th Rd

Most League Points	Goals	Record win	Player highest number of goals		Most League appearances	Most capped player
			Aggregate	Individual		
				WEST BROMWICH ALBION		
60, Div. 1 1919–20	105, Div. 2 1929–30	12–0 v Darwen Div. 1 4 April 1892	Tony Brown 218, 1963–79	William Richardson 39 Div. 1 1935–36	Tony Brown 574, 1963–80	Stuart Williams 33, Wales 1954–62
				WEST HAM UNITED		
57, Div. 2 1957–58	101, Div. 2 1957–58	8–0 v Rotherham United Div. 2 8 March 1958 Sunderland Div. 1 19 October 1968	Vic Watson 306, 1920–35	Vic Watson 41 Div. 1 1929–30	Bobby Moore 544, 1958–74	Bobby Moore 108, England 1962–73
				WIGAN ATHLETIC		
55, Div. 4 1978–79, 1979–80	76, Div. 4 1979–80	4–1 v Bradford City 29 September 1979 Scunthorpe United 17 November 1979	Peter Houghton 28, 1978–80	Peter Houghton 15, Div. 4 1979–80	Tommy Gore, Jeff Wright, 92, 1978–80	None
				WIMBLEDON		
61, Div. 4 1978–79	78, Div. 4 1978–79	15–2 v Polytechnic FA Cup Pr Rd 7 February 1929	John Leslie 44, 1977–80	Alan Cork 22, Div. 4 1978–79	John Leslie 129, 1977–80	None
				WOLVERHAMPTON WANDERERS		
64, Div. 1 1957–58	115, Div. 2 1931–32	14–0 v Crosswell's Brewery FA Cup 2nd Rd 1886–87	Bill Hartill 164, 1928–35	Dennis Westcott 37 Div. 1 1946–47	Billy Wright 491, 1946–59	Billy Wright 105, England 1946–59
				WREXHAM		
61, Div. 4 1969–70 Div. 3 1977–78	106, Div. 3(N) 1932–33	10–1 v Hartlepool United Div. 4 3 March 1962	Tom Bamford 175, 1928–34	Tom Bamford 44 Div. 3(N) 1933–34	Arfon Griffiths 592, 1959–61 1962–79	Horace Blew 22, Wales 1899–1910
				YORK CITY		
62, Div. 4 1964–65	92, Div. 3(N) 1954–55	9–1 v Southport Div. 3(N) 2 February 1957	Norman Wilkinson 125, 1954–66	Bill Fenton 31 Div. 3(N) 1951–52 Arthur Bottom 31 Div. 3(N) 1955–56	Barry Jackson 481, 1958–70	Peter Scott 7, N Ireland 1976–78

Goalscoring

Since the Second World War, Tottenham Hotspur have been concerned in both the FA Cup tie and the Football League match which produced the highest aggregate of goals in those competitions. On 11 October 1958 they beat Everton 10–4 in a Division One match and the following season on 3 February 1960 in a fourth round Cup replay they defeated Crewe Alexandra 13–2.

Since the introduction of substitutes in the Football League at the start of the 1965–66 season, only two players have achieved hat-tricks when filling that role. Geoff Vowden did it for Birmingham City in a Division Two match against Huddersfield Town on 7 September 1968 and Keith Allen for Luton Town against Ware in the FA Cup on 16 November 1968 in a first round match. Both players went on to the field after the interval.

Of the players still active in the Football League during the 1979–80 season only Derby County's Roger Davies ever scored more than four times in one match in the competition. He hit five against Luton Town in March 1975.

Colin Viljoen, when with Ipswich Town, is the only player in recent years who has marked his Football League debut with a hat-trick, when he did so against Portsmouth on 25 March 1967; there have been several instances of players scoring twice on their initial outing. They are

Tom Cheetham scored six goals in the first two League matches of his career during the 1935–36 season for Queen's Park Rangers in Division Three (Southern). A former regular soldier he scored 35 goals in 34 matches and played in an international trial.

Left: Hat-trick scoring substitutes have understandably been rather thin on the ground and doubtless even thinner in the air. But one such treble-shooter was **Geoff Vowden for Birmingham City.** (Syndication International.) *Right:* **Roger Davies achieved a nap hand for Derby County** more than five years ago against Luton Town. His experience as a striker in recent years has included a spell in **Belgium with FC Bruges.** (Syndication International)

Fred Pickering (light shirt) playing for Everton against his former team, Blackburn Rovers, at Ewood Park on 24 March 1964 and obviously receiving close attention. (Syndication International)

Left: **Tom Cheetham gave up a rifle to become a marksman of a different nature with Queen's Park Rangers and proved to be something of an instant success in his new role. (Colorsport)**

Paul Mariner (with Plymouth Argyle), Neil Whatmore (Bolton Wanderers), Austin Hayes (Southampton), Alastair Brown (Leicester City), Alan Young (Oldham Athletic), Tom Finney (Luton Town), Joe Waters (Leicester City) and John Lathan (Mansfield Town).

In the 1963–64 season Fred Pickering achieved two hat-tricks in Division One at Goodison Park but for different teams. He scored the first for Blackburn Rovers on 9 November against Everton who signed him later and for whom he repeated the feat on 14 March against Nottingham Forest.

When Sheffield Wednesday won the championship of Division Two in the 1925–26 season Jimmy Trotter scored 37 goals in 41 matches. In Division One, a year later, he finished with exactly 37 in 41 games again.

There have been only seven instances in the period since the Second World War of a player scoring five times in an away Football League match, and near neighbours Fulham and Chelsea can each claim two of them. Fulham achieved it with Jimmy Hill and Steve Earle and Chelsea with Jimmy Greaves and Bobby Tambling.

During the 1948–49 season in Division Three (Southern) Tommy Lawton and Jackie Sewell each scored four times in two Football League matches against Exeter City on 16 October and Newport County on 16 January.

The last time a player scored as many as six goals in a Football League match was when present Chelsea manager Geoff Hurst did so for West Ham United in an 8–0 win over Sunderland in Division One on 19 October 1968.

'Bunny' Bell was the only player to average more than a goal per game in both Division One and Three in the same season. In 1935–36 in Division Three (Northern) with Tranmere Rovers he

Jackie Sewell *(above)* **was in rampant scoring form for Notts County in the 1948–49 season along with Tommy Lawton. Geoff Hurst** *(below)* **was the last player in the Football League to score as many as six goals in the competition in one match. (Syndication International)**

Bryan Robson *(centre, top)* **appears to have been on the receiving end of this accidental kick from Brian Stubbs (Notts County), but it was against Newcastle United that this former West Ham United striker invariably found the scoring target himself. Bunny Bell** *(below)* **once scored nine times in one match for Tranmere Rovers and missed a second half penalty! (Syndication International and Colorsport)**

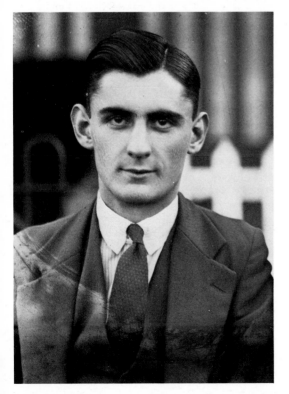

scored 33 in 28 matches before a transfer to Everton for whom he added three goals in two Division One games before the end of the season.

Of the players still active in the Football League during the 1979–80 season only Newport County striker Dave Gwyther, formerly with Swansea City, Halifax Town and Rotherham United could claim at one time or another to have headed a hat-trick of goals as many as four times. No other current player claims more than two such feats.

During the last 50 years only two players have achieved hat-tricks in three consecutive Football League matches. Frank Wrightson did it with Chester in February 1936 and Jack Balmer with Liverpool in November 1946.

Between September 1971 and March 1979 Bryan Robson scored for West Ham United against his original club Newcastle United in five different League matches.

Among those still active in the Football League during the 1979–80 season only Chris Jones of Rochdale could claim to have scored goals in Football League matches for as many as nine different League clubs. He began his career with Manchester City and subsequently played for

Trevor Francis seen here being congratulated by Nottingham Forest colleague Garry Birtles after scoring in the 1979 European Cup Final, was the youngest player to score as many as four goals in one Football League match while with Birmingham City. (Syndication International)

Swindon Town, Oldham Athletic, Walsall, York City, Huddersfield Town, Doncaster Rovers, Darlington (on loan) and then Rochdale.

Trevor Francis scored all four goals for Birmingham City against Bolton Wanderers on 20 February 1971 in a 4–0 win to become the first under-17 player in history to score as many times in a Football League match. He was not 17 until the following April.

Only one player in recent times scored a century of goals in the Scottish League and then in the Football League. He was Neil Martin who achieved this feat over a decade and a half with Alloa Athletic, Queen of the South and Hibernian and then with Sunderland, Coventry City, Nottingham Forest, Brighton and Hove Albion and Crystal Palace whom he left in November 1976.

Ted MacDougall was the most prolific scoring player still active in Football League matches during the 1979–80 season with Bournemouth and then Blackpool. He scored his 250th League goal for Bournemouth against Rochdale on 3 November 1979 in a 4–0 win. Though his first League club had been Liverpool he made his League debut with York City and subsequently played for Bournemouth, Manchester United, West Ham United, Norwich City and Southampton before returning to Bournemouth. He joined Blackpool as player-coach in January 1980.

Wrexham striker Dixie McNeil with more than 200 League goals and five other clubs behind him in his career has never played in Division One. Between the wars centre-forward Harry Morris scored 294 goals in 421 League matches with Fulham, Brentford, Millwall, Swansea Town, Swindon Town and Clapton Orient of which 14 were in Division Two, the remainder in Division Three. Between 1926 and 1933 he scored 216 alone for Swindon.

Wolverhampton Wanderers centre-forward John Richards was discovered playing in the England Grammar Schools trials at Butlin's Holiday Camp in Bognor Regis at Easter 1969. He had scored eight goals in two games and two days later was playing in Wolves Central League side. In July he signed as a professional at 18 and at the end of the 1979–80 season was still an active player in the first team having scored more than 125 League goals for the club.

The most successive seasons in which a player

scored 20 Football League goals or more was established by Arthur Rowley with Leicester City and Shrewsbury Town over a period of 13 seasons ending in 1962–63. His record was in scoring 28, 38, 39, 30, 23, 29, 44, 20, 38, 32, 28, 23 and 24. In 1952–53 he achieved two separate hat-tricks for Leicester against his former club Fulham.

Rodney Marsh twice scored more than three goals in a Football League Cup match for Queen's Park Rangers. He scored two fours, one against Colchester United in a first round tie in the 1966–67 season and the other against Tranmere Rovers in the third round in 1969–70. In 1966–67 he had also achieved hat-tricks against Middlesbrough and Mansfield Town in Division Three and Poole in the FA Cup.

Alf Lythgoe scored five goals in each of two Football League matches with different clubs in different divisions in the same season. He scored five for Stockport County against Southport in a Division Three (Northern) match on 25 August 1934 and five for Huddersfield Town against Blackburn Rovers in Division One on 13 April 1935.

Preston North End twice have had five goals scored against them on their own Deepdale ground in the period since the Second World War. In Division One matches there Jimmy McIntosh achieved five for Blackpool on 1 May 1948 and Jimmy Greaves emulated this feat for Chelsea on 19 December 1959.

John O'Rourke scored hat-tricks in all four divisions of the Football League, with Luton Town in Division Four in 1965–66, Middlesbrough in Division Three in 1966–67 and in Division Two in 1967–68 and Coventry City in Division One in 1969–70.

David Helliwell scored the first three Football League goals of his career with different clubs in different seasons, firstly for Blackburn Rovers in 1968–69, then Lincoln City in 1969–70 and Workington in 1970–71.

William Pendergast scored in 12 successive Division Three (Northern) matches for Chester in the 1938–39 season. He finished with 26 goals in 34 games.

Tommy Lawton was the youngest player to finish a season as the leading scorer in Division One when he scored 28 goals for Everton in 1937–38, during which he reached his 18th birthday on 6 October 1937.

Nottingham Forest manager Brian Clough scored 82 League goals in two seasons for Middlesbrough achieving 43 in 1958–59 and 39 in 1959–60.

FOOTBALL LEAGUE GOALSCORERS

(Division One from 1888–89, other divisions since 1919–20 because of the difficulty in checking earlier scorers).

Leading League Goalscorers 1888-1915

Season	Leading scorer	Team	Goals
1888–89	John Goodall	Preston NE	21
1889–90	Jimmy Ross	Preston NE	24
1890–91	Jack Southworth	Blackburn Rovers	26
1891–92	John Campbell	Sunderland	32
1892–93	John Campbell	Sunderland	31
1893–94	Jack Southworth	Everton	27
1894–95	John Campbell	Sunderland	22
1895–96	Johnny Campbell	Aston Villa	20
	Steve Bloomer	Derby County	20
1896–97	Steve Bloomer	Derby County	22
1897–98	Fred Wheldon	Aston Villa	21
1898–99	Steve Bloomer	Derby County	23
1899–1900	Bill Garratt	Aston Villa	27
1900–01	Steve Bloomer	Derby County	24
1901–02	James Settle	Everton	18
	Fred Priest	Sheffield Utd	18
1902–03	Alec Raybould	Liverpool	31
1903–04	Steve Bloomer	Derby County	20
1904–05	Arthur Brown	Sheffield Utd	23

Season	Leading scorer	Team	Goals
1905–06	Bullet Jones	Birmingham	26
	Albert Shepherd	Bolton W	26
1906–07	Alec Young	Everton	30
1907–08	Enoch West	Nottingham F	27
1908–09	Bert Freeman	Everton	38
1909–10	John Parkinson	Liverpool	29
1910–11	Albert Shepherd	Newcastle Utd	25
1911–12	Harold Hampton	Aston Villa	25
	Dave McLean	Sheffield Wed	25
	George Holley	Sunderland	25
1912–13	Dave McLean	Sheffield Wed	30
1913–14	George Elliott	Middlesbrough	31
1914–15	Bobby Parker	Everton	35

Division One 1919-39

Season	Leading scorer	Team	Goals
1919–20	Fred Morris	WBA	37
1920–21	Joe Smith	Bolton W	38
1921–22	Andy Wilson	Middlesbrough	31
1922–23	Charlie Buchan	Sunderland	30
1923–24	Wilf Chadwick	Everton	28
1924–25	Fred Roberts	Manchester City	31
1925–26	Ted Harper	Blackburn Rovers	43

Division One 1946-80

Season	Leading scorer	Team	Goals
1926–27	Jimmy Trotter	Sheffield Wed	37
1927–28	Dixie Dean	Everton	60
1928–29	Dave Halliday	Sunderland	43
1929–30	Vic Watson	West Ham Utd	41
1930–31	Pongo Waring	Aston Villa	49
1931–32	Dixie Dean	Everton	44
1932–33	Jack Bowers	Derby County	35
1933–34	Jack Bowers	Derby County	35
1934–35	Ted Drake	Arsenal	42
1935–36	Ginger Richardson	WBA	39
1936–37	Freddie Steele	Stoke City	33
1937–38	Tommy Lawton	Everton	28
1938–39	Tommy Lawton	Everton	35
1946–47	Dennis Westcott	Wolverhampton W	37
1947–48	Ronnie Rooke	Arsenal	33
1948–49	Willie Moir	Bolton W	25
1949–50	Dickie Davis	Sunderland	25
1950–51	Stan Mortensen	Blackpool	30
1951–52	George Robledo	Newcastle U	33
1952–53	Charlie Wayman	Preston NE	24
1953–54	Jimmy Glazzard	Huddersfield Town	29
	Johnny Nicholls	WBA	29
1954–55	Ronnie Allen	WBA	27
1955–56	Nat Lofthouse	Bolton W	33
1956–57	John Charles	Leeds United	38
1957–58	Bobby Smith	Tottenham Hotspur	36
1958–59	Jimmy Greaves	Chelsea	32
1959–60	Dennis Viollet	Manchester United	32
1960–61	Jimmy Greaves	Chelsea	41
1961–62	Ray Crawford	Ipswich Town	33
	Derek Kevan	WBA	33
1962–63	Jimmy Greaves	Tottenham Hotspur	37
1963–64	Jimmy Greaves	Tottenham Hotspur	35
1964–65	Jimmy Greaves	Tottenham Hotspur	29
	Andy McEvoy	Blackburn Rovers	29
1965–66	Roger Hunt	Liverpool	30
1966–67	Ron Davies	Southampton	37
1967–68	George Best	Manchester United	28
	Ron Davies	Southampton	28
1968–69	Jimmy Greaves	Tottenham Hotspur	27
1969–70	Jeff Astle	WBA	25
1970–71	Tony Brown	WBA	28
1971–72	Francis Lee	Manchester City	33
1972–73	Bryan Robson	West Ham United	28
1973–74	Mick Channon	Southampton	21
1974–75	Malcolm Macdonald	Newcastle U	21
1975–76	Ted MacDougall	Norwich City	23
1976–77	Malcolm Macdonald	Arsenal	25
	Andy Gray	Aston Villa	25
1977–78	Bob Latchford	Everton	30
1978–79	Frank Worthington	Bolton W	24
1979–80	Phil Boyer	Southampton	23

Division Two 1919-39

Season	Leading scorer	Team	Goals
1919–20	Sam Taylor	Huddersfield Town	35
1920–21	Syd Puddefoot	Huddersfield Town	29
1921–22	Jimmy Broad	Stoke City	25
1922–23	Harry Bedford	Blackpool	32
1923–24	Harry Bedford	Blackpool	34
1924–25	Arthur Chandler	Leicester City	33
1925–26	Bob Turnbull	Chelsea	39
1926–27	George Camsell	Middlesbrough	59
1927–28	Jimmy Cookson	WBA	38
1928–29	Jimmy Hampson	Blackpool	40
1929–30	Jimmy Hampson	Blackpool	45
1930–31	Dixie Dean	Everton	39
1931–32	Cyril Pearce	Swansea Town	35

Division Two 1919-39

Season	Leading Scorer	Team	Goals
1932–33	Ted Harper	Preston NE	37
1933–34	Pat Glover	Grimsby Town	42
1934–35	Jack Milsom	Bolton W.	31
1935–36	Jock Dodds	Sheffield Utd	34
	Bob Finan	Blackpool	34
1936–37	Jack Bowers	Leicester City	33
1937–38	George Henson	Bradford PA	27
1938–39	Hugh Billington	Luton Town	28

Division Two 1946–80

Season	Leading scorer	Team	Goals
1946–47	Charlie Wayman	Newcastle U	30
1947–48	Eddie Quigley	Sheffield W	23
1948–49	Charlie Wayman	Southampton	32
1949–50	Tommy Briggs	Grimsby Town	35
1950–51	Cecil McCormack	Barnsley	33
1951–52	Derek Dooley	Sheffield W	46
1952–53	Arthur Rowley	Leicester City	39
1953–54	John Charles	Leeds United	42
1954–55	Tommy Briggs	Blackburn Rovers	33
1955–56	Bill Gardiner	Leicester City	34
1956–57	Arthur Rowley	Leicester City	44
1957–58	Brian Clough	Middlesbrough	40
1958–59	Brian Clough	Middlesbrough	42
1959–60	Brian Clough	Middlesbrough	39
1960–61	Ray Crawford	Ipswich Town	39
1961–62	Roger Hunt	Liverpool	41
1962–63	Bobby Tambling	Chelsea	35
1963–64	Ron Saunders	Portsmouth	33
1964–65	George O'Brien	Southampton	34
1965–66	Martin Chivers	Southampton	30
1966–67	Bobby Gould	Coventry City	24
1967–68	John Hickton	Middlesbrough	24
1968–69	John Toshack	Cardiff City	22
1969–70	John Hickton	Middlesbrough	24
1970–71	John Hickton	Middlesbrough	25
1971–72	Bob Latchford	Birmingham City	23
1972–73	Don Givens	QPR	23
1973–74	Duncan McKenzie	Nottingham Forest	26
1974–75	Brian Little	Aston Villa	20
1975–76	Derek Hales	Charlton Athletic	28
1976–77	Mickey Walsh	Blackpool	26
1977–78	Bob Hatton	Blackpool	22
1978–79	Bryan Robson	West Ham United	24
1979–80	Clive Allen	QPR	28

Division Three (South) 1920-39

Season	Leading scorer	Team	Goals
1920–21	John Connor	Crystal Palace	28
	Ernie Simms	Luton Town	28
	George Whitworth	Northampton Town	28
1921–22	Frank Richardson	Plymouth Argyle	31
1922–23	Fred Pagnam	Watford	30
1923–24	Billy Haines	Portsmouth	28
1924–25	Jack Fowler	Swansea Town	28
1925–26	Jack Cock	Plymouth Argyle	32
1926–27	Harry Morris	Swindon Town	47
1927–28	Harry Morris	Swindon Town	38
1928–29	Andrew Rennie	Luton Town	43
1929–30	George Goddard	QPR	37
1930–31	Peter Simpson	Crystal Palace	46
1931–32	Clarrie Bourton	Coventry City	49
1932–33	Clarrie Bourton	Coventry City	40
1933–34	Cyril Pearce	Charlton Athletic	26
1934–35	Ralph Allen	Charlton Athletic	32
1935–36	Albert Dawes	Crystal Palace	38
1936–37	Joe Payne	Luton Town	55
1937–38	Harry Crawshaw	Mansfield Town	25
1938–39	Ben Morton	Swindon Town	28

Division Three (South) 1946–58

Season	Leading scorer	Team	Goals
1946–47	Don Clark	Bristol City	36
1947–48	Len Townsend	Bristol City	29
1948–49	Don McGibbon	Bournemouth	30
1949–50	Tommy Lawton	Notts County	31
1950–51	Wally Ardron	Nottingham Forest	36
1951–52	Ronnie Blackman	Reading	39
1952–53	Geoff Bradford	Bristol Rovers	33
1953–54	Jack English	Northampton Town	28
1954–55	Ernie Morgan	Gillingham	31
1955–56	Sammy Collins	Torquay United	40
1956–57	Ted Phillips	Ipswich Town	42
1957–58	Sam McCrory	Southend United	31
	Derek Reeves	Southampton	31

Division Three (North) 1921-39

Season	Leading scorer	Team	Goals
1921–22	Jim Carmichael	Grimsby Town	37
1922–23	George Beel	Chesterfield	23
	Jim Carmichael	Grimsby Town	23
1923–24	David Brown	Darlington	27
1924–25	David Brown	Darlington	39
1925–26	Jimmy Cookson	Chesterfield	44
1926–27	Albert Whitehurst	Rochdale	44
1927–28	Joe Smith	Stockport County	38
1928–29	Jimmy McConnell	Carlisle United	43
1929–30	Frank Newton	Stockport County	36
1930–31	Jimmy McConnell	Carlisle United	37
1931–32	Alan Hall	Lincoln City	42
1932–33	Bill McNaughton	Hull City	39
1933–34	Alf Lythgoe	Stockport County	46
1934–35	Gilbert Alsop	Walsall	40
1935–36	Bunny Bell	Tranmere Rovers	33
1936–37	Ted Harston	Mansfield Town	55
1937–38	John Roberts	Port Vale	28
1938–39	Sam Hunt	Carlisle United	32

Division Three (North) 1946–58

Season	Leading scorer	Team	Goals
1946–47	Clarrie Jordan	Doncaster Rovers	42
1947–48	Jimmy Hutchinson	Lincoln City	32
1948–49	Wally Ardron	Rotherham United	29
1949–50	Peter Doherty	Doncaster Rovers	26
1950–51	Jack Shaw	Rotherham United	37
1951–52	Andy Graver	Lincoln City	36
1952–53	Jimmy Whitehouse	Carlisle United	29
1953–54	Jack Connor	Stockport County	31
1954–55	Jack Connor	Stockport County	30
	Arthur Bottom	York City	30
1955–56	Bob Crosbie	Grimsby Town	36
1956–57	Ray Straw	Derby County	37
1957–58	Alf Ackerman	Carlisle United	35

Division Three 1958–80

Season	Leading scorer	Team	Goals
1958–59	Jim Towers	Brentford	32
1959–60	Derek Reeves	Southampton	39

Division Three 1958–80

Season	Leading scorer	Team	Goals
1960–61	Tony Richards	Walsall	36
1961–62	Cliff Holton	Northampton T (36) and Walsall (1)	37
1962–63	George Hudson	Coventry City	30
1963–64	Alf Biggs	Bristol Rovers	30
1964–65	Ken Wagstaff	Mansfield Town (8) and Hull City (23)	31
1965–66	Les Allen	QPR	30
1966–67	Rodney Marsh	QPR	30
1967–68	Don Rogers	Swindon Town	25
	Bobby Owen	Bury	25
1968–69	Brian Lewis	Luton Town	22
	Don Rogers	Swindon Town	22
1969–70	George Jones	Bury	26
1970–71	Gerry Ingram	Preston NE	22
	Dudley Roberts	Mansfield Town	22
1971–72	Ted MacDougall	Bournemouth	35
	Alf Wood	Shrewsbury Town	35
1972–73	Bruce Bannister	Bristol Rovers	25
	Arthur Horsfield	Charlton Athletic	25
1973–74	Billy Jennings	Watford	26
1974–75	Dixie McNeil	Hereford United	31
1975–76	Dixie McNeil	Hereford United	35
1976–77	Peter Ward	Brighton & HA	32
1977–78	Alex Bruce	Preston NE	27
1978–79	Ross Jenkins	Watford	29
1979–80	Andy Rowland	Swindon Town	20

Division Four 1958–80

Season	Leading scorer	Team	Goals
1958–59	Arthur Rowley	Shrewsbury Town	37
1959–60	Cliff Holton	Watford	42
1960–61	Terry Bly	Peterborough U	52
1961–62	Bobby Hunt	Colchester United	41
1962–63	Ken Wagstaff	Mansfield Town	34
	Colin Booth	Doncaster Rovers	34
1963–64	Hugh McIlmoyle	Carlisle United	39
1964–65	Alick Jeffrey	Doncaster Rovers	36
1965–66	Kevin Hector	Bradford PA	34
1966–67	Ernie Phythian	Hartlepools United	23
1967–68	Roy Chapman	Port Vale	25
	Les Massie	Halifax Town	25
1968–69	Gary Talbot	Chester	22
1969–70	Albert Kinsey	Wrexham	27
1970–71	Ted MacDougall	Bournemouth	42
1971–72	Peter Price	Peterborough U	28
1972–73	Fred Binney	Exeter City	28
1973–74	Brian Yeo	Gillingham	31
1974–75	Ray Clarke	Mansfield Town	28
1975–76	Ronnie Moore	Tranmere Rovers	34
1976–77	Brian Joicey	Barnsley	25
1977–78	Steve Phillips	Brentford	32
	Alan Curtis	Swansea City	32
1978–79	John Dungworth	Aldershot	26
1979–80	Colin Garwood	Portsmouth (17) and Aldershot (10)	27

NORTH LONDON DERBY MATCHES
Arsenal v. Tottenham Hotspur

The rivalry between Arsenal and Tottenham Hotspur has become an established part of the Football League scene. But when this team group of the former was taken in 1895 they were known as Woolwich Arsenal and had yet to do battle with Spurs. Arsenal were seventh in Division Two that season. The cloth capped era it was with a vengeance, and not like the apeing view taken by present-day Tottenham midfield player Glenn Hoddle. (Syndication International)

Arsenal founded in 1886 as Royal Arsenal, becoming Woolwich Arsenal in 1891 and Arsenal from 1914.

In League matches the results of Arsenal's home matches with their score first:

Season	Score	Season	Score
1909–10	1–0	1958–59	3–1
1910–11	2–0	1959–60	1–1
1911–12	3–1	1960–61	2–3
1912–13	0–3	1961–62	2–1
1920–21	3–2	1962–63	2–3
1921–22	1–0	1963–64	4–4
1922–23	0–2	1964–65	3–1
1923–24	1–1	1965–66	1–1
1924–25	1–0	1966–67	0–2
1925–26	0–1	1967–68	4–0
1926–27	2–4	1968–69	1–0
1927–28	1–1	1969–70	2–3
1933–34	1–3	1970–71	2–0
1934–35	5–1	1971–72	0–2
1950–51	2–2	1972–73	1–1
1951–52	1–1	1973–74	0–1
1952–53	4–0	1974–75	1–0
1953–54	0–3	1975–76	0–2
1954–55	2–0	1976–77	1–0
1955–56	0–1	1978–79	1–0
1956–57	3–1	1979–80	1–0
1957–58	4–4		

Tottenham Hotspur founded in 1882 as Hotspur Football Club becoming Tottenham Hotspur in 1885.

In League matches the results of Tottenham's home matches with their score first:

Season	Score	Season	Score
1909–10	1–1	1958–59	1–4
1910–11	3–1	1959–60	3–0
1911–12	5–0	1960–61	4–2
1912–13	1–1	1961–62	4–3
1920–21	2–1	1962–63	4–4
1921–22	2–0	1963–64	3–1
1922–23	1–2	1964–65	3–1
1923–24	3–0	1965–66	2–2
1924–25	2–0	1966–67	3–1
1925–26	1–1	1967–68	1–0
1926–27	0–4	1968–69	1–2
1927–28	2–0	1969–70	1–0
1933–34	1–1	1970–71	0–1
1934–35	0–6	1971–72	1–1
1950–51	1–0	1972–73	1–2
1951–52	1–2	1973–74	2–0
1952–53	1–3	1974–75	2–0
1953–54	1–4	1975–76	0–0
1954–55	0–1	1976–77	2–2
1955–56	3–1	1978–79	0–5
1956–57	1–3	1979–80	1–2
1957–58	3–1		

Above: **Nottingham Forest's new stand at the City Ground with Notts County's Meadow Lane across the Trent on the left. (J Sumpter: Belvoir Studios)**

Below: **Chelsea players pose for a sweater advertisement at Stamford Bridge.** *Back row, left to right,* **Mike Fillery, Micky Droy, Ron Harris, Eamonn Bannon (before his transfer to Dundee Utd).** *Middle row,* **Lee Frost, Gary Locke, John Bumstead, Graham Wilkins, Ian Britton.** *Front row,* **Gary Johnson, Gary Chivers. (Syndication International)**

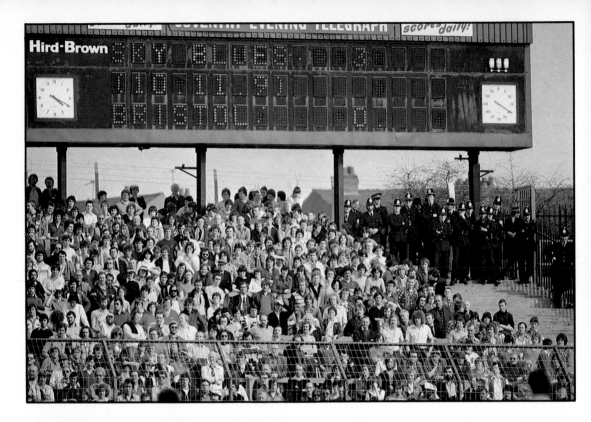

Above: **The type of scoreboard information to please Coventry City followers at Highfield Road. (Provincial Sports Photography)**

Left: **But for the colours it might be the Boat Race. (Colorsport)**

The name plate is all that remains of this steam locomotive preserved at Hull City's Boothferry Park ground. (Courtesy Hull City AFC)

Celebration and consolation. The two extremes of the game. Arsenal goalkeeper Pat Jennings is congratulated by happy fans after their **FA Cup** semi-final victory over **Wolves** while the opposing midfield player Peter **D**aniel receives a friendly hug. (**P**rovincial **S**ports Photography)

Scenes from the **FA Cup** third round tie between **Yeovil Town** and **Norwich City** at the **Huish. Yeovil** in their traditional green shirts and **Norwich** sporting their canary yellow.

The Paxton Road end at Tottenham Hotspur's White Hart Lane ground. (Colorsport)

Red and white stripe-shirted Sheffield United players find themselves having to contend with a black and white dog as well as their blue and white Leicester City opponents. (Colorsport)

A group of typically shy and retiring English
supporters. (Colorsport)

A crowded scene at **The Den**, with a floodlight
pylon giving some fans at the **Millwall v Ipswich
Town** match a vantage point for the highlights.
(Colorsport)

The ton-up boys and girls of West Ham. (Colorsport)

A Newcastle United supporter at the 1974 FA Cup Final against Liverpool whose headgear might have been just as acceptable at Ascot. (Colorsport)

Arsenal fans go to Wembley loaded with ammunition and a suitable firing piece. (Colorsport)

SHEFFIELD DERBY MATCHES
Sheffield United v. Sheffield Wednesday

The 91st Sheffield derby at Hillsborough provided Wednesday with a 4–0 win over their United neighbours. It also produced a record attendance for a match in the Third Division. A crowd of 49 309 watched this Boxing Day encounter. (Sheffield Newspapers Ltd)

United founded in 1889.

In League matches the results of United's home matches with their score first:

Season	Score	Season	Score
1893–94	1–1	1927–28	1–1
1894–95	1–0	1928–29	1–1
1895–96	1–1	1929–30	2–2
1896–97	2–0	1930–31	1–1
1897–98	1–1	1931–32	1–1
1898–99	2–1	1932–33	2–3
1900–01	1–0	1933–34	5–1
1901–02	3–0	1937–38	2–1
1902–03	2–3	1938–39	0–0
1903–04	1–1	1949–50	2–0
1904–05	4–2	1951–52	7–3
1905–06	0–2	1953–54	2–0
1906–07	2–1	1954–55	1–0
1907–08	1–3	1958–59	1–0
1908–09	2–1	1961–62	1–0
1909–10	3–3	1962–63	2–2
1910–11	0–1	1963–64	1–1
1911–12	1–1	1964–65	2–3
1912–13	0–2	1965–66	1–0
1913–14	0–1	1966–67	1–0
1914–15	0–1	1967–68	0–1
1919–20	3–0	1970–71	3–2
1926–27	2–0	1979–80	1–1

Wednesday founded in 1867.

In League matches the results of Wednesday's home matches with their score first:

Season	Score	Season	Score
1893–94	1–2	1927–28	3–3
1894–95	2–3	1928–29	5–2
1895–96	1–0	1929–30	1–1
1896–97	1–1	1930–31	1–3
1897–98	0–1	1931–32	2–1
1898–99	1–1	1932–33	3–3
1900–01	1–0	1933–34	0–1
1901–02	1–0	1937–38	0–1
1902–03	0–1	1938–39	1–0
1903–04	3–0	1949–50	2–1
1904–05	1–3	1951–52	1–3
1905–06	1–0	1953–54	3–2
1906–07	2–2	1954–55	1–2
1907–08	2–0	1958–59	2–0
1908–09	1–0	1961–62	1–2
1909–10	1–3	1962–63	3–1
1910–11	2–0	1963–64	3–0
1911–12	1–1	1964–65	0–2
1912–13	1–0	1965–66	2–2
1913–14	2–1	1966–67	2–2
1914–15	1–1	1967–68	1–1
1919–20	2–1	1970–71	0–0
1926–27	2–3	1979–80	4–0

19,138 — Aldershot v. Carlisle FA Cup 4th round replay 28/1/70

73,295 — Arsenal v. Sunderland Division one 9/3/35

76,588 — Aston Villa v. Derby County FA Cup 6th round 2/3/46

40,255 — Barnsley v. Stoke City FA Cup 5th round 15/2/36

66,844 — Birmingham City v. Everton FA Cup 5th round 11/2/39

61,783 — Blackburn Rovers v. Bolton Wanderers FA Cup 6th round 2/3/29

39,118 — Blackpool v. Manchester United Division one 19/4/52

69,912 — Bolton Wanderers v. Manchester City FA Cup 5th round 18/2/33

28,799 — AFC Bournemouth v. Manchester United FA Cup 6th round 2/3/57

39,146 — Bradford City v. Burnley FA Cup 4th round 11/3/11

39,626 — Brentford v. Preston NE FA Cup 6th round 5/3/38

36,747 — Brighton & Hove Albion v. Fulham Division two 27/12/58

43,335 — Bristol City v. Preston NE FA Cup 5th round 16/2/35

38,472 — Bristol Rovers v. Preston NE FA Cup 4th round 30/1/60

54,775 — Burnley v. Huddersfield Town FA Cup 3rd round 23/2/24

35,000 — Bury v. Bolton Wanderers FA Cup 3rd round 9/1/60

14,000 — Cambridge United v. Chelsea Friendly 1/5/70

57,800 — Cardiff City v. Arsenal Division one 22/4/53

27,500 — Carlisle United v. Birmingham City FA Cup 3rd round 5/1/57 and Middlesbrough FA Cup 5th round 7/2/70

75,031 — Charlton Athletic v. Aston Villa FA Cup 5th round 12/2/38

82,905 — Chelsea v. Arsenal Division one 12/10/35

20,500 — Chester v Chelsea FA Cup 3rd round replay 16/1/52

ECORD
TTENDANCES for the
2 FOOTBALL LEAGUE
LUBS

equals 10,000 crowd

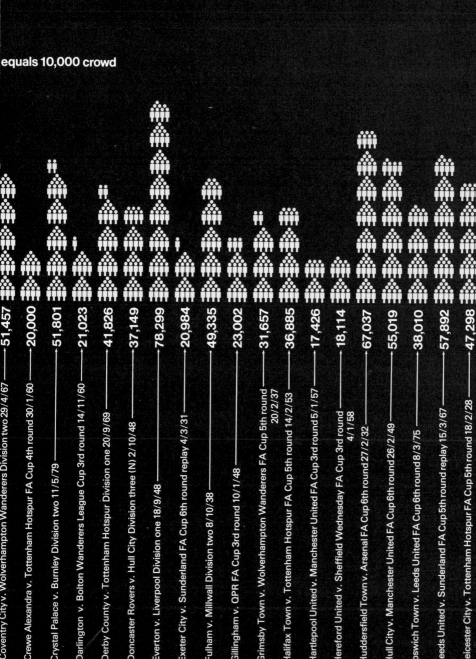

Attendance	Match
51,457	Coventry City v. Wolverhampton Wanderers Division two 29/4/67
20,000	Crewe Alexandra v. Tottenham Hotspur FA Cup 4th round 30/1/60
51,801	Crystal Palace v. Burnley Division two 11/5/79
21,023	Darlington v. Bolton Wanderers League Cup 3rd round 14/11/60
41,826	Derby County v. Tottenham Hotspur Division one 20/9/69
37,149	Doncaster Rovers v. Hull City Division three (N) 2/10/48
78,299	Everton v. Liverpool Division one 18/9/48
20,984	Exeter City v. Sunderland FA Cup 6th round replay 4/3/31
49,335	Fulham v. Millwall Division two 8/10/38
23,002	Gillingham v. QPR FA Cup 3rd round 10/1/48
31,657	Grimsby Town v. Wolverhampton Wanderers FA Cup 5th round 20/2/37
36,885	Halifax Town v. Tottenham Hotspur FA Cup 5th round 14/2/53
17,426	Hartlepool United v. Manchester United FA Cup 3rd round 5/1/57
18,114	Hereford United v. Sheffield Wednesday FA Cup 3rd round 4/1/58
67,037	Huddersfield Town v. Arsenal FA Cup 6th round 27/2/32
55,019	Hull City v. Manchester United FA Cup 6th round 26/2/49
38,010	Ipswich Town v. Leeds United FA Cup 6th round 8/3/75
57,892	Leeds United v. Sunderland FA Cup 5th round replay 15/3/67
47,298	Leicester City v. Tottenham Hotspur FA Cup 5th round 18/2/28
23,196	Lincoln City v. Derby County League Cup 4th round 15/11/67
61,905	Liverpool v. Wolverhampton Wanderers FA Cup 4th round 2/2/52
30,069	Luton Town v. Blackpool FA Cup 6th round replay 4/3/59

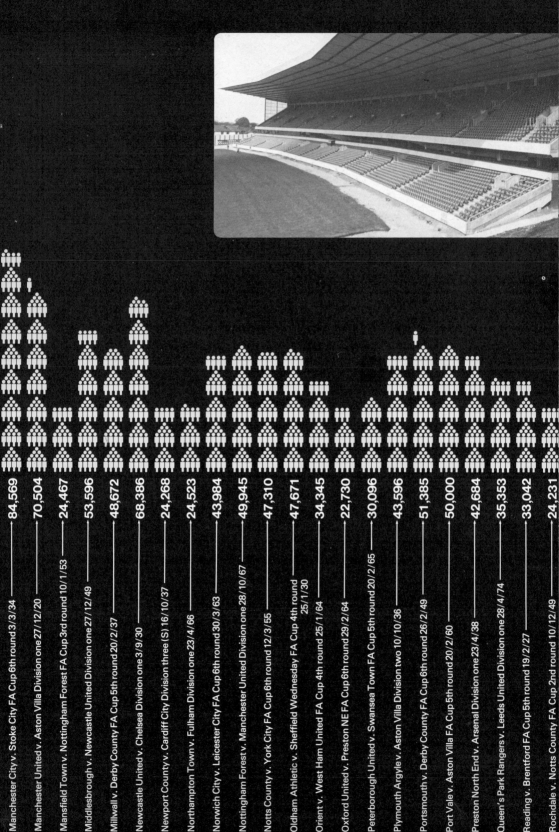

Manchester City v. Stoke City FA Cup 6th round 3/3/34 — **84,569**

Manchester United v. Aston Villa Division one 27/12/20 — **70,504**

Mansfield Town v. Nottingham Forest FA Cup 3rd round 10/1/53 — **24,467**

Middlesbrough v. Newcastle United Division one 27/12/49 — **53,596**

Millwall v. Derby County FA Cup 5th round 20/2/37 — **48,672**

Newcastle United v. Chelsea Division one 3/9/30 — **68,386**

Newport County v. Cardiff City Division three (S) 16/10/37 — **24,268**

Northampton Town v. Fulham Division one 23/4/66 — **24,523**

Norwich City v. Leicester City FA Cup 6th round 30/3/63 — **43,984**

Nottingham Forest v. Manchester United Division one 28/10/67 — **49,945**

Notts County v. York City FA Cup 6th round 12/3/55 — **47,310**

Oldham Athletic v. Sheffield Wednesday FA Cup 4th round 25/1/30 — **47,671**

Orient v. West Ham United FA Cup 4th round 25/1/64 — **34,345**

Oxford United v. Preston NE FA Cup 6th round 29/2/64 — **22,730**

Peterborough United v. Swansea Town FA Cup 5th round 20/2/65 — **30,096**

Plymouth Argyle v. Aston Villa Division two 10/10/36 — **43,596**

Portsmouth v. Derby County FA Cup 6th round 26/2/49 — **51,385**

Port Vale v. Aston Villa FA Cup 5th round 20/2/60 — **50,000**

Preston North End v. Arsenal Division one 23/4/38 — **42,684**

Queen's Park Rangers v. Leeds United Division one 28/4/74 — **35,353**

Reading v. Brentford FA Cup 5th round 19/2/27 — **33,042**

Rochdale v. Notts County FA Cup 2nd round 10/12/49 — **24,231**

ECORD
TTENDANCES for the
2 FOOTBALL LEAGUE
LUBS

equals 10,000 crowd

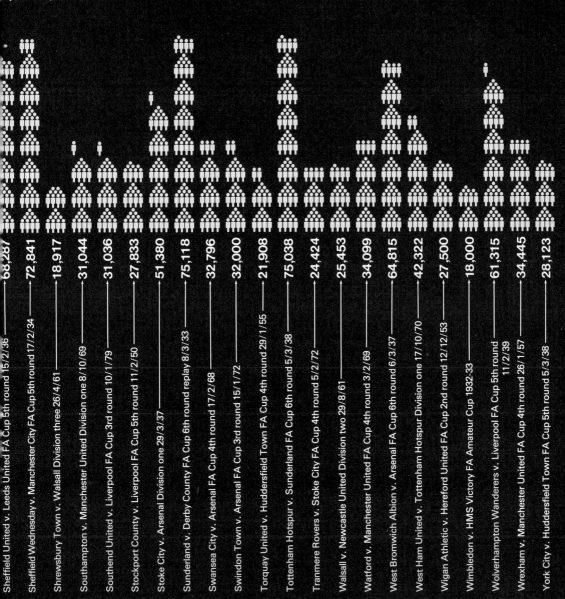

Attendance	Match
68,287	Sheffield United v. Leeds United FA Cup 5th round 15/2/36
72,841	Sheffield Wednesday v. Manchester City FA Cup 5th round 17/2/34
18,917	Shrewsbury Town v. Walsall Division three 26/4/61
31,044	Southampton v. Manchester United Division one 8/10/69
31,036	Southend United v. Liverpool FA Cup 3rd round 10/1/79
27,833	Stockport County v. Liverpool FA Cup 5th round 11/2/50
51,380	Stoke City v. Arsenal Division one 29/3/37
75,118	Sunderland v. Derby County FA Cup 6th round replay 8/3/33
32,796	Swansea City v. Arsenal FA Cup 4th round 17/2/68
32,000	Swindon Town v. Arsenal FA Cup 3rd round 15/1/72
21,908	Torquay United v. Huddersfield Town FA Cup 4th round 29/1/55
75,038	Tottenham Hotspur v. Sunderland FA Cup 6th round 5/3/38
24,424	Tranmere Rovers v. Stoke City FA Cup 4th round 5/2/72
25,453	Walsall v. Newcastle United Division two 29/8/61
34,099	Watford v. Manchester United FA Cup 4th round 3/2/69
64,815	West Bromwich Albion v. Arsenal FA Cup 6th round 6/3/37
42,322	West Ham United v. Tottenham Hotspur Division one 17/10/70
27,500	Wigan Athletic v. Hereford United FA Cup 2nd round 12/12/53
18,000	Wimbledon v. HMS Victory FA Amateur Cup 1932-33
61,315	Wolverhampton Wanderers v. Liverpool FA Cup 5th round 11/2/39
34,445	Wrexham v. Manchester United FA Cup 4th round 26/1/57
28,123	York City v. Huddersfield Town FA Cup 5th round 5/3/38

MAJOR RECORDS

Highest scores – Teams
First-class match
Arbroath 36 Bon Accord 0, Scottish Cup first round, 5 September 1885
International
England 13 Northern Ireland 0, 18 February 1882
FA Cup
Preston North End 26 Hyde United 0, first round, 15 October 1887.
Football League
Newcastle United 13 Newport County 0, Division Two, 5 October 1946
Stockport County 13 Halifax Town 0, Division Three (Northern), 6 January 1934
Scottish League
Celtic 11 Dundee 0, Division One, 26 October 1895
East Fife 13 Edinburgh City 2, Division Two, 11 December 1937
Aggregate
Tranmere Rovers 13 Oldham Athletic 4, Division Three (Northern) 26 December 1935
Most goals in a season
Football League
134 goals by Peterborough United, Division Four, 1960–61 in 46 matches
Scottish League
142 goals by Raith Rovers, Division Two, 1937–38 in 34 matches
Most goals – Individual
Match
13 goals by John Petrie for Arbroath v Bon Accord, Scottish Cup first round, 5 September 1885
Career
1 329 goals by Artur Friedenreich in Brazilian football between 1910–1930
Most League appearances
The record for Football League appearances is the 824 by Terry Paine for Southampton and Hereford United, 1957 to 1977.

ATTENDANCE RECORDS

Any match
205 000 (199 854 paid) for the Brazil v Uruguay match in the 1950 World Cup final series on 16 July 1950 at the Maracana Stadium, Rio de Janeiro.

European Cup
136 505 for the Celtic v Leeds United semi-final at Hampden Park, Glasgow, on 15 April 1970.

International
149 547 for the Scotland v England inter-

Year	Winners	Runners-up
1961	Aston Villa 3	¶Rotherham U 2
1962	Norwich C 4	¶Rochdale 0
1963	¶Birmingham C 3	Aston Villa 1
1964	Leicester C 4	¶Stoke C 3
1965	¶Chelsea 3	Leicester C 2
1966	West Bromwich A 5	¶West Ham U 3
1967	Queen's Park R 3	West Bromwich A 2
1968	Leeds U 1	Arsenal 0*
1969	Swindon T 3	Arsenal 1*
1970	Manchester C 2	West Bromwich A 1
1971	Tottenham H 2	Aston Villa 0
1972	Stoke C 2	Chelsea 1
1973	Tottenham H 1	Norwich C 0
1974	Wolverhampton W 2	Manchester C 1
1975	Aston Villa 1	Norwich C 0
1976	Manchester C 2	Newcastle U 1
1977	Aston Villa 3	Everton 2*
	(after first replay 1–1*, Hillsborough, 55 000)	
	(after 0–0, Wembley, 100 000)	
1978	Nottingham F 1	Liverpool 0
	(after 0–0*, Wembley, 100 000)	
1979	Nottingham F 3	Southampton 2
1980	Wolverhampton W 1	Nottingham F 0

* after extra time   ¶ home team in first leg

national at Hampden Park, Glasgow, on 17 April 1937.

FA Cup final
160 000 (estimated) for the Bolton Wanderers v West Ham United match at Wembley on 28 April 1923 (counted admissions were 126 047).

Scottish Cup final
146 433 for the Celtic v Aberdeen final at Hampden Park, Glasgow, on 24 April 1937.

Football League
Division One: Manchester United v Arsenal at Maine Road, 17 January 1948, 83 260.
   Division Two: Aston Villa v Coventry City at Villa Park, 30 October 1937, 68 029.
   Division Three (Southern): Cardiff City v Bristol City at Ninian Park, 7 April 1947, 51 621.
   Division Three (Northern): Hull City v Rotherham United at Boothferry Park, 25 December 1948, 49 655.
   Division Three: Sheffield Wednesday v Sheffield United at Hillsborough, 26 December 1979, 49 309.
   Division Four: Crystal Palace v Millwall at Selhurst Park, 31 March 1961, 37 774.
   Scottish League: Rangers v Celtic, Ibrox Park, 2 January 1939, 118 567.

Football League Cup winners

Venue	Attendances	Facts and Feats
0–2; 3–0*	12 226; 27 000	Villa recover first leg deficit; matches played in August and September 1961.
3–0; 1–0	11 123; 19 708	Rochdale from Division Four beaten by Second Division Norwich City.
3–1; 0–0	31 850; 37 921	The first all-midlands and all-First Division League Cup Final.
1–1; 3–2	22 309; 25 372	Leicester City achieve their first major trophy after 80 years.
3–2; 0–0	20 690; 26 957	Ten years after their first League Championship, Chelsea add another honour.
1–2; 4–1	28 341; 31 925	West Bromwich establish a record score for one leg after losing the first.
Wembley	97 952	Rangers, two goals down at half-time, become first Division Three winners.
Wembley	97 887	Extra time and the winning goal comes from Leeds full-back Terry Cooper.
Wembley	98 189	Arsenal lose again in extra time to Third Division Swindon Town.
Wembley	97 963	Manchester City recover from being behind in Albion's third League Cup Final.
Wembley	100 000	Martin Chivers scores twice in the last ten minutes for Spurs success.
Wembley	100 000	Stoke's 12th game in the tournament brings them their first major honour.
Wembley	100 000	Tottenham substitute Ralph Coates is the goalscoring hero in their second win.
Wembley	100 000	Wolves' goalkeeper Gary Pierce celebrates his 23rd birthday with a winners' medal.
Wembley	100 000	Ray Graydon's late penalty is punched onto a post, but he follows up to score.
Wembley	100 000	A spectacular overhead kick by Dennis Tueart gives City their second win.
Old Trafford	54 749	The marathon final, but it provides Villa with their record third League Cup win.
Old Trafford	54 375	A John Robertson penalty late in the replay gives Forest their victory.
Wembley	100 000	Forest become the first to retain the trophy after being one down at half-time.
Wembley	100 000	An Andy Gray goal from a defensive mix-up ends Forest's hopes of a treble.

AWARDS

The Football Writers Association founded in 1947 has elected a Footballer of the Year at the end of each season since 1947–48. Terry McDermott (Liverpool) was the choice in 1979–80. He was the fifth Liverpool player to have won the honour in the last seven years.

McDermott was also the winner of the Professional Footballers Association's award as their Player of the Year for 1980. This was the seventh occasion the competition had been held by the players' own union.

The annual award organised by France Football and selected in December by a panel of journalists from various European countries gave the 1979 award to Kevin Keegan (SV Hamburg and England) for the second year in succession.

Diego Maradona (Argentinos Juniors and Argentina) won the title of South American Footballer of the Year in 1979. This competition has been held since 1971.

The African Footballer of the Year in 1979 was Thomas N'Kono from the Cameroun.

League Cup Final receipts at Wembley

1967	£57 000	1974	£165 500
1968	£95 000	1975	£196 000
1969	£104 000	1976	£299 601
1970	£123 000	1977	£301 000
1971	£132 000	1978	£425 000
1972	£132 000	1979	£425 000
1973	£132 000	1980	£641 000

The highest aggregate of attendances for one season of the League Cup was achieved in 1971–72 when 2 397 154 watched the 123 matches in the competition.

In 1979–80 when the second round was expanded to include home and away legs the overall attendances for the tournament went up to 2 324 838 compared with 1 827 464 in 1978–79.

League cup goalscorers

Gerry Hitchens (Aston Villa) with eleven goals in the 1960–61 season established an individual record in the first League Cup competition. Three other players have equalled the figure: Tony Brown (West Bromwich Albion) and Geoff Hurst (West Ham United) in 1965–66 and Rodney Marsh (Queen's Park Rangers) in 1966–67.

Scottish Club directory

Ground	Honours League	Scottish FA Cup	League Cup

ABERDEEN (1903) Scarlet/scarlet

Pittodrie Park Aberdeen	Premier Div. Champions 1979–80 Premier Div. runners-up 1977–78 Div. 1 Champions 1954–55 Runners-up 1910–11, 1936–37, 1955–56, 1970–71, 1971–72	Winners 1947, 1970 Runners-up 1937, 1953, 1954, 1959, 1967, 1978	Winners 1946, 1956, 1977 Runners-up 1979, 1980

AIRDRIEONIANS (1878) White/white

Broomfield Park Airdrie	Div. 1 runners-up 1922–23, 1923–24, 1924–25, 1925–26, 1979–80 Div. 2 Champions 1902–03, 1954–55, 1973–74 Runners-up 1900–01, 1946–47, 1949–50, 1965–66	Winners 1924 Runners-up 1975	

ALBION ROVERS (1882) Yellow/white

Cliftonhill Park Coatbridge	Div. 2 Champions 1933–34 Runners-up 1913–14, 1937–38, 1947–48	Runners-up 1920	

ALLOA (1883) Gold/black

Recreation Ground Alloa	Div. 2 Champions 1921–22 Runners-up 1938–39, 1976–77		

ARBROATH (1878) Maroon/white

Gayfield Park Arbroath	Div. 2 runners-up 1934–35, 1958–59, 1967–68, 1971–72		

AYR UNITED (1910) White/black

Somerset Park Ayr	Div. 2 Champions 1911–12, 1912–13, 1927–28, 1936–37, 1958–59, 1965–66 Runners-up 1910–11, 1955–56, 1968–69		

BERWICK RANGERS (1881) Gold/black

Shielfield Park Tweedmouth Berwick-on-Tweed	Div. 2 Champions 1978–79		

BRECHIN CITY (1906) Red/red

Glebe Park Brechin	Highest League placing 5th, Div. 2, 1958–59		

CELTIC (1888) Green, white/white

Celtic Park Glasgow SE	Prem. Div. Champions 1976–77, 1978–79 Premier Div. runners-up 1979–80 Div. 1 Champions 1892–93, 1893–94, 1895–96, 1897–98, 1904–05, 1905–06, 1906–07, 1907–08, 1908–09, 1909–10, 1913–14, 1914–15, 1915–16, 1916–17, 1918–19, 1921–22, 1925–26, 1935–36, 1937–38, 1953–54, 1965–66, 1966–67, 1967–68, 1968–69, 1969–70, 1970–71, 1971–72, 1972–73, 1973–74 Runners-up 16 times Premier Div. Runners-up 1975–76	Winners 1892, 1899, 1900, 1904, 1907, 1908, 1911, 1912, 1914, 1923, 1925, 1927, 1931, 1933, 1937, 1951, 1954, 1965, 1967, 1969, 1971, 1972, 1974, 1975, 1977, 1980 Runners-up 14 times	Winners 1957, 1958, 1966, 1967, 1968, 1969, 1970, 1975 Runners-up 8 times

League career			Record win	Highest number of league goals
				ABERDEEN
1904–05 Div. 2	1919–75 Div. 1	1975– Pr. Div.	13–0 v Peterhead,	Benny Yorston, 38, 1929–30
1905–17 Div. 1			Scottish Cup, 1922–23	
				AIRDRIEONIANS
1894–1903 Div. 2	1948–50 Div. 2	1965–66 Div. 2	11–1 v Falkirk, Div. 1,	Bert Yarnall, 39, 1916–17
1903–36 Div. 1	1950–54 Div. 1	1966–73 Div. 1	1950–51	
1936–47 Div. 2	1954–55 Div. 2	1973–74 Div. 2		
1947–48 Div. 1	1955–65 Div. 1	1974–80 Div. 1		
		1980– Pr. Div.		
				ALBION ROVERS
1903–15 Div. 2	1934–37 Div. 1	1946–48 Div. 2	10–0 v Brechin City,	Jim Renwick, 41, 1932–33
1919–23 Div. 1	1937–38 Div. 2	1948–49 Div. 1	Div. 2, 1937–38	
1923–34 Div. 2	1938–39 Div. 1	1949– Div. 2		
				ALLOA
1921–22 Div. 2	1923–77 Div. 2	1978– Div. 2	9–2 v Forfar, Div. 2,	Wee Crilley, 49, 1921–22
1922–23 Div. 1	1977–78 Div. 1		1932–33	
				ARBROATH
1921–35 Div. 2	1959–60 Div. 1	1969–72 Div. 2	36–0 v Bon Accord,	Dave Easson, 45, 1958–59
1935–39 Div. 1	1960–68 Div. 2	1972–80 Div. 1	Scottish Cup, 1885–86	
1946–59 Div. 2	1968–69 Div. 1	1980– Div. 2		
				AYR UNITED
1897–1913 Div. 2	1946–56 Div. 2	1967–69 Div. 2	11–1 v Dumbarton,	Jimmy Smith, 66, 1927–28
1913–25 Div. 1	1956–57 Div. 1	1969–75 Div. 1	League Cup, 1952–53	
1925–28 Div. 2	1957–59 Div. 2	1975–78 Pr. Div.		
1928–36 Div. 1	1959–61 Div. 1	1978– Div. 1		
1936–37 Div. 2	1961–66 Div. 2			
1937–39 Div. 1	1966–67 Div. 1			
				BERWICK RANGERS
1955–79 Div. 2	1979– Div. 1		8–1 v Forfar Athletic, Div. 2,	Ken Bowron, 38, 1963–64
			1965–66; 8–1 v Vale of Leithen,	
			Scottish Cup, 1966–67	
				BRECHIN CITY
1929–39 Div. 2	1954– Div. 2		12–1 v Thornhill,	Willie McIntosh, 26, 1959–60
			Scottish Cup, 1925–26	
				CELTIC
1890–1975 Div. 1	1975– Pr. Div.		11–0 v Dundee, Div. 1,	Jimmy McGrory, 50, 1935–36
			1895–96	

Ground	Honours League	Scottish FA Cup	League Cup
CLYDE (1878) White/black			
Shawfield Stadium Glasgow C5	Div. 2 Champions 1904–05, 1951–52, 1956–57, 1961–62, 1972–73, 1977–78 Runners-up 1903–04, 1905–06, 1925–26, 1963–64	Winners 1939, 1955, 1958 Runners-up 1910, 1912, 1949	
CLYDEBANK (1965) White/white			
Kilbowie Park Clydebank	Div. 1 runners-up 1976–77 Div. 2 Champions 1975–76		
COWDENBEATH (1881) Blue/white			
Central Park Cowdenbeath	Div. 2 Champions 1913–14, 1914–15, 1938–39 Runners-up 1921–22, 1923–24, 1969–70		
DUMBARTON (1872) White/white			
Boghead Park Dumbarton	Div. 1 Champions 1890–91 (shared), 1891–92 Div. 2 Champions 1910–11, 1971–72 Runners-up 1907–08	Winners 1883 Runners-up 1881, 1882, 1887, 1891, 1897	
DUNDEE (1893) Blue/white			
Dens Park Dundee	Div. 1 Champions 1961–62, 1978–79 Runners-up 1902–03, 1906–07, 1908–09, 1948–49 Div. 2 Champions 1946–47	Winners 1910 Runners-up 1925, 1952, 1964	Winners 1952, 1953, 1974 Runners-up 1968
DUNDEE UNITED (1910) Tangerine/tangerine			
Tannadice Park Dundee	Div. 2 Champions 1924–25, 1928–29 Runners-up 1930–31, 1959–60	Runners-up 1974	Winners 1980
DUNFERMLINE ATHLETIC (1885) White, black/black			
East End Park Dunfermline	Div. 2 Champions 1925–26 Runners-up 1912–13, 1933–34, 1954–55, 1957–58, 1972–73, 1978–79	Winners 1961, 1968 Runners-up 1965	Runners–up 1950
EAST FIFE (1903) Gold/black			
Bayview Park Methil	Div. 2 Champions 1947–48 Runners-up 1929–30, 1970–71	Winners 1938 Runners-up 1927, 1950	Winners 1948, 1950, 1954
EAST STIRLING(SHIRE) (1881) Black, white/black			
Firs Park Falkirk	Div. 2 Champions 1931–32 Runners-up 1962–63, 1979–80		
FALKIRK (1876) Blue/white			
Brockville Park Falkirk	Div. 1 runners-up 1907–08, 1909–10 Div. 2 Champions 1935–36, 1969–70, 1974–75, 1979–80 Runners-up 1904–05, 1951–52, 1960–61	Winners 1913, 1957	Runners-up 1948

League career			Record win	Highest number of league goals
				CLYDE
1891–93 Div. 1	1951–52 Div. 2	1964–72 Div. 1	11–1 v Cowdenbeath,	Bill Boyd, 32, 1932–33
1893–94 Div. 2	1952–56 Div. 1	1972–73 Div. 2	Div. 2, 1951–52	
1894–1900 Div. 1	1956–57 Div. 2	1973–76 Div. 1		
1900–06 Div. 2	1957–61 Div. 1	1976–78 Div. 2		
1906–24 Div. 1	1961–62 Div. 2	1978–80 Div. 1		
1924–26 Div. 2	1962–63 Div. 1	1980– Div. 2		
1926–51 Div. 1	1963–64 Div. 2			
				CLYDEBANK
1966–76 Div. 2	1977–78 Pr. Div.	1978– Div. 1	8–1 v Arbroath, Div. 2,	Blair Millar, 28, 1978–79
1976–77 Div. 1			1975–76	
				COWDENBEATH
1905–24 Div. 2	1934–70 Div. 2	1971– Div. 2	12–0 v St Johnstone,	Willie Devlin, 40, 1925–26
1924–34 Div. 1	1970–71 Div. 1		Scottish Cup, 1927–28	
				DUMBARTON
1890–96 Div. 1	1913–22 Div. 1	1972– Div. 1	8–0 v Cowdenbeath,	Kenny Wilson, 38, 1971–72
1896–97 Div. 2	1922–54 Div. 2		Div. 2, 1963–64	
1906–13 Div. 2	1955–72 Div. 2			
				DUNDEE
1893–1917 Div. 1	1947–75 Div. 1	1979–80 Pr. Div.	10–0 v Alloa, Div. 2, 1946–47 and	Dave Halliday, 38, 1923–24
1919–38 Div. 1	1975–76 Pr. Div.	1980– Div. 1	v Dunfermline, Div. 2, 1946–47	
1938–47 Div. 2	1976–79 Div. 1			
				DUNDEE UNITED
1910–15 Div. 2	1929–30 Div. 1	1960–75 Div. 1	14–0 v Nithsdale,	John Coyle, 41, 1955–56
1923–25 Div. 2	1930–31 Div. 2	1975– Pr. Div.	Scottish Cup, 1930–31	
1925–27 Div. 1	1931–32 Div. 1			
1927–29 Div. 2	1932–60 Div. 2			**DUNFERMLINE**
1912–15 Div. 2	1934–37 Div. 1	1958–72 Div. 1	11–2 v Stenhousemuir,	Bobby Skinner, 55, 1925–26
1921–26 Div. 2	1937–55 Div. 2	1972–73 Div. 2	Div. 2, 1930–31	
1926–28 Div. 1	1955–57 Div. 1	1973–76 Div. 1		
1928–34 Div. 2	1957–58 Div. 2	1976–79 Div. 2		
		1979– Div. 1		
				EAST FIFE
1921–30 Div. 2	1948–58 Div. 1	1974–75 Div. 2	13–2 v Edinburgh City,	Henry Morris, 41, 1947–48
1930–31 Div. 1	1958–71 Div. 2	1975–78 Div. 1	Div. 2, 1937–38	
1931–48 Div. 2	1971–74 Div. 1	1978– Div. 2		
				EAST STRILING(SHIRE)
1900–15 Div. 2	1924–39 Div. 2	1963–64 Div 1	8–2 v Brechin City, Div. 2,	Malcolm Morrison, 36, 1938–39
1921–23 Div. 2	1955–63 Div. 2	1964–80 Div. 2	1961–62	
		1980– Div. 1		
				FALKIRK
1902–05 Div. 2	1952–59 Div. 1	1974–75 Div. 2	10–0 v Breadalbane,	Evelyn Morrison, 43, 1928–29
1905–35 Div. 1	1959–61 Div. 2	1975–77 Div. 1	Scottish Cup, 1922–23	
1935–36 Div. 2	1961–69 Div. 1	1977–80 Div. 2	and 1925–26	
1936–51 Div. 1	1969–70 Div. 2	1980– Div. 1		
1951–52 Div. 2	1970–74 Div. 1			

Ground	Honours League	Scottish FA Cup	League Cup

FORFAR ATHLETIC (1884) Blue/blue

Station Park
Forfar — Highest League placing 3rd, Div. 2, 1979–80

HAMILTON ACADEMICAL (1875) Red, white/white

Douglas Park
Hamilton — Div. 2 Champions 1903–04 Runners-up 1952–53, 1964–65 — Runners-up 1911, 1935

HEART OF MIDLOTHIAN (1874) Maroon/white

Tynecastle Park
Edinburgh — Div. 1 Champions 1894–95, 1896–97, 1957–58, 1959–60, 1979–80 Runners-up 1893–94, 1898–99, 1903–04, 1905–06, 1914–15, 1937–38 1953–54, 1956–57, 1958–59, 1964–65, 1977–78 — Winners 1891, 1896, 1901, 1906, 1956 Runners-up 1903, 1907, 1968, 1976 — Winners 1955, 1959, 1960, 1963 Runners-up 1962

HIBERNIAN (1875) Green/white

Easter Road Park
Edinburgh — Div. 1 Champions 1902–03, 1947–48, 1950–51, 1951–52 Runners-up 1896–97, 1946–47, 1949–50, 1952–53, 1973–74, 1974–75 Div. 2 Champions 1893–94, 1894–95, 1932–33 — Winners 1887, 1902 Runners-up 1896, 1914, 1923, 1924, 1947, 1958, 1972, 1979 — Winners 1973 Runners-up 1951, 1969, 1975

KILMARNOCK (1869) Blue, white/blue

Rugby Park
Kilmarnock — Div. 1 Champions 1964–65 Runners-up 1959–60, 1960–61, 1962–63, 1963–64, 1975–76, 1978–79 Div. 2 Champions 1897–98, 1898–99 Runners-up 1953–54, 1973–74 — Winners 1920, 1929 Runners-up 1898, 1932, 1938, 1957, 1960 — Runners-up 1953, 1961, 1963

MEADOWBANK THISTLE (1974) Amber/black

Meadowbank
Stadium
Edinburgh — Highest League placing 11th, Div. 2, 1976–77

MONTROSE (1879) Blue/blue

Links Park
Montrose — Highest League placing 3rd, Div. 1, 1975–76

MORTON (1874) Blue, white/white

Cappielow Park
Greenock — Div. 1 Champions 1977–78 Div. 1 runners-up 1916–17 Div. 2 Champions 1949–50, 1963–64, 1966–67 Runners-up 1899–1900, 1928–29, 1936–37 — Winners 1922 Runners-up 1948 — Runners-up 1964

MOTHERWELL (1886) Amber/amber

Fir Park
Motherwell — Div. 1 Champions 1931–32 Runners-up 1926–27, 1929–30, 1932–33, 1933–34 Div. 2 Champions 1953–54, 1968–69 Runners-up 1894–95, 1902–03 — Winners 1952 Runners-up 1931, 1933, 1939, 1951 — Winners 1951 Runners-up 1955

PARTICK THISTLE (1876) Red, yellow/black

Firhill Park
Glasgow NW — Div. 1 Champions 1975–76 Div. 2 Champions 1896–97 1899–1900, 1970–71 Runners-up 1901–02 — Winners 1921 Runners-up 1930 — Winners 1972 Runners-up 1954, 1957, 1959

League career			Record win	Highest number of league goals
				FORFAR ATHLETIC
1921–25 Div. 2	1926–39 Div. 2	1949– Div. 2	9–1 v Stenhousemuir, Div. 2, 1968–69	Davie Kilgour, 45, 1929–30
				HAMILTON ACADEMICAL
1897–1906 Div. 2	1953–54 Div. 1	1966–75 Div. 2	10–2 v Cowdenbeath, Div. 1, 1932–33	David Wilson, 34, 1936–37
1906–47 Div. 1	1954–65 Div. 2	1975– Div. 1		
1947–53 Div. 2	1965–66 Div. 1			
				HEART OF MIDLOTHIAN
1890–1975 Div. 1	1977–78 Div. 1	1979–80 Div. 1	15–0 v King's Park, Scottish Cup, 1936–37	Barney Battles, 44, 1930–31
1975–77 Pr. Div.	1978–79 Pr. Div.	1980– Pr. Div.		
				HIBERNIAN
1893–95 Div. 2	1931–33 Div. 2	1975–80 Pr. Div.	15–1 v Peebles Rovers, Scottish Cup, 1960–61	Joe Baker, 42, 1959–60
1895–1931 Div. 1	1933–75 Div. 1	1980– Div. 1		
				KILMARNOCK
1895–99 Div. 2	1954–73 Div. 1	1976–77 Pr. Div.	11–1 v Paisley Academicals, Scottish Cup, 1929–30	Peerie Cunningham, 35, 1927–28
1899–1947 Div 1	1973–74 Div. 2	1977–79 Div. 1		
1947–54 Div. 2	1974–76 Div. 1	1979– Pr. Div.		
				MEADOWBANK THISTLE
1974– Div. 2			4–1 v Albion Rovers, Div. 2, 1975–76 and v Forfar, League Cup, 1975–76	John Jobson, 17, 1979–80
				MONTROSE
1929–39 Div. 2	1975–79 Div. 1	1979– Div. 2	12–0 v Vale of Leithen, Scottish Cup, 1974–75	Brian Third, 29, 1972–73
1955–75 Div. 2				
				MORTON
1893–1900 Div. 2	1937–38 Div. 1	1952–64 Div. 2	11–0 v Carfin Shamrock, Scottish Cup, 1886–87	Allan McGraw, 41, 1963–64
1900–27 Div. 1	1938–39 Div. 2	1964–66 Div. 1		
1927–29 Div. 2	1946–49 Div. 1	1966–67 Div. 2		
1929–33 Div. 1	1949–50 Div. 2	1967–78 Div. 1		
1933–37 Div. 2	1950–52 Div. 1	1978– Pr. Div.		
				MOTHERWELL
1893–1903 Div. 2	1954–68 Div. 1	1975–79 Pr. Div.	12–1 v Dundee United, Div. 2, 1953–54	Willie MacFayden, 52, 1931–32
1903–53 Div. 1	1968–69 Div. 2	1979– Div. 1		
1953–54 Div. 2	1969–75 Div. 1			
				PARTICK THISTLE
1893–97 Div. 2	1900–01 Div. 1	1970–71 Div. 2	16–0 v Royal Albert, Scottish Cup, 1930–31	Alec Hair, 41, 1926–27
1897–99 Div. 1	1901–02 Div. 2	1971–76 Div. 1		
1899–1900 Div. 2	1902–70 Div. 1	1976– Pr. Div.		

Ground	Honours League	Scottish FA Cup	League Cup

QUEEN OF THE SOUTH (1919) Blue/white

Palmerston Park Dumfries	Div. 2 Champions 1950–51 Runners-up 1932–33, 1961–62, 1974–75		

QUEEN'S PARK (1867) Black, white/white

Hampden Park Glasgow G42 9BA	Div. 2 Champions 1922–23, 1955–56	Winners 1874, 1875, 1876, 1880, 1881, 1882, 1884, 1886, 1890, 1893 Runners-up 1892, 1900 English FA Cup runners-up 1884, 1885	

RAITH ROVERS (1893) Blue/white

Stark's Park Kirkcaldy	Div. 2 Champions 1907–08, 1909–10 (shared), 1937–38, 1948–49 Runners-up 1908–09, 1926–27, 1966–67, 1975–76, 1977–78	Runners-up 1913	Runners-up 1949

RANGERS (1873) Blue/white

Ibrox Stadium Glasgow SW	Premier Div. Champions 1975–76, 1977–78 Premier Div. Runners-up 1976–77, 1978–79 Div. 1 Champions 1890–91 (shared), 1898–99, 1899–1900, 1900–01, 1901–02, 1910–11, 1911–12, 1912–13, 1917–18, 1919–20, 1920–21, 1922–23, 1923–24, 1924–25, 1926–27, 1927–28, 1928–29, 1929–30, 1930–31, 1932–33, 1933–34, 1934–35, 1936–37, 1938–39, 1946–47, 1948–49, 1949–50, 1952–53, 1955–56, 1956–57, 1958–59, 1960–61, 1962–63, 1963–64, 1974–75 Runners-up 21 times	Winners 1894, 1897, 1898, 1903, 1928, 1930, 1932, 1934, 1935, 1936, 1948, 1949, 1950, 1953, 1960, 1962, 1963, 1964, 1966, 1973, 1976, 1978, 1979 Runners-up 12 times	Winners 1947, 1949, 1961, 1962, 1964, 1965, 1971, 1976, 1978, 1979 Runners-up 5 times

ST JOHNSTONE (1884) Blue/white

Muirton Park Perth	Div. 2 Champions 1923–24, 1959–60, 1962–63 Runners-up 1931–32		Runners-up 1970

ST MIRREN (1876) Black, white/white

St Mirren Park Paisley	Div. 1 Champions 1976–77 Div. 2 Champions 1967–68 Runners-up 1935–36	Winners 1926, 1959 Runners-up 1908, 1934, 1962	Runners-up 1956

STENHOUSEMUIR (1884) Maroon/white

Ochilview Park Larbert	Highest League placing 3rd, Div. 2, 1958–59, 1960–61		

STIRLING ALBION (1945) Red/red

Annfield Park Stirling	Div. 2 Champions 1952–53, 1957–58, 1960–61, 1964–65, 1976–77 Runners-up 1948–49, 1950–51		

STRANRAER (1870) Blue/white

Stair Park Stranraer	Highest League placing 4th, Div. 2, 1960–61, 1976–77		

League career			Record win	Highest number of league goals

QUEEN OF THE SOUTH
Jimmy Gray, 33, 1927–28

1925–33 Div. 2	1951–59 Div. 1	1964–75 Div. 2	11–1 v Stranraer,
1933–50 Div. 1	1959–62 Div. 2	1975–79 Div. 1	Scottish Cup, 1931–32
1950–51 Div. 2	1962–64 Div. 1	1979– Div. 2	

QUEEN'S PARK
Willie Martin, 30, 1937–38

1900–22 Div. 1	1923–48 Div. 1	1956–58 Div. 1	16–0 v St Peter's,
1922–23 Div. 2	1948–56 Div. 2	1958– Div. 2	Scottish Cup, 1885–86

RAITH ROVERS
Norman Haywood, 38, 1937–38

1902–10 Div. 2	1929–38 Div. 2	1967–70 Div. 1	10–1 v Coldstream,
1910–17 Div. 1	1938–39 Div. 1	1970–76 Div. 2	Scottish Cup, 1953–54
1919–26 Div. 1	1946–49 Div. 2	1976–77 Div. 1	
1926–27 Div. 2	1949–63 Div. 1	1977–78 Div. 2	
1927–29 Div. 1	1963–67 Div. 2	1978– Div. 1	

RANGERS
Sam English, 44, 1931–32

1890–1975 Div. 1	1975– Pr. Div.	14–2 v Blairgowrie,
		Scottish Cup, 1933–34

ST JOHNSTONE
Jimmy Benson, 36, 1931–32

1911–15 Div. 2	1932–39 Div. 1	1963–75 Div. 1	8–1 v Partick Thistle,
1921–24 Div. 2	1946–60 Div. 2	1975–76 Pr. Div.	Scottish Cup, 1969–70
1924–30 Div. 1	1960–62 Div. 1	1976– Div. 1	
1930–32 Div. 2	1962–63 Div. 2		

ST MIRREN
Dunky Walker, 45, 1921–22

1890–1935 Div. 1	1967–68 Div. 2	1975–77 Div. 1	15–0 v Glasgow University,
1935–36 Div. 2	1968–71 Div. 1	1977– Pr. Div.	Scottish Cup, 1959–60
1936–67 Div. 1	1971–75 Div. 2		

STENHOUSEMUIR
Evelyn Morrison, 29, 1927–28

1921– Div. 2	9–2 v Dundee United,
	Div. 2, 1936–37

STIRLING ALBION
Michael Lawson, 26, 1975–76

1947–49 Div. 2	1953–56 Div. 1	1962–65 Div. 2	7–0 v Albion Rovers, Div. 2,
1949–50 Div. 1	1956–58 Div. 2	1965–68 Div. 1	1947–48 ; v Montrose, Div. 2,
1950–51 Div. 2	1958–60 Div. 1	1968–77 Div. 2	1957–58 ; v St Mirren, Div. 1,
1951–52 Div. 1	1960–64 Div. 2	1977– Div. 1	1959–60 and v Arbroath,
1952–53 Div. 2	1961–62 Div. 1		Div. 2, 1964–65

STRANRAER
Derek Frye, 27, 1977–78

1955– Div. 2	7–0 v Brechin City, Div. 2,
	1964–65

SCOTTISH LEAGUE INFORMATION

Gordon Smith was the first player to appear for three different clubs in the European Cup. He was with Hibernian in the 1955–56 season and later played for Heart of Midlothian in 1960–61 and Dundee in 1962–63.

He had joined Hibernian from Dundee North End in April 1941 for only £40. By the next season he had established himself and was in the team which routed Rangers 8–1 on 27 September 1941, though Rangers dominated football during the Second World War. That day four goals by Bobby Combe, and two each from Arthur Milne and Smith himself achieved the success.

Already an experienced right-winger by the time normal football was resumed in 1946–47, Smith made 310 post-war League appearances for Hibs before moving across Edinburgh to play for Hearts where he remained for two seasons before linking up with Dundee in 1961 and helping them to the Scottish League championship in his first season. He completed his Scottish League career in 1963–64 with a total of 423 League games and 146 goals. For Scotland he made 18 appearances at full level.

When Doug Rougvie was sent off playing for Aberdeen against Rangers on 31 March 1979 in the Scottish League Cup Final at Hampden Park he became only the second player dismissed in a major Scottish final. Jock Buchanan (Rangers) had been the first, ordered off in the 1929 Scottish Cup Final. In both matches the depleted teams were beaten, Rangers 2–0 by Kilmarnock and Aberdeen 2–1 by Rangers.

Andy Gray, who became the most expensive player on the transfer market in the 1979–80 season (see Milestones), had a rapid rise to seniority in his native Scotland. He was playing for Clydebank Strollers at 15, and a year later was on the ground staff of Dundee United. He had three matches with United's reserves before making his first team debut as a substitute in a Scottish League Cup match at Motherwell on 18 August 1973; he became a regular choice during the club's League programme that season, finishing as top scorer with 16 League goals. He joined Aston Villa for £110 000 in September 1975.

Gordon Smith was one of the outstanding wingers in his day and established a fast record of appearances for different clubs in the European Cup. (Popperfoto)

The first substitute used in a Scottish League match was Archie Gemmill who replaced Jim Clunie for St Mirren against Clyde after 25 minutes of their Division One match on 13 August 1966. In the 1979–80 season Gemmill was captain of Scotland and a member of Birmingham City's promotion team while Clunie was manager of St Mirren as the first Scottish winners of the Anglo-Scottish Cup.

Archie Gemmill, the first player with a number 12 shirt to appear in a Scottish League match (All Sport/Don Morley)

Welsh/Irish Soccer

WALES

Newport County qualified for the European Cup Winners Cup by winning the Welsh Cup for the first time in their history in the 1979–80 season. They were also promoted from Division Four after finishing third in the table following 18 years in the division. Between 22 February and 12 April 1980 they won ten successive League matches.

Bryn Jones was the most expensive player to feature in a transfer deal spanning the Second World War. He joined Arsenal from Wolverhampton Wanderers in the summer of 1938 for £14 000, and this record stood until Billy Steel moved from Morton to Derby County in 1947 for £15 000.

Jones might well have joined Tottenham Hotspur in June 1937, but their bid of £12 000 was turned down by Wolves. He had had spells with Merthyr Amateurs, trials with Southend United, one season with Glenavon and then joined Aberaman without much distinction until moving to Molineux in November 1933 for £1500. He made his League debut at inside-right against Everton on 18 November 1933. One of his brothers Emlyn had seven seasons with Southend United while another brother Ivor played for Swansea and West Bromwich Albion. Bryn made 17 appearances for Wales.

NORTHERN IRELAND

Northern Ireland won the British International Championship in the 1979–80 season for only the second time in their history to celebrate the Irish Football Association's Centenary. Their earlier success in the tournament had been in 1913–14.

Ireland can also claim to have produced the best individual goalscoring achievement in a British International Championship match when centre-forward Joe Bambrick scored six of the seven goals with which Northern Ireland beat Wales on 1 February 1930 at Celtic Park, Belfast.

On 29 March Bambrick had another triumph on the same ground when he scored all four of Linfield's goals in their 4–3 Irish Cup Final win over Ballymena. His goals in all matches that season totalled 94 and besides his six included one 5, five 4's, ten 3's and seven 2's accounting for 75 alone. Bambrick later played for Chelsea and Walsall and for Ireland he scored 12 goals in eleven appearances.

British International Soccer

Scotland's most successful run came in the 1880s when they had 12 wins in a row, beating England and Wales five times each and Ireland twice. They actually went 21 games without defeat after beating England 5–4 on 13 March 1880 and ended it with a 5–1 win against Wales on 10 March 1888.

England's most successful run came in the following decade. It started when they beat Wales 3–1 on 15 March 1890 and ended after they again defeated the Welsh 9–1 on 16 March 1896, following a sequence of 20 matches. It comprised 16 wins and four draws and at one time produced nine successive wins.

Northern Ireland's best sequence of results began on 1 May 1957 against Portugal in a 3–0 win and ended after a 1–0 win against Czechoslovakia in the World Cup on 8 June 1958. It produced four wins and three draws.

Former Arsenal goalkeeper Jack Kelsey created a record for Wales by keeping goal in 12 consecutive international matches in the 1957–58 season. It began with a 4–0 defeat by England on 19 October 1957 and ended with a 2–2 draw also against the English on 26 November 1958. During this run Wales went eight matches without defeat.

Pat Jennings made 27 consecutive appearances in goal for Northern Ireland, starting with the match against Portugal on 14 November 1973 which was drawn 1–1 and it ended against Belgium on 16 November 1977 in a 3–0 win. During this run he created a record for his country of keeping his goal intact for three consecutive matches during the 1974–75 season: against Sweden (2–0), Yugoslavia (1–0) and England (0–0).

Scotland's best defensive sequence was established when they went seven matches without conceding a goal starting with a 3–0 win over Northern Ireland on 28 February 1925 and continued against England (2–0), Wales (3–0), Northern Ireland (4–0), England (1–0), Wales (3–0) until ending again with Northern Ireland (2–0) on 26 February 1927.

Ron Springett of Sheffield Wednesday made 21 consecutive appearances in goal for England starting with a 9–3 win against Scotland on 15

April 1961 and ending on 25 February 1963 against France in a 5–2 defeat.

Northern Ireland played 50 international matches before including a player from a Football League club in their side. It was their 51st game on 4 March 1899 against Wales in, Belfast when Archie Goodall (Derby County), Bill Taggart (Walsall) and Tom Morrison (Burnley) played in a 1–0 win.

Scotland first used a player from the Football League in their 59th international match on 4 April 1894 against England at Celtic Park. They had five Anglo-Scots in their side which won 2–1.

Scotland included ten Anglo-Scots in their team which started the match against East Germany in East Berlin on 7 September 1977. Later they brought on two more Anglos as substitutes. The only Scottish League player in the side was Danny McGrain the Celtic full-back.

There have been only two occasions during this century when Scotland have not included a player from a Glasgow club in a full international match against England. It happened at Newcastle in April 1907 when they drew 1–1 and at Wembley in May 1979 when they lost 3–1.

Only once since the Second World War has Scotland fielded a team in a British International Championship match that did not include a player from either Celtic or Rangers. On 2 April 1955 they lost 7–2 to England at Wembley, but had two players each from Clyde and Partick Thistle in their side.

Prior to the war a similar situation arose without Glasgow based players in October 1933, when they lost 3–2 to Wales. They had been unable to field a number of regular players owing to injuries and other causes.

Northern Ireland is the only home country to have included a non-British player in a British International Championship match. He was Willie Andrews, a half-back who played for Glentoran and Grimsby Town. He was born in Kansas City, USA and played against Scotland twice and England between 1908 and 1913.

Johnny Carey, when a Manchester United player, turned out against England in two full international matches within three days and for different countries. He appeared for Northern Ireland in Belfast on 28 September 1946 and for the Republic of Ireland in Dublin on 30 September.

Later, in the same season, he played in four countries in eight days. The sequence began with a Division One match for Manchester United at

Johnny Carey believed in making the most of himself as a footballer. And in these days of overworked professional footballers, it is a sobering reminder of the not-so-long ago when it was just the same! (Colorsport)

Liverpool on 3 May 1947, a Saturday, and was followed by playing for the Republic of Ireland against Portugal in Dublin the next day. He then played in a Dutch trial match at The Hague on 6 May and for the Rest of Europe against Great Britain at Hampden Park on 10 May.

When Celtic and former Liverpool and St Mirren forward Frank McGarvey made his debut as a Liverpool player in a full international match on

The Irish have more than once placed their faith in youth and Sammy McIlroy of Manchester United and Northern Ireland is just one who has justified this trust on the football field. (Syndication International)

22 May 1979, he went on as a last minute substitute for Scotland against Northern Ireland at Hampden Park and had not touched the ball at the finish of the game.

The only hat-trick to have been achieved for Northern Ireland in a British International Championship match during the last 75 years was a double one: a six goals feat by Linfield centre-forward Joe Bambrick in a 7–0 win against Wales in Belfast on 1 February 1930.

Only four players in this century have achieved hat-tricks when making their debuts for England in full international matches: George Mills (Chelsea) v Northern Ireland in October 1937, Wilf Mannion (Middlesbrough) v Northern Ireland in September 1946, Stan Mortensen (Blackpool) v Portugal in May 1947 and Fred Pickering (Everton) v USA in May 1964.

A post-war record which no current player is even anywhere near equalling is that of Jimmy Greaves who achieved six hat-tricks for England in full international matches while with Chelsea and Tottenham Hotspur. They were v Luxembourg in October 1960, v Scotland in April 1961, v Peru in May 1962, v Northern Ireland in November 1963 (when his total was four goals), v Northern Ireland in October 1964 and v Norway in June 1966 (when he scored another four times).

No other player scored as many goals in full international matches in one season as Tommy Lawton when with Chelsea in the 1946–47 season. Playing for England he scored four each against Holland and Portugal and one each v Northern Ireland and Wales and added two for Great Britain against the Rest of Europe for a total of 12 goals.

Since the mid-1970s the equivalent of a complete team of English-born players have appeared for the Republic of Ireland in full international matches. They have included: Terry Mancini, John Dempsey, Mick Kearns, Gerry Peyton, Ron Healey, David O'Leary, Tony Grealish, Mickey Walsh, Chris Hughton, Mark Lawrenson and Austin Hayes.

No teenage goalkeeper has played for England or Scotland in a full international match, but they have been included by all the other home countries. Gary Sprake played for Wales when he was 18 years and 231 days old and Pat Jennings for Northern Ireland when 18 and 316 days. Paddy Roche was capped for the Republic of Ireland when 19 and Alan Kelly when only 18 years of age.

Three Irishmen are among the youngest of international players: Sammy McIlroy (Manchester United) who was given his debut when 17 years and 198 days old and George Best (Hibernian) when 17 and 328 days, both by Northern Ireland, and Jimmy Holmes (Tottenham Hotspur) by the Republic of Ireland when 17 years and 200 days.

When Jack and Bobby Charlton first played together in the same international side against Scotland at Wembley in April 1965 they became the first pair of brothers to appear together for England in a full international since Nottingham Forest's Frank and Fred Forman had done so in 1899.

Several contemporary England international players have earned reputations as lucky mascots in rarely having been on the losing side, but few past or present, have equalled Jack Charlton in that respect. In his 35 international appearances only two against Austria and Scotland were lost and in 23 of them not a goal was conceded.

British International Championship matches have been played during this century on six other London grounds besides Wembley: Stamford Bridge, Highbury, Crystal Palace, Craven Cottage, The Den and Selhurst Park.

In the 88 years of full international matches involving the four home countries up to 1961 no player had been sent off, but since then all these have suffered that fate: Pat Crerand, Tommy Gemmell, Peter Lorimer, Andy Gray and Willie Johnston (all Scotland), Alan Mullery, Alan Ball and Trevor Cherry (England), Billy Ferguson, Jimmy Nicholson and George Best (Northern Ireland) and Trevor Hockey and Byron Stevenson (Wales).

BRITISH INTERNATIONAL CHAMPIONSHIP

The British International Championship began when all four home countries started playing each other. Previously matches between some of them had only been regarded as friendlies. The tournament itself began in 1883–84. If countries were level on points at the top they shared the title, as goal average or goal difference did not count in determining the winner until the latter system was introduced in 1978–79.

The Charlton brothers Jack (left) and Bobby celebrated an almost unique achievement when they appeared together in the England side in 1965. The record books had to be thumbed back many years . . . (Syndication International)

England have won the title outright on 32 occasions, Scotland 24, Wales seven and Ireland once. England have been concerned in all the 20 shared titles, Scotland 17, Wales and Ireland in five each.

In the overall record of matches between the four home countries, in addition to the friendlies played before the International Championship started, England and Wales met each other twice in qualifying matches for the 1974 World Cup, as did Scotland and Wales in the 1978 World Cup, Scotland played England as part of their Centenary in 1973 and Wales met England in their Centenary match in 1976.

England also played Ireland in the qualifying competition of the 1980 European Championship.

England v Scotland

First match	Scotland 0 England 0 30 November 1872 Glasgow
Overall record	98 matches: Scotland 38 wins, England 38, drawn 22. Goals: England 179, Scotland 164
Record win	England 9 Scotland 3 15 April 1961 Wembley
Best individual performance	Dennis Wilshaw (England) 4 goals v Scotland, 2 April 1955, Wembley
Most appearances	Billy Wright (England) 13

Wales v Scotland

First match	Scotland 4 Wales 0 25 March 1876 Glasgow
Overall record	95 matches: Scotland 57 wins, Wales 16, drawn 22. Goals: Scotland 232, Wales 106
Record win	Scotland 9 Wales 0 23 March 1878 Old Hampden
Best individual performance	Willie Paul (Scotland) 4 goals v Wales 22 March 1890, Paisley. John Madden (Scotland) 4 goals v Wales 18 March 1883, Wrexham
Most appearances	Billy Meredith (Wales) 12, Ivor Allchurch (Wales) 12

England v Wales

First match	England 2 Wales 1 18 January 1879 Kennington Oval
Overall record	93 matches: England 60 wins, Wales 13, drawn 20. Goals: England 236, Wales 88
Record win	Wales 1 England 9 16 March 1896 Cardiff
Best individual performance	Steve Bloomer (England) 5 goals v Wales, 16 March 1896, Cardiff
Most appearances	Billy Meredith (Wales) 20

Ireland v Wales

First match	Wales 7 Ireland 1 25 February 1882 Wrexham
Overall record	87 matches: Wales 40 wins, Ireland 27, drawn 20. Goals: Wales 176, Ireland 125
Record win	Wales 11, Ireland 0 3 March 1888 Wrexham
Best individual performance	Joe Bambrick (Ireland) 6 goals v Wales, 1 February 1930, Belfast
Most appearances	Billy Meredith (Wales) 16

Ireland v England

First match	Ireland 0 England 13 18 February 1882 Belfast
Overall record	89 matches: England 69 wins, Ireland 6, drawn 14. Goals: England 308, Ireland 80
Record win	Ireland 0 England 13 18 February 1882 Belfast
Best individual performance	Willie Hall (England) 5 goals v Ireland, 16 November 1938, Old Trafford
Most appearances	Pat Jennings (Ireland) 16

Scotland v Ireland

First match	Ireland 0 Scotland 5 26 January 1884 Belfast

Overall record	85 matches: Scotland 59 wins, Ireland 14, drawn 12. Goals: Scotland 249, Ireland 77
Record win	Scotland 11 Ireland 0 23 February 1901 Hampden Park
Best individual performance	Charles Heggie (Scotland) 5 goals v Ireland, 20 March 1886, Belfast
Most appearances	Danny Blanchflower (Ireland) 13

Youngest international players

England: Duncan Edwards (Manchester United) 18 years 183 days, left-half v Scotland, 2 April 1955

Ireland: Norman Kernaghan (Belfast Celtic) 17 years 80 days, outside-right v Wales, 11 March 1936

Scotland: Denis Law (Huddersfield Town) 18 years 236 days, inside-forward v Wales, 18 October 1958

Wales: John Charles (Leeds United) 18 years 71 days, centre-half v Ireland, 8 March 1950

(There are claims that other players have been younger, but the above examples are the ones which have so far been proved satisfactorily.)

FULL INTERNATIONAL RECORD OF THE HOME COUNTRIES

ENGLAND

Opponents	P	W	D	L	F	A
Argentina	8	4	3	1	12	7
Austria	15	8	3	4	54	25
Australia	1	1	0	0	2	1
Belgium	17	12	4	1	66	24
Bohemia	1	1	0	0	4	0
Brazil	11	1	4	6	9	18
Bulgaria	5	3	2	0	7	1
Chile	2	2	0	0	4	1
Colombia	1	1	0	0	4	0
Cyprus	2	2	0	0	6	0
Czechoslovakia	9	5	2	2	17	11
Denmark	7	6	1	0	21	7
Ecuador	1	1	0	0	2	0
Finland	5	5	0	0	22	3
France	18	13	2	3	57	24
East Germany (GDR)	3	2	1	0	6	3
West Germany	14	8	2	4	30	19
Greece	2	2	0	0	5	0
Hungary	11	6	0	5	36	26
Northern Ireland	89	69	14	6	308	80
Republic of Ireland	8	4	3	1	14	7
Italy	14	6	4	4	23	18
Luxembourg	5	5	0	0	25	3

Opponents	P	W	D	L	F	A
Malta	2	2	0	0	6	0
Mexico	4	2	1	1	11	2
Netherlands (Holland)	6	3	2	1	11	5
Norway	4	4	0	0	20	2
Peru	2	1	0	1	5	4
Poland	4	1	2	1	3	4
Portugal	14	8	5	1	35	16
Rumania	4	2	2	0	4	1
Scotland	98	38	22	38	179	164
Spain	13	9	1	3	30	15
Sweden	10	6	2	2	23	13
Switzerland	12	8	2	2	33	9
USA	4	3	0	1	24	5
USSR	7	3	3	1	14	7
Uruguay	6	2	2	2	7	8
Wales	93	60	20	13	236	88
Yugoslavia	11	2	5	4	15	18
Rest of Europe	1	1	0	0	3	0
FIFA	1	0	1	0	4	4
Rest of the World	1	1	0	0	2	1

SCOTLAND

Opponents	P	W	D	L	F	A
Argentina	2	0	1	1	2	4
Austria	14	3	4	7	18	28
Belgium	8	3	0	5	11	12
Brazil	5	0	2	3	1	5
Bulgaria	1	1	0	0	2	1
Cyprus	2	2	0	0	13	0
Chile	1	1	0	0	4	2
Czechoslovakia	10	5	1	4	18	16
Denmark	9	8	0	1	17	5
England	98	38	22	38	164	179
Finland	4	4	0	0	13	3
France	7	5	0	2	10	6
East Germany (GDR)	2	1	0	1	3	1
West Germany	9	3	4	2	16	13
Hungary	6	1	2	3	11	15
Northern Ireland	85	59	12	14	249	77
Republic of Ireland	4	2	1	1	8	3
Italy	3	1	0	2	1	6
Iran	1	0	1	0	1	1
Luxembourg	1	1	0	0	6	0
Netherlands (Holland)	7	4	1	2	11	9
Norway	8	6	1	1	27	12
Paraguay	1	0	0	1	2	3
Peru	3	1	1	1	4	4
Poland	5	1	1	3	6	8
Portugal	9	4	1	4	12	9
Rumania	2	0	2	0	2	2
Spain	6	2	2	2	13	11
Sweden	4	1	1	2	6	7
Switzerland	7	5	0	2	13	9
Turkey	1	0	0	1	2	4
Uruguay	2	0	0	2	2	10
USA	1	1	0	0	6	0
USSR	2	0	0	2	0	3
Wales	95	57	22	16	232	106
Yugoslavia	5	1	4	0	8	6
Zaire	1	1	0	0	2	0

WALES

Opponents	P	W	D	L	F	A
Austria	4	1	0	3	3	6
Belgium	2	1	0	1	6	4
Brazil	5	0	0	5	3	11
Chile	1	0	0	1	0	2
Czechoslovakia	6	2	0	4	5	7
Denmark	2	1	0	1	4	3
England	93	13	20	60	88	236
Finland	2	2	0	0	4	0
France	3	0	1	2	3	9
East Germany	4	1	0	3	7	8
West Germany	6	0	3	3	4	12
Greece	2	1	0	1	4	3
Hungary	7	3	2	2	11	10
Iceland	1	1	0	0	4	0
Luxembourg	2	2	0	0	8	1
Northern Ireland	87	40	20	27	176	125
Republic of Ireland	2	2	0	0	5	3
Iran	1	1	0	0	1	0
Israel	2	2	0	0	4	0
Italy	3	0	0	3	2	9
Kuwait	2	0	2	0	0	0
Malta	2	2	0	0	9	0
Mexico	2	0	1	1	2	3
Poland	2	1	0	1	2	3
Portugal	2	1	0	1	4	4
Rumania	2	0	1	1	0	2
Scotland	95	16	22	57	106	232
Spain	2	0	1	1	2	3
Sweden	1	0	1	0	0	0
Switzerland	2	1	0	1	3	6
Turkey	2	1	0	1	4	1
Rest of the UK	2	1	0	1	3	3
USSR	2	1	0	1	3	3
Yugoslavia	4	0	1	3	4	11

NORTHERN IRELAND

Opponents	P	W	D	L	F	A
Albania	2	1	1	0	5	2
Argentina	1	0	0	1	1	3
Australia	3	2	1	0	5	3
Belgium	2	1	0	1	3	2
Bulgaria	4	2	1	1	4	3
Cyprus	4	3	0	1	11	1
Czechoslovakia	2	2	0	0	3	1
Denmark	2	1	0	1	2	5
England	89	6	14	69	80	308
France	3	0	1	2	3	9
Greece	2	1	0	1	3	2
Netherlands (Holland)	5	1	2	2	4	8
Israel	3	1	2	0	4	3
Iceland	2	1	0	1	2	1
Republic of Ireland	2	1	1	0	1	0
Italy	4	1	1	2	6	7
Mexico	1	1	0	0	4	1
Norway	2	1	0	1	4	2
Poland	2	2	0	0	4	0
Portugal	4	1	3	0	6	3
Scotland	85	14	12	59	77	249
Spain	5	0	2	3	4	12
Sweden	2	1	0	1	3	2
Switzerland	2	1	0	1	2	2
Turkey	2	2	0	0	7	1
Uruguay	1	1	0	0	3	0
USSR	4	0	2	2	1	4
Wales	87	27	20	40	125	176
West Germany	5	0	1	4	6	15
Yugoslavia	2	1	0	1	1	1

Bobby Moore, the player with
the most England international
appearances.
(All Sport/Don Morley)

INTERNATIONAL APPEARANCES OF THE HOME COUNTRIES

INTERNATIONAL APPEARANCES (ENGLAND) 50 or more

		Int. Champ.	Others	Total
Bobby Moore (West Ham United)	1962–1973	30	78	108
Bobby Charlton (Manchester United)	1958–1970	32	74	106
Billy Wright (Wolverhampton Wanderers)	1946–1959	38	67	105
Tom Finney (Preston North End)	1946–1956	29	47	76
Gordon Banks (Leicester City, Stoke City)	1963–1972	23	50	73
Alan Ball (Blackpool, Everton, Arsenal)	1965–1975	20	52	72
Martin Peters (West Ham United, Tottenham Hotspur)	1966–1974	19	48	67
Ray Wilson (Huddersfield Town, Everton)	1960–1968	15	48	63
Emlyn Hughes (Liverpool, Wolverhampton Wanderers)	1969–	21	41	62
Jimmy Greaves (Chelsea, Tottenham Hotspur)	1959–1967	14	43	57
Johnny Haynes (Fulham)	1954–1962	16	40	56
Dave Watson (Manchester City, Werder Bremen, Southampton)	1974–	15	40	55
Stanley Matthews (Stoke City, Blackpool)	1934–1956	24	30	54*
Kevin Keegan (Liverpool, Hamburg)	1972–	11	43	54
Ray Clemence (Liverpool)	1972–	13	38	51

* Matthews' total does not include the 29 war-time and Victory internationals in which he appeared.

INTERNATIONAL APPEARANCES (SCOTLAND) 50 or more

		Int. Champ.	Others	Total
Kenny Dalglish (Celtic, Liverpool)	1971–	23	52	75
Denis Law (Huddersfield T, Manchester City, Torino, Manchester Utd)	1958–1974	26	29	55
Billy Bremner (Leeds United)	1965–1976	19	35	54
George Young (Rangers)	1946–1957	29	24	53

INTERNATIONAL APPEARANCES (NORTHERN IRELAND) 50 or more

		Int. Champ.	Others	Total
Pat Jennings (Watford, Tottenham Hotspur, Arsenal)	1964–	40	43	83
Terry Neill (Arsenal, Hull City)	1961–1973	30	30	60
Danny Blanchflower (Barnsley, Aston Villa, Tottenham Hotspur)	1949–1962	37	19	56
Billy Bingham (Sunderland, Luton Town, Everton)	1951–1963	34	22	56
Jimmy McIlroy (Burnley)	1951–1965	36	19	55
Allan Hunter (Blackburn Rovers, Ipswich Town)	1969–	23	30	53
Bryan Hamilton (Linfield, Ipswich Town, Everton, Millwall, Swindon Town)	1968–	22	28	50

INTERNATIONAL APPEARANCES (WALES) 50 or more

		Int. Champ.	Others	Total
Ivor Allchurch (Swansea, Newcastle United, Cardiff City)	1950–1966	37	31	68
Cliff Jones (Swansea, Tottenham Hotspur, Fulham)	1954–1969	31	28	59
Terry Yorath (Leeds United, Coventry City, Tottenham Hotspur)	1969–	27	27	54
Leighton Phillips (Cardiff City, Aston Villa, Swansea City)	1971–	21	29	50

EUROPEAN FOOTBALL CHAMPIONSHIP
1980 final tournament

...tion from the West Germany v. Czechoslovakia ...opean Championship match in Italy during 1980. ...ndication International)

The final stages of the sixth European Championship (formerly known as the Nations Cup) were held in Italy from 11 June to 22 June 1980. The seven-group qualifiers had joined Italy, the host nation, for the final tournament organised for the first time on the lines of the World Cup. The draw split the eight teams into two groups of four with the winners of each group meeting in the final and the respective runners-up in the match for third and fourth places.

In previous competitions the eight group qualifiers had been drawn in home and away quarter-finals with the semi-finalists meeting in a sudden death situation again in one country. There was no seeding or exemption for the host nation.

This time England, Belgium, Spain and Italy were in one group with Czechoslovakia, West Germany, Greece and Holland forming the second one.

Four venues were used for the matches: Rome, Naples, Turin and Milan with the match for third place being staged in Naples and the final in Rome.

The European Football Championship is for the Henri Delaunay Cup and became known under its present title from the 1966–68 tournament.

EUROPEAN CHAMPIONSHIP FINALS

Series	Final						No of entries
1958–60	(10 July 1960, Paris att. 17,966)						
	USSR (Metreveli, Ponedelnik)	(0)	(1) 2	Yugoslavia (Netto o.g.)	(1)	(1) 1	17
1962–64	(21 June 1964, Madrid att. 120,000)						
	Spain (Pereda, Marcelino)		(1) 2	USSR (Khusainov)		(1) 1	29
1966–68	(8 June 1968, Rome att. 75,000)						
	Italy (Domenghini)	(0)	(1) 1	Yugoslavia (Dzajic)	(1)	(1) 1	31
Replay	(10 June 1968, Rome att. 60,000)						
	Italy (Riva, Anastasi)		(2) 2	Yugoslavia		(0) 0	
1970–72	(18 June 1972, Brussels att. 43,437)						
	West Germany (Muller (G) 2, Wimmer)		(1) 3	USSR		(0) 0	32
1974–76	(20 June 1976, Belgrade att. 45,000)						
	Czechoslovakia (Svehlik, Dobias) Czechoslovakia won 5–3 on penalties	(2)	(2) 2	West Germany (Muller (D), Holzenbein)	(1)	(2) 2	32
1978–80	West Germany (Hrubesch 2) (22 June 1980, Rome att. 47,864)		(1) 2	Belgium (Vandereycken)		(0) 1	32

EUROPEAN FOOTBALL CHAMPIONSHIP
RESULTS 1958–1980

(formerly EUROPEAN NATIONS' CUP)

Key: *—Semi-final   Czecho'ia—Czechoslovakia
      ●—Final
      †—Third-placed match

ALBANIA

1958–60	1962–64	1966–68	1970–72	1974–76	1978–80
	Greece (wdn)	Yugoslavia 0–2 / 0–4	Poland 0–3 / 1–1		
	Denmark 0–4 / 1–0	W. Germany 0–6 / 0–0	Turkey 1–2 / 3–0		
			W. Germany 0–1 / 0–2		

AUSTRIA

1958–60	1962–64	1966–68	1970–72	1974–76	1978–80
Norway 1–0 / 5–2	Eire 0–0 / 2–3	Finland 0–0 / 2–1	Italy 1–2 / 2–2	Wales 2–1 / 0–1	Norway 2–0 / 4–0
France 2–5 / 2–4		USSR 3–4 / 1–0	Eire 4–1 / 6–0	Luxembourg 2–1 / 6–2	Scotland 3–2 / 1–1
		Greece 1–4 / 1–1	Sweden 0–1 / 1–0	Hungary 0–0 / 1–2	Portugal 1–2 / 2–1
					Belgium 1–1 / 0–0

BELGIUM

1958–60	1962–64	1966–68	1970–72	1974–76	1978–80
	Yugoslavia 2–3 / 0–1	Luxembourg 5–0 / 3–0	Denmark 2–0 / 2–1	Iceland 2–0 / 1–0	Norway 1–1 / 2–1
		Poland 1–3 / 2–4	Scotland 3–0 / 0–1	France 2–1 / 0–0	Portugal 1–1 / 2–0
		France 2–1 / 1–1	Portugal 3–0 / 1–1	E. Germany 0–0 / 1–2	Austria 1–1 / 0–0
			Italy 0–0 / 2–1	Holland 0–5 / 1–2	Scotland 2–0 / 3–1
			W. Germany 1–2		England 1–1
			Hungary 2–1		Spain 2–1
					Italy 0–0
					W. Germany 1–2

BULGARIA

1958–60	1962–64	1966–68	1970–72	1974–76	1978–80
Yugoslavia 0–2 / 1–1	Portugal 3–1 / 1–3 / 1–0	Norway 0–0 / 4–2	Norway 1–1 / 4–1	Greece 3–3 / 1–2	Denmark 2–2 / 3–0
	France 1–0 / 1–3	Sweden 2–0 / 3–0	Hungary 3–0 / 0–2	W. Germany 1–1 / 0–1	N. Ireland 0–2 / 0–2
		Portugal 1–0 / 0–0	France 1–2 / 2–1	Malta 5–0 / 2–0	Eire 1–0 / 0–3
		Italy 3–2 / 0–2			England 0–3 / 0–2

CYPRUS

1958–60	1962–64	1966–68	1970–72	1974–76	1978–80
		Rumania 1–5 / 0–7	N. Ireland 0–3 / 0–5	Czecho'ia 0–4 / 0–3	Spain 0–5 / 1–3
		Italy 0–2 / 0–5	USSR 1–3 / 1–6	England 0–5 / 0–1	Yugoslavia 0–3 / 0–5
		Switzerland 0–5 / 2–1	Spain 0–2 / 0–7	Portugal 0–2 / 0–1	Rumania 1–1 / 0–2

	1958–60	1962–64	1966–68	1970–72	1974–76	1978–80
CZECHOSLOVAKIA	Eire 0–2 / 4–0 Denmark 2–2 / 5–1 Rumania 2–0 / 3–0 USSR 0–3* France 2–0†	E. Germany 1–2 / 1–1	Eire 2–0 / 1–2 Spain 1–0 / 1–2 Turkey 3–0 / 0–0	Finland 1–1 / 4–0 Wales 3–1 / 1–0 Rumania 1–0 / 1–2	England 0–3 / 2–1 Cyprus 4–0 / 3–0 Portugal 5–0 / 1–1 USSR 2–0 / 2–2 Holland 3–1* W. Germany 2–2• (5–3 on penalties)	Sweden 3–1 / 4–1 Luxembourg 3–0 / 4–0 France 2–0 / 1–2 W. Germany 0–1 Greece 3–1 Netherlands 1–1 Italy 1–1
DENMARK	Czecho'ia 2–2 / 1–5	Malta 6–1 / 3–1 Albania 4–0 / 0–1 Luxembourg 3–3 / 2–2 / 1–0 USSR 0–3* Hungary .–3†	Hungary 0–6 / 0–2 Holland 0–2 / 3–2 E. Germany 1–1 / 2–3	Portugal 0–1 / 0–5 Scotland 0–1 / 1–0 Belgium 1–2 / 2–3	Spain 1–2 / 0–2 Rumania 0–0 / 1–6 Scotland 0–1 / 1–3	England 3–4 / 0–1 Eire 3–3 / 0–2 Bulgaria 2–2 / 0–3 N. Ireland 1–2 / 4–0
ENGLAND		France 1–1 / 2–5	N. Ireland 2–0 / 2–0 Wales 5–1 / 3–0 Scotland 2–3 / 1–1 Spain 1–0 / 2–1 Yugoslavia 0–1* USSR 2–0†	Malta 1–0 / 5–0 Greece 3–0 / 2–0 Switzerland 3–2 / 1–1 W. Germany 1–3 / 0–0	Czecho'ia 3–0 / 1–2 Portugal 0–0 / 1–1 Cyprus 5–0 / 1–0	Denmark 4–3 / 1–0 Eire 1–1 / 2–0 N. Ireland 4–0 / 5–1 Bulgaria 3–0 / 2–0 Belgium 1–1 Italy 0–1 Spain 2–1
FINLAND			Austria 0–0 / 1–2 Greece 1–2 / 1–1 USSR 0–2 / 2–5	Czecho'ia 1–1 / 0–4 Rumania 0–3 / 0–4 Wales 0–1 / 0–3	Poland 1–2 / 0–3 Holland 1–3 / 1–4 Italy 0–1 / 0–0	Greece 3–0 / 1–8 Hungary 2–1 / 1–3 USSR 1–1 / 2–2
FRANCE	Greece 7–1 / 1–1 Austria 5–2 / 4–2 Yugoslavia 4–5* Czecho'ia 0–2†	England 1–1 / 5–2 Bulgaria 3–1 / 0–1 Hungary 1–3 / 1–2	Poland 2–1 / 4–1 Luxembourg 3–0 / 3–1 Belgium 1–2 / 1–1 Yugoslavia 1–1 / 1–5	Norway 3–1 / 3–1 Hungary 1–1 / 0–2 Bulgaria 2–1 / 1–2	Belgium 1–2 / 0–0 E. Germany 2–2 / 1–2 Iceland 0–0 / 3–0	Sweden 2–2 / 3–1 Luxembourg 3–1 / 3–0 Czecho'ia 0–2 / 2–1
E. GERMANY	Portugal 2–3 / 0–2	Czecho'ia 2–1 / 1–1 Hungary 1–2 / 3–3	Holland 4–3 / 0–1 Denmark 1–1 / 3–2 Hungary 1–3 / 1–0	Holland 1–0 / 2–3 Luxembourg 5–0 / 2–1 Yugoslavia 1–2 / 0–0	Iceland 1–1 / 1–2 France 2–2 / 2–1 Belgium 0–0 / 2–1	Iceland 3–1 / 3–0 Holland 0–3 / 2–3 Poland 2–1 / 1–1 Switzerland 2–0 / 5–2

W. GERMANY

1958–60	1962–64	1966–68		1970–72		1974–76		1978–80	
		Albania	6–0	Turkey	1–1	Greece	2–2	Malta	0–0
			0–0		3–0		1–1		8–0
		Yugoslavia	0–1	Albania	1–0	Malta	1–0	Turkey	0–0
			3–1		2–0		8–0		2–0
				Poland	3–1	Bulgaria	1–1	Wales	2–0
					0–0		1–0		5–1
				England	3–1	Spain	1–1	Czecho'ia	1–0
					0–0		2–0	Netherlands	3–2
				Belgium	2–1*	Yugoslavia	4–2*	Greece	0–0
				USSR	3–0●	(a.e.t.)		Belgium	2–1
						Czecho'ia	2–2●		
						(3–5 on penalties)			

GREECE

1958–60		1962–64	1966–68		1970–72		1974–76		1978–80	
France	1–7	Withdrew v	Finland	2–1	Switzerland	0–1	Bulgaria	3–3	Finland	0–3
	1–1	Albania		1–1		0–1		2–1		8–1
			Austria	4–1	England	0–3	W. Germany	2–2	USSR	0–2
				1–1		0–2		1–1		1–0
			USSR	0–4	Malta	1–1	Malta	0–2	Hungary	4–1
				0–1		2–0		4–0		0–0
									Netherlands	0–1
									Czecho'ia	1–3
									W. Germany	0–0

HUNGARY

1958–60		1962–64		1966–68		1970–72		1974–76		1978–80	
USSR	1–3	Wales	3–1	Holland	2–2	Norway	3–1	Luxembourg	4–2	Finland	1–2
	0–1		1–1		2–1		4–0		8–1		3–1
		E. Germany	2–1	Denmark	2–0	France	1–1	Wales	0–2	USSR	2–0
			3–3		6–0		2–0		1–2		2–2
		France	3–1	E. Germany	3–1	Bulgaria	0–3	Austria	0–0	Greece	1–4
			2–1		0–1		2–0		2–1		0–0
		Spain	1–2*	USSR	2–0	Rumania	1–1				
		Denmark	3–1†		0–3		2–2				
							2–1				
						USSR	0–1*				
						Belgium	1–2†				

ICELAND

1958–60	1962–64		1966–68	1970–72	1974–76		1978–80	
	Eire	2–4			Belgium	0–2	Poland	0–2
		1–1				0–1		0–2
					E. Germany	1–1	Holland	0–3
						2–1		0–4
					France	0–0	E. Germany	1–3
						0–3		0–3
							Switzerland	0–2
								1–2

REPUBLIC OF IRELAND

1958–60		1962–64		1966–68		1970–72		1974–76		1978–80	
Czecho'ia	2–0	Iceland	4–2	Spain	0–0	Sweden	1–1	USSR	3–0	N. Ireland	0–0
	0–4		1–1		0–2		0–1		1–2		0–1
		Austria	0–0	Turkey	2–1	Italy	0–3	Turkey	1–1	Denmark	3–3
			3–2		1–2		1–2		4–0		2–0
		Spain	1–5	Czecho'ia	0–2	Austria	1–4	Switzerland	2–1	England	1–1
			0–2		2–1		0–6		0–1		0–2
										Bulgaria	0–1
											3–0

1958–60	1962–64	1966–68	1970–72	1974–76	1978–80
ITALY					
	Turkey 6–0 / 1–0	Rumania 3–1 / 1–0	Austria 2–1 / 2–2	Holland 1–3 / 1–0	Spain 0–0
	USSR 0–2 / 1–1	Cyprus 2–0 / 5–0	Eire 3–0 / 2–1	Poland 0–0 / 0–0	England 1–0
		Switzerland 2–2 / 4–0	Sweden 0–0 / 3–0	Finland 1–0 / 0–0	Belgium 0–0 / 0–0
		Bulgaria 2–3 / 2–0	Belgium 0–0 / 1–2		Czecho'ia 1–1
		USSR 0–0* (Italy won toss)			
		Yugoslavia 1–1• replayed 2–0			
LUXEMBOURG					
	Holland 1–1 / 2–1	Poland 0–4 / 0–0	E. Germany 0–5 / 1–2	Hungary 2–4 / 1–8	France 1–3 / 0–3
	Denmark 2–2 / 3–3 / 0–1	France 0–3 / 1–3	Yugoslavia 0–2 / 0–0	Wales 0–5 / 1–3	Czecho'ia 0–3 / 0–4
		Belgium 0–5 / 0–3	Holland 0–6 / 0–8	Austria 1–2 / 2–6	Sweden 0–3 / 1–1
MALTA					
	Denmark 1–6 / 1–3		Switzerland 1–2 / 0–5	W. Germany 0–1 / 0–8	Wales 0–7 / 0–2
			England 0–1 / 0–5	Greece 2–0 / 0–4	W. Germany 0–0 / 0–8
			Greece 1–1 / 0–2	Bulgaria 0–5 / 0–2	Turkey 1–2 / 1–2
NETHERLANDS					
	Switzerland 3–1 / 1–1	Hungary 2–2 / 1–2	Yugoslavia 1–1 / 0–2	Finland 3–1 / 4–1	Iceland 3–0 / 4–0
	Luxembourg 1–1 / 1–2	Denmark 2–0 / 2–3	E. Germany 0–1 / 3–2	Italy 3–1 / 0–1	Switzerland 3–1 / 3–0
		E. Germany 3–4 / 1–0	Luxembourg 6–0 / 8–0	Poland 1–4 / 3–0	Poland 0–2 / 1–1
				Belgium 5–0 / 2–1	Greece 1–0
				Czecho'ia 1–3* (a.e.t.)	W. Germany 2–3
				Yugoslavia 3–2† (a.e.t.)	Czecho'ia 1–1
NORTHERN IRELAND					
	Poland 2–0 / 2–0	England 0–2 / 0–2	Spain 0–3 / 1–1	Norway 1–2 / 3–0	Eire 0–0 / 1–0
	Spain 1–1 / 0–1	Scotland 1–2 / 1–0	Cyprus 3–0 / 5–0	Sweden 2–0 / 1–2	Denmark 2–1 / 0–4
		Wales 0–0 / 0–2	USSR 0–1 / 1–1	Yugoslavia 1–0 / 0–1	Bulgaria 2–0 / 2–0
					England 0–4 / 1–5
NORWAY					
Austria 0–1 / 2–5	Sweden 0–2 / 1–1	Bulgaria 0–0 / 2–4	Hungary 1–3 / 0–4	N. Ireland 2–1 / 0–3	Austria 0–2 / 0–4
		Portugal 1–2 / 1–2	France 1–3 / 1–3	Yugoslavia 1–3 / 1–3	Belgium 1–1 / 1–2
		Sweden 3–1 / 2–5	Bulgaria 1–1 / 1–4	Sweden 1–3 / 0–2	Scotland 2–3 / 0–4
					Portugal 0–1 / 1–3

POLAND

1958–60	1962–64	1966–68	1970–72	1974–76	1978–80
Spain 2–4 0–3	N. Ireland 0–2 0–2	Luxembourg 4–0 0–0	Albania 3–0 1–1	Finland 2–1 3–0	Iceland 2–0 2–0
		France 1–2 1–4	Turkey 5–1 0–1	Italy 0–0 0–0	Switzerland 2–0 2–0
		Belgium 3–1 4–2	W. Germany 1–3 0–0	Holland 4–1 0–3	E. Germany 1–2 1–1
					Holland 2–0 1–1

PORTUGAL

1958–60	1962–64	1966–68	1970–72	1974–76	1978–80
E. Germany 2–3 2–0	Bulgaria 1–3 3–1	Sweden 1–2 1–1	Denmark 1–0 5–0	England 0–0 1–1	Belgium 1–1 0–2
Yugoslavia 2–1 1–5	0–1	Norway 2–1 2–1	Belgium 0–3 1–1	Czecho'ia 0–5 1–1	Austria 2–1 1–2
		Bulgaria 0–1 0–0	Scotland 2–0 1–2	Cyprus 2–0 1–0	Scotland 1–0 1–4
					Norway 1–0 3–1

RUMANIA

1958–60	1962–64	1966–68	1970–72	1974–76	1978–80
Turkey 3–0 0–2	Spain 0–6 3–1	Cyprus 5–1 7–0	Finland 3–0 4–0	Denmark 0–0 6–1	Yugoslavia 3–2 1–2
Czecho'ia 0–2 0–3		Switzerland 4–2 1–7	Wales 0–0 2–0	Spain 1–1 2–2	Spain 0–1 2–2
		Italy 1–3 0–1	Czecho'ia 0–1 2–1	Scotland 1–1 1–1	Cyprus 1–1 2–0
			Hungary 1–1 2–2 1–2		

SCOTLAND

1958–60	1962–64	1966–68	1970–72	1974–76	1978–80
		Wales 1–1 3–2	Denmark 1–0 0–1	Spain 1–2 1–1	Austria 2–3 1–1
		N. Ireland 2–1 0–1	Belgium 0–3 1–0	Rumania 1–1 1–1	Norway 3–2 4–0
		England 3–2 1–1	Portugal 0–2 2–1	Denmark 1–0 3–1	Portugal 0–1 4–1
					Belgium 0–2 1–3

SPAIN

1958–60	1962–64	1966–68	1970–72	1974–76	1978–80
Poland 4–2 3–0	Rumania 6–0 1–3	Eire 0–0 2–0	N. Ireland 3–0 1–1	Denmark 2–1 2–0	Yugoslavia 2–1 0–1
Withdrew v Russia	N. Ireland 1–1 1–0	Turkey 0–0 2–0	Cyprus 2–0 7–0	Scotland 2–1 1–1	Rumania 1–0 2–2
	Eire 5–1 2–0	Czecho'ia 0–1 2–1	USSR 1–2 0–0	Rumania 1–1 2–2	Cyprus 5–0 3–1
	Hungary 2–1*	England 0–1 1–2		W. Germany 1–1 0–2	Italy 0–0
	USSR 2–1●				Belgium 1–2
					England 1–2

SWEDEN

1958–60	1962–64	1966–68	1970–72	1974–76	1978–80
	Norway 2–0 1–1	Portugal 2–1 1–1	Eire 1–1 1–0	N. Ireland 0–2 2–1	France 2–2 1–3
	Yugoslavia 0–0 3–2	Bulgaria 0–2 0–3	Austria 1–0 0–1	Yugoslavia 1–2 0–3	Czecho'ia 1–3 1–4
	USSR 1–1 1–3	Norway 1–3 5–2	Italy 0–0 0–3	Norway 3–1 2–0	Luxembourg 3–0 1–1

	1958–60		1962–64		1966–68		1970–72		1974–76		1978–80	

SWITZERLAND

1962–64		1966–68		1970–72		1974–76		1978–80	
Holland	1–3	Rumania	2–4	Greece	1–0	Turkey	1–2	Holland	1–3
	1–1		7–1		1–0		1–1		0–3
		Cyprus	5–0	Malta	2–1	Eire	1–2	Poland	0–2
			1–2		5–0		1–0		0–2
		Italy	2–2	England	2–3	USSR	0–1	E. Germany	0–2
			0–4		1–1		1–4		2–5
								Iceland	2–0
									2–1

TURKEY

1958–60		1962–64		1966–68		1970–72		1974–76		1978–80	
Rumania	0–3	Italy	0–6	Eire	1–2	W. Germany	1–1	Eire	1–1	Wales	0–1
	2–0		0–1		2–1		0–3		0–4		1–0
				Spain	0–0	Albania	2–1	Switzerland	2–1	Malta	2–1
					0–2		0–3		1–1		2–1
				Czecho'ia	0–3	Poland	1–5	USSR	0–3	W. Germany	0–0
					0–0		1–0		1–0		0–2

USSR

1958–60		1962–64		1966–68		1970–72		1974–76		1978–80	
Hungary	3–1	Italy	2–0	Austria	4–3	Cyprus	3–1	Eire	0–3	Greece	2–0
	1–0		1–1		0–1		6–1		2–1		0–1
Walkover v		Sweden	1–1	Finland	2–0	Spain	2–1	Turkey	3–0	Hungary	0–2
Spain (withdrew)			3–1		5–2		0–0		0–1		2–2
Czecho'ia	3–0*	Denmark	3–0*	Greece	1–0	N. Ireland	1–0	Switzerland	4–1	Finland	1–1
Yugoslavia	2–1●	Spain	1–2●		4–0		1–1		1–0		2–2
(a.e.t.)				Hungary	0–2	Yugoslavia	0–0	Czecho'ia	0–2		
					3–0		3–0		2–2		
				Italy	0–0*	Hungary	1–0*				
				(Italy won toss)		W. Germany	0–3●				
				England	0–2†						

WALES

1962–64		1966–68		1970–72		1974–76		1978–80	
Hungary	1–3	Scotland	1–1	Rumania	0–0	Austria	1–2	Malta	7–0
	1–1		2–3		0–2		1–0		2–0
		England	1–5	Czecho'ia	1–3	Hungary	2–0	Turkey	1–0
			0–3		0–1		2–1		0–1
		N. Ireland	0–0	Finland	1–0	Luxembourg	5–0	W. Germany	0–2
			2–0		3–0		3–1		1–5
						Yugoslavia	0–2		
							1–1		

YUGOSLAVIA

1958–60		1962–64		1966–68		1970–72		1974–76		1978–80	
Bulgaria	2–0	Belgium	3–2	Albania	2–0	Holland	1–1	Norway	3–1	Spain	1–2
	1–1		1–0		4–0		2–0		3–1		1–0
Portugal	1–2	Sweden	0–0	W. Germany	1–0	Luxembourg	2–0	N. Ireland	1–0	Cyprus	3–0
	5–1		2–3		1–3		0–0		0–1		5–0
France	5–4*			France	1–1	E. Germany	2–1	Sweden	2–1	Rumania	2–3
USSR	1–2●				5–1		0–0		3–0		2–1
(a.e.t.)				England	1–0*	USSR	0–0	Wales	2–0		
				Italy	1–1●		0–3		1–1		
				replayed	0–2			W. Germany	2–4*		
								(a.e.t.)			
								Holland	2–3†		

THE 11 WINNERS OF THE
EUROPEAN CHAMPION CLUBS CUP

 Each cup denotes one win

CELTIC

LIVERPOOL

MANCHESTER UTD.

NOTTM FOREST

AJAX

FEYENOORD

BAYERN MUNICH

A C MILAN

INTER MILAN

BENFICA

REAL MADRID
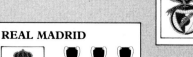

European Cup Records

EUROPEAN CHAMPION CLUBS CUP

Season	Games	Goals	The Final	Attendances Overall	Average
1955–56	29	127	13.6.56, Paris, 38,000 **Real Madrid (2) 4, Stade de Reims (2) 3** Di Stefano, Rial 2, Marquitos; Leblond, Templin, Hidalgo	912,000	31,450
1956–57	44	170	30.5.57, Madrid, 124,000 **Real Madrid (0) 2, Fiorentina (0) 0** Di Stefano (pen), Gento	1,786,000	40,590
1957–58	48	189	28.5.58, Brussels, 67,000 **Real Madrid (0) (2) 3, AC Milan (0) (2) 2 (a.e.t.)** Di Stefano, Rial, Gento; Schiaffino, Grillo	1,790,000	37,290
1958–59	55	199	2.6.59, Stuttgart, 80,000 **Real Madrid (1) 2, Stade de Reims (0) 0** Mateos, Di Stefano	2,010,000	36,545
1959–60	52	218	18.5.60, Glasgow, 135,000 **Real Madrid (3) 7, Eintracht Frankfurt (1) 3** Di Stefano 3, Puskas 4; Kress, Stein 2	2,780,000	50,545
1960–61	51	166	31.3.61, Berne, 28,000 **Benfica (2) 3, Barcelona (1) 2** Aguas, Ramallets (og), Coluna; Kocsis, Czibor	1,850,000	36,274
1961–62	55	221	2.5.62, Amsterdam, 65,000 **Benfica (2) 5, Real Madrid (3) 3** Aguas, Cavem, Coluna, Eusebio 2; Puskas 3	2,135,000	45,727
1962–63	59	214	22.5.63, London, 45,000 **AC Milan (0) 2, Benfica (1) 1** Altafini 2; Eusebio	2,158,000	36,593
1963–64	61	212	27.5.64, Vienna, 74,000 **Inter Milan (1) 3, Real Madrid (0) 1** Mazzola 2, Milani; Felo	2,180,000	35,737
1964–65	62	215	28.5.65, Milan, 80,000 **Inter Milan (1) 1, Benfica (0) 0** Jair	2,577,000	41,564
1965–66	58	234	11.5.66, Brussels, 55,000 **Real Madrid (0) 2, Partizan Belgrade (1) 1** Amancio, Serena; Vasovic	2,112,000	36,431
1966–67	65	211	25.5.67, Lisbon, 56,000 **Celtic (0) 2, Inter Milan (1) 1** Gemmell, Chalmers; Mazzola (pen)	2,248,000	34,584
1967–68	60	162	29.5.68, London, 100,000 **Manchester United (0) (1) 4, Benfica (0) (1) 1 (a.e.t.)** Charlton 2, Best, Kidd; Graca	2,544,000	42,500
1968–69	52	176	28.5.69, Madrid, 50,000 **AC Milan (2) 4, Ajax (0) 1** Prati 3, Sormani; Vasovic (pen)	2,056,000	39,540
1969–70	63	202	6.5.70, Milan, 50,000 **Feyenoord (1) (1) 2, Celtic (1) (1) 1 (a.e.t.)** Israel, Kindvall; Gemmell	2,345,000	37,222
1970–71	63	210	2.6.71, London, 90,000 **Ajax (1) 2, Panathinaikos (0) 0** Van Dijk, Kapsis (og)	2,124,000	33,714
1971–72	64	175	31.5.72, Rotterdam, 67,000 **Ajax (0) 2, Inter Milan (0) 0** Cruyff 2	2,066,976	32,280
1972–73	58	160	30.5.73, Belgrade, 93,500 **Ajax (0) 1, Juventus (0) 0** Rep	1,712,277	30,000
1973–74	60	180	15.5.74, Brussels, 65,000 **Bayern Munich (0) (0) 1, Atletico Madrid (0) (0) 1 (a.e.t.)** Schwarzenbeck; Luis		
		replay:	17.5.74, Brussels, 65,000 **Bayern Munich (1) 4, Atletico Madrid (0) 0** Muller 2, Hoeness 2	1,586,852	26,448
1974–75	55	174	28.5.75, Paris, 50,000 **Bayern Munich (0) 2, Leeds United (0) 0** Roth, Muller	1,380,254	25,096
1975–76	61	202	12.5.76, Glasgow, 54,864 **Bayern Munich (0) 1, St Etienne (0) 0** Roth	1,736,087	28,460
1976–77	61	155	25.5.77, Rome, 57,000 **Liverpool (1) 3, Borussia Moenchengladbach (0) 1** McDermott, Smith, Neal (pen); Simonsen	2,010,000	34,325
1977–78	59	172	10.5.78, London, 92,000 **Liverpool (0) 1, FC Bruges (0) 0** Dalglish	1,509,471	25,584
1978–79	63	185	30.5.79, Munich, 57,500 **Nottingham Forest (1) 1, Malmo (0) 0** Francis	1,551,291	24,624
1979–80		*	28.5.80, Madrid, 50,000 **Nottingham Forest (1) 1, SV Hamburg (0) 0** Robertson	*	

*Figures not available at the time of going to press

Manchester United in 1968 with the European Cup they won as the first English winners of the trophy. (Colorsport)

Liverpool capture the European Cup for the second year running in 1978.

Celtic pictured in 1966–67, the year of their triumph in the European Cup. (Syndication International)

Rangers pictured in 1971–72, during the season in which they won the Cup Winners Cup. (Syndication International)

EUROPEAN CUP-WINNERS CUP

Season	Games	Goals	The Final	Attendances Overall	Average
1960–61	18	60	1st leg, 17.5.61, Glasgow, 80,000 **Rangers (0) 0, Fiorentina (1) 2** Milan 2		
			2nd leg, 27.5.61, Florence, 50,000 **Fiorentina (1) 2, Rangers (1) 1** Milan, Hamrin ; Scott	290,000	16,111
1961–62	44	174	10.5.62, Glasgow, 27,389 **Fiorentina (1) 1, Atletico Madrid (1) 1** Hamrin ; Piero		
		replay :	5.9.62, Stuttgart, 45,000 **Atletico Madrid (2) 3, Fiorentina (0) 0** Jones, Mendonca, Piero	650,000	14,733

Season	Games	Goals	The Final	Attendances Overall	Average
1962–63	48	169	15.5.63, Rotterdam, 25,000 **Tottenham Hotspur (2) 5, Atletico Madrid** **(0) 1** Greaves 2, White, Dyson 2 ; Collar (pen)	1,100,000	22,916
1963–64	62	202	13.5.64, Brussels, 9,000 **MTK Budapest (1) (3) 3, Sporting Lisbon** **(1) (3) 3 (a.e.t.)** Sandor 2, Kuti ; Figueiredo 2, Dansky (og)		
		replay :	15.5.64, Antwerp, 18,000 **Sporting Lisbon (1) 1, MTK Budapest (0) 0** Mendes	1,300,000	20,967
1964–65	61	163	19.5.65, London, 100,000 **West Ham United (0) 2, Munich 1860 (0) 0** Sealey 2	1 100,000	18,032
1965–66	59	188	5.5.66, Glasgow, 41,657 **Borussia Dortmund (0) (1) 2, Liverpool (0)** **(1) 1 (a.e.t.)** Held, Yeats (og) ; Hunt	1,546,000	26,203
1966–67	61	170	31.5.67, Nuremberg, 69,480 **Bayern Munich (0) (0) 1, Rangers (0)** **(0) 0 (a.e.t.)** Roth	1,556,000	25,508
1967–68	64	200	23.5.68, Rotterdam, 60,000 **AC Milan (2) 2, SV Hamburg (0) 0** Hamrin 2	1,683,000	26,269
1968–69	51	157	21.5.69, Basle, 40,000 **Slovan Bratislava (3) 3, Barcelona (1) 2** Cvetler, Hrivnak, Jan Capkovic ; Zaldua, Rexach	957.000	18,765
1969–70	64	179	29.4.70, Vienna, 10,000 **Manchester City (2) 2, Gornik Zabrze (0) 1** Young, Lee (pen) ; Ozlizlo	1,675,000	25,890
1970–71	67	203	19.5.71, Athens, 42,000 **Chelsea (0) (1) 1, Real Madrid (0) (1) 1** Osgood ; Zoco		
		replay :	21.5.71, Athens, 24,000 **Chelsea (2) 2, Real Madrid (0) 1** Dempsey, Osgood ; Fleitas	1,570,000	23,582
1971–72	65	186	24.5.72, Barcelona, 35,000 **Rangers (2) 3, Dynamo Moscow (0) 2** Stein, Johnston 2 ; Estrekov, Makovikov	1,145,211	17,615
1972–73	61	174	16.5.73, Salonika, 45,000 **AC Milan (1) 1, Leeds United (0) 0** Chiarugi	908,564	15,000
1973–74	61	169	8.5.74, Rotterdam, 5,000 **FC Magdeburg (1) 2, AC Milan (0) 0** Lanzi (og), Seguin	1,105,494	18,123
1974–75	59	177	14.5.75, Basle, 13,000 **Dynamo Kiev (2) 3, Ferencvaros (0) 0** Onischenko 2, Blokhin	1,298,850	22,014
1975–76	61	189	5.5.76, Brussels, 58,000 **Anderlecht (1) 4, West Ham United (1) 2** Rensenbrink 2 (1 pen), Van der Elst 2 ; Holland, Robson	1,128,962	18,508
1976–77	63	198	11.5.77, Amsterdam, 65,000 **SV Hamburg (0) 2, Anderlecht (0) 0** Volkert (pen), Magath	1,537,000	24,400
1977–78	63	179	3.5.78, Amsterdam, 48,679 **Anderlecht (3) 4, Austria/WAC (0) 0** Rensenbrink 2 (1 pen), Van Binst 2	1,161,383	18,434
1978–79	59	160	16.5.79, Basle, 58,000 **Barcelona (2) (2) 4, Fortuna Dusseldorf (2)** **(2) 3 (a.e.t.)** Sanchez, Asensi, Rexach, Krankl; Klaus Allofs, Seel 2	1,041,135	17,646
1979–80		*	14.5.80, Brussels, 40,000 **Valencia (0) 0, Arsenal (0) 0 (a.e.t.)** (Valencia won 5–4 on penalties)	*	

*Figures not available at the time of going to press

FAIRS CUP/UEFA CUP

1955–58 First leg : 5.3.58, London, 45,466
London (1) 2, Barcelona (2) 2
Greaves, Langley (pen) ; Tejada, Martinez
Second leg : 1.5.58, Barcelona, 62,000
Barcelona (3) 6, London (0) 0
Suarez 2, Evaristo 2, Martinez, Verges

1958–60 First leg : 29.3.60, Birmingham, 40,500
Birmingham City (0) 0, Barcelona (0) 0
Second leg : 4.5.60, Barcelona, 70,000
Barcelona (2) 4, Birmingham City (0) 1
Martinez, Czibor 2, Coll ; Hooper

1960–61 First leg : 27.9.61, Birmingham, 21,005
Birmingham City (0) 2, AS Roma (1) 2
Hellawell, Orritt ; Manfredini 2
Second leg : 11.10.61, Rome, 60,000
AS Roma (0) 2, Birmingham City (0) 0
Farmer (og), Pestrin

1961–62 First leg : 8.9.62, Valencia, 65,000
Valencia 6, Barcelona 2
Yosu 2, Guillot 3, Nunez ; Kocsis 2
Second leg : 12.9.62, Barcelona, 60,000
Barcelona 1, Valencia 1
Kocsis ; Guillot

1962–63 First leg : 12.6.63, Zagreb, 40,000
Dynamo Zagreb (1) 1, Valencia (0) 2
Zambata ; Waldo, Urtiaga
Second leg : 26.6.63, Valencia, 55,000
Valencia (1) 2, Dynamo Zagreb (0) 0
Mano, Nunez

1963–64	Final:	Barcelona, 24.6.64, 50,000 **Real Zaragoza (1) 2, Valencia (1) 1** Villa, Marcelino; Urtiaga
1964–65	Final:	23.6.65, Turin, 25,000 **Ferencvaros(1)1, Juventus(0)0** Fenyvesi
1965–66	First leg:	14.9.66, Barcelona, 70,000 **Barcelona (0) 0, Real Zaragoza (1) 1** Canario
	Second leg:	21.9.66, Zaragoza, 70,000 **Real Zaragoza (1) 2, Barcelona (1) 4** Marcelino 2; Pujol 3, Zabella
1966–67	First leg:	30.8.67, Zagreb, 40,000 **Dynamo Zagreb (1) 2, Leeds United (0) 0** Cercer 2
	Second leg:	6.9.67, Leeds, 35,604 **Leeds United (0) 0, Dynamo Zagreb (0) 0**
1967–68	First leg:	7.8.68, Leeds, 25,368 **Leeds United (1) 1, Ferencvaros (0) 0** Jones
	Second leg:	11.9.68, Budapest, 70,000 **Ferencvaros (0) 0, Leeds United (0) 0**
1968–69	First leg:	25.5.69, Newcastle, 60,000 **Newcastle United (0) 3, Ujpest Dozsa (0) 0** Moncur 2, Scott
	Second leg:	11.6.69, Budapest, 37,000 **Ujpest Dozsa (2) 2, Newcastle United (0) 3** Bene, Gorocs; Moncur, Arentoft, Foggon
1969–70	First leg:	22.4.70, Brussels, 37,000 **Anderlecht (2) 3, Arsenal (0) 1** Devrindt, Mulder 2; Kennedy
	Second leg:	28.4.70, London, 51,612 **Arsenal (1) 3, Anderlecht (0) 0** Kelly, Radford, Sammels
1970–71	First leg:	26.5.71, Turin, 65,000 **Juventus (0) 0, Leeds United (0) 0** (game abandoned after 51 minutes) 28.5.71, Turin, 65,000 **Juventus (1) 2, Leeds United (0) 2** Bettega, Capello; Madeley, Bates
	Second leg:	3.6.71, Leeds, 42,483 **Leeds United (1) 1, Juventus (1) 1** Clarke; Anastasi Leeds won on away goals rule.
1971–72	First leg:	3.5.72, Wolverhampton, 45,000 **Wolverhampton Wanderers (0) 1, Tottenham Hotspur (0) 2** McCalliog; Chivers 2
	Second leg:	17.5.72, London, 48,000 **Tottenham Hotspur (1) 1, Wolverhampton Wanderers (0) 1** Mullery; Wagstaffe
1972–73	First leg:	10.5.73, Liverpool, 41,169 **Liverpool (3) 3, Borussia Moenchengladbach (0) 0**

		Keegan 2, Lloyd
	Second leg:	25.5.73, Moenchengladbach, 35,000 **Borussia Moenchengladbach (2) 2, Liverpool (0) 0** Heynckes 2
1973–74	First leg:	21.5.74, London, 46,281 **Tottenham Hotspur (1) 2, Feyenoord (1) 2** England, Van Daele (og); Van Hanegem, De Jong
	Second leg:	29.5.74, Rotterdam, 68,000 **Feyenoord (1) 2, Tottenham Hotspur (0) 0** Rijsbergen, Ressel
1974–75	First leg:	7.5.75, Dusseldorf, 45,000 **Borussia Moenchengladbach (0) 0, Twente Enschede (0) 0**
	Second leg:	21.5.75, Enschede, 24,500 **Twente Enschede (0) 1, Borussia Moenchengladbach (2) 5** Drost; Heynckes 3, Simonsen 2 (1 pen)
1975–76	First leg:	28.4.76, Liverpool, 56,000 **Liverpool (0) 3, Bruges (2) 2** Kennedy, Case, Keegan (pen); Lambert, Cools
	Second leg:	19.5.76, Bruges, 32,000 **Bruges (1) 1, Liverpool (1) 1** Lambert (pen); Keegan
1976–77	First leg:	4.5.77, Turin, 75,000 **Juventus (1) 1, Athletic Bilbao (0) 0** Tardelli
	Second leg:	18.5.77, Bilbao, 43,000 **Athletic Bilbao (1) 2, Juventus (1) 1** Iruerta, Carlos; Bettega
1977–78	First leg:	26.4.78, Bastia, 15,000 **Bastia (0) 0, PSV Eindhoven (0) 0**
	Second leg:	9.5.78, Eindhoven, 27,000 **PSV Eindhoven (1) 3, Bastia (0) 0** Willy Van der Kerkhof, Deijkers, Van der Kuylan
1978–79	First Leg:	9.5.79, Belgrade, 87,500 **Red Star Belgrade (1) 1, Borussia Moenchengladbach (0) 1** Sestic; Jurisic (og)
	Second leg:	23.5.79, Dusseldorf, 45,000 **Borussia Moenchengladbach (1) 1, Red Star Belgrade (0) 0** Simonsen
1979–80	First leg:	7.5.80, Moenchengladbach, 25,000 **Borussia Moenchengladbach (1) 3, Eintracht Frankfurt (1) 2** Kulik 2, Matthaus; Karger, Holzenbein
	Second leg:	21.5.80, Frankfurt, 60,000 **Eintracht Frankfurt (0) 1, Borussia Moenchengladbach (0) 0** Schaub (Eintracht won on away goals rule)

British Clubs in Europe

FOOTBALL LEAGUE CLUBS

Season	Competition	Round	Date	Opponents (Country)	Venue	Result		Scorers
ARSENAL								
1971–72	European Cup	1	15.9.71	Stromsgodset (Norway)	A	W	3-1	Simpson, Marinello, Kelly
			29.9.71		H	W	4-0	Kennedy, Radford 2, Armstrong
		2	20.10.71	Grasshoppers	A	W	2-0	Kennedy, Graham
			3.11.71	(Switzerland)	H	W	3-0	Kennedy, George, Radford
		QF	8.3.72	Ajax (Holland)	A	L	1-2	Kennedy
			22.3.72		H	L	0-1	
1979–80	Cup-Winners' Cup	1	19.9.79	Fenerbahce (Turkey)	H	W	2-0	Sunderland, Young
			3.10.79		A	D	0-0	
		2	24.10.79	Magdeburg (East	H	W	2-1	Young, Sunderland
			7.11.79	Germany)	A	D	2-2	Price, Brady
		QF	5.3.80	Gothenburg (Sweden)	H	W	5-1	Sunderland 2, Price, Brady, Young
			19.3.80		A	D	0-0	
		SF	9.4.80	Juventus (Italy)	H	D	1-1	Bettega own goal
			23.4.80		A	W	1-0	Vaessen
		F	14.5.80	Valencia (Spain)†	N	D	0-0	
1963–64	Fairs Cup	1	25.9.63	Staevnet (Denmark)	A	W	7-1	Strong 3, Baker 3, MacLeod
			22.10.63		H	L	2-3	Skirton, Barnwell
		2	13.11.63	Liege (Belgium)	H	D	1-1	Anderson
			18.12.63		A	L	1-3	McCullough
1969–70	Fairs Cup	1	9.9.69	Glentoran (Northern	H	W	3-0	Graham 2, Gould
			29.9.69	Ireland)	A	L	0-1	
		2	29.10.69	Sporting Lisbon (Portugal)	A	D	0-0	
			26.11.69		H	W	3-0	Radford, Graham 2
		3	17.12.69	Rouen (France)	A	D	0-0	
			13.1.70		H	W	1-0	Sammels
		QF	11.3.70	Dynamo Bacau	A	W	2-0	Sammels, Radford
			18.3.70	(Rumania)	H	W	7-1	George 2, Sammels 2, Radford 2, Graham
		SF	8.4.70	Ajax (Holland)	H	W	3-0	George 2 (1 pen), Sammels
			15.4.70		A	L	0-1	
		F	22.4.70	Anderlecht (Belgium)	A	L	1-3	Kennedy
			28.4.70		H	W	3-0	Kelly, Radford, Sammels
1970–71	Fairs Cup	1	16.9.70	Lazio (Italy)	A	D	2-2	Radford 2
			23.9.70		H	W	2-0	Radford, Armstrong
		2	21.10.70	Sturm Graz (Austria)	A	L	0-1	
			4.11.70		H	W	2-0	Storey (pen), Kennedy
		3	2.12.70	Beveren (Belgium)	H	W	4-0	Graham, Kennedy 2, Sammels
			16.12.70		A	D	0-0	
		QF	9.3.71	FC Cologne (West	H	W	2-1	McLintock, Storey
			23.3.71	Germany) *	A	L	0-1	
1978–79	UEFA Cup	1	13.9.78	Lokomotive Leipzig (East	H	W	3-0	Stapleton 2, Sunderland
			27.9.78	Germany)	A	W	4-1	Brady, Stapleton 2, Sunderland
		2	18.10.78	Hajduk Split	A	L	1-2	Brady
			1.11.78	(Yugoslavia)	H	W	1-0	Young
		3	22.11.78	Red Star Belgrade	A	L	0-1	
			6.12.78	(Yugoslavia)	H	D	1-1	Sunderland
ASTON VILLA								
1975–76	UEFA Cup	1	17.9.75	Antwerp (Belgium)	A	L	1-4	Graydon
			1.10.75		H	L	0-1	
1977–78	UEFA Cup	1	14.9.77	Fenerbahce (Turkey)	H	W	4-0	Gray, Deehan 2, Little
			28.9.77		A	W	2-0	Deehan, Little
		2	19.10.77	Gornik Zabrze (Poland)	H	W	2-0	McNaught 2
			2.11.77		A	D	1-1	Gray
		3	23.11.77	Athletic Bilbao (Spain)	H	W	2-0	Iribar own goal, Deehan
			7.12.77		A	D	1-1	Mortimer
		QF	1.3.78	Barcelona (Spain)	H	D	2-2	McNaught, Deehan
			15.3.78		A	L	1-2	Little

Season	Competition	Round	Date	Opponents (Country)	Venue	Result		Scorers

BIRMINGHAM CITY

Season	Competition	Round	Date	Opponents (Country)	Venue	Result		Scorers
1955–56	Fairs Cup	Gp.D	15.5.56	Inter-Milan (Italy)	A	D	0–0	
			17.4.57		H	W	2–1	Govan 2
			22.5.56	Zagreb (Yugoslavia)	A	W	1–0	Brown
			3.12.56		H	W	3–0	Orritt, Brown, Murphy
		SF	23.10.57	Barcelona (Spain	H	W	4–3	Murphy 2, Brown, Orritt
			13.11.57		A	L	0–1	
			26.11.57		N	L	1–2	Murphy
1958–60	Fairs Cup	1	14.10.58	FC Cologne (West	A	D	2–2	Neal, Hooper
			11.11.58	Germany)	H	W	2–0	Larkin, Taylor
		QF	6.5.59	Zagreb (Yugoslavia)	H	W	1–0	Larkin
			25.5.59		A	D	3–3	Larkin 2, Hooper
		SF	7.10.59	Union St Gillosie	A	W	4–2	Hooper, Gordon, Barrett, Taylor
			11.11.59	(Belgium)	H	W	4–2	Gordon 2, Larkin, Hooper
		F	29.3.60	Barcelona (Spain)	H	D	0–0	
			4.5.60		A	L	1–4	Hooper
1960–61	Fairs Cup	1	19.10.60	Ujpest Dosza (Hungary)	H	W	3–2	Gordon 2, Astall
			26.10.60		A	W	2–1	Rudd, Singer
		QF	23.11.60	Copenhagen (Denmark)	A	D	4–4	Gordon 2, Singer 2
			7.12.60		H	W	5–0	Stubbs 2, Harris, Hellawell, own goal!
		SF	19.4.61	Inter-Milan (Italy)	A	W	2–1	Harris, own goal
			3.5.61		H	W	2–1	Harris 2
		F	27.9.61	AS Roma (Italy)	H	D	2–2	Hellawell, Orritt
			11.10.61		A	L	0–2	
1961–62	Fairs Cup	1		bye				
		2	15.11.61	Espanol (Spain)	A	L	2–5	Bloomfield, Harris (pen)
			7.12.61		H	W	1–0	Auld

BURNLEY

Season	Competition	Round	Date	Opponents (Country)	Venue	Result		Scorers
1960–61	European Cup	Pr		bye				
		1	16.11.60	Reims (France)	H	W	2–0	Robson, McIlroy
			30.11.60		A	L	2–3	Robson, Connelly
		QF	18.1.61	SV Hamburg (West	H	W	3–1	Pilkington 2, Robson
			15.3.61	Germany)	A	L	1–4	Harris
1966–67	Fairs Cup	1	20.9.66	Stuttgart (West Germany)	A	D	1–1	Irvine
			27.9.66		H	W	2–0	Coates, Lochhead
		2	19.10.66	Lausanne (Switzerland)	A	W	3–1	Coates, Harris, Lochhead
			25.10.66		H	W	5–0	Lochhead 3, O'Neil, Irvine
		3	18.1.67	Napoli (Italy)	H	W	3–0	Coates, Latcham, Lochhead
			8.2.67		A	D	0–0	
		QF	4.4.67	Eintracht Frankfurt	A	D	1–1	Miller
			18.4.67	(West Germany)	H	L	1–2	Miller

CARDIFF CITY

Season	Competition	Round	Date	Opponents (Country)	Venue	Result		Scorers
1964–65	Cup Winners' Cup	1	9.9.64	Esbjerg (Denmark)	A	D	0–0	
			13.10.64		H	W	1–0	King
		2	16.12.64	Sporting Lisbon (Portugal)	A	W	2–1	Farrell, Tapscott
			23.12.64		H	D	0–0	
		QF	20.1.65	Real Zaragoza (Spain)	A	D	2–2	Williams, King
			3.2.65		H	L	0–1	
1965–66	Cup Winners' Cup	1	8.9.65	Standard Liege (Belgium)	H	L	1–2	Johnston
			20.10.65		A	L	0–1	
1967–68	Cup Winners' Cup	1	20.9.67	Shamrock Rovers (Eire)	A	D	1–1	King
			4.10.67		H	W	2–0	Toshack, Brown (pen)
		2	15.11.67	NAC Breda (Holland)	A	D	1–1	King
			29.11.67		H	W	4–1	Brown, Barrie Jones, Clark, Toshack
		QF	6.3.68	Moscow Torpedo	H	W	1–0	Barrie Jones
			19.3.68	(USSR)	A	L	0–1	
			3.4.68		H	W	1–0	Dean
		SF	24.4.68	SV Hamburg (West	A	D	1–1	Dean
			1.5.68	Germany)	H	L	2–3	Dean, Harris
1968–69	Cup-Winners' Cup	1	18.9.68	Porto (Portugal)	H	D	2–2	Toshack, Bird (pen)
			2.10.68		A	L	1–2	Toshack
1969–70	Cup-Winners' Cup	1	17.9.69	Mjoendalen (Norway)	A	W	7–1	Clark 2, Toshack 2, Lea, Sutton, King

Season	Competition	Round	Date	Opponents (Country)	Venue	Result	Scorers

CARDIFF CITY continued

			1.10.69		H	W 5–1	King 2, Allan 3
		2	12.11.69	Goztepe Izmir (Turkey)	A	L 0–3	
			16.11.69		H	W 1–0	Bird
1970–71	Cup-Winners' Cup	1	16.9.70	Pezoporikos (Cyprus)	H	W 8–0	Toshack 2, Clark 2, Sutton, Gibson, King, Woodruff
			30.9.70		A	D 0–0	
		2	21.10.70	Nantes (France)	H	W 5–1	Toshack 2, Gibson, King, Phillips
			4.11.70		A	W 2–1	Toshack, Clark
		QF	10.3.70	Real Madrid (Spain)	H	W 1–0	Clark
			24.3.71		A	L 0–2	
1971–72	Cup-Winners Cup	1	15.9.71	Dynamo Berlin (East Germany) †	A	D 1–1	Gibson
			29.9.71		H	D 1–1	Clark
1973–74	Cup-Winners' Cup	1	19.9.73	Sporting Lisbon (Portugal)	H	D 0–0	
			3.10.73		A	L 1–2	Vincent
1974–75	Cup-Winners Cup	1	18.9.74	Ferencvaros (Hungary)	A	L 0–2	
			2.10.74		H	L 1–4	Dwyer
1976–77	Cup-Winners' Cup	Pr	4.8.76	Servette (Switzerland)	H	W 1–0	Evans
			11.8.76		A	L 1–2*	Showers
		1	15.9.76	Dynamo Tbilisi (USSR)	H	W 1–0	Alston
			29.9.76		A	L 0–3	
1977–78	Cup-Winners Cup	1	14.9.77	Austria/WAC (Austria)	H	D 0–0	
			28.9.77		A	L 0–1	

CHELSEA

1970–71	Cup-Winners' Cup	1	16.9.70	Aris Salonika (Greece)	A	D 1–1	Hutchinson
			30.9.70		H	W 5–1	Hutchinson 2, Hollins 2, Hinton
		2	21.10.70	CSKA Sofia (Bulgaria)	A	W 1–0	Baldwin
			4.11.70		H	W 1–0	Webb
		QF	10.3.71	FC Bruges (Belgium)	A	L 0–2	
			24.3.71		H	W 4–0	Houseman, Osgood 2, Baldwin
		SF	14.4.71	Manchester City (England)	H	W 1–0	Smethurst
			28.4.71		A	W 1–0	Weller
		F	19.5.71	Real Madrid (Spain)	N	D 1–1	Osgood
			21.5.71		N	W 2–1	Dempsey, Osgood
1971–72	Cup-Winners' Cup	1	15.9.71	Jeunesse Hautcharage (Luxembourg)	A	W 8–0	Osgood 3, Houseman 2, Hollins, Webb, Baldwin
			29.9.71		H	W 13–0	Osgood 5, Baldwin 3, Hollins (pen), Hudson, Webb, Houseman, Harris
		2	20.10.71	Atvidaberg (Sweden) *	A	D 0–0	
			3.11.71		H	D 1–1	Hudson
1958–59	Fairs Cup	1	30.9.58	Frem Copenhagen (Denmark)	A	W 3–1	Harrison, Greaves, Nicholas
			4.11.58		H	W 4–1	Greaves 2, Sillett (P), own goal
		QF	29.4.59	Belgrade (Yugoslavia)	H	W 1–0	Brabrook
			13.5.59		H	L 1–4	Brabrook
1965–66	Fairs Cup	1	22.9.65	AS Roma (Italy)	H	W 4–1	Venables 3, Graham
			6.10.65		A	D 0–0	
		2	17.11.65	Weiner SK (Austria)	A	L 0–1	
			1.12.65		H	W 2–0	Murray, Osgood
		3	9.2.66	AC Milan (Italy)	A	L 1–2	Graham
			16.2.66		H	W 2–1	Graham, Osgood
			2.3.66		A	D 1–1 ‡	Bridges
		QF	15.3.66	Munich 1860 (West Germany)	A	D 2–2	Tambling 2
			29.3.66		H	W 1–0	Osgood
		SF	27.4.66	Barcelona (Spain)	A	L 0–2	
			11.5.66		H	W 2–0	own goals 2
			25.5.66		A	L 0–5	
1968–69	Fairs Cup	1	18.9.68	Morton (Scotland)	H	W 5–0	Osgood, Birchenall, Cooke, Boyle, Hollins
			30.9.68		A	W 4–3	Baldwin, Birchenall Houseman, Tambling
		2	23.10.68	DWS Amsterdam (Holland) ‡	H	D 0–0	
			30.10.68		A	D 0–0	

Season	Competition	Round	Date	Opponents (Country)	Venue	Result		Scorers

COVENTRY CITY

Season	Competition	Round	Date	Opponents (Country)	Venue	Result		Scorers
1970–71	Fairs Cup	1	16.9.70	Trakia Plovdiv (Bulgaria)	A	W	4–1	O'Rourke 3, Martin
			30.9.70		H	W	2–0	Joicey, Blockley
		2	20.10.70	Bayern Munich (West	A	L	1–6	Hunt
			3.11.70	Germany)	H	W	2–1	Martin, O'Rourke

DERBY COUNTY

Season	Competition	Round	Date	Opponents (Country)	Venue	Result		Scorers
1972–73	European Cup	1	13.9.72	Zeljeznicar (Yugoslavia)	H	W	2–0	McFarland, Gemmill
			27.9.72		A	W	2–1	Hinton, O'Hare
		2	25.10.72	Benfica (Portugal)	H	W	3–0	McFarland, Hector, McGovern
			8.11.72		A	D	0–0	
		QF	7.3.73	Spartak Trnava	A	D	0–0	
			21.3.73	(Czechoslovakia)	H	W	2–0	Hector 2
		SF	11.4.73	Juventus (Italy)	A	L	1–3	Hector
			25.4.73		H	D	0–0	
1975–76	European Cup	1	17.9.75	Slovan Bratislava	A	L	0–1	
			1.10.75	(Czechoslovakia)	H	W	3–0	Bourne, Lee 2
		2	22.10.75	Real Madrid (Spain)	H	W	4–1	George 3 (2 pen), Nish
			5.11.75		A	L	1–5	George
1974–75	UEFA Cup	1	18.9.74	Servette (Switzerland)	H	W	4–1	Hector 2, Daniel, Lee
			2.10.74		A	W	2–1	Lee, Hector
		2	23.10.74	Atletico Madrid (Spain)	H	D	2–2	Nish, Rioch (pen)
			6.11.74		A	D	2–2†	Rioch, Hector
		3	27.11.74	Velez (Yugoslavia)	H	W	3–1	Bourne 2, Hinton
			11.12.74		A	L	1–4	Hector
1976–77	UEFA Cup	1	15.9.76	Finn Harps (Eire)	H	W	12–0	Hector 5, James 3, George 3, Rioch
			29.9.76		A	W	4–1	Hector 2, George 2
		2	20.10.76	AEK Athens (Greece)	A	L	0–2	
			3.11.76		H	L	2–3	George, Rioch

EVERTON

Season	Competition	Round	Date	Opponents (Country)	Venue	Result		Scorers
1963–64	European Cup	1	18.9.63	Inter-Milan (Italy)	H	D	0–0	
			25.9.63		A	L	0–1	
1970–71	European Cup	1	16.9.70	Keflavik (Iceland)	H	W	6–2	Ball 3, Royle 2, Kendall
			30.9.70		A	W	3–0	Royle 2, Whittle
		2	21.10.70	Borussia Moenchenglad-	A	D	1–1	Kendall
			4.11.70	bach (West Germany)	H	D	1–1†	Morrissey
		QF	9.3.71	Panathinaikos (Greece) *	H	D	1–1	Johnson
			24.3.71		A	D	0–0	
1966–67	Cup-Winners' Cup	1	28.9.66	Aalborg (Denmark)	A	D	0–0	
			11.10.66		H	W	2–1	Morrissey, Ball
		2	9.11.66	Real Zaragoza (Spain)	A	L	0–2	
			23.11.66		H	W	1–0	Brown
1962–63	Fairs Cup	1	24.10.62	Dunfermline Athletic	H	W	1–0	Stevens
			31.10.62	(Scotland)	A	L	0–2	
1964–65	Fairs Cup	1	23.9.64	Valerengen (Norway)	A	W	5–2	Pickering 2, Harvey, Temple 2
			14.10.64		H	W	4–2	Young 2, Vernon, own goal
		2	11.11.64	Kilmarnock (Scotland)	A	W	2–0	Temple, Morrissey
			23.11.64		H	W	4–1	Harvey, Pickering 2, Young
		3	20.1.65	Manchester United	A	D	1–1	Pickering
			9.2.65	(England)	H	L	1–2	Pickering
1965–66	Fairs Cup	1	28.9.65	IFC Nuremberg (West	A	D	1–1	Harris
			12.10.65	Germany)	H	W	1–0	Gabriel
		2	3.11.65	Ujpest Dosza (Hungary)	A	L	0–3	
			16.11.65		H	W	2–1	Harris, own goal
1975–76	UEFA Cup	1	17.9.75	AC Milan (Italy)	H	D	0–0	
			1.10.75		A	L	0–1	
1978–79	UEFA Cup	1	12.9.78	Finn Harps (Eire)	A	W	5–0	Thomas, King 2, Latchford, Walsh
			26.9.78		H	W	5–0	King, Latchford, Walsh, Ross, Dobson
		2	18.10.78	Dukla Prague	H	W	2–1	Latchford, King
			1.11.78	(Czechoslovakia)	A	L	0–1	
1979–80	UEFA Cup	1	19.9.79	Feyenoord (Holland)	A	L	0–1	
			3.10.79		H	L	0–1	

Season	Competition	Round	Date	Opponents (Country)	Venue	Result	Scorers
IPSWICH TOWN							
1962–63	European Cup	Pr	18.9.62	Floriana (Malta)	A	W 4–1	Crawford 2, Phillips 2
			25.9.62		H	W 10–0	Crawford 5, Moran 2, Phillips 2, Elsworthy
		1	14.11.62	AC Milan (Italy)	A	L 0–3	
			28.11.62		H	W 2–1	Crawford, Blackwood
1973–74	UEFA Cup	1	19.9.73	Real Madrid (Spain)	H	W 1–0	own goal
			3.10.73		A	D 0–0	
		2	24.10.73	Lazio (Italy)	H	W 4–0	Whymark 4
			7.11.73		A	L 2–4	Viljoen (pen), Johnson
		3	28.11.73	Twente Enschede	H	W 1–0	Whymark
			12.12.73	(Holland)	A	W 2–1	Morris, Hamilton
		QF	6.3.74	Lokomotive Leipzig	H	W 1–0	Beattie
			20.3.74	(East Germany) †	H	L 0–1	
1974–75	UEFA Cup	1	18.9.74	Twente Enschede	H	D 2–2	Hamilton, Talbot
			2.10.74	(Holland) *	A	D 1–1	Hamilton
1975–76	UEFA Cup	1	17.9.75	Feyenoord (Holland)	A	W 2 1	Whymark, Johnson
			1.10.75		H	W 2 0	Woods, Whymark
		2	22.10.75	FC Bruges (Belgium)	H	W 3–0	Gates, Peddelty, Austin
			5.11.75		A	L 0–4	
1977–78	UEFA Cup	1	14.9.77	Landskrona (Sweden)	A	W 1–0	Whymark
			28.9.77		H	W 5–0	Whymark 4 (1 pen), Mariner
		2	19.10.77	Las Palmas (Spain)	H	W 1–0	Gates
			2.11.77		A	D 3–3	Mariner 2, Talbot
		3	23.11.77	Barcelona (Spain)	H	W 3 -0	Gates, Whymark, Talbot
			7.12.77		A	L 0–3 †	
1979–80	UEFA Cup	1	19.9.79	Skeid Oslo (Norway)	A	W 3–1	Mills, Turner, Mariner
			3.10.79		H	W 7–0	Muhren 2, McCall 2, Wark, Thijssen, Mariner
		2	24.10.79	Grasshoppers	A	D 0–0	
			7.11.79	(Switzerland)	H	D 1–1*	Beattie
1978–79	Cup-Winners' Cup	1	13.9.78	AZ 67 (Holland)	A	D 0–0	
			27.9.78		H	W 2–0	Mariner, Wark (pen)
		2	18.10.78	SW Innsbruck (Austria)	H	W 1–0	Wark (pen)
			1.11.78		A	D 1- 1	Burley
		QF	7.3.79	Barcelona (Spain)	H	W 2–1	Gates 2
			21.3.79		A	L 0- 1	
LEEDS UNITED							
1969–70	European Cup	1	17.9.69	Lyn Oslo (Norway)	H	W 10–0	Jones 3, Clarke 2, Giles 2, Bremner 2, O'Grady
			1.10.69		A	W 6–0	Belfitt 2, Hibbitt 2, Jones, Lorimer
		2	12.11.69	Ferencvaros (Hungary)	H	W 3–0	Giles, Jones 2
			26.11.69		A	W 3–0	Jones 2, Lorimer
		QF	4.3.70	Standard Liege (Belgium)	A	W 1–0	Lorimer
			18.3.70		H	W 1–0	Giles (pen)
		SF	1.4.70	Celtic (Scotland)	H	L 0–1	
			15.4.70		A	L 1–2	Bremner
1974–75	European Cup	1	28.9.74	Zurich (Switzerland)	H	W 4–1	Clarke 2, Lorimer (pen), Jordan
			2.10.74		A	L 1–2	Clarke
		2	23.10.74	Ujpest Dozsa (Hungary)	A	W 2–1	Lorimer, McQueen
			6.11.74		H	W 3–0	McQueen, Bremner, Yorath
		QF	5.3.75	Anderlecht (Belgium)	H	W 3–0	Jordan, McQueen, Lorimer
			19.3.75		A	W 1–0	Bremner
		SF	9.4.75	Barcelona (Spain)	H	W 2–1	Bremner, Clarke
			24.4.75		A	D 1–1	Lorimer
		F	28.5.75	Bayern Munich (West Germany)	N	L 0–2	
1972–73	Cup-Winners' Cup	1	13.9.72	Ankaragucu (Turkey)	A	D 1–1	Jordan
			28.9.72		H	W 1–0	Jones
		2	25.10.72	Carl Zeiss Jena (East Germany	A	D 0–0	
			8.11.72		H	W 2 -0	Cherry, Jones

Season	Competition	Round	Date	Opponents (Country)	Venue	Result	Scorers
LEEDS UNITED continued							
		QF	7.3.73	Rapid Bucharest	H	W 5–0	Giles, Clarke, Lorimer 2, Jordan
			23.3.73	(Rumania)	A	W 3–1	Jones, Jordan, Bates
		SF	11.4.73	Hajduk Split (Yugoslavia)	H	W 1–0	Clarke
			25.4.73		A	D 0–0	
		F	16.5.73	AC Milan (Italy)	N	L 0–1	
1965–66	Fairs Cup	1	29.9.65	Torino (Italy)	H	W 2–1	Bremner, Peacock
			6.10.65		A	D 0–0	
		2	24.11.65	Lokomotive Leipzig	A	W 2–1	Lorimer, Bremner
			1.12.65	(East Germany)	H	D 0–0	
		3	2.2.66	Valencia (Spain)	H	D 1–1	Lorimer
			16.2.66		A	W 1–0	O'Grady
		QF	2.3.66	Ujpest Dosza (Hungary)	H	W 4–1	Cooper, Bell, Storrie, Bremner
			9.3.66		A	D 1–1	Lorimer
		SF	20.4.66	Real Zaragoza (Spain)	A	L 0–1	
			27.4.66		H	W 2–1	Johanneson, Charlton
			11.5.66		N	L 1–3	Charlton
1966–67	Fairs Cup	1	bye				
		2	18.10.66	DWS Amsterdam	A	W 3–1	Bremner, Johanneson, Greenhoff
				(Holland)			
			26.10.66		H	W 5–1	Johanneson 3, Giles, Madeley
		3	18.1.67	Valencia (Spain)	H	D 1–1	Greenhoff
			8.2.67		A	W 2–0	Giles, Lorimer
		QF	22.3.67	Bologna (Italy)	A	L 0–1	
			19.4.67		H	W 1–0‡	Giles (pen)
		SF	19.5.67	Kilmarnock (Scotland)	H	W 4–2	Belfitt 3, Giles (pen)
			24.5.67		A	D 0–0	
		F	30.8.67	Dynamo Zagreb	A	L 0–2	
			6.9.67	(Yugoslavia)	H	D 0–0	
1967–68	Fairs Cup	1	3.10.67	Spora Luxembourg	A	W 9–0	Lorimer 4, Greenhoff 2, Madeley, Jones, Bremner
				(Luxembourg)			
			17.10.67		H	W 7–0	Johanneson 3, Greenhoff 2, Cooper, Lorimer
		2	29.11.67	Partizan Belgrade	A	W 2–1	Lorimer, Belfitt
			6.12.67	(Yugoslavia)	H	D 1–1	Lorimer
		3	20.12.67	Hibernian (Scotland)	H	W 1–0	Gray (E)
			10.1.68		A	D 0–0	
		QF	26.3.68	Rangers (Scotland)	A	D 0·0	
			9.4.68		H	W 2–0	Lorimer, Giles (pen)
		SF	1.5.68	Dundee (Scotland)	A	D 1–1	Madeley
			15.5.68		H	W 1–0	Gray (E)
		F	7.8.68	Ferencvaros (Hungary)	H	W 1–0	Charlton
			11.9.68		A	D 0–0	
1968–69	Fairs Cup	1	18.9.68	Standard Liege (Belgium)	A	D 0–0	
			23.10.68		H	W 3–2	Charlton, Lorimer, Bremner
		2	13.11.68	Napoli (Italy)	H	W 2–0	Charlton 2
			27.11.68		A	L 0–2‡	
		3	18.12.68	Hanover 96 (West	H	W 5–1	O'Grady, Hunter, Lorimer 2, Charlton
				Germany)			
			4.2.69		A	W 2–1	Belfitt, Jones
		QF	5.3.69	Ujpest Dosza (Hungary)	A	L 0–1	
			19.3.69		A	L 0–2	
1970–71	Fairs Cup	1	15.9.70	Sarpsborg (Norway)	H	W 1–0	Lorimer
			29.9.70		H	W 5–0	Charlton 2, Bremner 2, Lorimer
		2	21.10.70	Dynamo Dresden	A	W 1–0	Lorimer
			4.11.70	(East Germany)	A	L 1–2*	Jones
		3	2.12.70	Sparta Prague	H	W 6–0	Clarke, Bremner, Gray (E) 2, Charlton own goal
				(Czechoslovakia)			
			9.12.70		A	W 3–2	Gray (E), Clarke, Belfitt
		QF	10.3.71	Setubal (Portugal)	H	W 2–1	Lorimer, Giles (pen)
			24.3.71		A	D 1–1	Lorimer
		SF	14.4.71	Liverpool (England)	A	W 1–0	Bremner
			28.4.71		H	D 0–0	
		F	28.5.71	Juventus (Italy)	A	D 2–2	Madeley, Bates
			3.6.71		H	D 1–1*	Clarke
1971–72	UEFA Cup	1	15.9.71	Lierse (Belgium)	A	W 2–0	Galvin, Lorimer
			29.9.71		H	L 0–4	

Season	Competition	Round	Date	Opponents (Country)	Venue	Result		Scorers

LEEDS UNITED continued

Season	Competition	Round	Date	Opponents (Country)	Venue	Result		Scorers
1973–74	UEFA Cup	1	19.9.73	Stromsgodset (Norway)	A	D	1–1	Clarke
			3.10.73		H	W	6–1	Clarke 2, Jones 2, Gray (F), Bates
		2	24.10.73	Hibernian (Scotland)	H	D	0–0	
			7.11.73		A	D	0–0†	
		3	28.11.73	Setubal (Portugal)	H	W	1–0	Cherry
			12.12.73		A	L	1–3	Liddell
1979–80	UEFA Cup	1	19.9.79	Valetta (Malta)	A	W	4–0	Graham 3, Hart
			3.10.79		H	W	3–0	Curtis, Hankin, Hart
		2	24.10.79	Uni. Craiova (Rumania)	A	L	0–2	
			7.11.79		H	L	0–2	

N.B. Leeds met Barcelona in Spain on 22.9.71 in a match to determine who should hold the Fairs Cup trophy permanently. Barcelona, the first winners beat Leeds, the holders 2–1 (Jordan was the United scorer).

LEICESTER CITY

Season	Competition	Round	Date	Opponents (Country)	Venue	Result		Scorers
1961–62	Cup-Winners Cup	1	13.9.61	Glenavon (Northern	A	W	4–1	Walsh 2, Appleton, Keyworth
			27.9.61	Ireland)	H	W	3–1	Wills, Keyworth, McIlmoyle
		2	25.10.61	Atletico Madrid (Spain)	H	D	1–1	Keyworth
			15.11.61		A	L	0–2	

LIVERPOOL

Season	Competition	Round	Date	Opponents (Country)	Venue	Result		Scorers
1964–65	European Cup	Pr	17.8.64	KR Reykjavik (Iceland)	A	W	5–0	Wallace 2, Hunt 2, Chisnall
			14.9.64		H	W	6–1	Byrne, St John 2, Graham, Hunt, Stevenson
		1	25.11.64	Anderlecht (Belgium)	H	W	3–0	St John, Hunt, Yeats
			16.12.64		A	W	1–0	Hunt
		QF	10.2.65	FC Cologne (West	A	D	0–0	
			17.3.65	Germany)	H	D	0–0	
			24.3.65		N	D	2–2‡	St John, Hunt
		SF	4.5.65	Inter-Milan (Italy)	H	W	3–1	Hunt, Callaghan, St John
			12.5.65		A	L	0–3	
1966–67	European Cup	1	28.9.66	Petrolul Ploesti (Rumania)	H	W	2–0	St John, Callaghan
			12.10.66		A	L	1–3	Hunt
			19.10.66		N	W	2–0	St John, Thompson (P)
		2	7.12.66	Ajax (Holland)	A	L	1–5	Lawler
			14.12.66		H	D	2–2	Hunt 2
1973–74	European Cup	1	19.9.73	Jeunesse D'Esch	A	D	1–1	Hall
			3.10.73	(Luxembourg)	H	W	2–0	Toshack, own goal
		2	24.10.73	Red Star Belgrade	A	L	1–2	Lawler
			6.11.73	(Yugoslavia)	H	L	1–2	Lawler
1976–77	European Cup	1	14.9.76	Crusaders (Northern	H	W	2–0	Neal (pen), Toshack
			28.9.76	Ireland)	A	W	5–0	Johnson 2, Keegan, McDermott, Heighway
		2	20.10.76	Trabzonspor (Turkey)	A	L	0–1	
			3.11.76		H	W	3–0	Heighway, Johnson, Keegan
		QF	2.3.77	St Etienne (France)	A	L	0–1	
			16.3.77		H	W	3–1	Keegan, Kennedy, Fairclough
		SF	6.4.77	Zurich (Switzerland)	A	W	3–1	Neal 2 (1 pen), Heighway
			20.4.77		H	W	3–0	Case 2, Keegan
		F	25.5.77	Borussia Moenchenglad-	N	W	3–1	McDermott, Smith, Neal (pen)
				bach (West Germany)				
1977–78	European Cup	1		bye				
		2	19.10.77	Dynamo Dresden	H	W	5–1	Hansen, Case 2, Neal (pen), Kennedy
				(East Germany)				
			2.11.77		A	L	1–2	Heighway
		QF	1.3.78	Benfica (Portugal)	A	W	2–1	Case, Hughes
			15.3.78		H	W	4–1	Callaghan, Dalglish, McDermott, Neal
		SF	29.3.78	Borussia Moenchenglad-	A	L	1–2	Johnson
			12.4.78	bach (West Germany)	H	W	3–0	Kennedy, Dalglish, Case
		F	10.5.78	FC Bruges (Belgium)	N	W	1–0	Dalglish

Season	Competition	Round	Date	Opponents (Country)	Venue	Result		Scorers

LIVERPOOL continued

Season	Competition	Round	Date	Opponents (Country)	Venue	Result		Scorers
1978–79	European Cup	1	13.9.78	Nottingham Forest	A	L	0–2	
			27.9.78	(England)	H	D	0–0	
1979–80	European Cup	1	19.9.79	Dynamo Tbilisi (USSR)	H	W	2–1	Johnson, Case
			3.10.79		A	L	0–3	
1965–66	Cup-Winners' Cup	1	29.9.65	Juventus (Italy)	A	L	0–1	
			13.10.65		H	W	2–0	Lawler, Strong
		2	1.12.65	Standard Liege (Belgium)	H	W	3–1	Lawler 2, Thompson (P)
			15.12.65		A	W	2–1	Hunt, St John
		QF	1.3.66	Honved (Hungary)	A	D	0–0	
			8.3.66		H	W	2–0	Lawler, St John
		SF	14.4.66	Celtic (Scotland)	A	L	0–1	
					H	W	2–0	Lawler, St John
		F	5.5.66	Borussia Dortmund (West Germany)	N	L	1–2	Hunt
1971–72	Cup-Winners' Cup	1	15.9.71	Servette (Switzerland)	A	L	1–2	Lawler
			29.9.71		H	W	2–0	Hughes, Heighway
		2	20.10.71	Bayern Munich	H	D	0–0	
			3.11.71	(West Germany)	A	L	1–3	Evans
1974–75	Cup-Winners' Cup	1	17.9.74	Stromsgodset (Norway)	H	W	11–0	Lindsay (pen), Boersma 2, Heighway, Thompson (P B) 2, Smith, Cormack, Hughes, Callaghan, Kennedy
			1.10.74	Barcelona (Spain)	A	W	1–0	Kennedy
		2	23.10.74	Ferencvaros (Hungary) *	H	D	1–1	Keegan
			5.11.74		A	D	0–0	
1967–68	Fairs Cup	1	19.9.67	Malmo FF (Sweden)	A	W	2–0	Hateley 2
			4.10.67		H	W	2–1	Yeats, Hunt
		2	7.11.67	Munich 1860 (West Germany)	H	W	8–0	St John, Hateley, Thompson (P), Smith (pen), Hunt 2, Callaghan 2
			14.11.67		A	L	1–2	Callaghan
		3	28.11.67	Ferencvaros (Hungary)	A	L	0–1	
			9.1.68		H	L	0–1	
1968–69	Fairs Cup	1	18.9.68	Atletico Bilbao (Spain) ‡	A	L	1–2	Hunt
			2.10.68		H	W	2–1	Lawler, Hughes
1969–70	Fairs Cup	1	16.9.69	Dundalk (Eire)	H	W	10–0	Evans 2, Smith 2, Graham 2, Lawler, Lindsay, Thompson (P) Callaghan
			30.9.69		A	W	4–0	Thompson (P) 2, Graham, Callaghan
		3	11.11.69	Setubal (Portugal) *	A	L	0–1	
			26.11.69		H	W	3–2	Smith (pen), Evans, Hunt
1970–71	Fairs Cup	1	15.9.70	Ferencvaros (Hungary)	H	W	1–0	Graham
			29.9.70		A	D	1–1	Hughes
		2	21.10.70	Dynamo Bucharest	H	W	3–0	Lindsay, Lawler, Hughes
			4.11.70	(Rumania)	A	D	1–1	Boersma
		3	9.12.70	Hibernian (Scotland)	A	W	1–0	Toshack
			22.12.70		H	W	2–0	Heighway, Boersma
		QF	10.3.71	Bayern Munich	H	W	3–0	Evans 3
			24.3.71	(West Germany)	A	D	1–1	Ross
		SF	14.4.71	Leeds United (England)	H	L	0–1	
			28.4.71		A	D	0–0	
1972–73	UEFA Cup	1	12.9.72	Eintracht Frankfurt	H	W	2–0	Keegan, Hughes
			26.9.72	(West Germany)	A	D	0–0	
		2	24.10.72	AEK Athens (Greece)	H	W	3–0	Boersma, Cormack, Smith(pen)
			7.11.72		A	W	3–1	Hughes 2, Boersma
		3	29.11.72	Dynamo Berlin (East Germany)	A	D	0–0	
			12.12.72		H	W	3–1	Boersma, Heighway, Toshack
		QF	7.3.73	Dynamo Dresden	H	W	2–0	Hall, Boersma
			21.3.73	(East Germany)	A	W	1–0	Keegan
		SF	10.4.73	Tottenham Hotspur	H	W	1–0	Lindsay
			25.4.73	(England)	A	L	1–2 *	Heighway
		F	10.5.73	Borussia Moenchenglad-bach (West Germany)	H	W	3–0	Keegan 2, Lloyd
			23.5.73		A	L	2–0	
1975–76	UEFA Cup	1	17.9.75	Hibernian (Scotland)	A	L	0–1	
			30.9.75		H	W	3–1	Toshack 3

Season	Competition	Round	Date	Opponents (Country)	Venue	Result	Scorers
LIVERPOOL continued							
		2	22.10.75	Real Sociedad (Spain)	A	W 3–1	Heighway, Callaghan, Thompson (P B)
			4.11.75		H	W 6–0	Toshack, Kennedy 2, Fairclough, Heighway, Neal
		3	26.11.75	Slask Wroclaw (Poland)	A	W 2–1	Kennedy, Toshack
			10.12.75		H	W 3–0	Case 3
		QF	3.3.76	Dynamo Dresden	A	D 0–0	
			17.3.76	(East Germany)	H	W 2–1	Case, Keegan
		SF	30.3.76	Barcelona (Spain)	A	W 1–0	Toshack
			14.4.76		H	D 1–1	Thompson (P B)
		F	28.4.76	FC Bruges (Belgium)	H	W 3–2	Kennedy, Case, Keegan (pen)
			19.5.76		A	D 1–1	Keegan
1977–78	Super Cup	F	22.11.77	SV Hamburg (West	A	D 1–1	Fairclough
			6.12.77	Germany)	H	W 6–0	Thompson, McDermott 3, Fairclough, Dalglish
1978–79	Super Cup	F	4.12.78	Anderlecht (Belgium)	A	L 1–3	Case
			19.12.78		H	W 2–1	Hughes, Fairclough
MANCHESTER CITY							
1968–69	European Cup	1	18.9.68	Fenerbahce (Turkey)	H	D 0–0	
			2.10.68		A	L 1–2	Coleman
1969–70	Cup-Winners' Cup	1	17.9.69	Atletico Bilbao (Spain)	A	D 3–3	Young, Booth, own goal
			1.10.69		H	W 3–0	Oakes, Bell, Bowyer
		2	12.11.69	Lierse (Belgium)	A	W 3–0	Lee 2, Bell
			26.11.69		H	W 5–0	Bell 2, Lee 2, Summerbee
		QF	4.3.70	Academica Coimbra	A	D 0–0	
			18.3.70	(Portugal)	H	W 1–0	Towers
		SF	1.4.70	Schalke 04 (West	A	L 0–1	
			15.4.70	Germany)	H	W 5–1	Young 2, Doyle, Lee, Bell
		F	29.4.70	Gornik Zabrze (Poland)	N	W 2–1	Young, Lee (pen)
1970–71	Cup-Winners' Cup	1	16.9.70	Linfield (Northern	H	W 1–0	Bell
			30.9.70	Ireland)	A	L 1–2 *	Lee
		2	21.10.70	Honved (Hungary)	A	W 1–0	Lee
			4.11.70		H	W 2–0	Bell, Lee
		QF	10.3.71	Gornik Zabrze (Poland)	A	L 0–2	
			24.3.71		H	W 2–0	Mellor, Doyle
			31.3.71		N	W 3–1	Young, Booth, Lee
		SF	14.4.71	Chelsea (England)	A	L 0–1	
			28.4.71		H	L 0–1	
1972–73	UEFA Cup	1	13.9.72	Valencia (Spain)	H	D 2–2	Mellor, Marsh
			27.9.72		A	L 1–2	Marsh
1976–77	UEFA Cup	1	15.9.76	Juventus (Italy)	H	W 1–0	Kidd
			29.9.76		A	L 0–2	
1977–78	UEFA Cup	1	14.9.77	Widzew Lodz (Poland) *	H	D 2–2	Barnes, Channon
			28.9.77		A	D 0–0	
1978–79	UEFA Cup	1	13.9.78	Twente Enschede	A	D 1–1	Watson
			27.9.78	(Holland)	H	W 3–2	Kidd, Bell, own goal
		2	18.10.78	Standard Liege (Belgium)	H	W 4–0	Hartford, Kidd 2 (1 pen), Palmer
			1.11.78		A	L 0–2	
		3	23.11.78	AC Milan (Italy)	A	D 2–2	Kidd, Power
			6.12.78		H	W 3–0	Booth, Hartford, Kidd
		QF	7.3.79	Borussia Moenchenglad-	H	D 1–1	Channon
			21.3.79	bach (West Germany)	A	L 1–3	Deyna
MANCHESTER UNITED							
1956–57	European Cup	Pr	12.9.56	Anderlecht (Belgium)	A	W 2–0	Viollet, Taylor (T)
			26.9.56		H	W 10–0	Viollet 4, Taylor (T) 3, Whelan 2, Berry
		1	17.10.56	Borussia Dortmund	H	W 3–2	Viollet 2, Pegg
			21.11.56	(West Germany)	A	D 0–0	
		QF	16.1.57	Atletico Bilbao (Spain)	A	L 3–5	Taylor (T), Viollet, Whelan
			6.2.57		H	W 3–0	Viollet, Taylor (T), Berry
		SF	11.4.57	Real Madrid (Spain)	A	L 1–3	Taylor (T)
			24.4.57		H	D 2–2	Taylor (T), Charlton

Season	Competition	Round	Date	Opponents (Country)	Venue	Result		Scorers

MANCHESTER UNITED continued

Season	Competition	Round	Date	Opponents (Country)	Venue	Result		Scorers
1957–58	European Cup	Pr	25.9.57	Shamrock Rovers (Eire)	A	W	6–0	Whelan 2. Taylor (T) 2, Berry, Pegg
			2.10.57		H	W	3–2	Viollet 2, Pegg
		1	20.11.57	Dukla Prague	H	W	3–0	Webster, Taylor (T), Pegg
			4.12.57	(Czechoslovakia)	A	L	0–1	
		QF	14.1.58	Red Star Belgrade	H	W	2–1	Charlton, Colman
			5.2.58	(Yugoslavia)	A	D	3–3	Viollet, Charlton 2
		SF	8.5.58	AC Milan (Italy)	H	W	2–1	Viollet, Taylor (E) (pen)
			14.5.58		A	L	0–4	
1965–66	European Cup	Pr	22.9.65	HJK Helsinki (Finland)	A	W	3–2	Herd, Connelly, Law
			6.10.65		H	W	6–0	Connelly 3, Best 2, Charlton
		1	17.11.65	Vorwaerts Berlin	A	W	2–0	Law, Connelly
			1.12.65	(East Germany)	H	W	3–1	Herd 3
		QF	2.2.66	Benfica (Portugal)	H	W	3–2	Herd, Law, Foulkes
			9.3.66		A	W	5–1	Best 2, Connelly, Crerand, Charlton
		SF	13.4.66	Partizan Belgrade	A	L	0–2	
			20.4.66	(Yugoslavia)	H	W	1–0	own goal
1967–68	European Cup	1	20.9.67	Hibernians (Malta)	H	W	4–0	Sadler 2, Law 2
			27.9.67		A	D	0–0	
		2	15.11.67	Sarajevo (Yugoslavia)	A	D	0–0	
			29.11.67		H	W	2–1	Aston, Best
		QF	28.2.68	Gornik Zabrze (Poland)	H	W	2–0	Kidd, own goal
			13.3.68		A	L	0–1	
		SF	24.4.68	Real Madrid (Spain)	H	W	1–0	Best
			15.5.68		A	D	3–3	Sadler, Kidd, Foulkes
		F	29.5.68	Benfica (Portugal)	N	W	4–1	Charlton 2, Best, Kidd
1968–69	European Cup	1	18.9.68	Waterford (Eire)	A	W	3–1	Law 3
			2.10.68		H	W	7–1	Stiles, Law 4, Burns, Charlton
		2	13.11.68	Anderlecht (Belgium)	H	W	3–0	Kidd, Law 2
			27.11.68		A	L	1–3	Sartori
		QF	26.2.69	Rapid Vienna (Austria)	H	W	3–0	Best 2, Morgan
			5.3.69		A	D	0–0	
		SF	23.4.69	AC Milan (Italy)	A	L	0–2	
			15.5.69		H	W	1–0	Charlton
1963–64	Cup-Winners' Cup	1	25.9.63	Tilburg Willem II (Holland)	A	D	1–1	Herd
			15.10.63		H	W	6–1	Setters, Law 3, Charlton, Chisnall
		2	3.12.63	Tottenham Hotspur	A	L	0–2	
			10.12.63	(England)	H	W	4–1	Herd 2, Charlton 2
		QF	26.2.64	Sporting Lisbon	H	W	4–1	Law 3 (2 pens), Charlton
			18.3.64	(Portugal)	A	L	0–5	
1977–78	Cup-Winners' Cup	1	14.9.77	St. Etienne (France)	A	D	1–1	Hill
			5.10.77		H	W	2–0	Pearson, Coppell
		2	19.10.77	Porto (Portugal)	A	L	0–4	
			2.11.77		H	W	5–2	Coppell 2, own goals 2, Nicholl
1964–65	Fairs Cup	1	23.9.64	Djurgaarden (Sweden)	A	D	1–1	Herd
			27.10.64		H	W	6–1	Law 3 (1 pen), Charlton 2, Best
		2	11.11.64	Borussia Dortmund	A	W	6–1	Herd, Charlton 3, Best, Law
			2.12.64	(West Germany)	H	W	4–0	Charlton 2, Law, Connelly
		3	20.1.65	Everton (England)	H	D	1–1	Connelly
			9.2.65		A	W	2–1	Connelly, Herd
		QF	12.5.65	Strasbourg (France)	A	W	5–0	Connelly, Herd, Law 2, Charlton
			19.5.65		H	D	0–0	
		SF	31.5.65	Ferencvaros (Hungary)	H	W	3–2	Law (pen), Herd 2
			6.6.65		A	L	0–1	
			16.6.65		A	L	1–2	Connelly
1976–77	UEFA Cup	1	15.9.76	Ajax (Holland)	A	L	0–1	
			29.9.76		H	W	2–0	Macari, McIlroy
		2	20.10.76	Juventus (Italy)	H	W	1–0	Hill
			3.11.76		A	L	0–3	

NEWCASTLE UNITED

Season	Competition	Round	Date	Opponents (Country)	Venue	Result		Scorers
1968–69	Fairs Cup	1	11.9.68	Feyenoord (Holland)	H	W	4–0	Scott, Robson(B), Gibb, Davies
			17.9.68		A	L	0–2	

Season	Competition	Round	Date	Opponents (Country)	Venue	Result		Scorers

NEWCASTLE UNITED continued

Season	Competition	Round	Date	Opponents (Country)	Venue	Result		Scorers
		2	30.10.68	Sporting Lisbon	A	D	1–1	Scott
			20.11.68	(Portugal)	H	W	1–0	Robson (B)
		3	1.1.69	Real Zaragoza (Spain)	A	L	2–3	Robson (B), Davies
			15.1.69		H	W	2–1*	Robson (B), Gibb
		QF	12.3.69	Setubal (Portugal)	H	W	5–1	Robson (B) 2, Gibb, Davies, Foggon
			26.3.69		A	L	1–3	Davies
		SF	14.5.69	Rangers (Scotland)	A	D	0–0	
			22.5.69		H	W	2–0	Scott, Sinclair
		F	29.5.69	Ujpest Dosza (Hungary)	H	W	3–0	Moncur 2, Scott
			11.6.69		A	W	3–2	Moncur, Arentoft, Foggon
1969–70	Fairs Cup	1	15.9.69	Dundee United (Scotland)	A	W	2–1	Davies 2
			1.10.69		H	W	1–0	Dyson
		2	19.11.69	Porto (Portugal)	A	D	0–0	
			26.11.69		H	W	1–0	Scott
		3	17.12.69	Southampton (England)	H	D	0–0	
			13.1.70		A	D	1–1*	Robson (B)
		QF	11.3.70	Anderlecht (Belgium) *	A	L	0–2	
			18.3.70		H	W	3–1	Robson (B) 2, Dyson
1970–71	Fairs Cup	1	23.9.70	Inter-Milan (Italy)	A	D	1–1	Davies
			30.9.70		H	W	2–0	Moncur, Davies
		2	21.10.70	Pecs Dosza (Hungary) †	H	W	2–0	Davies 2
			4.11.70		A	L	0–2	
1977–78	UEFA Cup	1	14.9.77	Bohemians (Eire)	A	D	0–0	
			28.9.77		H	W	4–0	Gowling 2, Craig 2
		2	19.10.77	Bastia (France)	A	L	1–2	Cannell
			2.11.77		H	L	1–3	Gowling

NOTTINGHAM FOREST

Season	Competition	Round	Date	Opponents (Country)	Venue	Result		Scorers
1961–62	Fairs Cup	1	13.9.61	Valencia (Spain)	A	L	0–2	
			4.10.61		H	L	1–5	Cobb
1967–68	Fairs Cup	1	20.9.67	Eintracht Frankfurt	A	W	1–0	Baker
			17.10.67	(West Germany)	H	W	4–0	Baker 2, Chapman, Lyons
		2	31.10.67	Zurich (Switzerland)*	H	W	2–1	Newton, Moore (pen)
			14.11.67		A	L	0–1	
1978–79	European Cup	1	13.9.78	Liverpool (England)	H	W	2–0	Birtles, Barrett
			27.9.78		A	D	0–0	
		2	18.10.78	AEK Athens (Greece)	A	W	2–1	McGovern, Birtles
			1.11.78		H	W	5–1	Needham, Woodcock, Anderson, Birtles 2
		QF	7.3.79	Grasshoppers	H	W	4–1	Birtles, Robertson (pen), Gemmill, Lloyd
			21.3.79	(Switzerland)	A	D	1–1	O'Neill
		SF	11.4.79	IFC Cologne (West	H	D	3–3	Birtles, Bowyer, Robertson
			25.4.79	Germany)	A	W	1–0	Bowyer
			30.5.79	Malmo (Sweden)	N	W	1–0	Francis
1979–80	European Cup	1	19.9.79	Osters (Sweden)	H	W	2–0	Bowyer, Hallan own goal
			3.10.79		A	D	1–1	Woodcock
		2	24.10.79	Arges Pitesti (Rumania)	H	W	2–0	Woodcock, Birtles
			7.11.79		A	W	2–1	Bowyer, Birtles
		QF	5.3.80	Dynamo Berlin (East	H	L	0–1	
			19.3.80	Germany)	A	W	3–1	Francis 2, Robertson (pen)
		SF	9.4.80	Ajax (Holland)	H	W	2–0	Francis, Robertson (pen)
			23.4.80		A	L	0–1	
		F	28.5.80	SV Hamburg (West	N	W	1–0	Robertson
				Germany)				
1979–80	Super Cup		30.1.80	Barcelona (Spain)	H	W	1–0	George
			5.2.80		A	D	1–1	Burns

QUEEN'S PARK RANGERS

Season	Competition	Round	Date	Opponents (Country)	Venue	Result		Scorers
1976–77	UEFA Cup	1	15.9.76	Brann Bergen (Norway)	H	W	4–0	Bowles 3, Masson
			29.9.76		A	W	7–0	Bowles 3, Givens 2, Thomas, Webb

Season	Competition	Round	Date	Opponents (Country)	Venue	Result		Scorers

QUEEN'S PARK RANGERS continued

Season	Competition	Round	Date	Opponents (Country)	Venue	Result		Scorers
		2	20.10.76	Slovan Bratislava	A	D	3–3	Bowles 2, Givens
			3.11.76	(Czechoslovakia)	H	W	5–2	Givens 3, Bowles, Clement
		3	24.11.76	IFC Cologne (West	H	W	3–0	Givens, Webb, Bowles
			7.12.76	Germany)	A	L	1–4*	Masson
		QF	2.3.77	AEK Athens (Greece)	H	W	3–0	Francis (2 pens), Bowles
			16.3.77		A	L	0–3†	

SHEFFIELD WEDNESDAY

Season	Competition	Round	Date	Opponents (Country)	Venue	Result		Scorers
1961–62	Fairs Cup	1	12.9.61	Lyon (France)	A	L	2–4	Ellis, Young
			4.10.61		H	W	5–2	Fantham 2, Griffin, McAnearney (pen), Dobson
		2	29.11.61	AS Roma (Italy)	H	W	4–0	Fantham, Young 3
			13.12.61		A	L	0–1	
		QF	28.2.62	Barcelona (Spain)	H	W	3–2	Fantham 2, Finney
			28.3.62		A	L	0–2	
1963–64	Fairs Cup	1	25.9.63	DOS Útrecht (Holland)	A	W	4–1	Holliday, Layne, Quinn, own goal
			15.10.63		H	W	4–1	Layne 3 (1 pen), Dobson
		2	6.11.63	IFC Cologne (West	A	L	2–3	Pearson 2
			27.11.63	Germany)	H	L	1–2	Layne

SOUTHAMPTON

Season	Competition	Round	Date	Opponents (Country)	Venue	Result		Scorers
1976–77	Cup-Winners' Cup	1	15.9.76	Marseille (France)	H	W	4–0	Waldron, Channon 2 (1pen), Osgood
			29.9.76		A	L	1–2	Peach
		2	20.10.76	Carrick Rangers (Northern Ireland)	A	W	5–2	Stokes, Channon 2, McCalliog, Osgood
			3.11.76		H	W	4–1	Williams, Hayes 2, Stokes
		QF	2.3.77	Anderlecht (Belgium)	A	L	0–2	
			16.3.77		H	W	2–1	Peach (pen), MacDougall
1969–70	Fairs Cup	1	17.9.69	Rosenborg (Norway)	A	L	0–1	
			1.10.69		H	W	2–0	Davies, Paine
		2	4.11.69	Vitoria Guimaraes (Portugal)	A	D	3–3	Channon, Davies, Paine
			12.11.69		H	W	5–1	Gabriel, Davies 2 (1 pen), Channon, own goal
		3	17.12.69	Newcastle United (England)*	A	D	0–0	
			13.1.70		H	D	1–1	Channon
1971–72	UEFA Cup	1	15.9.71	Atletico Bilbao (Spain)	H	W	2–1	Jenkins, Channon (pen)
			29.9.71		A	L	0–2	

STOKE CITY

Season	Competition	Round	Date	Opponents (Country)	Venue	Result		Scorers
1972–73	UEFA Cup	1	13.9.72	Kaiserslautern (West	H	W	3–1	Conroy, Hurst, Ritchie
			27.9.72	Germany)	A	L	0–4	
1974–75	UEFA Cup	1	18.9.74	Ajax (Holland) *	H	D	1–1	Smith
			2.10.74		A	D	0–0	

SUNDERLAND

Season	Competition	Round	Date	Opponents (Country)	Venue	Result		Scorers
1973–74	Cup-Winners' Cup	1	19.9.73	Vasas-Budapest (Hungary)	A	W	2–0	Hughes, Tueart
			3.10.73		H	W	1–0	Tueart (pen)
		2	24.10.73	Sporting Lisbon (Portugal)	H	W	2–1	Kerr, Horswill
			7.11.73		A	L	0–2	

SWANSEA CITY

Season	Competition	Round	Date	Opponents (Country)	Venue	Result		Scorers
1961–62	Cup-Winners' Cup	1	16.9.61	Motor Jena (East Germany) (in Linz, Austria)	H	D	2–2	Reynolds, Nurse (pen)
			18.10.61		A	L	1–5	Reynolds
1966–67	Cup-Winners' Cup	1	21.9.66	Slavia Sofia (Bulgaria)	H	D	1–1	Todd
			5.10.66		A	L	0–4	

TOTTENHAM HOTSPUR

Season	Competition	Round	Date	Opponents (Country)	Venue	Result		Scorers
1961–62	European Cup	Pr	13.9.61	Gornik Zabrze (Poland)	A	L	2–4	Jones, Dyson
			20.9.61		H	W	8–1	Blanchflower (pen), Jones 3, Smith 2, Dyson, White

Season	Competition	Round	Date	Opponents (Country)	Venue	Result	Scorers
TOTTENHAM HOTSPUR continued							
		1	1.11.61	Feyenoord (Holland)	A	W 3–1	Dyson, Saul 2
			15.11.61		H	D 1–1	Dyson
		QF	14.2.62	Dukla Prague	A	L 0–1	
			26.2.62	(Czechoslovakia)	H	W 4–1	Smith 2, Mackay 2
		SF	21.3.62	Benfica (Portugal)	A	L 1–3	Smith
			5.4.62		H	W 2–1	Smith, Blanchflower (pen)
1962–63	Cup-Winners' Cup	1		bye			
		2	31.10.62	Rangers (Scotland)	H	W 5–2	White, Greaves, Allen, Norman, own goal
			11.12.62		A	W 3–2	Greaves, Smith 2
		QF	5.3.63	Slovan Bratislava	A	L 0–2	
			14.3.63	(Czechoslovakia)	H	W 6–0	Mackay, Smith, Greaves 2, Jones, White
		SF	24.4.63	OFK Belgrade	A	W 2–1	White, Dyson
			1.5.63	(Yugoslavia)	H	W 3–1	Mackay, Jones, Smith
		F	15.5.63	Atletico Madrid (Spain)	N	W 5–1	Greaves 2, White, Dyson 2
1963–64	Cup-Winners' Cup	1		exempt			
		2	3.12.63	Manchester United	H	W 2–0	Mackay, Dyson
			10.12.63	(England)	A	L 1–4	Greaves
1967–68	Cup-Winners' Cup	1	20.9.67	Hajduk Split (Yugoslavia)	A	W 2–0	Robertson, Greaves
			27.9.67		H	W 4–3	Robertson 2, Gilzean, Venables
		2	29.11.67	Lyon (France) *	A	L 0–1	
			13.12.67		H	W 4–3	Greaves 2 (1 pen), Jones, Gilzean
1971–72	UEFA Cup	1	14.9.71	Keflavik (Iceland)	A	W 6–1	Gilzean 3, Coates, Mullery 2
			28.9.71		H	W 9–0	Chivers 3, Gilzean 2, Perryman, Coates, Knowles, Holder
		2	20.10.71	Nantes (France)	A	D 0–0	
			2.11.71		H	W 1–0	Peters
		3	8.12.71	Rapid Bucharest	H	W 3–0	Peters, Chivers 2
			15.12.71	(Rumania)	A	W 2–0	Pearce, Chivers
		QF	7.3.72	UT Arad (Rumania)	A	W 2–0	Morgan, England
			21.3.72		H	D 1–1	Gilzean
		SF	5.4.72	AC Milan (Italy)	H	W 2–1	Perryman 2
			19.4.72		A	D 1–1	Mullery
		F	3.5.72	Wolverhampton	A	W 2–1	Chivers 2
			17.5.72	Wanderers (England)	H	D 1–1	Mullery
1972–73	UEFA Cup	1	13.9.72	Lyn Oslo (Norway)	A	W 6–3	Peters, Pratt, Gilzean 2, Chivers 2
			27.9.72		H	W 6–0	Chivers 3, Coates 2, Pearce
		2	25.10.72	Olympiakos Piraeus	H	W 4–0	Pearce 2, Chivers, Coates
			8.11.72	(Greece)	A	L 0–1	
		3	29.11.72	Red Star Belgrade	H	W 2–0	Chivers, Gilzean
			13.12.72	(Yugoslavia)	A	L 0–1	
		QF	7.3.73	Setubal (Portugal)	H	W 1–0	Evans
			21.3.73		A	L 1–2 *	Chivers
		SF	10.4.73	Liverpool (England) *	A	L 0–1	
			25.4.73		H	W 2–1	Peters 2
1973–74	UEFA Cup	1	19.9.73	Grasshoppers	A	W 5–1	Chivers 2, Evans, Gilzean 2
			3.10.73	(Switzerland)	H	W 4–1	Peters 2, England, own goal
		2	24.10.73	Aberdeen (Scotland)	A	D 1–1	Coates
			7.11.73		H	W 4–1	Peters, Neighbour, McGrath 2
		3	28.11.73	Dynamo Tbilisi (USSR)	A	D 1–1	Coates
			12.12.73		H	W 5–1	McGrath, Chivers 2, Peters 2
		QF	6.3.74	IFC Cologne	A	W 2–1	McGrath, Peters
			20.3.74	(West Germany)	H	W 3–0	Chivers, Coates, Peters
		SF	10.4.74	Lokomotive Leipzig	A	W 2–1	Peters, McGrath
			24.4.74	(East Germany)	H	W 2–0	McGrath, Chivers
		F	21.5.74	Feyenoord (Holland)	H	D 2–2	England, own goal
			29.5.74		A	L 0–2	
WEST BROMWICH ALBION							
1968–69	Cup-Winners' Cup	1	18.9.68	FC Bruges (Belgium)	A	L 1–3	Hartford
			2.10.68		H	W 2–0 *	Brown (T), Hartford

Season	Competition	Round	Date	Opponents (Country)	Venue	Result		Scorers

WEST BROMWICH ALBION continued

		2	13.11.68	Dynamo Bucharest	A	D	1–1	Hartford
			27.11.68	(Rumania)	H	W	4–0	Lovett, Astle, Brown (T) 2 (1 pen)
		QF	15.1.69	Dunfermline Athletic	A	D	0–0	
			19.2.69	(Scotland)	H	L	0–1	
1966–67	Fairs Cup	1		bye				
		2	2.11.66	DOS Utrecht (Holland)	A	D	1–1	Hope
			9.11.66		H	W	5–2	Brown (T) 3 (1 pen), Clark, Kaye
		3	2.2.67	Bologna (Italy)	A	L	0–3	
			8.3.67		H	L	1–3	Fairfax
1978–79	UEFA Cup	1	13.9.78	Galatasaray (Turkey)	A	W	3–1	Robson, Regis, Cunningham
			27.9.78		H	W	3–1	Robson, Cunningham (pen), Trewick
		2	18.10.78	Sporting Braga	A	W	2–0	Regis 2
			1.11.78	(Portugal)	H	W	1–0	Brown (A)
		3	22.11.78	Valencia (Spain)	A	D	1–1	Cunningham
			6.12.78		H	W	2–0	Brown (T) 2, (1 pen)
		QF	7.3.79	Red Star Belgrade	A	L	0–1	
			21.3.79	(Yugoslavia)	H	D	1–1	Regis
1979–80	UEFA Cup	1	19.9.79	Carl Zeiss Jena	A	L	0–2	
			3.10.79	(East Germany)	H	L	1–2	Wile

WEST HAM UNITED

1964–65	Cup-Winners' Cup	1	23.9.64	La Gantoise (Belgium)	A	W	1–0	Boyce
			7.10.64		H	D	1–1	Byrne
		2	25.11.64	Sparta Prague	H	W	2–0	Bond, Sealey
			9.12.64	(Czechoslovakia)	A	L	1–2	Sissons
		QF	16.3.65	Lausanne (Switzerland)	A	W	2–1	Dear, Byrne
			23.3.65		H	W	4–3	Dear 2, Peters, own goal
		SF	7.4.65	Real Zaragoza (Spain)	H	W	2–1	Dear, Byrne
			28.4.65		A	D	1–1	Sissons
		F	19.5.65	Munich 1860 (West Germany)	N	W	2–0	Sealey 2
1965–66	Cup-Winners' Cup	1		bye				
		2	24.11.65	Olympiakos Piraeus	H	W	4–0	Hurst 2, Byrne, Brabrook
			1.12.65	(Greece)	A	D	2–2	Peters 2
		QF	2.3.66	Magdeburg (East Germany)	H	W	1–0	Byrne
			16.3.66		A	D	1–1	Sissons
		SF	5.4.66	Borussia Dortmund	H	L	1–2	Peters
			13.4.66	(West Germany)	A	L	1–3	Byrne
1975–76	Cup-Winners' Cup	1	17.9.75	Lahden Reipas (Finland)	A	D	2–2	Brooking, Bonds
			1.10.75		H	W	3–0	Robson (K), Holland, Jennings
		2	22.10.75	Ararat Erevan (USSR)	A	D	1–1	Taylor (A)
			5.11.75		H	W	3–1	Paddon, Robson(K), Taylor(A)
		QF	3.3.76	Den Haag (Holland)	A	L	2–4	Jennings 2
			17.3.76		H	W	3–1 *	Taylor (A), Lampard, Bonds (pen)
		SF	31.3.76	Eintracht Frankfurt	A	L	1–2	Paddon
			14.4.76	(West Germany)	H	W	3–1	Brooking 2, Robson (K)
		F	5.5.76	Anderlecht (Belgium)	N	L	2–4	Holland, Robson (K)

WOLVERHAMPTON WANDERERS

1958–59	European Cup	Pr		bye				
		1	12.11.58	Schalke 04	H	D	2–2	Broadbent 2
			18.11.58	(West Germany)	A	L	1–2	Jackson
1959–60	European Cup	Pr	30.9.59	Vorwaerts (East Germany)	A	L	1–2	Broadbent
			7.10.59		H	W	2–0	Broadbent, Mason
		1	11.11.59	Red Star Belgrade	A	D	1–1	Deeley
			24.11.59	(Yugoslavia)	H	W	3–0	Murray, Mason 2
		QF	10.2.60	Barcelona (Spain)	A	L	0–4	
			2.3.60		H	L	2–5	Murray, Mason
1960–61	Cup-Winners' Cup	Pr		bye				

Season	Competition	Round	Date	Opponents (Country)	Venue	Result	Scorers
WOLVERHAMPTON WANDERERS continued							
		QF	12.10.60	FK Austria (Austria)	A	L 0–2	
			30.11.60		H	W 5–0	Kirkham 2, Mason, Broadbent 2
		SF	29.3.61	Rangers (Scotland)	A	L 0–2	
			19.4.61		H	D 1–1	Broadbent
1971–72	UEFA Cup	1	15.9.71	Academica Coimbra	H	W 3–0	McAlle, Richards, Dougan
			29.9.71	(Portugal)	A	W 4–1	Dougan 3, McAlle
		2	20.10.71	Den Haag (Holland)	A	W 3–1	Dougan, McCalliog, Hibbitt
			3.11.71		H	W 4–0	Dougan, own goals 3
		3	24.11.71	Carl Zeiss Jena	A	W 1–0	Richards
			8.12.71	(East Germany)	H	W 3–0	Hibbitt, Dougan 2
		QF	7.3.72	Juventus (Italy)	A	D 1–1	McCalliog
			21.3.72		H	W 2–1	Hegan, Dougan
		SF	5.4.72	Ferencvaros (Hungary)	A	D 2–2	Richards, Munro
			19.4.72		H	W 2–1	Bailey, Munro
		F	3.5.72	Tottenham Hotspur	H	L 1–2	McCalliog
			17.5.72	(England)	A	D 1–1	Wagstaffe
1973–74	UEFA Cup	1	26.9.73	Belenenses (Portugal)	A	W 2–0	Richards, Dougan
			3.10.73		H	W 2–1	Eastoe, McCalliog
		2	24.10.73	Lokomotive Leipzig	A	L 0–3	
			7.11.73	(East Germany)	H	W 4–1	Kindon, Munro, Dougan. Hibbitt
1974–75	UEFA Cup	1	18.9.74	Porto (Portugal)	A	L 1–4	Bailey
			2.10.74		H	W 3–1	Bailey, Daley, Dougan
WREXHAM							
1972–73	Cup-Winners' Cup	1	13.9.72	Zurich (Switzerland)	A	D 1–1	Kinsey
			27.9.72		H	W 2–1	Ashcroft, Sutton
		2	25.10.72	Hajduk Split	H	W 3–1	Tinnion, Smallman, own goal
			8.11.72	(Yugoslavia) *	A	L 0–2	
1975–76	Cup-Winners' Cup	1	17.9.75	Djurgaarden (Sweden)	H	W 2–1	Griffiths, Davis
			1.10.75		A	D 1–1	Whittle
		2	22.10.75	Stal Rzeszow (Poland)	H	W 2–0	Ashcroft 2
			5.11.75		A	D 1–1	Sutton
		QF	3.3.76	Anderlecht (Belgium)	A	L 0–1	
			17.3.76		H	D 1–1	Lee
1978–79	Cup-Winners' Cup	1	13.9.78	Rijeka (Yugoslavia)	A	L 0–3	
			27.9.78		H	W 2–0	McNeil, Cartwright
1979–80	Cup-Winners' Cup	1	19.9.79	Magdeburg (East	H	W 3–2	McNeil, Fox, Buxton
			3.10.79	Germany)	A	L 2–5	Vinter, Hill

*won on away goals counting double
†won on penalties
‡won on the toss of a coin

SCOTTISH LEAGUE CLUBS

Season	Competition	Round	Date	Opponents (Country)	Venue	Result	Scorers
ABERDEEN							
1967–68	Cup-Winners'	1	6.9.67	KR Reykjavik (Iceland)	H	W 10–1	Munro 3, Storrie 2, Smith 2, McMillan, Petersen, Taylor
			13.9.67		A	W 4–1	Storrie 2, Buchan, Munro
		2	29.11.67	Standard Liege (Belgium)	A	L 0–3	
			6.12.67		H	W 2–0	Munro, Melrose
1970–71	Cup-Winners' Cup	1	16.9.70	Honved (Hungary) †	H	W 3–1	Graham, Harper, Murray (S)
			30.9.70		A	L 1–3	Murray (S)
1978–79	Cup-Winners'	1	13.9.78	Marek Stanke (Bulgaria)	A	L 2–3	Jarvie, Harper
			27.9.78		H	W 3–0	Strachan, Jarvie, Harper

Season	Competition	Round	Date	Opponents (Country)	Venue	Result		Scorers

ABERDEEN continued

Season	Competition	Round	Date	Opponents (Country)	Venue	Result		Scorers
		2	18.10.78	Fortuna Dusseldorf	A	L	0–3	
			1.11.78	(West Germany)	H	W	2–0	McLelland, Jarvie
1968–69	Fairs Cup	1	17.9.68	Slavia Sofia (Bulgaria)	A	D	0–0	
			2.10.68		H	W	2–0	Robb, Taylor
		2	23.10.68	Real Zaragoza (Spain)	H	W	2–1	Forrest, Smith
			30.10.68		A	L	0–3	
1971–72	UEFA Cup	1	15.9.71	Celta Vigo (Spain)	A	W	2–0	Harper, own goal
			29.9.71		H	W	1–0	Harper
		2	27.10.71	Juventus (Italy)	A	L	0–2	
			17.11.71		H	D	1–1	Harper
1972–73	UEFA Cup	1	13.9.72	Borussia Moenchenglad-	H	L	2–3	Harper, Jarvie
			27.9.72	bach (West Germany)	A	L	3–6	Harper 2, Jarvie
1973–74	UEFA Cup	1	19.9.73	Finn Harps (Eire)	H	W	4–1	Miller (R), Jarvie 2, Graham
			3.10.73		A	W	3–1	Robb, Graham, Miller (R)
		2	24.10.73	Tottenham Hotspur	H	D	1–1	Hermiston (pen)
			7.11.73	(England)	A	L	1–4	Jarvie
1977-78	UEFA Cup	1	14.9.77	RWD Molenbeek	A	D	0–0	
			28.9.77	(Belgium)	H	L	1–2	Jarvie
1979–80	UEFA Cup	1	19.9.79	Eintracht Frankfurt (West	H	D	1–1	Harper
			3.10.79	Germany)	A	L	0–1	

CELTIC

Season	Competition	Round	Date	Opponents (Country)	Venue	Result		Scorers
1966-67	European Cup	1	28.9.66	Zurich (Switzerland)	H	W	2–0	Gemmell, McBride
			5.10.66		A	W	3–0	Gemmell 2 (1 pen), Chalmers
		2	30.11.66	Nantes (France)	A	W	3–1	McBride, Lennox, Chalmers
			7.12.66		H	W	3–1	Johnstone, Lennox, Chalmers
		QF	1.3.66	Vojvodina (Yugoslavia)	A	L	0–1	
			8.3.66		H	W	2–0	Chalmers, McNeill
		SF	12.4.67	Dukla Prague	H	W	3–1	Johnstone, Wallace 2
			25.4.67	(Czechoslovakia)	A	D	0–0	
		F	25.5.67	Inter-Milan (Italy)	N	W	2–1	Gemmell, Chalmers
1967–68	European Cup	1	20.9.67	Dynamo Kiev (USSR)	H	L	1–2	Lennox
			4.10.67		A	D	1–1	Lennox
1968–69	European Cup	1	18.8.68	St Etienne (France)	A	L	0–2	
			2.10.68		H	W	4–0	Gemmell(pen), Craig, Chalmers McBride
		2	13.11.68	Red Star Belgrade (Yugoslavia)	H	W	5–1	Murdoch, Johnstone 2, Lennox, Wallace
			27.11.68		A	D	1–1	Wallace
		QF	19.2.69	AC Milan (Italy)	A	D	0–0	
			12.3.69		H	L	0–1	
1969–70	European Cup	1	17.9.69	Basle (Switzerland)	A	D	0–0	
			1.10.69		H	W	2–0	Hood, Gemmell
		2	12.11.69	Benfica (Portugal)	H	W	3–0	Gemmell, Wallace, Hood
			26.11.69		A	L	0–3‡	
		QF	4.3.70	Fiorentina (Italy)	H	W	3–0	Auld, Wallace, own goal
			18.3.70		A	L	0–1	
		SF	1.4.70	Leeds United (England)	A	W	1–0	Connolly
			15.4.70		H	W	2–1	Hughes, Murdoch
		F	6.5.70	Feyenoord (Holland)	N	L	1–2	Gemmell
1970–71	European Cup	1	16.9.70	KPV Kokkola (Finland)	H	W	9–0	Hood 3, Wilson 2, Hughes, McNeill, Johnstone, Davidson
			30.9.70		A	W	5–0	Wallace 2, Callaghan, Davidson, Lennox
		2	21.10.70	Waterford (Eire)	A	W	7–0	Wallace 3, Murdoch 2, Marari 2
			4.11.70		H	W	3–2	Hughes, Johnstone 2
		QF	10.3.70	Ajax (Holland)	A	L	0–3	
			24.3.71		H	W	1–0	Johnstone
1971–72	European Cup	1	15.9.71	BK 1903 Copenhagen	A	L	1-2	Macari
			29.9.71	(Denmark)	H	W	3–0	Wallace 2, Callaghan
		2	20.10.71	Sliema Wanderers (Malta)	H	W	5–0	Gemmell, Macari 2, Hood, Brogan
			3.11.71		A	W	2–1	Hood, Lennox
		QF	8.3.72	Ujpest Dozsa (Hungary)	A	W	2–1	Macari, own goal
			22.3.72		H	D	1–1	Macari

Season	Competition	Round	Date	Opponents (Country)	Venue	Result		Scorers

CELTIC continued

Season	Competition	Round	Date	Opponents (Country)	Venue	Result		Scorers
		SF	5.4.72	Inter-Milan (Italy) †	A	D	0–0	
			19.4.72		H	D	0–0	
1972–73	European Cup	1	13.9.72	Rosenborg (Norway)	H	W	2–1	Macari, Deans
			27.9.72		A	W	3–1	Macari, Hood, Dalglish
		2	25.10.72	Ujpest Dozsa (Hungary)	H	W	2–1	Dalglish 2
			8.11.72		A	L	0–3	
1973–74	European Cup	1	19.9.73	Turun (Finland)	A	W	6–1	Callaghan 2, Hood, Johnstone, Connelly (pen), Deans
			3.10.73		H	W	3–0	Deans, Johnstone 2
		2	24.10.73	Vejle (Denmark)	H	D	0–0	
			6.11.73		A	W	1–0	Lennox
		QF	27.2.74	Basle (Switzerland)	A	L	2–3	Wilson, Dalglish
			20.3.74		H	W	4–2	Dalglish, Deans, Callaghan, Murray
		SF	10.4.74	Atletico Madrid (Spain)	H	D	0–0	
			24.4.74		A	L	0–2	
1974–75	European Cup	1	18.9.74	Olympiakos Piraeus (Greece)	H	D	1–1	Wilson
			2.10.74		A	L	0–2	
1977–78	European Cup	1	14.9.77	Jeunesse D'Esch (Luxembourg)	H	W	5–0	McDonald, Wilson, Craig 2, McLaughlin
			28.9.77		A	W	6–1	Lennox 2, Edvaldsson 2, Glavin, Craig
		2	19.10.77	SW Innsbruck (Austria)	H	W	2–1	Craig, Burns
			2.11.77		A	L	0–3	
1979–80	European Cup	1	19.9.79	Partizan Tirana (Albania)	A	L	0–1	
			3.10.79		H	W	4–1	McDonald, Aitken 2, Davidson
		2	24.10.79	Dundalk (Eire)	H	W	3–2	McDonald, McCluskey, Burns
			7.11.79		A	D	0–0	
		QF	5.3.80	Real Madrid (Spain)	H	W	2–0	McCluskey, Doyle
			19.3.80		A	L	0–3	
1963–64	Cup-Winners' Cup	1	17.9.63	Basle (Switzerland)	A	W	5–1	Divers, Hughes 3, Lennox
			9.10.63		H	W	5–0	Johnstone, Divers 2, Murdoch, Chalmers
		2	4.12.63	Dynamo Zagreb (Yugoslavia)	H	W	3–0	Chalmers 2, Hughes
			11.12.63		A	L	1–2	Murdoch
		QF	26.2.64	Slovan Bratislava (Czechoslovakia)	H	W	1–0	Murdoch (pen)
			4.3.64		A	W	1–0	Hughes
		SF	15.4.64	MTK Budapest (Hungary)	H	W	3–0	Johnstone, Chalmers 2
			29.4.64		A	L	0–4	
1965–66	Cup-Winners' Cup	1	29.9.65	Go Ahead Deventer (Holland)	A	W	6–0	Gallagher 2, Hughes, Johnston 2, Lennox
			7.10.65		H	W	1–0	McBride
		2	3.11.65	Aarhus (Denmark)	A	W	1–0	McBride
			17.11.65		H	W	2–0	McNeill, Johnstone
		QF	12.1.66	Dynamo Kiev (USSR)	H	W	3–0	Gemmell, Murdoch 2
			26.1.66		A	D	1–1	Gemmell
		SF	14.4.66	Liverpool (England)	H	W	1–0	Lennox
			19.4.66		A	L	0–2	
1975–76	Cup-Winners' Cup	1	16.9.75	Valur Reykjavik (Iceland)	A	W	2–0	Wilson, McDonald
			1.10.75		H	W	7–0	Edvaldsson, Dalglish, McCluskey (P) (pen), Hood 2, Deans, Callaghan
		2	22.10.75	Boavista (Portugal)	A	D	0–0	
			5.11.75		H	W	3–1	Dalglish, Edvaldsson, Deans
		QF	3.3.76	Sachsenring Zwickau (West Germany)	H	D	1–1	Dalglish
			17.3.76		A	L	0–1	
1962–63	Fairs Cup	1	26.9.62	Valencia (Spain)	A	L	2–4	Carrol 2
			24.10.62		H	D	2–2	Crerand, own goal
1964–65	Fairs Cup	1	23.9.64	Leixoes (Portugal)	A	D	1–1	Murdoch
			7.10.64		H	W	3–0	Murdoch (pen) Chalmers 2
		2	18.11.64	Barcelona (Spain)	A	L	1–3	Hughes
			2.12.64		H	D	0–0	
1976–77	UEFA Cup	1	15.9.76	Wisla Krakow (Poland)	H	D	2–2	McDonald, Dalglish
			29.9.76		A	L	0–2	

Season	Competition	Round	Date	Opponents (Country)	Venue	Result		Scorers

DUNDEE

Season	Competition	Round	Date	Opponents (Country)	Venue	Result		Scorers
1962–63	European Cup	Pr	5.9.62	IFC Cologne (West Germany)	H	W	8–1	Gilzean 3, own goal, Wishart, Robertson, Smith, Penman
			26.9.62		A	L	0–4	
		1	24.10.62	Sporting Lisbon	A	L	0–1	
			31.10.62	(Portugal)	H	W	4–1	Gilzean 3, Cousin
		QF	6.3.63	Anderlecht (Belgium)	A	W	4–1	Gilzean 2, Cousin, Smith
			13.3.63		H	W	2–1	Cousin, Smith
		SF	24.4.63	AC Milan (Italy)	A	L	1–5	Cousin
			1.5.63		H	W	1–0	Gilzean
1964–65	Cup-Winners' Cup	1		bye				
		2	18.11.64	Real Zaragoza (Spain)	H	D	2–2	Murray, Houston
			8.12.64		A	L	1–2	Robertson
1967–68	Fairs Cup	1	27.9.67	DWS Amsterdam	A	L	1–2	McLean (G)
			4.10.67	(Holland)	H	W	3–0	Wilson (S), McLean 2 (1 pen)
		2	1.11.67	Liege (Belgium)	H	W	3–1	Stuart 2, Wilson (S)
			14.11.67		A	W	4–1	McLean (G) 4
		3		bye				
		QF	27.3.68	Zurich (Switzerland)	H	W	1–0	Easton
			3.4.68		A	W	1–0	Wilson (S)
		SF	1.5.68	Leeds United (England)	H	D	1–1	Wilson (R)
			15.5.68		A	L	0–2	
1971–72	UEFA Cup	1	15.9.71	Akademisk Copenhagen	H	W	4–2	Bryce 2, Wallace, Lambie
			29.9.71	(Denmark)	A	W	1–0	Duncan
		2	19.10.71	IFC Cologne (West	A	L	1–2	Kinninmouth
			3.11.71	Germany)	H	W	4–2	Duncan 3, Wilson (R)
		3	24.11.71	AC Milan (Italy)	A	L	0–3	
			8.12.71		H	W	2–0	Wallace, Duncan
1973–74	UEFA Cup	1	19.9.73	Twente Enschede	H	L	1–3	Stewart
			3.10.73	(Holland)	A	L	2–4	Johnston, Scott (J)
1974–75	UEFA Cup	1	18.9.74	RWD Molenbeek	A	L	0–1	
			2.10.74	(Belgium)	H	L	2–4	Duncan, Scott (J)

DUNDEE UNITED

Season	Competition	Round	Date	Opponents (Country)	Venue	Result		Scorers
1974–75	Cup-Winners' Cup	1	18.9.74	Juil Petrosani (Rumania)	H	W	3–0	Narey, Copland, Gardner
			2.10.74		A	L	0–2	
		2	23.10.74	Bursaspor (Turkey)	H	D	0–0	
			6.10.74		A	L	0–1	
1966–67	Fairs Cup	1		bye				
		2		Barcelona (Spain)	A	W	2–1	Hainey, Seeman
			16.11.66		H	W	2–0	Mitchell, Hainey
		3	8.2.67	Juventus (Italy)	A	L	0–3	
			8.3.67		H	W	1–0	Dossing
1969–70	Fairs Cup	1	15.9.69	Newcastle United	H	L	1–2	Scott
			1.10.69	(England)	A	L	0–1	
1970–71	Fairs Cup	1	15.9.70	Grasshoppers	H	W	3–2	Reid (I), Markland, Reid (A)
			30.9.70	(Switzerland)	A	D	0–0	
		2	21.10.70	Sparta Prague	A	L	1–3	Traynor
			4.11.70	(Czechoslovakia)	H	W	1–0	Gordon
1975–76	UEFA Cup	1	23.9.75	Keflavik (Iceland)	A	W	2–0	Narey 2
			30.9.75		H	W	4–0	Hall 2, Hegarty (pen), Sturrock
		2	22.10.75	Porto (Portugal)	H	L	1–2	Rennie
			5.11.75		A	D	1–1	Hegarty
1977–78	UEFA Cup	1	14.9.77	KB Copenhagen	H	W	1–0	Sturrock
			27.9.77	(Denmark)	A	L	0–3	
1978–79	UEFA Cup	1	12.9.78	Standard Liege	A	L	0–1	
			27.9.78	(Belgium)	H	D	0–0	
1979–80	UEFA Cup	1	19.9.79	Anderlecht (Belgium)	H	D	0–0	
			2.10.79		A	D	1–1*	Kopel
		2	24.10.79	Diosgyor (Hungary)	H	L	0–1	
			7.11.79		A	L	1–3	Kopel

DUNFERMLINE ATHLETIC

Season	Competition	Round	Date	Opponents (Country)	Venue	Result		Scorers
1961–62	Cup-Winners' Cup	1	12.9.61	St Patrick's Athletic (Eire)	H	W	4–1	Melrose, Peebles, Dickson, Macdonald
			27.9.61		A	W	4–0	Peebles 2, Dickson 2

Season	Competition	Round	Date	Opponents (Country)	Venue	Result	Scorers

DUNFERMLINE ATHLETIC continued

Season	Competition	Round	Date	Opponents (Country)	Venue	Result	Scorers
		2	25.10.61	Vardar Skoplje (Yugoslavia)	H	W 5–0	Smith, Dickson 2, Melrose, Peebles
			8.11.61		A	L 0–2	
		QF	13.2.62	Ujpest Dozsa (Hungary)	A	L 3–4	Smith, Macdonald 2
			20.2.62		H	L 0–1	
1967–68	Cup-Winners' Cup	1	18.9.68	Apoel (Cyprus)	H	W 10–1	Robertson 2, Renton 2, Barry, Callaghan (W) 2, Gardner, Edwards, Callaghan (T)
			2.10.68		A	W 2–0	Gardner, Callaghan (W)
		2	13.11.68	Olympiakos Pireaeus	H	W 4–0	Edwards 2, Fraser, Mitchell
			27.11.68	(Greece)	A	L 0–3	
		QF	15.1.69	West Bromwich Albion	H	D 0–0	
			19.2.69	(England)	A	W 1–0	Gardner
		SF	9.4.69	Slovan Bratislava	H	D 1–1	Fraser
			23.4.69	(Czechoslovakia)	A	L 0–1	
1962–63	Fairs Cup	1	24.10.62	Everton (England)	A	L 0–1	
			31.10.62		H	W 2–0	Miller, Melrose
		2	12.12.62	Valencia (Spain)	A	L 0–4	
			19.12.62		H	W 6–2	Melrose, Sinclair 2, McLean, Peebles, Smith
			6.2.63		N	L 0–1	
1964–65	Fairs Cup	1	13.10.64	Oergryte (Sweden)	H	W 4–2	McLaughlin 2, Sinclair 2
			20.10.64		A	D 0–0	
		2	17.11.64	Stuttgart (West Germany)	H	W 1–0	Callaghan (T)
			1.12.64		A	D 0–0	
		3	27.1.65	Atletico Bilbao (Spain)	A	L 0–1	
			3.3.65		H	W 1–0	Smith
			16.3.65		A	L 1–2	Smith
1965–66	Fairs Cup	1		bye			
		2	3.11.65	KB Copenhagen (Denmark)	H	W 5–0	Fleming, Paton 2, Robertson, Callaghan (T)
			17.11.65		A	W 4–2	Edwards, Paton, Fleming, Ferguson
		3	26.1.66	Spartak Brno	H	W 2–0	Paton, Ferguson (pen)
			16.2.66	(Czechoslovakia)	A	D 0–0	
		QF	16.3.66	Real Zaragoza (Spain)	H	W 1–0	Paton
			20.3.66		A	L 2–4	Ferguson 2
1966–67	Fairs Cup	1	24.8.66	Frigg Oslo (Norway)	A	W 3–1	Fleming 2, Callaghan (T)
			28.9.66		H	W 3–1	Delaney 2, Callaghan (T)
		2	26.10.66	Dynamo Zagreb *	H	W 4–2	Delaney, Edwards, Ferguson 2
			11.11.66		A	L 0–2	
1969–70	Fairs Cup	1	16.9.69	Bordeaux (France)	H	W 4–0	Paton 2, Mitchell, Gardner
			30.9.69		A	L 0–2	
		2	5.11.69	Gwardia Warsaw	A	W 2–1	McLean, Gardner
			18.11.69	(Poland)	A	W 1–0	Renton
		3	17.12.69	Anderlecht (Belgium) *	A	L 0–1	
			14.1.70		H	W 3–2	McLean 2, Mitchell

HEARTS

Season	Competition	Round	Date	Opponents (Country)	Venue	Result	Scorers
1958–59	European Cup	Pr	3.9.58	Standard Liege	A	L 1–5	Crawford
			9.9.58	(Belgium)	H	W 2–1	Bauld 2
1960–61	European Cup	Pr	29.9.60	Benfica (Portugal)	H	L 1–2	Young
			5.10.60		A	L 0–3	
1976–77	Cup-Winners' Cup	1	15.9.76	Lokomotive Leipzig	A	L 0–2	
			29.9.76	(East Germany)	H	W 5–1	Kay, Gibson 2, Brown, Busby
		2	20.10.76	SV Hamburg (West	A	L 2–4	Park, Busby
			3.11.76	Germany)	H	L 1–4	Gibson
1961–62	Fairs Cup	1	27.9.61	Union St Gilloise	A	W 3–1	Blackwood, Davidson 2
			4.10.61	(Belgium)	H	W 2–0	Wallace, Stenhouse
		2	6.11.61	Inter-Milan (Italy)	H	L 0–1	
			22.11.61		A	L 0–4	
1963–64	Fairs Cup	1	25.9.63	Lausanne (Switzerland)	A	D 2–2	Traynor, Ferguson
			9.10.63		H	D 2–2	Cumming, Hamilton (J)
			15.10.63		A	L 2–3	Wallace, Ferguson
1965–66	Fairs Cup	1		bye			

Season	Competition	Round	Date	Opponents (Country)	Venue	Result		Scorers

HEARTS continued

Season	Competition	Round	Date	Opponents (Country)	Venue	Result		Scorers
		2	18.10.65	Valerengen (Norway)	H	W	1–0	Wallace
			27.10.65		A	W	3–1	Kerrigan 2, Trayner
		3	12.1.66	Real Zaragoza (Spain)	H	D	3–3	Anderson, Wallace, Kerrigan
			26.1.66		A	D	2–2	Anderson, Wallace
			2.3.66		A	L	0–1	

HIBERNIAN

Season	Competition	Round	Date	Opponents (Country)	Venue	Result		Scorers
1955–56	European Cup	1	14.9.55	Rot-Weiss Essen	A	W	4–0	Turnbull 2, Reilly, Ormond
			12.10.55	(West Germany)	H	D	1–1	Buchanan (J)
		QF	23.11.55	Djurgaarden (Sweden)	H	W	3–1	Combe, Mulkerrin, own goal
			28.11.55		A	W	1–0	Turnbull (pen)
		SF	4.4.56	Reims (France) *	A	L	0–2	
			18.4.56		H	L	0–1	
1972–73	Cup-Winners' Cup	1	13.9.72	Sporting Lisbon	A	L	1–2	Duncan
			27.9.72	(Portugal)	H	W	6–1	Gordon 2, O'Rourke 3, own goal
		2	25.10.72	Besa (Albania)	H	W	7–1	Cropley, O'Rourke 3, Duncan 2, Brownlie
			8.11.72		A	D	1–1	Gordon
		QF	7.3.73	Hajduk Split (Yugoslavia)	H	W	4–2	Gordon 3, Duncan
			21.3.73		A	L	0–3	
1960–61	Fairs Cup	1		Lausanne (Switzerland) Lausanne withdrew				
		QF	27.12.60	Barcelona (Spain)	A	D	4–4	McLeod, Preston, Baker 2
			22.2.61		H	W	3–2	Kinloch 2 (1 pen), Baker
		SF	19.4.61	AS Roma (Italy)	H	D	2–2	Baker, McLeod
			26.4.61		A	D	3–3	Baker 2, Kinloch
			27.5.61		A	L	0–6	
1961–62	Fairs Cup	1	4.9.61	Belenenses (Portugal)	H	D	3–3	Fraser 2, Baird (pen)
			27.9.61		A	W	3–1	Baxter 2, Stevenson
		2	1.11.61	Red Star Belgrade	A	L	0–4	
			15.11.61	(Yugoslavia)	H	L	0–1	
1962–63	Fairs Cup	1	3.10.62	Stavenet (Denmark)	H	W	4–0	Byrne 2, Baker, own goal
			23.10.62		A	W	3–2	Stevenson 2, Bryne
		2	27.11.62	DOS Utrecht (Holland)	A	W	1–0	Falconer
			12.12.62		H	W	2–1	Baker, Stevenson
		QF	13.3.63	Valencia (Spain)	A	L	0–5	
			3.4.63		H	W	2–1	Preston, Baker
1965–66	Fairs Cup	1	8.9.65	Valencia (Spain)	H	W	2–0	Scott, McNamme
			12.10.65		A	L	0–2	
			3.11.65		A	L	0–3	
1967–68	Fairs Cup	1	20.9.67	Porto (Portugal)	H	W	3–0	Cormack 2, Stevenson
			4.10.67		A	L	1–3	Stanton (pen)
		2	22.11.67	Napoli (Italy)	A	L	1–4	Stein
			29.11.67		H	W	5–0	Duncan, Quinn, Cormack, Stanton, Stein
		3	20.12.67	Leeds United (England)	A	L	0–1	
			10.1.68		H	D	1–1	Stein
1968–69	Fairs Cup	1	18.9.68	Ljubljana (Yugoslavia)	A	W	3–0	Stevenson, Stein, Marinello
			2.10.68		H	W	2–1	Davis (2 pen)
		2	13.11.68	Lokomotive Leipzig	H	W	3–1	McBride 3
			20.11.68	(East Germany)	A	W	1–0	Grant
		3	18.12.68	SV Hamburg (West	A	L	0–1	
			15.1.69	Germany) *	H	W	2–1	McBride 2
1970–71	Fairs Cup	1	16.9.70	Malmo (Sweden)	H	W	6–0	McBride 3, Duncan 2, Blair
			30.9.70		A	W	3–2	Duncan, McEwan, Stanton
		2	14.10.70	Vitoria Guimaraes	H	W	2–0	Duncan, Stanton
			28.10.70	(Portugal)	A	L	1–2	Graham
		3	9.12.70	Liverpool (England)	H	L	0–1	
			22.12.70		A	L	0–2	
1973–74	UEFA Cup	1	19.9.73	Keflavik (Iceland)	H	W	2–0	Black, Higgins
			3.10.73		A	D	1–1	Stanton
		2	24.10.73	Leeds United (England) †	A	D	0–0	
			2.10.74		H	D	0–0	

Season	Competition	Round	Date	Opponents (Country)	Venue	Result		Scorers

HIBERNIAN continued

Season	Competition	Round	Date	Opponents (Country)	Venue	Result		Scorers
1974–75	UEFA Cup	1	18.9.74	Rosenborg (Norway)	A	W	3–2	Stanton, Gordon, Cropley
			2.10.74		H	W	9–1	Harper 2, Munro 2, Stanton 2, Cropley 2 (pens), Gordon
		2	23.10.74	Juventus (Italy)	H	L	2–4	Stanton, Cropley
			6.11.74		A	L	0–4	
1975–76	UEFA Cup	1	17.9.75	Liverpool (England)	H	W	1–0	Harper
			30.9.75		A	L	1–3	Edwards
1976–77	UEFA Cup	1	15.9.76	Sochaux (France)	H	W	1–0	Brownlie
			29.9.76		A	D	0–0	
		2	20.10.76	Oesters Vaxjo (Sweden)	H	W	2–0	Blackley, Brownlie (pen)
			3.11.76		A	L	1–4	Smith
1978–79	UEFA Cup	1	13.9.78	Norrkoping (Sweden)	H	W	3–2	Higgins 2, Temperley
			27.9.78		A	D	0–0	
		2	18.10.78	Strasbourg (France)	A	L	0–2	
			1.11.78		H	W	1–0	McLeod (pen)

KILMARNOCK

Season	Competition	Round	Date	Opponents (Country)	Venue	Result		Scorers
1965–66	European Cup	Pr	8.9.65	Nendori Tirana (Albania)	A	D	0–0	
			29.6.65		H	W	1–0	Black
		1	17.11.65	Real Madrid (Spain)	H	D	2–2	McLean (pen), McInally
			1.12.65		A	L	1–5	McIlroy
1964–65	Fairs Cup	1	2.9.64	Eintracht Frankfurt	A	L	0–3	
			22.9.64	(West Germany)	H	W	5–1	Hamilton, McIlroy, McFadzean McInally, Sneddon
		2	11.11.64	Everton (England)	H	L	0–2	
			23.11.64		A	L	1–4	McIlroy
1966–67	Fairs Cup	1		bye				
		2	25.10.66	Antwerp (Belgium)	A	W	1–0	McInally
			2.11.66		H	W	7–2	McInally 2, Queen 2, McLean 2 Watson
		3	14.12.66	La Gantoise (Belgium)	H	W	1–0	Murray
			21.12.66		A	W	2–1	McInally, McLean
		QF	19.4.67	Lokomotive Leipzig	A	L	0–1	
			26.4.67	(East Germany)	H	W	2–0	McFadzean, McIlroy
		SF	19.5.67	Leeds United (England)	A	L	2–4	McIlroy 2
			24.5.67		H	D	0–0	
1969–70	Fairs Cup	1	16.9.69	Zurich (Switzerland)	A	L	2–3	McLean (J), Mathie
			30.9.69		H	W	3–1	McGrory, Morrison, McLean(T)
		2	19.11.69	Slavia Sofia (Bulgaria)	H	W	4–1	Mathie 2, Cook, Gilmour
			26.11.69		A	L	0–2	
		3	17.12.69	Dynamo Bacau	H	D	1–1	Mathie
			13.1.70	(Yugoslavia)	A	L	0–2	
1970–71	Fairs Cup	1	15.9.70	Coleraine (Northern	A	D	1–1	Mathie
			29.9.70	Ireland)	H	L	2–3	McLean (T), Morrison

MORTON

Season	Competition	Round	Date	Opponents (Country)	Venue	Result		Scorers
1968–69	Fairs Cup	1	18.9.68	Chelsea (England)	A	L	0–5	
			30.9.68		H	L	3–4	Thorop, Mason, Taylor

PARTICK THISTLE

Season	Competition	Round	Date	Opponents (Country)	Venue	Result		Scorers
1963–64	Fairs Cup	1	16.9.63	Glentoran (Northern	A	W	4–1	Hainey, Yard 2, Wright
			30.9.63	Ireland)	H	W	3–0	Smith 2, Harvey (pen)
		2	18.11.63	Spartak Brno	H	W	3–2	Yard, Harvey (pen), Ferguson
			27.11.63	(Czechoslovakia)	A	L	0–4	
1972–73	UEFA Cup	1	13.9.72	Honved (Hungary)	A	L	0–1	
			27.9.72		H	L	0–3	

RANGERS

Season	Competition	Round	Date	Opponents (Country)	Venue	Result		Scorers
1956–57	European Cup	Pr		bye				
		1	24.10.56	Nice (France)	H	W	2–1	Murray, Simpson
			14.11.56		A	L	1–2	Hubbard (pen)
			28.11.56		N	L	1–3	own goal

Season	Competition	Round	Date	Opponents (Country)	Venue	Result		Scorers

RANGERS continued

Season	Competition	Round	Date	Opponents (Country)	Venue	Result		Scorers
1957–58	European Cup	Pr	4.9.57	St Etienne (France)	H	W	3–1	Kichenbrand, Scott, Simpson
			25.9.57		A	L	1–2	Wilson
		1	27.11.57	AC Milan (Italy)	H	L	1–4	Murray
			11.12.57		A	L	0–2	
1959–60	European Cup	Pr	16.9.59	Anderlecht (Belgium)	H	W	5–2	Millar, Scott, Matthew, Baird 2
			24.9.59		A	W	2–0	Matthew, McMillan
		1	11.11.59	Red Star Belgrade	H	W	4–3	McMillan, Scott, Wilson, Millar
			18.11.59	(Czechoslovakia)	A	D	1–1	Scott
		QF	9.3.60	Sparta Rotterdam	A	W	3–2	Wilson, Baird, Murray
			16.3.60	(Holland)	H	L	0–1	
			30.3.60		N	W	3–2	Baird 2, own goal
		SF	13.4.60	Eintracht Frankfurt	A	L	1–6	Caldow (pen)
			5.5.60	(West Germany)	H	L	3–6	McMillan 2, Wilson
1961–62	European Cup	Pr	5.9.61	Monaco (France)	A	W	3–2	Baxter, Scott 2
			12.9.61		H	W	3–2	Christie 2, Scott
		1	15.11.61	Vorwaerts (East Germany)	A	W	2–1	Caldow (pen,) Brand
			23.11.61		H	W	4–1	McMillan 2, Henderson, own goal
		QF	7.2.62	Standard Liege (Belgium)	A	L	1–4	Wilson
			14.2.62		H	W	2–0	Brand, Caldow (pen)
1963–64	European Cup	Pr	25.9.63	Real Madrid (Spain)	H	L	0–1	
			9.10.63		A	L	0–6	
1964–65	European Cup	Pr	2.9.64	Red Star Belgrade	H	W	3–1	Brand 2, Forrest
			9.9.64	(Yugoslavia)	A	L	2–4	Grieg, McKinnon
			4.11.64		N	W	3–1	Forrest 2, Brand
		1	18.11.64	Rapid Vienna (Austria)	H	W	1–0	Wilson
			8.12.64		A	W	2–0	Forrest, Wilson
		QF	17.2.65	Inter-Milan (Italy)	A	L	1–3	Forest
			3.3.65		H	W	1–0	Forrest
1975–76	European Cup	1	17.9.75	Bohemians (Eire)	H	W	4–1	Fyfe, Johnstone, O'Hara, own goal
			1.10.75		A	D	1–1	Johnstone
		2	22.10.75	St Etienne (France)	H	L	0–2	
			5.11.75		A	L	1–2	MacDonald
1976–77	European Cup	1	15.9.76	Zurich (Switzerland)	H	D	1–1	Parlane
			29.9.76		A	L	0–1	
1978–79	European Cup	1	13.9.78	Juventus (Italy)	A	L	0–1	
			27.9.78		H	W	2–0	MacDonald, Smith
		2	18.10.78	PSV Eindhoven (Holland)	H	D	0–0	
			1 11.78		A	W	3–2	MacDonald, Johnstone, Russell
		QF	6.3.79	FC Cologne (West	A	L	0–1	
			22.3.79	Germany)	H	D	1–1	McLean
1960–61	Cup-Winners' Cup	Pr	28.9.60	Ferencvaros (Hungary)	H	W	4–2	Davis, Millar 2, Brand
			12.10.60		A	L	1–2	Wilson
		QF	15.11.60	Borussia Moenchenglad-	A	W	3–0	Millar, Scott, McMillan
			30.11.60	bach (West Germany)	H	W	8–0	Baxter, Brand 3, Millar 2, Davis, own goal
		SF	29.3.61	Wolverhampton	H	W	2–0	Scott, Brand
			19.4.61	Wanderers (England)	A	D	1–1	Scott
		F	17.5.61	Fiorentina (Italy)	H	L	0–2	
			27.5.61		A	L	1–2	Scott
1962–63	Cup-Winners' Cup	1	5.9.62	Seville (Spain)	H	W	4–0	Millar 3, Brand
			26.9.62		A	L	0–2	
		2	31.10.62	Tottenham Hotspur	A	L	2–5	Brand, Millar
			11.12.62	(England)	H	L	2–3	Brand, Wilson
1966–67	Cup-Winners' Cup	1	27.9.66	Glentoran (Northern	A	D	1–1	McLean
			5.10.66	Ireland)	H	W	4–0	Johnston, Smith (D), Setterington, McLean
		2	23.11.66	Borussia Dortmund	H	W	2–1	Johansen, Smith (A)
			6.12.66	(West Germany)	A	D	0–0	
		QF	1.3.67	Real Zaragoza (Spain) ‡	H	W	2–0	Smith, Willoughby
			22.3.67		A	L	0–2	
		SF	19.4.67	Slavia Sofia (Bulgaria)	A	W	1–0	Wilson
			3.5.67		H	W	1–0	Henderson
		F	31.5.67	Bayern Munich (West Germany)	N	L	0–1	

Season	Competition	Round	Date	Opponents (Country)	Venue	Result		Scorers

RANGERS continued

Season	Competition	Round	Date	Opponents (Country)	Venue	Result		Scorers
1969–70	Cup-Winners' Cup	1	17.9.69	Steaua Bucharest	H	W	2–0	Johnston 2
			1.10.69	(Rumania)	A	D	0–0	
		2	12.11.69	Gornik Zabrze (Poland)	A	L	1–3	Persson
			26.11.69		H	L	1–3	Baxter
1971–72	Cup-Winners' Cup	1	15.9.71	Rennes (France)	A	D	1–1	Johnston
			28.9.71		H	W	1–0	MacDonald
		2	20.10.71	Sporting Lisbon	H	W	3–2	Stein 2, Henderson
			3.11.71	(Portugal)	A	L	3–4*	Stein 2, Henderson
		QF	8.3.72	Torino (Italy)	A	D	1–1	Johnston
			22.3.72		H	W	1–0	MacDonald
		SF	5.4.72	Bayern Munich	A	D	1–1	own goal
			19.4.72	(West Germany)	H	W	2–0	Jardine, Parlane
		F	24.5.72	Dynamo Moscow (USSR)	N	W	3–2	Johnstone 2, Stein
1973–74	Cup-Winners' Cup	1	19.9.73	Ankaragucu (Turkey)	A	W	2–0	Conn, McLean
			3.10.73		H	W	4–0	Greig 2, O'Hara, Johnstone
		2	24.10.73	Borussia Moenchenglad-	A	L	0–3	
			7.11.73	bach (West Germany)	H	W	3–2	Conn, Jackson, MacDonald
1977–78	Cup-Winners' Cup	Pr	17.8.77	Young Boys (Switzerland)	H	W	1–0	Greig
			31.8.77		A	D	2–2	Johnstone, Smith
		1	14.9.77	Twente Enschede	H	D	0–0	
			28.9.77	(Holland)	A	L	0–3	
1979–80	Cup-Winners' Cup	Pr	21.8.79	Lillestrom (Norway)	H	W	1–0	Smith
			5.9.79		A	W	2–0	MacDonald (A), Johnstone
		1	19.9.79	Fortuna Dusseldorf (West	H	W	2–1	MacDonald (A), McLean
			3.10.79	Germany)	A	D	0–0	
		2	24.10.79	Valencia (Spain)	A	D	1–1	McLean
			7.11.79		H	L	1–3	Johnstone
1967–68	Fairs Cup	1	21.9.67	Dynamo Dresden	A	D	1–1	Ferguson
			4.10.67	(East Germany)	H	W	2–1	Penman, Greig
		2	8.11.67	IFC Cologne (West	H	W	3–0	Ferguson 2, Henderson
			28.11.67	Germany)	A	L	1–3	Henderson
		3		bye				
		QF	26.3.68	Leeds United (England)	H	D	0–0	
			9.4.68		A	L	0–2	
1968–69	Fairs Cup	1	18.9.68	Vojvodina (Yugoslavia)	H	W	2–0	Greig (pen), Jardine
			2.10.68		A	L	0–1	
		2	30.10.68	Dundalk (Eire)	H	W	6–1	Henderson 2, Ferguson 2, Greig, own goal
			13.11.68		A	W	3–0	Mathieson, Stein 2
		3	11.1.69	DWS Amsterdam	A	W	2–0	Johnston, Henderson
			22.1.69	(Holland)	H	W	2–1	Smith, Stein
		QF	19.3.69	Atletico Bilbao (Spain)	H	W	4–1	Ferguson, Penman, Persson, Stein
			2.4.69		A	L	0–2	
		SF	14.5.69	Newcastle United	H	D	0–0	
			22.5.69	(England)	A	L	0–2	
1970–71	Fairs Cup	1	16.9.70	Bayern Munich	A	L	0–1	
			30.9.70	(West Germany)	H	D	1–1	Stein
1972–73	Super Cup	F	16.1.73	Ajax (Holland)	H	L	1–3	MacDonald
			24.1.73		A	L	2–3	MacDonald, Young

At the end of the 1979–80 season Rangers had played more matches in Europe of any club in the British Isles. Including two matches in the Super Cup they had played 111 times. Liverpool had played 105 including four matches in the Super Cup.

ST JOHNSTONE

Season	Competition	Round	Date	Opponents (Country)	Venue	Result		Scorers
1971–72	UEFA Cup	1	15.9.71	SV Hamburg	A	L	1–2	Pearson
			29.9.71	(West Germany)	H	W	3–0	Hall, Pearson, Whitelaw
		2	20.10.71	Vasas Budapest (Hungary)	H	W	2–0	Connolly (pen), Pearson
			2.11.71		A	L	0–1	
		3	24.11.71	Zeljeznicar (Yugoslavia)	H	W	1–0	Connolly
			8.12.71		A	L	1–5	Rooney

IRISH LEAGUE CLUBS

Season	Competition	Round	Date	Opponents (Country)	Venue	Result		Scorers

ARDS

Season	Competition	Round	Date	Opponents (Country)	Venue	Result		Scorers
1958–59	European Cup	Pr	17.9.58	Reims (France)	H	L	1–4	Lowry
			8.10.58		A	L	2–6	Lawther, Quee
1969–70	Cup-Winners'	1	17.9.69	AS Roma (Italy)	H	D	0–0	
	Cup		1.10.69		A	L	1–3	Crothers
1974–75	Cup-Winners'	1	18.9.74	PSV Eindhoven (Holland)	A	L	0–10	
	Cup		2.10.74		H	L	1–4	Guy
1973–74	UEFA Cup	1	12.9.73	Standard Liege (Belgium)	H	W	3–2	Cathcart, McAvoy (pen), McAteer (pen)
			19.9.73		A	L	1–6	Guy

BALLYMENA UNITED

Season	Competition	Round	Date	Opponents (Country)	Venue	Result		Scorers
1978–79	Cup-Winners'	1	13.9.78	Beveren (Belgium)	A	L	0–3	
	Cup		27.9.78		H	L	0–3	

CARRICK RANGERS

Season	Competition	Round	Date	Opponents (Country)	Venue	Result		Scorers
1976–77	Cup-Winners'	1	15.9.76	Aris Bonnevoie	H	W	3–1	Prenter 2, Connor
	Cup		6.10.76	(Luxembourg)	A	L	1–2	Irwin
		2	20.10.76	Southampton (England)	H	L	2–5	Irwin, Prenter
			3.11.76		A	L	1–4	Reid

CLIFTONVILLE

Season	Competition	Round	Date	Opponents (Country)	Venue	Result		Scorers
1979–80	Cup-Winners'	1	20.9.79	Nantes (France)	H	L	0–1	
	Cup		3.10.79		A	L	0–7	

COLERAINE

Season	Competition	Round	Date	Opponents (Country)	Venue	Result		Scorers
1974–75	European Cup	1	18.11.74	Feyenoord (Holland)	A	L	0–7	
			2.10.74		H	L	1–4	Simpson
1965–66	Cup-Winners'	1	2.9.65	Dynamo Kiev (USSR)	H	L	1–6	Curley
	Cup		8.9.65		A	L	0–4	
1975–76	Cup-Winners'	1	16.9.75	Eintracht Frankfurt	A	L	1–5	Cochrane
	Cup		30.9.75	(West Germany)	H	L	2–6	McCurdy, Cochrane
1969–70	Fairs Cup	1	17.9.69	Jeunesse D'Esch	A	L	2–3	Hunter, Murray
			1.10.69	(Luxembourg)	H	W	4–0	Dickson 2, Wilson, Jennings
		2	11.11.69	Anderlecht (Belgium)	A	L	1–6	Murray
			20.11.69		H	L	3–7	Dickson 2, Irwin
1970–71	Fairs Cup	1	15.9.70	Kilmarnock (Scotland)	H	D	1–1	Mullan
			29.9.70		A	W	3–2	Dickson 3
		2	20.10.70	Sparta Rotterdam	A	L	0–2	
			4.11.70	(Holland)	H	L	1–2	Jennings
1977–78	Cup-Winners'	1	14.9.77	Lokomotive Leipzig	H	L	1–4	Tweed
	Cup			(East Germany)	A	D	2–2	Guy 2

CRUSADERS

Season	Competition	Round	Date	Opponents (Country)	Venue	Result		Scorers
1973–74	European Cup	1	19.9.73	Dynamo Bucharest	H	L	0–1	
			3.10.73	(Rumania)	A	L	0–11	
1976–77	European Cup	1	14.9.76	Liverpool (England)	A	L	0–2	
			28.9.76		H	L	0–5	
1967–68	Cup-Winners'	1	20.9.67	Valencia (Spain)	A	L	0–4	
	Cup		11.10.67		H	L	2–4	Trainor, Magill
1968–69	Cup-Winners'	1	18.9.68	Norrkoping (Sweden)	H	D	2–2	Jameson, Parke
	Cup		2.10.68		A	L	1–4	McPolin

DERRY CITY

Season	Competition	Round	Date	Opponents (Country)	Venue	Result		Scorers
1965–66	European Cup	Pr	31.8.65	Lyn Oslo (Norway)	A	L	3–5	Wood (R), Gilbert 2
			9.9.65		H	W	5–1	Wilson 2, Crossan, Wood (R), McGeough

Season	Competition	Round	Date	Opponents (Country)	Venue	Result		Scorers
DERRY CITY continued								
		1	23.11.65	Anderlecht (Belgium)	A	L	0–9	
				Derry City	withdrew			
1964–65	Cup-Winners'	1	9.9.64	Steaua Bucharest	A	L	0–3	
	Cup		16.9.64	(Rumania)	H	L	0–2	
DISTILLERY								
1963–64	European Cup	Pr	25.9.63	Benfica (Portugal)	H	D	3–3	John Kennedy, Hamilton, Ellison
			2.10.63		A	L	0–5	
1971–72	Cup-Winners'	1	15.9.71	Barcelona (Spain)	H	L	1–3	O'Neill
	Cup		29.9.71		A	L	0–4	
GLENAVON								
1957–58	European Cup	Pr	11.9.57	Aarhus (Denmark)	A	D	0–0	
			25.9.57		H	L	0–3	
1960–61	European Cup	Pr		withdrew				
1961–62	Cup-Winners'	1	13.9.61	Leicester City (England)	H	L	1–4	Jones
	Cup		27.9.61		A	L	1–3	Wilson
1977–78	UEFA Cup	1	14.9.77	PSV Eindhoven	H	L	2–6	Malone (pen), McDonald
			28.9.77	(Holland)	A	L	0–5	
1979–80	UEFA Cup	1	18.9.79	Standard Liege (Belgium)	H	L	0–1	
			3.10.79		A	L	0–1	
GLENTORAN								
1964–65	European Cup	Pr	16.9.64	Panathinaikos (Greece)	H	D	2–2	Turner, Thompson
			30.9.64		A	L	2–3	Turner, Pavis
1967–68	European Cup	1	13.9.67	Benfica (Portugal) *	H	D	1–1	Colrain (pen)
			4.10.67		A	D	0–0	
1968–69	European Cup	1	18.9.68	Anderlecht (Belgium)	A	L	0–3	
			2.10.68		H	D	2–2	Morrow, Johnston
1970–71	European Cup	1	16.9.70	Waterford (Eire)	H	L	1–3	Hall
			30.9.70		A	L	0–1	
1977–78	European Cup	1	15.9.77	Valur (Iceland)	A	L	0–1	
			29.9.77		H	W	2–0	Robson, Jamison
		2	19.10.77	Juventus (Italy)	H	L	0–1	
			2.11.77		A	L	0–5	
1966–67	Cup-Winners'	1	27.9.66	Rangers (Scotland)	H	D	1–1	Sinclair
	Cup		5.10.66		A	L	0–4	
1973–74	Cup-Winners'	1	19.9.73	Chimia Ramnicu	A	D	2–2	Jamison, McCreary
	Cup		3.10.73	(Rumania)	H	W	2–0	Hamison, Craig
		2	24.10.73	Brann Bergen (Norway)	A	D	1–1	Feeney
			7.11.73		H	W	3–1	Feeney, Jamison 2
		QF	5.3.74	Borussia Moenchenglad-	H	L	0–2	
			20.3.74	bach (West Germany)	A	L	0–5	
1962–63	Fairs Cup	1	26.9.62	Real Zaragoza (Spain)	H	L	0–2	
			10.10.62		A	L	2–6	Doherty 2
1963–64	Fairs Cup	1	16.9.63	Partick Thistle (Scotland)	H	L	1–4	Thompson
			30.9.63		A	L	0–3	
1965–66	Fairs Cup	1	28.9.65	Antwerp (Belgium)	A	L	0–1	
			6.10.65		H	D	3–3	Hamilton, Thompson 2
1969–70	Fairs Cup	1	9.9.69	Arsenal (England)	A	L	0–3	
			29.9.69		H	W	1–0	Henderson
1971–72	UEFA Cup	1	14.9.71	Eintracht Brunswick	H	L	0–1	
			28.9.71	(West Germany)	A	L	1–6	McCaffrey
1975–76	UEFA Cup	1	16.9.75	Ajax (Holland)	H	L	1–6	Jamison
			1.10.75		A	L	0–8	
1976–77	UEFA Cup	1	14.9.76	Basle (Switzerland)	H	W	3–2	Feeney 2, Dickenson
			29.9.76		A	L	0–3	
1978–79	UEFA Cup	1	5.9.78	IBV Westmann (Iceland)	A	D	0–0	
			14.9.78		H	D	1–1	Caskey (W)
LINFIELD								
1959–60	European Cup	Pr	9.9.59	Gothenburg (Sweden)	H	W	2–1	Milburn 2
			23.9.59		A	L	1–6	Dickson
1961–62	European Cup	Pr	30.8.61	Vorwaerts (East Germany)	A	L	0–3	
					withdrew			

Season	Competition	Round	Date	Opponents (Country)	Venue	Result		Scorers

LINFIELD continued

Season	Competition	Round	Date	Opponents (Country)	Venue	Result		Scorers
1962–63	European Cup	Pr	5.9.62	Esbjerg (Denmark)	H	L	1–2	Dickson
			19.9.62		A	A	0–0	
1966–67	European Cup	1	7.9.66	Aris Bonnevoie	A	D	3–3	Hamilton, Pavis, Scott
			16.9.66	(Luxembourg)	A	W	6–1	Thomas 3, Scott 2, Pavis
		2	26.10.66	Valerengen (Norway)	A	W	4–1	Scott, Pavis, Thomas, Shields
			8.11.66		H	D	1–1	Thomas
		QF	1.3.67	CSKA Sofia (Bulgaria)	H	D	2–2	Hamilton, Shields
			15.3.67		A	L	0–1	
1969–70	European Cup	1	17.9.69	Red Star Belgrade	A	L	0–8	
			1.10.69	(Yugoslavia)	H	L	2–4	McGraw 2
1971–72	European Cup	1	15.9.71	Standard Liege (Belgium)	A	L	0–2	
			29.9.71		H	L	2–3	Magee, Larmour
1975–76	European Cup	1	17.9.75	PSV Eindhoven (Holland)	H	L	1–2	Malone (P)
			1.10.75		A	L	0–8	
1978–79	European Cup	1	13.9.78	Lillestrom (Norway)	H	D	0–0	
			27.9.78		A	L	0–1	
1979–80	European Cup	Pr	29.8.79	Dundalk (Eire)	A	D	1–1	Feeney
			5.9.79	(in Haarlem, Holland)	H	L	0–2	
1963–64	Cup-Winners'	1		bye				
	Cup	2	13.11.63	Fenerbahce (Turkey)	A	L	1–4	Dickson
			11.12.63		H	W	2–0	Craig, Ferguson
1970–71	Cup-Winners'	1	16.9.70	Manchester City	A	L	0–1	
	Cup		30.9.70	(England) *	H	W	2–1	Millen 2
1967–68	Fairs Cup	1	19.9.67	Lolomotive Leipzig	A	L	1–5	Pavis
			4.10.67	(East Germany)	H	W	1–0	Hamilton
1968–69	Fairs Cup	1	18.9.68	Setubal (Portugal)	A	L	0–3	
			9.10.68		H	L	1–3	Scott

PORTADOWN

Season	Competition	Round	Date	Opponents (Country)	Venue	Result		Scorers
1962–63	Cup-Winners'	1		bye				
	Cup	2	7.11.62	OFK Belgrade	A	L	1–5	Clements
			22.11.62	(Yugoslavia)	H	W	3–2	Burke, Jones, Cush
1974–75	UEFA Cup	1	18.9.74	Valur (Iceland)	A	D	0–0	
			1.10.74		H	W	2–1	MacFaul, Morrison (pen)
		2	23.10.74	Partizan Belgrade	A	L	0–5	
			6.11.74	(Yugoslavia)	H	D	1–1	Malcolmson

LEAGUE OF IRELAND CLUBS

ATHLONE TOWN

Season	Competition	Round	Date	Opponents (Country)	Venue	Result		Scorers
1975–76	UEFA Cup	1	18.9.75	Valerengen (Norway)	H	W	3–0	Martin, Davis 2
			1.10.75		A	D	1–1	Martin
		2	22.10.75	AC Milan (Italy)	H	D	0–0	
			5.11.75		A	L	0–3	

BOHEMIANS

Season	Competition	Round	Date	Opponents (Country)	Venue	Result		Scorers
1975–76	European Cup	1	17.9.75	Rangers (Scotland)	A	L	1–4	Flanagan
			1.10.75		H	D	1–1	O'Connor (T)
1978–79	European Cup	1	13.9.78	Omonia Nicosia (Cyprus)	A	L	1–2	O'Connor (P)
			27.9.78		H	W	1–0	Joyce
		2	18.10.78	Dynamo Dresden	H	D	0–0	
			1.11.78	(East Germany)	A	L	0–6	
1970–71	Cup-Winners'	Pr	26.8.70	Gottwaldov	H	L	1–2	Swan (pen)
	Cup		2.9.70	(Czechoslovakia)	A	D	2–2	O'Connell, Dunne
1976–77	Cup-Winners'	1	15.9.76	Esbjerg (Denmark	H	W	2–1	Ryan (B), own goal
	Cup		29.9.76		A	W	1–0	Mitten
		2	20.10.76	Slask Wroclaw (Poland)	A	L	0–3	
			3.11.76		H	L	0–1	
1972–73	UEFA Cup	1	13.9.72	IFC Cologne (West	A	L	1–2	Daly
			27.9.72	Germany)	H	L	0–3	
1974–75	UEFA Cup	1	18.9.74	SV Hamburg (West	A	L	0–3	
			2.10.74	Germany)	H	L	0–1	
1979–80	UEFA Cup	1	19.9.79	Sporting Lisbon	A	L	0–2	
			3.10.79	(Portugal)	H	D	0–0	

Season	Competition	Round	Date	Opponents (Country)	Venue	Result		Scorers

CORK CELTIC

Season	Competition	Round	Date	Opponents (Country)	Venue	Result		Scorers
1974–75	European Cup	1		walkover				
		2	23.10.74	Ararat Erevan (USSR)	H	L	1–2	Tambling
			6.11.74		A	L	0–5	
1964–65	Cup-Winners' Cup	1	30.9.64	Slavia Sofia (Bulgaria)	A	D	1–1	Leahy
			7.10.64		H	L	0–2	

CORK HIBS

Season	Competition	Round	Date	Opponents (Country)	Venue	Result		Scorers
1971–72	European Cup	1	15.9.71	Borussia Moenchenglad-	H	L	0–5	
			29.9.71	bach (West Germany)	A	L	1–2	Dennehy
1972–73	Cup-Winners' Cup	1	10.9.72	Pezoporikos (Cyprus)	A	W	2–1	Lawson (pen), Sheehan
			13.9.72		H	W	4–1	Wallace, Lawson 2, Dennehy
		2	25.10.72	Schalke 04 (West	H	D	0–0	
			8.11.72	Germany)	A	L	0–3	
1973–74	Cup-Winners' Cup	1	19.9.73	Banik Ostrava	A	L	0–1	
			3.10.73	(Czechoslovakia)	H	L	1–2	Humphries
1970–71	Fairs Cup	1	16.9.70	Valencia (Spain)	H	L	0–3	
			26.9.70		A	L	1–3	Wigginton

DRUMCONDRA

Season	Competition	Round	Date	Opponents (Country)	Venue	Result		Scorers
1958–59	European Cup	Pr	17.9.58	Atletico Madrid (Spain)	A	L	0–8	
			1.10.58		H	L	1–5	Fullam (pen)
1961–62	European Cup	Pr	23.8.61	IFC Nuremberg (West	A	L	0–5	
			13.9.61	Germany)	H	L	1–4	Fullam
1965–66	European Cup	Pr	15.9.65	Vorwaerts (East Germany)	H	W	1–0	Morrissey
			22.9.65		A	L	0–3	
1962–63	Fairs Cup	1	3.10.62	Odense BK 09 (Denmark)	H	W	4–1	Dixon 2, Morrissey, McCann
			17.10.62		A	L	2–4	Rice, Morrissey
		2	4.12.62	Bayern Munich (West	A	L	0–6	
			12.12.62	Germany)	H	W	1–0	Dixon
1966–67	Fairs Cup	1	21.9.66	Eintracht Frankfurt	H	L	0–2	
			5.10.66	(West Germany)	A	L	1–6	Whelan

DUNDALK

Season	Competition	Round	Date	Opponents (Country)	Venue	Result		Scorers
1963–64	European Cup	Pr	11.9.63	Zurich (Switzerland)	H	L	0–3	
			25.9.63		A	W	2–1	Cross, Hasty
1967–68	European Cup	1	20.9.67	Vasas Budapest (Hungary)	H	L	0–1	
			11.10.67		A	L	1–8	Hale
1976–77	European Cup	1	15.9.76	PSV Eindhoven (Holland)	H	D	1–1	McDowell
			29.9.76		A	L	0–6	
1979–80	European Cup	Pr	29.8.79	Linfield (Northern Ireland)	H	D	1–1	Devine
			5.9.79	(in Haarlem, Holland)	A	W	2–0	Muckian 2
		1	19.9.79	Hibernians (Malta)	H	W	2–0	Carlyle, Devine
			26.9.79		A	L	0–1	
		2	24.10.79	Celtic (Scotland)	A	L	2–3	Muckian, Lawlor
			7.11.79		H	D	0–0	
1968–69	Fairs Cup	1	11.9.68	DOS Utrecht (Holland)	A	D	1–1	Stokes
			1.10.68		H	W	2–1	Stokes, Morrissey
		2	30.10.68	Rangers (Scotland)	A	L	1–6	Murray (pen)
			13.11.68		H	L	0–3	
1969–70	Fairs Cup	1	16.9.69	Liverpool (England)	A	L	0–10	
			30.9.69		H	L	0–4	

FINN HARPS

Season	Competition	Round	Date	Opponents (Country)	Venue	Result		Scorers
1974–75	Cup-Winners' Cup	1	18.11.74	Bursaspor (Turkey)	A	L	2–4	Ferry, Bradley
					H	D	0–0	
1973–74	UEFA Cup	1	19.9.73	Aberdeen (Scotland)	A	L	1–4	Harkin
			3.10.73		H	L	1–3	Harkin
1976–77	UEFA Cup	1	15.9.76	Derby County (England)	A	L	0–12	
			29.9.76		H	L	1–4	own goal
1978–79	UEFA Cup	1	12.9.78	Everton (England)	H	L	0–5	
			26.9.78		A	L	0–5	

HOME FARM

Season	Competition	Round	Date	Opponents (Country)	Venue	Result		Scorers
1975–76	Cup-Winners' Cup	1	17.9.75	Lens (France)	H	D	1–1	Brophy
			1.10.75		A	L	0–6	

Season	Competition	Round	Date	Opponents (Country)	Venue	Result		Scorers

LIMERICK

Season	Competition	Round	Date	Opponents (Country)	Venue	Result		Scorers
1960–61	European Cup	Pr	31.8.60	Young Boys (Switzerland)	H	L	0–5	
			5.10.60		A	L	2–4	Lynam, O'Reilly
1965–66	Cup-Winners' Cup	1	7.10.65	CSKA Sofia (Bulgaria)	H	L	1–2	O'Connor
			13.10.65		A	L	0–2	
1971–72	Cup-Winners' Cup	1	15.9.71	Torino (Italy)	H	L	0–1	
			29.9.71		A	L	0–4	

SHAMROCK ROVERS

Season	Competition	Round	Date	Opponents (Country)	Venue	Result		Scorers
1957–58	European Cup	Pr	25.9.57	Manchester United (England)	H	L	0–6	
			2.10.57		A	L	2–3	McCann, Hamilton
1959–60	European Cup	Pr	26.8.59	Nice (France)	A	L	2–3	Hamilton, Tuohy
			23.9.59		H	D	1–1	Hennessy
1964–65	European Cup	Pr	16.9.64	Rapid Vienna (Austria)	A	L	0–3	
			30.9.64		H	L	0–2	
1962–63	Cup-Winners' Cup	1	bye					
		2	24.10.62	Botev Plovdiv (Bulgaria)	H	L	0–4	
			14.11.62		A	L	0–1	
1966–67	Cup-Winners' Cup	1	28.9.66	Spora (Luxembourg)	H	W	4–1	Fullam, Dixon, Kearin, O'Neill (pen)
			5.10.66		A	W	4–1	Kearin, Dixon 2, O'Neill
		2	9.11.66	Bayern Munich (West Germany)	H	D	1–1	Dixon
			23.11.66		A	L	2–3	Gilbert, O'Neill
1967–68	Cup-Winners' Cup	1	20.9.67	Cardiff City (Wales)	H	D	1–1	Gilbert
			4.10.67		A	L	0–2	
1968–69	Cup-Winners' Cup	1	18.9.68	Randers Freja (Denmark)	A	L	0–1	
			2.10.68		H	L	1–2	Fullam
1969–70	Cup-Winners' Cup	1	17.9.69	Schalke 04 (West Germany)	H	W	2–1	Barber 2
			1.10.69		A	L	0–3	
1978–79	Cup-Winners' Cup	1	13.9.78	Apoel Nicosia (Cyprus)	H	W	2–0	Giles, Lynex
			27.9.78		A	W	1–0	Lynex
		2	18.10.78	Banik Ostrava (Czechoslovakia)	A	L	0–3	
			1.11.78		H	L	1–3	Giles
1963–64	Fairs Cup	1	18.9.63	Valencia (Spain)	H	L	0–1	
			10.10.63		A	D	2–2	O'Neill, Mooney
1965–66	Fairs Cup	1	bye					
		2	17.11.65	Real Zaragoza (Spain)	H	D	1–1	Tuohy
			24.11.65		A	L	1–2	Fullam

SHELBOURNE

Season	Competition	Round	Date	Opponents (Country)	Venue	Result		Scorers
1962–63	European Cup	Pr	19.9.62	Sporting Lisbon (Portugal)	H	L	0–2	
			27.9.62		A	L	1–5	Hennessy
1963–64	Cup-Winners' Cup	1	24.9.63	Barcelona (Spain)	H	L	0–2	
			15.10.63		A	L	1–3	Bonham (pen)
1964–65	Fairs Cup	1	16.9.64	Belenenses (Portugal)	A	D	1–1	Barber
			14.10.64		H	D	0–0	
			28.10.64		N	W	2–1	Hannigan, Conroy (M)
		2	25.11.64	Atletico Madrid (Spain)	H	L	0–1	
			2.12.64		A	L	0–1	
1971–72	UEFA Cup	1	15.9.71	Vasas Budapest (Hungary)	A	L	0–1	
			29.9.71		H	D	1–1	Murray

ST PATRICK'S ATHLETIC

Season	Competition	Round	Date	Opponents (Country)	Venue	Result		Scorers
1961–62	Cup-Winners' Cup	Pr	12.9.61	Dunfermline Athletic (Scotland)	A	L	1–4	O'Rourke
			27.9.61		H	L	0–4	
1967–68	Fairs Cup	1	13.9.67	Bordeaux (France)	H	L	1–3	Hennessy
			11.10.67		A	L	3–6	Campbell 2, Ryan

WATERFORD

Season	Competition	Round	Date	Opponents (Country)	Venue	Result		Scorers
1966–67	European Cup	Pr	31.8.66	Vorwaerts Berlin (East Germany)	H	L	1–5	Lynch
			9.9.66		A	L	0–6	
1968–69	European Cup	1	18.9.68	Manchester United (England)	H	L	1–3	Matthews
			2.10.68		A	L	1–7	Casey
1969–70	European Cup	1	17.9.69	Galatasaray (Turkey)	A	L	0–2	
			1.10.69		H	L	2–3	Buck, Morley
1970–71	European Cup	1	16.9.70	Glentoran (Northern Ireland)	A	W	3–1	O'Neil, McGeough, Casey
			30.9.70		H	W	1–0	Casey

Season	Competition	Round	Date	Opponents (Country)	Venue	Result	Scorers
WATERFORD continued							
		2	21.10.70	Celtic (Scotland)	H	L 0–7	
			4.11.70		A	L 2–3	Matthews, own goal
1972–73	European Cup	1	13.9.72	Omonia Nicosia (Cyprus)	H	W 2–1	Hale 2
			27.9.72		A	L 0–2	
1973–74	European Cup	1	19.9.73	Ujpest Dozsa (Hungary)	H	L 2–3	Kirby, O'Neill
			3.10.73		A	L 0–3	
1979–80	Cup-Winners' Cup	1	19.9.79	Gothenburg (Sweden)	A	L 0–1	
			3.10.79		H	D 1–1	Keane

European Club directory
(up to and including 1978-79)

Country	Championship wins	Cup wins	European and other honours
ALBANIA	(1945) Dinamo Tirana 14; Partizan Tirana 11; 17 Nendori 5; Vlaznia 4	(1948) Dinamo Tirana 12; Partizan Tirana 8; 17 Nendori 4; Vlaznia 2; Besa 1; Labinoti 1	None
AUSTRIA	(1912) Rapid Vienna 25; Austria/WAC (previously FK Austria and WAC) 14; Admira-Energie-Wacker (previously Sportklub Admira and Admira-Energie) 8; First Vienna 6; Tirol-Svarowski-Innsbruck (previously Wacker-Innsbruck) 5; Wiener Sportklub 3; FAC 1; Hakoah 1; Linz ASK 1; Wacker Vienna 1; WAF 1; Voest Linz 1	(1919) FK Austria 19; Rapid Vienna 9; Admira-Energie-Wacker 5; Tirol-Svarowski-Innsbruck 5; First Vienna 3; Linz ASK 1; Wacker Vienna 1; WAF 1; Wiener Sportklub 1	European Cup-Winners' Cup (runners-up) Austria/WAC 1978
BELGIUM	(1896) Anderlecht 16; Union St Gilloise 11; Beerschot 7; Standard Liege 6; RC Brussels 6; FC Liege 5; Daring Brussels 5; FC Bruges 5; Antwerp 4; Lierse SK 3; Malines 3; CS Bruges 3; RWD Molenbeek 1 Beveren 1	(1954) Anderlecht 5; Standard Liege 3; FC Bruges 3; Beerschot 2; Antwerp 1; La Gantoise 1; Lierse SK 1; Tournai 1; Waregem 1; Beveren 1	European Cup (runners-up) FC Bruges 1978 European Cup-Winners' Cup (winners) Anderlecht 1976, 1978 (runners-up) Anderlecht 1977. European Fairs Cup (runners-up) Anderlecht 1970. UEFA Cup (runners-up) FC Bruges 1976
BULGARIA	(1925) CSKA Sofia (previously CDNA) 19; Levski Spartak (previously Levski Sofia) 13; Slavia Sofia 6; Vladislav Varna 3; Lokomotiv Sofia 3; AS23 Sofia 1; Botev Plovdiv 1; SC Sofia 1; Sokol Varna 1; Spartak Plovdiv 1; Tichka Varna 1; Trakia Plovdiv 1; ZSK Sofia 1	(1946) Levski Spartak 13; CSKA Sofia 10; Slavia Sofia 5; Lokomotiv Sofia 2; Botev Plovdiv 1; Spartak Plovdiv 1; Spartak Sofia 1; Marek Stanke 1	None
CYPRUS	(1935) Apoel 11; Omonia 9; Anorthosis 6; AEL 5; EPA 3; Olympiakos 3; Chetin Kayal 1; Pezoporikos 1; Trast 1	(1935) Apoel 10; EPA 5; AEL 3; Trast 3; Chetin Kayal 2; Omonia 2; Apollon 2; Pezoporikos 2; Anorthosis 2; Paralimni 1; Olympiakos 1	None
CZECHOSLOVAKIA	(1926) * Sparta Prague 13; Slavia Prague 12; Dukla Prague (previously UDA) 10; Slovan Bratislava 6; Spartak Trnava 5; Inter-Bratislava 1; Spartak Hradec Kralove 1; Viktoria Zizkov 1; Banik Ostrava 1; Zbrojovka Brno 1	(1961) Dukla Prague 4; Slovan Bratislava 4; Spartak Trnava 3; Sparta Prague 3; Banik Ostrava 2; Lokomotiv Kosice 2; TJ Gottwaldov 1	European Cup-Winners' Cup (winners) Slovan Bratislava 1969

Country	Championship wins	Cup wins	European and other honours
DENMARK	(1913) KB Copenhagen 14 ; B93 Copenhagen 9 ; AB (Akademisk) 9 ; B 1903 Copenhagen 7 ; Frem 6 ; AGF Aarhus 4 ; Esbjergs FK 4 ; Vejle BK 4 ; B 1909 Odense 2 ; Hvidovre 2 ; Koge BK 2 ; Odense BK 1	(1955) AGF Aarhus 5 ; Vejile Bk 5 ; B 1909 Odense 3 ; Randers Freja 3 ; Aalborg BK 2 ; Ebsjergs BK 2 ; Frem 2 ; KB Copenhagen 1 ; Vanlose 1	None
FINLAND	(1949) * Turun Palloseura 5 ; Kuopion Palloseura 5 ; Valkeakosken Haka 4 ; Lahden Reipas 3 ; Helsinki JK 3 ; IF Kamraterna 2 ; Kotkan TP 2 ; Turun Pyrkiva 1 ; IF Kronohagens 1 ; Helsinki PS 1 ; Ilves-Kissat 1 ; Kokkolan PV 1 ; IF Kamraterna 1 ; Vasa 1	(1955) Lahden Reipas 7 ; Valkeakosken Haka 6 ; Kotkan TP 3 ; Mikkelin 2 ; IFK Abo 1 ; Drott 1 ; Helsinki JK 1 ; Helsinki PS 1 ; Kuopion Palloseura 1 ; Pallo-Peikot 1	None
FRANCE	(1933) Saint Etienne 9 ; Stade de Reims 6 ; OGC Nice 4 ; Olympique Marseille 4 ; Nantes 4 ; Lille OSC 3 ; AS Monaco 3 ; FC Sete 2 ; Sochaux 2 ; Racing Club Paris 1 ; Roubaix-Tourcoing 1 ; Girondins Bordeaux 1 ; Strasbourg 1	(1918) Olympique Marseille 9 ; Saint Etienne 6 ; Lille OSC 5 ; Racing Club Paris 5 ; Red Star 5 ; Olympique Lyon 3 ; CAS Generaux 2 ; AS Monaco 2 ; OGC Nice 2 ; Racing Club Strasbourg 2 ; Sedan 2 ; FC Sete 2 ; Stade de Reims 2 ; Stade Rennes 2 ; Nancy-Lorraine 2 ; AS Cannes 1 ; Club Francais 1 ; Excelsior Roubaix 1 ; Girondins Bordeaux 1 ; Le Havre 1 ; SO Montpelier 1 ; Olympique de Pantin 1 ; CA Paris 1 ; Sochaux 1 ; Toulouse 1 ; Nantes 1	European Champions' Cup (runners-up) Stade de Reims 1956, 1959 ; Saint Etienne 1976 UEFA Cup (runners-up) Bastia 1978
EAST GERMANY (GDR)	(1950) ASK Vorwaerts 6 ; Dynamo Dresden 5 ; Wismut Karl-Marx-Stadt 4 ; FC Magdeburg 4 ; Carl Zeiss Jena (previously Motor Jena) 3 ; Chemie Leipzig 2 ; Turbine Erfurt 2 ; Turbine Halle 1 ; Zwickau Horch 1 ; Empor Rostock 1 ; Dynamo Berlin 1	(1949) Carl Zeiss Jena 4 ; Dynamo Dresden 3 ; FC Magdeburg 3 ; Chemie Leipzig 2 ; Magdeburg Aufbau 2 ; Motor Zwickau 2 ; ASK Vorwaerts 2 ; Lokomotiv Leipzig 2 ; Dresden Einheit SC 1 ; Dresden PV 1 ; Dynamo Berlin 1 ; Halle Chemie SC 1 ; North Dessau Waggonworks 1 ; Thale EHW 1 ; Union East Berlin 1 ; Wismut Karl-Marx-Stadt 1 ; Sachsenring Zwickau 1	European Cup-Winners' Cup (winners) FC Magdeburg 1974
WEST GERMANY	(1903) 1 FC Nuremberg 9 ; Schalke 7 ; Bayern Munich 5 ; Borussia Moenchengladbach 5 ; SV Hamburg 4 ; VfB Leipzig 3 ; SpV Furth 3 ; Dorussia Dortmund 3 ; 1FC Cologne 3 ; Viktoria Berlin 2 ; Hertha Berlin 2 ; Hanover 96 2 ; Dresden SC 2 ; VfB Stuttgart 2 ; 1FC Kaiserslautern 2 ; Munich 1860 1 ; SV Werder Bremen 1 ; Union Berlin 1 ; FC Freibourg 1 ; Phoenix Karlsruhe 1 ; Karlsruhe FV 1 ; Holstein Kiel 1 ; Fortuna Dusseldorf 1 ; Rapid Vienna 1 ; VfR Mannheim 1 ; Rot-Weiss Essen 1 ; Eintracht Frankfurt 1 ; Eintracht Brunswick 1	(1935) Bayern Munich 5 ; 1FC Nuremberg 3 ; Dresden SC 2 ; Karlsruher SC 2 ; Munich 1860 2 ; Schalke 2 ; VfB Stuttgart 2 ; Borussia Moenchengladbach 2 ; Eintracht Frankfurt 2 ; 1FC Cologne 3 ; SV Hamburg 2 ; Borussia Dortmund 1 ; First Vienna 1 ; VfB Leipzig 1 ; Kickers Offenbach 1 ; Rapid Vienna 1 ; Rot-Weiss Essen 1 ; SW Essen 1 ; Werder Bremen 1 ; Fortuna Dusseldorf 1	World Club Championship (winners) Bayern Munich 1976. European Champions' Cup (winners) Bayern Munich 1974, 1975, 1976 ; (runners-up) Eintracht Frankfurt 1960, Borussia Moenchengladbach 1977 European Cup-Winners' Cup (winners) Borussia Dortmund 1966, Bayern Munich 1967, SV Hamburg 1977 ; (runners-up) Munich (1860) 1965, SV Hamburg 1968. Fortuna Dusseldorf 1979 UEFA Cup (winners) Borussia Moenchengladbach 1975, 1979 ; (runners-up) Borussia Moenchengladbach 1973

Country	Championship wins	Cup wins	European and other honours
GREECE	(1928) Olympiakos 20; Panathinaikos 12; AEK Athens 7; Aris Salonika 3; PAOK Salonika 1	(1932) Olympiakos 16; AEK Athens 7; Panathinaikos 6; PAOK Salonika 2; Aris Salonika 1; Ethnikos 1; Iraklis 1; Panionios 1	European Champions' Cup (runners-up) Panathinaikos 1971
HUNGARY	(1901) Ferencvaros (previously FTC) 22; MTK-VM Budapest (previously Hungaria, Bastya, and Voros Lobogo) 18; Ujpest Dozsa 18; Vasas Budapest 6; Honved 5; Csepel 4; BTC 2; Nagyvarad 1; Vasas Gyor 1	(1901) Ferencvaros 14; MTK-VM Budapest 9; Ujpest Dozsa 4; Raba (Vasas) Gyor 4; Vasas Budapest 1; Bocskai 1; Honved 1; III Ker 1; Kispesti AC 1; Soroksar 1; Szolnoki MAV 1; Diosgyor 1	European Cup-Winners Cup (runners-up) MTK Budapest 1964, Ferencvaros 1975. European Fairs Cup (winners) Ferencvaros 1965; (runners-up) Ferencvaros 1968, Ujpest Dozsa 1969
ICELAND	(1912) KR Reykjavik 20; Valur 16; IA Akranes 10; IBK Keflavik 3; Vikingur 2; IBV Vestmann 1	(1960) KR Reykjavik 7; Valur 4; IBV Vestmann 2; Fram 2; IBA Akureyri 1; Vikingur 1; IBK Keflavik 1; IA Akranes 1	None
IRELAND (Republic)	(1922) Shamrock Rovers 10; Shelbourne 7; Bohemians 7; Waterford 6; Cork United 5; Drumcondra 5; Dundalk 5; St Patrick's Athletic 3; St James's Gate 2; Cork Athletic 2; Sligo Rovers 2; Limerick 1; Dolphin 1; Cork Hibernians 1; Cork Celtic 1	(1922) Shamrock Rovers 21; Dundalk 6; Drumcondra 5; Bohemians 4; Shelbourne 3; Cork Athletic 2; Cork United 2; St James's Gate 2; St Patrick's Athletic 2; Cork Hibernians 2; Alton United 1; Athlone Town 1; Cork 1; Fordsons 1; Limerick 1; Transport 1; Waterford 1; Finn Harps 1; Home Farm 1	None
ITALY	(1898) Juventus 18; Inter-Milan 11; AC Milan 10; Genoa 9; Torino 8; Pro Vercelli 7; Bologna 7; Fiorentina 2; Casale 1; Novese 1; AS Roma 1; Cagliari 1; Lazio 1	(1922) Juventus 6; Torino 4; Fiorentina 4; AC Milan 4; Napoli 2; AS Roma 2; Bologna 2; Inter-Milan 2; Atalanta 1; Genoa 1; Lazio 1; Vado 1; Venezia 1	World Club Championship (winners) Inter-Milan 1964, 1965, AC Milan 1969. European Champions' Cup (winners) AC Milan 1963, 1969, Inter-Milan 1964, 1965; (runners-up) Fiorentina 1957, AC Milan 1958, Inter-Milan 1967, 1972, Juventus 1973. European Cup-Winners' Cup (winners) Fiorentina 1961, AC Milan 1968, 1973; (runners-up) Fiorentina 1962, AC Milan 1974. European Fairs Cup (winners) AS Roma 1961; (runners-up) Juventus 1965, 1971. UEFA Cup (winners) Juventus 1977
LUXEMBOURG	(1910) Jeunesse Esch 15; Spora Luxembourg 10; Stade Dudelange 10; Red Boys Differdange 6; US Hollerich-Bonnevoie 5; Fola Esch 5; US Luxembourg 3; Aris Bonnevoie 3; Sporting Luxembourg 2; Progres Niedercorn 2; Racing Luxembourg 1; National Schifflge 1; Avenir Breggen 1;	(1922) Red Boys Differdange 14; Spora Luxembourg 7; Jeunesse Esch 7; US Luxembourg 6; Stade Dudelange 4; Fola Esch 3; Progres Niedercorn 3; Alliance Dudelange 2; US Rumelange 2; Aris Bonnevoie 1; US Dudelange 1; Jeunesse Hautcharage 1; National Schifflge 1; Racing Luxembourg 1; SC Tetange 1	None

Country	Championship wins	Cup wins	European and other honours
MALTA	(1910) Floriana 24 ; Sliema Wanderers 21; Valletta 10; Hibernians 4; Hamrun Spartans 3; St George's 1; KOMR 1	(1935) Sliema Wanderers 16; Floriana 14; Valletta 5 ; Hibernians 3 ; Gzira United 1 ; Melita 1	None
NETHERLANDS	(1898) Ajax Amsterdam 18; Feyenoord 12; HVV The Hague 8; PSV Eindhoven 7; Sparta Rotterdam 6; Go Ahead Deventer 4; HBS The Hague 3; Willem II Tilburg 3; RCH Haarlem 2; RAP 2; Heracles 2; ADO The Hague 2; Quick the Hague 1; BVV Scheidam 1; NAC Breda 1; Eindhoven 1; Enschede 1; Volewijckers Amsterdam 1; Limburgia 1; Rapid JC Haarlem 1; DOS Utrecht 1; DWS Amsterdam 1; Haarlem 1; Be Quick Groningen 1; SVV Scheidam 1	(1899) Ajax Amsterdam 8; Feyenoord 4; Quick The Hague 4; PSV Eindhoven 4; HEC 3; Sparta Rotterdam 3; DFC 2; Fortuna Geleen 2; Haarlem 2; HBS The Hague 2; RCH 2; VOC 2; Wageningen 2; Willem II Tilburg 2; FC Den Haag 2; Concordia Rotterdam 1; CVV 1; Eindhoven 1; HVV The Hague 1; Longa 1; Quick Njimegen 1; RAP 1; Roermond 1; Schoten 1; Velocitas Breda 1; Velocitas Groningen 1; VSV 1; VUC 1; VVV 1; ZFC 1; NAC Breda 1; Twente Enschede 1; AZ 67 1	World Club Championship (winners) Feyenoord 1970, Ajax 1972. European Champions' Cup (winners) Feyenoord 1970, Ajax 1971, 1972, 1973; (runners-up) Ajax 1969. UEFA Cup (winners) Feyenoord 1974; PSV Eindhoven 1978; (runners-up) Twente Enschede 1975
NORWAY	(1938) Fredrikstad 9; Viking Stavanger 5; Lillestrom 3; Rosenborg Trondheim 3; Larvik Turn 3; Brann Bergen 2; Lyn Oslo 2; Valerengen 1; Friedig 1; Fram 1; Skeid Oslo 1; Stromsgodset Drammen 1; IK Start 1	(1902) Odds BK Skein 11; Fredrikstad 9; Lyn Oslo 8; Skeid Oslo 8; Sarpsborgs Fk 6; Orn Fk Horten 4; Brann Bergen 4; Mjondalens IF 3; Rosenborgs BK Trondheim 3; Stromsgodset Drammen 3; Mercantile 2; Viking Stavanger 2; Lillestrom 2; Grane Nordstrand 1; Kvik Halden 1; Sparta 1; Gjovik 1; Bodo-Glimt 1	None
POLAND	(1921) Ruch Chorzow 12; Gornik Zabrze 10; Wisla Krakow 6; Cracovia 5; Pogon Lwow 4; Legia Warsaw 4; Warta Poznan 2; Polonia Bytom 2; Stal Mielec 2; Garbarnia Krakow 1; Polonia Warsaw 1; LKS Lodz 1; Slask Wroclaw 1	(1951) Gornik Zabrze 6; Legia Warsaw 5; Zaglebie Sosnowiec 4; Ruch Chorzow 2; Gwardia Warsaw 1; LKS Lodz 1; Polonia Warsaw 1; Wisla Krakow 1; Stal Rzeszow 1; Slask Wroclaw 1; Arka Gydnia 1	European Cup-Winners' Cup (runners-up) Gornik Zabrze 1970
PORTUGAL	(1935) * Benfica 23; Sporting Lisbon 14; FC Porto 7; Belenenses 1	(1939) Benfica 15; Sporting Lisbon 9; FC Porto 4; Boavista 3; Belenenses 2; Vitoria Setubal 2; Academica Coimbra 1; Leixoes Porto 1; Sporting Braga 1	European Champions' Cup (winners) Benfica 1961, 1962; (runners-up) Benfica 1963, 1965, 1968 European Cup-Winners' Cup (winners) Sporting Lisbon 1964
RUMANIA	(1910) Dynamo Bucharest 9; Steaua Bucharest (previously CCA) 9; Venus Bucharest 7; CSC Temesvar 6; UT Arad 6; Rapid Bucharest 4; Ripensia Temesvar 3; Petrolul Ploesti 3; Olimpia Bucharest 2; CAC Bucharest 2; Arges 2; Soc RA Bucharest 1; Prahova Ploesti 1; CSC Brasov 1; Juventus Bucharest 1; SSUD Resita 1; Craiova Bucharest 1; Progresul 1; ; Ploesti United 1; University of Craiova 1	(1934) Steaua Bucharest 13; Rapid Bucharest 7; Dynamo Bucharest 3; UT Arad 2; CFR Bucharest 2; Progresul 2; RIP Timisoara 2; Uni Craiova 1; ICO Oradeo 1; Metal Ochimia Resita 1; Petrolul Ploesti 1; Stinta Cluj 1; Stinta Timisoara 1; Turnu Severin 1; Chimia Ramnicu 1; Jiul Petroseni 1	None
SPAIN	(1929) Real Madrid 19; Barcelona 9; Atletico Madrid 8; Athletic Bilbao 6; Valencia 4; Betis 1; Seville 1	(1902) Athletic Bilbao 22; Barcelona 18; Real Madrid 13; Atletico Madrid 5; Valencia 5; Real Union de Irun 3; Seville 3; Espanol 2; Real	European Champions' Cup (winners) Real Madrid 1956, 1957, 1958, 1959, 1960, 1966; (runners-up) Real

Country	Championship wins	Cup wins	European and other honours
SPAIN continued		Zaragoza 2 ; Arenas 1 ; Ciclista Sebastian 1 ; Racing de Irun 1 ; Vizcaya Bilbao 1 ; Real Betis 1	Madrid 1962, 1964, Barcelona 1961, Atletico Madrid 1974. World Club Championship (winners) Real Madrid 1960, Atletico Madrid 1974. European Cup-Winners' Cup (winners) Atletico Madrid 1962, Barcelona 1979; (runners-up) Atletico Madrid 1963, Barcelona 1969, Real Madrid 1971. European Fairs Cup (winners) Barcelona 1958, 1960, 1966 ; Valencia 1962, 1963, Zaragoza 1964 ; (runners-up) Barcelona 1962, Valencia 1964, Zaragoza 1966. UEFA Cup (runners-up) Athletic Bilbao 1977
SWEDEN	(1896) Malmo FF 14 ; Oergryte IS Gothenburg 13 ; IFK Norrkoping 11 ; Djurgaarden 8 ; AIK Stockholm 8 ; IFK Gothenburg 7: GAIS Gothenburg 6 ; IF Halsingborg 5 ; Boras IF Elfsborg 4 ; Atvidaberg 2 ; Oester Vaxjo 2 ; IFK Ekilstund 1 ; IF Gavle Brynas 1 ; IF Gothenburg Fassbergs 1 ; Norrkoping IK Sleipner 1 ; Halmstad 1	(1941) Malmo FF 11 ; IFK Norrkoping 3 ; AIK Stockholm 3 ; Atvidaberg 2 ; GAIS Gothenburg 1 ; IFK Halsingborg 1 ; Raa 1 ; Landskrona 1 ; Oster Vaxjo 1	European Champions' Cup (runners-up) Malmo FF 1979
SWITZERLAND	(1898) Grasshoppers 17 ; Servette 14 ; Young Boys Berne 10 ; FC Zurich 8 ; Lausanne 7 ; FC Basle 7 ; La Chaux-de-Fonds 3 ; FC Lugano 3 ; Winterthur 3 ; FC Aarau 2 ; FC Anglo-Americans 1 ; St Gallen 1 ; FC Bruhl 1 ; Cantonal-Neuchatel 1 ; Biel 1 ; Bellinzona 1 ; FC Etoile la Chaux de Fonds 1	(1926) Grasshoppers 13 ; La Chaux-de-Fonds 6 ; Lausanne 6 ; FC Basle 5 ; FC Zurich 5 ; Young Boys Berne 5 ; Servette 5 ; FC Lugano 2 ; FC Sion 2 ; FC Granges 1 ; Lucerne 1 ; St Gallen 1 ; Urania Geneva 1 ; Young Fellows Zurich 1	None
TURKEY	(1960) Fenerbahce 8 ; Galatasaray 5 ; Besiktas 3 ; Trabzonspor 3	(1963) Galatasaray 6 ; Fenerbahce 3 ; Goztepe Izmir 2 ; Trabzonspor 2 ; Altay Izmir 1 ; Ankaragucu 1 ; Eskisehirspor 1 ; Besiktas 1 ;	None
USSR	(1936) Dynamo Moscow 11 ; Spartak Moscow 9 ; Dynamo Kiev 8 ; CSKA Moscow 6 ; Torpedo Moscow 3 ; Dynamo Tbilisi 2 ; Saria Voroshilovgrad 1 ; Ararat Erevan 1	(1936) Spartak Moscow 9 ; Torpedo Moscow 5 ; Dynamo Moscow 5 ; Dynamo Kiev 5 ; CSKA Moscow 4 ; Donets Shaktyor 2 ; Lokomotiv Moscow 2 ; Ararat Erevan 2 ; Karpaty Lvov 1 ; Zenit Leningrad 1 ; Dynamo Tbilisi 1	European Cup-Winners' Cup (winners) Dynamo Kiev 1975 ; (runners-up) Dynamo Moscow 1972
YUGOSLAVIA	(1923) Red Star Belgrade 12 ; Hajduk Split 9 ; Partizan Belgrade 8 ; Gradjanski Zagreb 5 ; BSK Belgrade 5 ; Dynamo Zagreb 3 ; Jugoslovija Belgrade 2 ; Concordia Zagreb 2 ; HASK Zagreb 1 ; Vojvodina Novi Sad 1 ; FC Sarajevo 1 ; Zeljeznicar 1	(1947) Red Star Belgrade 9 ; Hajduk Split 6 ; Dynamo Zagreb 6 ; Partizan 4 ; BSK Belgrade 2 ; OFK Belgrade 2 ; Rijeka 2 ; Vardar Skoplje 1	European Champions' Cup (runners-up) Partizan Belgrade 1966. European Fairs Cup (winners) Dynamo Zagreb 1967 ; (runners-up) Dynamo Zagreb 1963 UEFA Cup (runners-up) Red Star Belgrade 1979

AROUND THE WORLD STORIES

With the assistance of a four-times taken penalty kick, Australia held Czechoslovakia to a 2–2 draw in Melbourne on 9 February 1980. Referee Barry Harwood penalised Czech defender Anton Ondrus for a foul on Peter Sharne after six minutes. Eddie Krncevic took the kick, but his shot was saved by goalkeeper Dusan Keketi only for a linesman standing alongside the goal to signal that the goalkeeper had moved before the kick was taken. Krncevic's second shot was also saved by Keketi, but again the linesman ruled that the goalkeeper had moved too quickly. The third attempt was entrusted to Ivo Prskalo, who merely succeeded in firing wildly past the post. This time referee Harwood insisted the kick be taken again as he had not given the signal. Prsalko eventually scored, though this time Keketi made no attempt to save the ball. Then Czechoslovakia themselves equalised two minutes later from the penalty spot.

Few full-timers
At the start of the 1979–80 season there were only 81 full-time professionals distributed among the ten clubs of the Austrian First Division. Austria/WAC, the champions, had 15, Admira/Wacker 14, Rapid and Voest Linz 13 each, and Austria Salzburg 12. Of 21 foreigners in the League Austria/WAC again had the most with six, followed by Rapid and Admira/Wacker with three each.

In and out success
Internazionale of Milan were the most active team in the 1979 Italian summer transfer transactions, signing nine new players and allowing eleven to move to other clubs. At the end of the season Inter were champions.

Long-time ending
The 1979 Bolivian championship finally ended on 19 March 1980, though it was a close event. Because of political and other upheavals many matches had had to be postponed so that some teams had to play as many as five matches in ten days to clear outstanding fixtures.

On the last day Oriente Petrolero had to play-off with The Strongest of La Paz for the title. Oriente won 2–1, but the losers had a penalty saved in the final minute of the match.

Pedal power
At the end of the 1979 Swedish season, Mjallby

IF won promotion to the First Division. The club, situated in a small fishing village on the south coast, have a modest ground with only a tiny stand. The approach road to it is a narrow country road, and the players usually arrive on bicycles for home matches. Four years earlier Mjallby had been in Division Four.

The Thirty-Niner
Erwin Van den Bergh of the Belgian club Lierse ended the 1979–80 season as the leading scorer in Europe with 39 goals, but it needed a whirlwind finish for him to achieve this total. He scored six of the seven goals by which Lierse beat Hasselt to equal the previous record, and then on the last day of the season he scored two more against Cercle Bruges to overhaul Jef Mermans 37 goals record achieved in 1949–50.

Six of the best
St Etienne staged a remarkably quick recovery in their second leg UEFA Cup second round match with PSV Eindhoven in 1979–80. Trailing 2–0 from the first leg in Holland, the French club scored in the second, third, fifth and 18th minutes to wipe out their opponents advantage before adding two more late goals, including a last minute penalty. The pick of their half dozen was a 35-yard free kick by Michel Platini, which produced goal number four.

Zoff's on target
Juventus goalkeeper Dino Zoff set up a new record of consecutive League appearances in Italy during the 1979–80 season, when he made his 230th in a row against Pescara, overtaking Alfredo Foni's previous total of 229. Zoff, as Italy's first choice goalkeeper as well, was concerned in an unusual happening in the match with Switzerland on 14 November 1979. He began the match as captain, handed over the skipper's armband at half-time to Franco Causio when he was substituted, and watched from the bench as the third captain of the day was appointed when Giancarlo Antognoni came on for Causio in the 70th minute.

Call me-Sister
Zico was the leading scorer in Brazil during 1979 with a total of 89 goals, comprised of 65 in League games, 16 in friendlies, seven for the national team and one for the Rest of Europe against Argentina. He had scored his first goal in a competitive match on 18 March 1970 for his only club Flamengo in a youth game against São

Cristobal. The youngest of five footballing brothers, he was christened Artur Antunes Coimbra and earned his nickname from his sister, calling him home from playing in the streets with a cry of 'Arturzico'.

Dynamo run down
West Germany's Eintracht Frankfurt won the UEFA Cup in 1979–80, beating fellow Bundesliga side Borussia Moenchengladbach in the final, but they had a narrow escape in the second round. In the first leg played in Bucharest against Dynamo, they were beaten 2–0 though the skill of goalkeeper Klaus Funk, and the intervention of the woodwork on three occasions kept the score down. In the second leg, the Rumanians had to play without their injured leading scorer Dudu Georgescu, and they had another player sent off during the match. With only seconds of normal time remaining, Dynamo were leading 2–1 on aggregate when their goalkeeper palmed a harmless cross on to the head of a German forward, and the ball bounced off him into the net. In extra time Dynamo had a man carried off injured, and lost 3–2 on aggregate.

Unreality for Real
When Real Sociedad of San Sebastian beat Espanol 1–0 in April 1980, it was their 28th unbeaten match in the Spanish League, and they established a new record previously held by Real Madrid with 27 in 1968–69. They stretched the run to 32 matches, but were still overhauled by Real Madrid for the title before the season ended. Worse for them, in the Spanish Cup quarter-finals Real Madrid were paired with Castilla, their affiliated Second Division club, and the unwritten procedure is to avoid such embarrassing ties. So the draw was made again, Real Sociedad were paired with Castilla who promptly beat them 2–1. In the Spanish Cup Final Real Madrid had to play Castilla and won 6–1.

Never a dull moment – abroad
Andras Torocsik and Tibor Nyilasi of Hungary were sent off in the 1978 World Cup against Argentina. They received a year's ban from their FA, which was subsequently lifted. Shortly afterwards Torocsik was badly injured in a car crash, and his footballing career seemed in doubt. In October 1979 Nyilasi, at the age of 24, announced his retirement because he was disillusioned and said that his nerves would no longer stand top class football. But in February 1980 he resumed playing again. Then on 26 March Torocsik, having recovered his fitness at club level, returned to the national team and scored the winning goal in a 2–1 win over Poland. Nyilasi also came back to the national team in subsequent matches.

Woman in black
Poland claim to have produced the first female referee at senior level with Miss Barbara Kozinova, who lives in Swidnice controlling Division Two matches in the 1979–80 season.

Few frozen assets
Only 983 spectators watched the European Championship match between the USSR and Finland in the 103 000 capacity Lenin Stadium in Moscow on 31 October 1979. The temperature was ten degrees below freezing and several players wore track suit trousers and bobble hats. The match ended in a 2–2 draw.

Flying Kiwis
New Zealand's national team undertook a hectic tour of Kuwait, Bahrain, Ireland, England and Scotland, playing ten matches in four weeks in October 1979. Their record was: Won 2, Drew 1 and Lost 7.

Eternally close
Argentina's most closely fought local rivalry exists between the Buenos Aires clubs Boca Juniors and River Plate. The two 1–1 draws, in which they were involved during the 1979 season, meant that Boca were leading 43 to 42 in victories in 116 official meetings since the 1930 introduction of professional football in the country.

Old Trafford Persian
Nasser Hedjazi who was in goal for Iran in the 1978 World Cup had a trial for Manchester United in September 1979. At 29 years of age he appeared in their Central League team against Burnley in a 5–0 win.

Evergreen Eberhard
East Germany's most experienced player at the start of the 1979–80 season was Eberhard Vogel of Carl Zeiss Jena, a left-winger who had made 379 League appearances and scored 169 goals during his career.

Bottoms up
Sponsorship of the Danish First Division in the last two years has been made by Carlsberg Breweries. In 1979 the aggregate of attendances went up from 661 000 to 882 000 for an average of 3425 spectators per match. Crowds ranged from a low of 237 to a high of 14 000 in this second season of professionalism.

New boys rule OK?
Deportivo Tachira won the championship of Venezuela in 1979 in only their second season in professional football, obtaining the title on a new rule which decided the winners on results between two teams level on points and not goal difference.

Rent-a-steak
Uruguayan First Division club Rentistas wanted to sign Daniel Allende from Second Division Central Espanol though they had no cash. But their president owned a slaughter house, and he agreed to a deal whereby Espanol received 550 beef steaks for the player at the rate of 25 a week plus 30 per cent of any subsequent transfer fee.

Sixty inglorious years
America of Cali won the 1979 Colombian championship for the first time in their history. Founded on 18 December 1918 it was their one notable honour in 60 years. But Millionarios of Bogota, once the wealthiest club in the country, was reporting itself on the verge of bankruptcy after poor results and the use of ten different coaches in three seasons.

North by north-east
OPS Oulu (Oulun Palloseura) won the 1979 championship in Finland for the first time in their history. The country's most northerly based winners, they achieved this feat after only four seasons in the top division. They had the assistance in seven matches of Newcastle United forward Keith Armstrong who scored five vital goals for them.

No Turkish delight
When Turkey visited Gelsenkirchen for a European Championship match with West Germany on 22 December 1979 the crowd of more than 70 000 included an estimated 20 000 Turks, most of them workers domiciled in Germany. West Germany won 2–0.

Irish double Dutch
Cathal Muckian, a £25-a-week part-time professional and local bank official with Dundalk, became the first player from the Republic of Ireland to score more than one goal in a European Cup match when he registered twice against Linfield in the preliminary round second leg in 1979–80. The match was played in Haarlem, Holland because of fear of disturbances following trouble in the first leg in Dundalk.

Dragan off
One of Yugoslavia's most famous international players left-winger Dragan Dzajic made his farewell in a 4–2 win over Argentina in September 1979, before a disappointing crowd of 20 000 in Belgrade. Dzajic had made 590 League appearances for Red Star Belgrade, scoring 287 goals before playing abroad with Bastia in the French First Division.

No Swiss Miss
Daniel Jeandupeux, manager of the Swiss club Sion, had retired two years before the 1979–80 season after a serious leg injury sustained while playing in France for Bordeaux. But he named himself as one of the substitutes for a Swiss Cup match with Grasshoppers and brought himself on in extra time. With the match still deadlocked, Jeandupeux was able to convert the decisive penalty kick to win the match.

No Dudu hoodoo
Dynamo Bucharest and Rumanian international centre-forward Dudu Georgescu set up a new aggregate record of League goals when he reached his 181st goal in 382 matches for the club in December 1979.

Sofia so good
CSKA Sofia, the Bulgarian Army club, allowed Bojil Kolev their long-serving defender who had made 56 appearances for his country to move to Tchernomore Bourgas, thinking his career was winding up. But Kolev flourished with them in 1979–80, taking his total of overall League games to 350 during which he had also scored 68 goals.

Pay by Czechs
Though attendances have never been high for League matches in Czechoslovakia, one weekend in the 1979–80 season saw only 1235 attending the ZTS Kosice v Sparta Prague game, and 1864 watching Slovan Bratislava play Lokomotiv Kosice.

The light that failed
When Holland met Spain for only the fourth time in 60 years in Vigo on 23 January 1980, it was an eventful night. The Dutch were unhappy about the rather obscure venue, and heavy rain caused them to ask that the match should not be played, though the decision of the referee under local official pressure made them start it. Though the rain had stopped in the 18th minute, one of the floodlight towers and a central bar of lights over the main stand went out. It took just under an hour to fix the fuse, but by that time the Dutch players had cleaned up, dressed and were on their way to the team coach. They were

prevailed upon to change and restart the match, which they subsequently lost by a penalty goal eight minutes from the end.

Tourist paradise?
Mexico had 31 Brazilian coaches in the country during 1979 and 40 others from various South American countries. Ten of the 20 First Division clubs were under the direction of foreigners.

Sporting conclusion
Sporting Club, Lisbon became the 1979–80 champions of Portugal, taking the title on the last day of the season by two points from Porto, who were beaten 2–0 by Espinho while Sporting were beating Leiria 3–0. It was Sporting's first title since 1974 and ended an odd sequence for them as their other recent honours in the League had come at four year intervals from 1958 up to 1974. In fact from 1962 it had been one Sporting success followed by three from Benfica for each four-year-period up to Benfica's third in a row in 1977. Porto ended the unusual sequence by winning the 1978 and 1979 titles.

Not all Greek
Olympiakos won the play-off for the championship in Greece after they had finished level on points with Aris Salonika. One of the decisive goals for the winners was scored by the Swedish international centre-forward Thomas Ahlstrom.

Melody lingers on
Chile's national team coach Luis Santibanez appointed a musical director for the squad in the South American Championship in the form of folklore singer Pedro Messone. They sang their way to the final, but then it ended on the wrong note: they were beaten by Paraguay.

Ding dong, the witch is dead
Officials of the Melgar club in Peru blamed the team's poor performances in the 1979 championship on witchcraft, exercised by a former member of the club against them. To counteract this, the players' shirts were soaked in an anti-witchcraft herbal solution. Alas, Melgar finished bottom of the table. But in the play-off, to avoid relegation among the bottom eight clubs, the spell worked and their final position was third.

Nothing changes
Ecuador decided to import foreign referees to control their First Division matches, so that the officials could earn more respect and be unbiased about the games they handled. Unfortunately, in successive weeks an Argentine referee was assaulted and a similar attack was made on a Uruguayan.

Ask the family
Olimpia appointed the ex-Uruguayan international forward, Luis Cubilla, as their coach after winning the 1978 Paraguayan championship. He helped them win the South American Cup, the World Club Championship and the Inter-American Cup in 1979, and then resigned to take up an appointment with the Argentine club Newell's Old Boys. So Olimpia appointed his brother Pedro in place of him.

THE EXPORT GAME

Players have been exported from British shores since before the turn of the century. And as the game abroad developed, coaches also played a significant role in spreading interest through their expertise around the world.

One of the earliest exports as a coach was Jimmy Hogan, whose modest playing career had embraced various clubs including Burnley and Fulham, and it was at only 30 years of age that he turned his attention to teaching others.

He did much to establish the game on the continent, especially in Austria and Hungary, becoming the tactical guidance behind the successful Austrian 'Wunderteam' of the 1930s.

Yet on frequent returns to this country he was not looked upon with much favour, in days when coaching was frowned upon and both Fulham and Aston Villa dismissed him after spells as their manager. But though well past the age of 60 he was still coaching at Brentford and in his 70th year he was a guest of the Hungarians when they beat England 6–3 at Wembley in 1953.

A player who had a much more illustrious career than Hogan was Steve Bloomer, but he also did well in a coaching capacity outside this country. In 1914 he retired after scoring 352 League goals and playing 23 times for his country. He went to Germany to coach and was interned throughout the First World War.

However, it was the adoption of professionalism on the continent between the two wars which led to more players from here finding an attractive source of income there. For example, the French introduced professionalism in 1932 and offered terms to several Football League players.

Hughie Gallacher and Tommy Law of Chelsea were offered £20 per week by the Nimes club. They could not obtain satisfactory guarantees, so they refused to sign, but a former teammate Andy Wilson, then with Queen's Park Rangers and Alex Cheyne still at Stamford Bridge, did join them with Harry Ward of Ramsgate.

At the time the Football Association was out of membership with FIFA over broken time payments, so were powerless to prevent the virtual poaching of their players. Another French team Racing Club of Paris sought the services of England international inside-forward David Jack as a coach, but he also refused the offer. Instead they secured Fred Phoenix, a player who had served Aston Villa, Torquay United and Bath City plus Fred Kennedy who had assisted Everton and Oldham Athletic. Kennedy returned to play for Blackburn Rovers in 1933–34, but went back to Racing in 1935.

Others who went to France around this period included Sam Jennings (Burnley), George Harkins (Southport), Hugh Vallance (Queen's Park Rangers, Aston Villa, Brighton, Kidderminster and Gillingham), Jock Paton and John Donoghue of Celtic.

The United States of America, which had been one of the first to tempt players from the British Isles before the 20th century, also renewed their efforts. Several players went to the USA for short spells like Alex Jackson from Dumbarton to Bethlehem Steel Company around 1923, Bill Harper from Arsenal to Fall River in 1930 and Mick O'Brien (Queen's Park Rangers, Leicester City, Hull City and Derby County) to Brooklyn Wanderers 1926, before returning to play for Walsall and Watford. Others, like Sam Chedgzoy from Everton in 1928, Cyril Hunter from Gateshead in the same year and Tommy Blair from Kilmarnock in 1923, also made the trip.

In 1894 it had been Baltimore who had sent an agent to this country to seek additions for a new professional league in the USA. As reported in the first edition of the *Guinness Book of Soccer Facts and Feats,* several Manchester City players sailed out, but the venture collapsed.

Other countries on the continent saw British players joining them in the 1930s, however, with Bob Douglas going to Switzerland from Aldershot in 1933, Jack Peacock moving to Sleipner, Sweden from Clapton Orient in the same year and Wilson Lennox making the journey to Holland from Accrington Stanley.

In the immediate years following the Second

Anglo-Italian soccer exports, *top:* **Joe Baker,** *middle:* **Jimmy Greaves,** *bottom:* **Gerry Hitchens. (Colorsport)**

World War, Italy became a different venue for a few of our players. Norman Adcock was one of them. He had arrived in the country with the liberation army in 1945 aged 22 with little senior experience in the game. Yet he signed for Padova as a professional, played centre-forward for them for three seasons, and then moved to Triestina in 1949. Later he became a player-coach and moved to Central Europe.

Johnny Jordan, who had played for Grays Athletic and Tottenham Hotspur as a forward, had a season with Juventus in 1948–49, but failed to settle and came back to play for Birmingham City and Sheffield Wednesday. Indeed the failure to adjust to the Italian scene was a continuing feature of connections between the two countries.

Frank Rawcliffe (Wolverhampton Wanderers, Newport County, Swansea Town and Aldershot) joined Alessandria in September 1949, but this centre-forward returned in 1950 to become player-coach to South Liverpool.

The next sphere of influence to be developed was an illegal one. In 1950 Colombia started a rebel league attracting leading foreign players chiefly from South America, but also offering large salaries without transfer fees to players from the British Isles.

The temptation was such that Neil Franklin (Stoke City and England), Bobby Flavell (Heart of Midlothian and Scotland), Jack Hedley (Everton), Roy Paul (Swansea Town and Wales), George Mountford (Stoke City) and Billy Higgins (Everton) flew to Bogota to join teams like Millonarios and Santa Fe, but found conditions were not to their liking and they returned home either immediately or after just a short stay. Only Charlie Mitten of Manchester United completed the season.

On their return most of them received periods of suspension as Colombia were outside FIFA's jurisdiction at the time. All were transferred by their clubs and in the case of Franklin who had been England's regular choice centre-half, his international career was ended.

In the middle of the 1950s the Italians were active again as far as this country was concerned and in 1955 Eddie Firmani, born in Cape Town, South Africa, of Italian extraction, signed for Sampdoria from Charlton Athletic who received £35 000 for his transfer. He subsequently played for Internazionale.

Another with Italian origin was Tony Marchi an England 'B' player who was transferred to Juventus in 1957 from Tottenham Hotspur, but as the Turin club who paid £40 000 for his services had one foreign player already on their books, they had to loan him to Lanerossi Vicenza. In 1958 he was transferred to Torino and he came back to Tottenham in 1959 for £24 000.

But of all the exports to Italy, John Charles was probably the most successful. As related in the Second edition of the *Guinness Book of Soccer Facts and Feats* he joined Juventus for a then record British fee of £65 000 in 1957 and scored 93 goals in 155 appearances before returning to Leeds United in August 1962, and having a shorter spell subsequently with Roma.

However, it was in 1961 when there was a flurry of activity in the transfer market between the two countries that players of the calibre of Denis Law, Jimmy Greaves, Gerry Hitchens and Joe Baker all made the move to Italy. Yet only Hitchens remained for any length of time.

Law cost Torino £100 000 but was back with Manchester City's neighbours United a year later at a cost of £115 000. Greaves had gone to AC Milan from Chelsea for £85 000 but came back within a few months to join Tottenham Hotspur in a £99 999 deal. Baker became a colleague of Law's at Torino having gone from Hibernian for £70 000 before coming back to Arsenal, while Hitchens who survived several years with various clubs had originally cost Internazionale £80 000.

The largely unsuccessful outcome of these moves tended to cease transfers to Italy and when towards the end of the 1960s the Italians banned foreigners anyway, it was back to the United States of America for the bulk of the moves outside this country. By 1978 there were 129 English born players alone playing regularly in the North American Soccer League, either on a season to season basis or on more of a permanent association.

But the continent was beckoning once again, especially Holland where Barry Hughes, a centre-half with West Bromwich Albion, first went as a player and then remained as a coach. In the 1979–80 season he was still in charge of Haarlem.

Ajax owed much of the development as a club to the coaching of Vic Buckingham prior to their days as three times European Cup holders in the early 1970s. And earlier still across the border in Belgium, Bill Gormlie a former Blackpool, Blackburn Rovers and Northampton Town goalkeeper was appointed national coach in 1947, and two years later found himself in charge of Anderlecht for a lengthy and successful period.

Again as reported in the previous edition of the *Guinness Book of Soccer Facts and Feats,* George Raynor became one of the most successful coaches in the world, leading Sweden to Olympic and World Cup successes of various kinds from 1948 to 1958.

During the war, Raynor had been a playing colleague with Aldershot of Jimmy Hagan, then guesting for the club on army service while with Sheffield United. And Hagan has earned his own reputation as a coach with several clubs in Portugal including Benfica.

It was in the same country that Tommy Docherty had a season in charge of Porto, while Manchester City team manager Malcolm Allison can claim to have coached in Turkey, Canada and the USA. Alec Stock, the Bournemouth manager, was in charge of the Italian club Roma at one time as well.

The drift of players to Holland has increased in recent years. One of the most successful of the exports was Ray Clarke who returned to Brighton and Hove Albion last season, after scoring regularly for Sparta Rotterdam and Ajax and then moving to FC Bruges in Belgium.

But it was to West Germany that the honour of the next major signing came when Hamburg paid £500 000 for the services of Kevin Keegan of Liverpool. In the summer of 1977 he was transferred and the move so enhanced his reputation that he became European Footballer of the Year in 1978 and 1979.

Anglo-Belgian soccer exports, *above right:* **Ray Clarke and** *below:* **Duncan McKenzie who had a spell with Anderlecht. (Colorsport/Syndication International)**

England international players, Tony Woodcock *above* **and Laurie Cunningham** *below*. **(Colorsport)**

Laurie Cunningham joined Real Madrid for £900 000 in 1979 from West Bromwich Albion and Cologne paid £650 000 for the services of Tony Woodcock of Nottingham Forest. Dave Watson had a short spell with Werder Bremen, also in West Germany, at the start of the 1979–80 season before returning to Keegan's new English club Southampton.

And so in the early part of the 1979–80 season four current England internationals were playing abroad among many British players and coaches earning their livelihood outside these islands.

Malmo, the Swedish club who reached the final of the European Cup in 1979, were coached by Bob Houghton while Roy Hodgson, a former colleague from his Croydon school days and subsequent player with him in South Africa, has had two championship successes in Sweden recently while in charge of Halmstad.

Also in Scandinavia, Tony Knapp was in charge of the Icelandic national team and in 1979 took over the coaching of the Norwegian club Viking Stavanger.

Malcolm Macdonald spent a season with Djurgaarden in 1979 before having to retire through injury after a goalscoring career with Fulham, Luton Town, Newcastle United and Arsenal. It was Macdonald who had equalled the record individual score in one match for England when he scored five times against Cyprus at Wembley in 1975.

The Manchester derby reached its centenary of matches in 1980. In last season's encounter at Maine Road, red-shirted United in aerial action against City men in their traditional sky blue. (Syndication International)

Terry McDermott, the Liverpool and England international midfield player who won the 1980 Professional Footballers Association award as Player of the Year. (Syndication International)

Trevor Francis heads the only goal of the 1979 European Cup Final for Nottingham Forest against Malmo in Munich. *Inset,* Forest captain John McGovern with the trophy. (Colorsport)

The eleven different winners of the first 24 European Cup finals. *Left to right:* **Real Madrid, Benfica, AC Milan, Internazionale, Celtic, Manchester United, Feyenoord, Ajax, Bayern Munich, Liverpool and Nottingham Forest.** (Artwork by Mick Hooker)

Wolves players celebrate at Wembley after their League Cup success. (All Sport Tony Duffy)

Martin O'Neill (red shirt) in a League Cup Final tussle with Wolves captain Emlyn Hughes. (All Sport Tony Duffy)

INTERNATIONAL CENTURIANS

Björn Nordqvist's career

IFK Norrkoping, PSV Eindhoven (Netherlands), IFK Gothenburg and Sweden (115 International appearances).

Date	Venue	Opponents	Result
1963			
4 May	Budapest	Hungary (Olmp qual)	L 0–4
24 Aug	Solna	Finland	D 0–0
1964			
20 Sep	Oslo	Norway	D 1–1
1965			
16 May	Gothenburg	England	L 1–2
20 Jun	Copenhagen	Denmark	L 1–2
31 Oct	Solna	Norway	D 0–0

Date	Venue	Opponents	Result
1966			
27 Apr	Leipzig	E. Germany	L 1–4
18 May	Wroclaw	Poland	D 1–1
4 Jun	Helsingfors	Finland	L 0–1
18 Sep	Oslo	Norway	W 4–2
5 Oct	Solna	Austria	W 4–1
6 Nov	Solna	Denmark	W 2–1
13 Nov	Lisbon	Portugal (Eur Nat)	W 2–1
1967			
17 May	Helsingfors	E. Germany	L 0–1
1 Jun	Solna	Portugal (EC)	D 1–1
11 Jun	Solna	Bulgaria (EC)	L 0–2
25 Jun	Copenhagen	Denmark	D 1–1
5 Nov	Solna	Norway (EC)	W 5–2
12 Nov	Solna	Bulgaria (EC)	L 0–3
1968			
19 Feb	Jaffa	Israel	W 3–0
28 Feb	Seville	Spain	L 1–3
2 May	Malmo	Spain	D 1–1
22 May	Wembley	England	L 1–3
22 Jun	Solna	Denmark	W 2–1
1 Aug	Gothenburg	USSR	D 2–2
11 Sep	Helsinki	Finland	W 3–0
15 Sep	Oslo	Norway	D 1–1
9 Oct	Solna	Norway (WC qual)	W 5–0
1969			
19 Feb	Tel Aviv	Israel	W 3–2
26 Feb	Split	Yugoslavia	L 1–2
1 May	Malmo	Mexico	W 1–0
22 May	Vaxjo	Finland	W 4–0
1 Jun	Gothenburg	Norway	W 4–2
19 Jun	Oslo	Norway (WC qual)	W 5–2
25 Jun	Copenhagen	Denmark	W 1–0
6 Aug	Malmo	USSR	W 1–0
25 Aug	Solna	Israel	W 3–1
24 Sep	Solna	Hungary	W 2–0
15 Oct	Solna	France (WC qual)	W 2–0
1 Nov	Paris	France (WC qual)	L 0–3
1970			
22 Feb	Mexico City	Mexico	D 0–0
1 Mar	Puebla	Mexico	W 1–0
16 May	Budapest	Hungary	W 2–1
3 Jun	Toluca	Italy (WC)	L 0–1
10 Jun	Puebla	Uruguay (WC)	W 1–0
25 Jun	Gothenburg	Denmark	D 1–1
13 Sep	Oslo	Norway	W 4–2
14 Oct	Dublin	R. of Ireland (EC)	D 1–1
28 Oct	Solna	R. of Ireland (EC)	W 1–0
1971			
3 Mar	Tel Aviv	Israel	L 1–2
19 May	Boras	Finland	W 4–1
26 May	Solna	Austria (EC)	W 1–0
9 Jun	Solna	Italy (EC)	D 0–0
20 Jun	Copenhagen	Denmark	W 3–1
27 Jun	Gothenburg	W. Germany	W 1–0
8 Aug	Malmo	Norway	W 3–0
4 Sep	Vienna	Austria	L 0–1
10 Oct	Milan	Italy (EC)	L 0–3

Date	Venue	Opponents	Result

Thorbjorn Svenssen's career

1972
Date	Venue	Opponents	Result
26 Apr	Geneva	Switzerland	D 1–1
14 May	Gothenburg	Czechoslovakia	L 1–2
25 May	Solna	Hungary (WC qual)	D 0–0
11 Jun	Vienna	Austria (WC qual)	L 0–2
29 Jun	Malmo	Denmark	W 2–1
15 Oct	Gothenburg	Malta (WC qual)	W 7–0

1973
26 Apr	Copenhagen	Denmark	W 2–1
23 May	Gothenburg	Austria (WC qual)	W 3–2
13 Jun	Budapest	Hungary (WC qual)	D 3–3
25 Jun	Solna	Brazil	W 1–0
26 Sep	Milan	Italy	L 0–2
11 Nov	Valetta	Malta (WC qual)	W 2–1
27 Nov	Gelsenkirchen	Austria (WC qual)	W 2–1

1974
3 Jun	Copenhagen	Denmark	W 2–0
9 Jun	Malmo	Switzerland	D 0–0
19 Jun	Dortmund	Holland (WC)	D 0–0
23 Jun	Düsseldorf	Uruguay (WC)	W 3–0
26 Jun	Stuttgart	Poland (WC)	L 0–1
30 Jun	Düsseldorf	W. Germany (WC)	L 2–4
3 Jul	Düsseldorf	Yugoslavia	W 2–1
30 Oct	Solna	N. Ireland	L 0–2

1975
16 Apr	Gothenburg	Scotland	D 1–1
19 May	Halmstad	Algeria	W 4–0
4 Jun	Solna	Yugoslavia (EC)	L 1–2
13 Aug	Oslo	Norway (EC)	W 2–0
3 Sep	Belfast	N. Ireland (EC)	W 2–1
25 Sep	Malmo	Denmark	D 0–0
15 Oct	Zagreb	Yugoslavia	L 0–3

1976
28 Feb	Tunis	Tunisia	D 1–1
12 Mar	Algiers	Algeria	W 2–0
28 Apr	Vienna	Austria	L 0–1
11 May	Gothenburg	Denmark	L 1–2
1 Jun	Helsinki	Finland	W 2–0
16 Jun	Solna	Norway (WC qual)	W 2–0
11 Aug	Malmo	Finland	W 6–0
8 Sep	Solna	Hungary	D 1–1
22 Sep	Oslo	Norway	L 2–3
9 Oct	Basle	Switzerland	W 2–1

1977
27 Apr	Glasgow	Scotland	L 1–3
26 May	Gothenburg	Norway	W 1–0
8 Jun	Solna	Switzerland (WC qual)	W 2–1
15 Jun	Copenhagen	Denmark	L 1–2
20 Jul	Reykjavik	Iceland	W 1–0
17 Aug	Solna	E. Germany	L 0–1
7 Sep	Oslo	Norway (WC qual)	L 1–2
5 Oct	Malmo	Denmark	W 1–0
12 Oct	Budapest	Hungary	L 0–3
12 Nov	Wroclaw	Poland	L 1–2

1978
4 Apr	Leipzig	E. Germany	W 1–0
20 May	Solna	Czechoslovakia	D 0–0
3 Jun	Mar del Plata	Brazil (WC)	D 1–1
7 Jun	Buenos Aires	Austria (WC)	L 0–1
11 Jun	Buenos Aires	Spain (WC)	L 0–1
28 Jun	Boras	Finland	W 2–1
16 Aug	Copenhagen	Denmark	L 1–2
1 Sep	Paris	France (EC)	D 2–2
4 Oct	Solna	Czechoslovakia (EC)	L 1–3

1947
11 Jun	Oslo	Poland	W 3–1
26 Jun	Helsinki	Finland	W 2–1
28 Jun	Helsinki	Sweden	L 1–5
24 Jul	Reykjavik	Iceland	W 4–2
7 Sep	Helsinki	Finland	D 3–3
21 Sep	Oslo	Denmark	L 3–5

1948
26 May	Oslo	Holland	L 1–2
12 Jun	Copenhagen	Denmark	W 2–1
6 Aug	Oslo	USA	W 11–0
5 Sep	Oslo	Finland	W 2–0
19 Sep	Oslo	Sweden	L 3–5
24 Dec	Cairo	Egypt	D 1–1

1949
18 May	Oslo	England	L 1–4
19 Jun	Oslo	Yugoslavia	L 1–3
8 Jul	Helsinki	Finland	D 1–1
2 Oct	Stockholm	Sweden	D 3–3

1950
22 Jun	Copenhagen	Denmark	L 0–4
15 Aug	Bergen	Luxembourg	D 2–2
10 Sep	Oslo	Finland	W 4–1
24 Sep	Oslo	Sweden	L 1–3
5 Nov	Belgrade	Yugoslavia	L 0–4
26 Nov	Dublin	R. of Ireland	D 2–2

1951
15 May	Middlesbrough	England (Amateurs)	L 1–2
30 May	Oslo	R. of Ireland	L 2–3
6 Jun	Rotterdam	Holland	W 3–2
26 Jul	Trondheim	Iceland	W 3–1
16 Aug	Helsinki	Finland	D 1–1
23 Aug	Oslo	Yugoslavia	L 2–4
16 Sep	Oslo	Denmark	W 2–0
30 Sep	Gothenburg	Sweden	W 4–3

1952
10 Jun	Oslo	Finland	L 1–2
21 Jun	Tammerfors	Sweden (Olymp)	L 1–4
31 Aug	Oslo	Finland	W 7–2
5 Oct	Oslo	Sweden	L 1–2
19 Oct	Copenhagen	Denmark	W 3–1

1953
19 May	Oslo	England (Amateurs)	D 1–1
24 Jun	Oslo	Saar (WC)	L 2–3
13 Aug	Bergen	Iceland	W 3–1
19 Aug	Oslo	W. Germany (WC)	D 1–1
30 Aug	Helsinki	Finland	W 4–1
13 Sep	Oslo	Denmark	L 0–1
27 Sep	Oslo	Holland	W 4–0
18 Oct	Stockholm	Sweden	D 0–0
8 Nov	Saarbrucken	Saar (WC)	D 0–0
22 Nov	Hamburg	W. Germany (WC)	L 1–5

1954
19 May	Oslo	Scotland	D 1–1
30 May	Vienna	Austria	L 0–5
4 Jun	Malmo	Denmark	W 2–1
7 Jun	Stockholm	Sweden	L 0–3
29 Aug	Oslo	Finland	W 3–1
19 Sep	Oslo	Sweden	D 1–1
31 Oct	Copenhagen	Denmark	W 1–0
8 Nov	Dublin	R. of Ireland	L 1–2

Sandefjord BK and Norway (104 International appearances).

Date	Venue	Opponents	Result
14 Aug	Helsinki	Finland	W 3–1
25 Sep	Stockholm	Sweden	D 1–1
6 Nov	Amsterdam	Holland	L 0–3
16 Nov	Karlsruhe	W. Germany	L 0–2
1956			
3 Jun	Oslo	Poland	D 0–0
13 Jun	Oslo	W. Germany	L 1–3
24 Jun	Copenhagen	Denmark	W 3–2
26 Jun	Bucharest	Rumania	L 0–2
26 Aug	Oslo	Finland	D 1–1
16 Sep	Oslo	Sweden	W 3–1
28 Oct	Warsaw	Poland	L 3–5
1957			
22 May	Oslo	Bulgaria (WC)	L 1–2
12 Jun	Oslo	Hungary (WC)	W 2–1
18 Jun	Turku	Sweden	D 0–0
19 Jun	Tammerfors	Denmark	L 0–2
8 Jul	Reykjavik	Iceland	W 3–0
1 Sep	Helsinki	Finland	W 4–0
22 Sep	Oslo	Denmark	D 2–2
13 Oct	Stockholm	Sweden	L 2–5
1958			
28 May	Oslo	Holland	D 0–0
15 Jun	Oslo	Finland	W 2–0
29 Jun	Copenhagen	Denmark	W 2–1
2 Nov	Leipzig	E. Germany	L 1–4
1959			
20 May	Oslo	Austria (Eur Nat)	L 0–1
17 Jun	Oslo	Luxembourg	W 1–0
28 Jun	Helsinki	Finland	W 4–2
2 Jul	Copenhagen	Denmark (Olymp)	L 1–2
7 Jul	Reykjavik	Iceland (Olymp)	L 0–1
21 Aug	Oslo	Iceland (Olymp)	W 2–1
13 Sep	Oslo	Denmark (Olymp)	L 2–4
23 Sep	Vienna	Austria (Eur Nat)	L 2–5
18 Oct	Gothenburg	Sweden	L 2–6
4 Nov	Rotterdam	Holland	L 1–7
1960			
26 May	Copenhagen	Denmark	L 0–3
9 Jun	Oslo	Iceland	W 4–0
22 Jun	Oslo	Austria	L 1–2
28 Aug	Oslo	Finland	W 6–3
18 Sep	Oslo	Sweden	W 3–1
1961			
16 May	Bergen	Mexico	D 1–1
1 Jun	Oslo	Turkey (WC)	L 0–1
27 Jun	Helsinki	Finland	L 1–4
1 Jul	Moscow	USSR (WC)	L 2–5
23 Aug	Oslo	USSR (WC)	L 0–3
17 Sep	Oslo	Denmark	L 0–4
22 Oct	Gothenburg	Sweden	L 0–2
29 Oct	Istanbul	Turkey (WC)	L 1–2
5 Nov	Valetta	Malta	D 1–1
1962			
16 May	Oslo	Holland	W 2–1

Date	Venue	Opponents	Result
1955			
8 May	Oslo	Hungary	L 0–5
25 May	Oslo	R. of Ireland	L 1–3
12 Jun	Oslo	Rumania	L 0–1

OUTSTANDING INTERNATIONAL PLAYERS

The following players have appeared in 100 or more matches for their countries:

Name	Country	From	To	Total
Franz Beckenbauer	West Germany	1965	1977	103
Josef Bozsik	Hungary	1947	1962	100
Bobby Charlton	England	1958	1970	106
Hector Chumpitaz	Peru	1963		140*
Gylmar	Brazil	1953	1969	100
Bobby Moore	England	1962	1973	108
Bjorn Nordqvist	Sweden	1963	1978	115
Pele	Brazil	1957	1971	111
Leonel Sanchez	Chile	1955	1967	104
Thorbjorn Svenssen	Norway	1947	1962	104
Djalma Santos	Brazil	1952	1968	100
Rivelino	Brazil	1968	1979	120
Billy Wright	England	1946	1959	105
Attouga	Tunisia	1963	1979	109
Kazimierz Deyna	Poland	1968	1978	102

* Still adding to total in 1980.

'Rudi' Krol and 'Sepp' Maier

Ruud 'Rudi' Krol established a record of 65 appearances for Holland when he played in the FIFA 75th anniversary game between the Dutch and the World Cup holders Argentina in Berne, Switzerland on 22 May 1979.

Captain of his club Ajax and his country, Krol had made his first appearance in national colours on 5 November 1969 against England in Amsterdam, and in the next few years not only established himself in the Dutch side, but assisted Ajax in their European Cup exploits.

Though a broken leg kept him out of the 1971 final, he won two European Cup winners medals in 1972 and 1973 playing at full-back, though in later years he has switched to playing as a sweeper in the middle of the defence.

In the summer of 1980 he accepted an offer of a three-year engagement from the North American Soccer League club Vancouver Whitecaps at the age of 31 after his contract with Ajax had expired. He played his 450th match for the club on 26 April 1980 against Den Haag.

Before Krol set the new Dutch record, the most made by 'Puck' Van Heel over a considerably longer period of time from 1925 to 1953 in the days of amateurism in Holland and far fewer fixtures. Gerard Van Heel captained his country on 29 occasions and, like Krol, was virtually a one-club man for most of his senior career, playing for the Rotterdam side Feyenoord and helping them to League honours in 1928, 1936, 1938 and 1940 and cup wins in 1930 and 1935.

Krol joined Ajax in 1967. He was a member of the Dutch national team which finished as runners-up in the 1974 World Cup and captained them in the 1978 when they were again beaten finalists.

Josef 'Sepp' Maier, the Bayern Munich goal-keeper, was forced to retire from the game in January 1980, having failed to return to fitness following a serious car accident sustained on 14 July 1979. His injuries including several broken bones and a torn diaphragm were worse that at first feared. Though he subsequently regained physical well being he was ruled out of a comeback to top class football.

Maier made his first appearance for West Germany in Dublin against the Republic of Ireland on 4 May 1966 and his 95th and record for a West German goalkeeper against Iceland in Reykjavik on 26 May 1979. His honours for his country included a World Cup winners medal in 1974, and a European Championship winners medal in 1972.

For Bayern, whom he joined at 14 in 1958 from TSV Haar, he established a run of 442 consecutive League appearances in the Bundesliga from August 1966 to June 1979. Between 1965 and the end of the 1978–79 season he was absent in only three of 476 games in the competition.

His club honours included three European Cup winners medals in 1974, 1975 and 1976, a World Club Championship winners medal in 1976 and a European Cup Winners Cup medal in 1967. On the domestic front he added four Bundesliga championships for Bayern in 1969, 1972, 1973 and 1974 and four German cup medals in 1966, 1967, 1969 and 1971.

He was Footballer of the Year in West Germany in 1975, 1977 and 1978. A locksmith by trade he developed business interests later on owning a tennis centre in Munich and a flourishing advertising agency.

At his farewell match in June 1980 a crowd of 77 850 watched him play the first 21 minutes of a match between Bayern and the West German national team, won 3–1 by the national side.

GROWTH OF FIFA

FIFA's membership of 146 nations, which was reached in 1978, has been complicated by several factors. The two separate associations of Vietnam have become one, but this has been offset in numbers by the admission of Mozambique in 1978. However, Rhodesia originally admitted in 1965 were suspended in 1970, but with the independence granted to Zimbabwe in 1979 the status quo should be restored there as well. But South Africa, which became a member in 1952 and was suspended in 1964, did not figure among the 146. The one notable exception to the number mentioned is the People's Republic of China.

The People's Republic of China was re-admitted to FIFA in 1979. Originally founded in 1924 as the China National Amateur Athletic Federation, it was first affiliated to the world governing body in 1931. It withdrew in 1958 ostensibly as a protest to FIFA's recognition of Nationalist China four years earlier. But the People's Republic itself, which came into being politically in 1949, had isolated its activities of a sporting nature from

West Bromwich Albion visited China in 1978 and the People's Republic made the reverse trip the following year. The Chinese are pictured limbering up at The Hawthorns and also in action against Chelsea at Stamford Bridge. (PA and Colorsport)

most of the rest of the world, Albania and North Korea being two exceptions, for many years before this period.

In 1974 China was admitted to the Asian Confederation and not only participated in the Asian Cup, but finished in third place. It was the first step towards full admission to FIFA.

Foreign teams at national and club level have visited China in recent years and these tours have been reciprocated. China has also entered the 1982 World Cup.

There are some 1 550 000 amateur players and another 700 000 at youth level in the country. There are 338 teams active in some 43 local associations and 560 youth teams as well.

Competitions organised include national and regional tournaments held on an annual basis in a season which runs from March to November.

World Soccer Competitions

Super Cup

Glasgow Rangers manager Willie Waddell approached Ajax to play in a friendly at Ibrox Park as part of the club's centenary celebrations in 1973. At the time Rangers were holders of the European Cup Winners Cup and Ajax the European Cup champions.

The Dutch newspaper *De Telegraaf* suggested a new cup for a fixture on a home and away basis and the tag Super Cup was attached to it. However UEFA said that they did not approve of such a competition and stated that only friendlies could be played.

On 16 January 1973 Ajax won 3–1 at Ibrox against Rangers and the colours of all the clubs that the Scottish club had played in Europe were paraded round the ground before the game. The return in Amsterdam on 24 January was also won 3–2 by Ajax but so successful were the matches that within a year official approval had been given for what was hoped would be an annual event.

1973 Ajax (Holland) beat Rangers (Scotland) 3–1, 3–2
1974 Ajax (Holland) beat AC Milan (Italy) 0–1, 6–0
1975 Dynamo Kiev (USSR) beat Bayern Munich (West Germany) 1–0, 2–0
1976 Anderlecht (Belgium) beat Bayern Munich (West Germany) 4–1, 1–2
1977 Liverpool (England) beat Hamburg SV (West Germany) 1–1, 6–0
1978 Anderlecht (Belgium) beat Liverpool (England) 3–1, 1–2
1979 Nottingham Forest (England) beat Barcelona (Spain) 1–0, 1–1

World Club Championship
year
1960 Real Madrid (Spain) beat Penarol (Uruguay) 0–0, 5–1

1961 Penarol (Uruguay) beat Benfica (Portugal) 0–1, 5–0, 2–1
1962 Santos (Brazil) beat Benfica (Portugal) 3–2, 5–2
1963 Santos (Brazil) beat AC Milan (Italy) 2–4, 4–2, 1–0
1964 Inter-Milan (Italy) beat Independiente (Argentina) 0–1, 2–0, 1–0
1965 Inter-Milan (Italy) beat Independiente (Argentina) 3–0, 0–0
1966 Penarol (Uruguay) beat Real Madrid (Spain) 2–0, 2–0
1967 Racing Club (Argentina) beat Celtic (Scotland) 0–1, 2–1, 1–0
1968 Estudiantes (Argentina) beat Manchester United (England) 1–0, 1–1
1969 AC Milan (Italy) beat Estudiantes (Argentina) 3–0, 1–2
1970 Feyenoord (Holland) beat Estudiantes (Argentina) 2–2, 1–0
1971 Nacional (Uruguay) beat Panathinaikos (Greece) 1–1, 2–1
1972 Ajax (Holland) beat Independiente (Argentina) 1–1, 3–0
1973 Independiente (Argentina) beat Juventus (Italy) 1–0
1974 Atletico Madrid (Spain) beat Independiente (Argentina) 0–1, 2–0
1975 Independiente (Argentina) and Bayern Munich (West Germany) could not agree on dates
1976 Bayern Munich (West Germany) beat Cruzeiro (Brazil) 2–0, 0–0
1977 Boca Juniors (Argentina) beat Borussia Moenchengladbach (West Germany) 2–2, 3–0
1978 Not contested
1979 Olimpia (Paraguay) beat Malmo (Sweden) 1–0, 2–1

Detailed background information on all the following cup competitions appears on pages 21 and 22 of the 1st Edition of *The Guinness Book of Soccer Facts and Feats.*

Mitropa Cup

The Mitropa Cup, the oldest international club competition in Europe, was revived in 1980 after one year's absence.

1927	Sparta Prague (Czechoslovakia)
1928	Ferencvaros (Hungary)
1929	Ujpest Dozsa (Hungary)
1930	Rapid Vienna (Austria)
1931	First Vienna (Austria)
1932	Bologna (Italy)
1933	FK Austria (Austria)
1934	Bologna (Italy)
1935	Sparta Prague (Czechoslovakia)
1936	FK Austria (Austria)
1937	Ferencvaros (Hungary)
1938	Slavia Prague (Czechoslovakia)
1939	Ujpest Dozsa (Hungary)
1951	Rapid Vienna (Austria)
1955	Voros Lobogo (Hungary)
1956	Vasas Budapest (Hungary)
1957	Vasas Budapest (Hungary)
1959	Honved (Hungary)
1960	not completed
1961	Bologna (Italy)
1962	Vasas Budapest (Hungary)
1963	MTK Budapest (Hungary)
1964	Sparta Prague (Czechoslovakia)
1965	Vasas Budapest (Hungary)
1966	Fiorentina (Italy)
1967	Spartak Trnava (Czechoslovakia)
1968	Red Star Belgrade (Yugoslavia)
1969	Inter Bratislava (Czechoslovakia)
1970	Vasas Budapest (Hungary)
1971	Celik Zenica (Yugoslavia)
1972	Celik Zenica (Yugoslavia)
1973	Tatabanya (Hungary)
1974	Tatabanya (Hungary)
1975	SW Innsbruck (Austria)
1976	SW Innsbruck (Austria)
1977	Vojvodina (Yugoslavia)
1978	Partizan Belgrade (Yugoslavia)
1979	not contested
1980	Udinese (Italy)

Asian Champion Clubs Cup

1967	Hapoel Tel Aviv (Israel)
1968	not played
1969	Maccabi Tel Aviv (Israel)
1970	Tai Teheran (Iran)
1971	Maccabi Tel Aviv (Israel)
1972–78	not played

World Military Championships

1950	Italy
1951	Italy
1952	Greece
1953	Belgium
1954	Belgium
1955	Turkey
1956	Italy
1957	France
1958	Portugal
1959	Italy
1960	Belgium
1961	not played, Turkey and Greece refused to meet
1962	Greece
1963	Greece
1964	France
1965	Spain
1966	Turkey
1967	Turkey
1968	Greece
1969	Greece
1970	not played
1971	not played
1972	Iraq
1973	Italy
1974–75	West Germany
1976–77	Iraq
1978–79	Iraq

Competition spread over two years from 1974.

African Cup Winners Cup

1975	Tonnerre Yaounde (Cameroun)
1976	Shooting Stars Club (Nigeria)
1977	Enugu Rangers (Nigeria)
1978	Horoya, Conakry (Guinea)
1979	Canon, Yaounde (Cameroun)

African Champion Clubs Cup

1964	Oryx, Douala (Cameroun)
1966	Stade d'Abidjan (Ivory Coast)
1967	TP Mazembe (Zaire)
1968	TP Mazembe (Zaire)
1969	Ismaili (Egypt)
1970	Kotoko (Ghana)
1971	Canon, Yaounde (Cameroun)
1972	Hafia, Conakry (Guinea)
1973	Vita Club, Kinshasa (Zaire)
1974	CARA, Brazzaville (Congo)
1975	Hafia, Conakry (Guinea)
1976	Mouloudia Chaabia Alger (Algeria)
1977	Hafia, Conakry (Guinea)
1978	Canon, Yaounde (Cameroun)
1979	Union, Douala (Cameroun)

AFRICAN NATIONS CUP

This competition for national teams began in 1957, and the original cup was donated by Lt General Mustapha of Egypt. It was given outright to Ghana in 1978 after they had won it for the third time. A new trophy, called the Africa Cup of Unity, was donated by the Supreme Council for Sport in Africa.

Nigeria won the 1980 competition when they defeated Algeria 3–0 in the final in Lagos before a crowd of over 80 000.

Previous winners: 1957 Egypt; 1959 Egypt; 1961 Ethiopia; 1963 Ghana; 1965 Ghana; 1968 Zaire; 1970 Sudan; 1972 Congo; 1974 Zaire; 1976 Morocco; 1978 Ghana.

AUSTRALIA

A national league was started in Australia in 1977 with a guaranteed sponsorship from Philips Industries for three years. Fourteen teams competed and on the same principle as the North American Soccer League, guest players from Europe appeared for clubs during the season.

Winners: 1977 Sydney City; 1978 West Adelaide; 1979 Marconi.

INTER-AMERICAN CUP

Played between the winners of the South American Cup (Libertadores Cup) and the Concacaf Cup it was first held in 1969, but was slow becoming a consistent competition because of failure of competing teams to agree to dates.

1969	Estudiantes (Argentina)
1972	Nacional (Uruguay)
1973	Independiente (Argentina)
1974	Independiente (Argentina)
1975	Independiente (Argentina)
1976	Independiente (Argentina)
1977	America (Mexico)
1978	America (Mexico)
1979	Olimpia (Paraguay)
1980	Olimpia (Paraguay)

THE CHAMPIONSHIP OF CONCACAF

The championship of the North and Central America and Caribbean Confederation was originally organised as the Championship of Central America and the Caribbean from 1941 to 1961 inclusive. Winners have been:

1941	Costa Rica
1943	El Salvador
1946	Costa Rica
1948	Costa Rica
1951	Panama
1953	Costa Rica
1955	Costa Rica
1957	Haiti
1960	Costa Rica
1961	Costa Rica
1963	Costa Rica
1965	Mexico
1967	Guatemala
1969	Costa Rica
1973	Haiti
1977	Mexico
1979	Haiti

The Championship of CONCACAF Club Champions

This club tournament for the Confederation began in 1963, but was only expanded into its latter form in 1967. Winners have been:

1963	Guadalajara (Mexico)
1964	Guadalajara
1965	Guadalajara
1966	Racing (Haiti)
1967	Alianza (El Salvador)
1968	Toluca (Mexico)
1969	Cruz Azul (Mexico)
1970	Three Zones:
	Cruz Azul (Mexico) in North
	Saprissa (Costa Rica) in Central
	Transvaal (Surinam) in Caribbean
1971	Cruz Azul (Mexico)
1972	Olimpia (Honduras)
1973	Transvaal (Surinam)
1974–75	Municipal (Guatemala)
1975–76	Atletico Espanol (Mexico)
1976–77	America (Mexico)
1977–78	Comunicaciones (Guatemala)

The Mediterranean Games held every four years since 1951 were won in 1979 by Yugoslavia, the host nation. Previous winners: 1951 Greece; 1955 Egypt; 1959 Italy; 1963 Italy; 1967 Italy; 1971 Yugoslavia; 1975 Algeria.

The Panamerican Games were won in 1979 by Brazil. The finals were held in Puerto Rico. Previous winners: 1937 (unofficial) Argentina; 1951 Argentina; 1955 Argentina; 1959 Argentina; 1963 Brazil; 1967 Mexico; 1971 Argentina; 1975 Mexico.

The Gulf Cup was won in 1979 by the host nation Iraq. Known as the Arabian Gulf tournament it was first won by Kuwait in 1970.

World Cup

The World Cup trophy itself is now the second in the lifetime of the competition. The first was named after Jules Rimet, the late Honorary President of FIFA from 1921 to 1954. Brazil won this cup outright in 1970.

A new trophy of solid gold 36cm high known as the FIFA World Cup and designed by an Italian from an entry of some 53 submitted for selection was used in 1974 for the first time.

Summary of Matches in World Cup Finals 1930-78

		P	W	D	L	F	A			P	W	D	L	F	A
1.	Brazil	52	33	10	9	119	56	25.	United States of America	7	3	0	4	12	21
2.	West Germany*	47	28	9	10	110	68	26.	Wales	5	1	3	1	4	4
3.	Italy	36	20	6	10	62	40	27.	Northern Ireland	5	2	1	2	6	10
4.	Uruguay	29	14	5	10	57	39	28.	Rumania	8	2	1	5	12	17
5.	Argentina	29	14	5	10	55	43	29.	Bulgaria	12	0	4	8	9	29
6.	Hungary	26	13	2	11	73	42	30.	Tunisia	3	1	1	1	3	2
7.	Sweden	28	11	6	11	48	46	31.	North Korea	4	1	1	2	5	9
8.	England	24	10	6	8	34	28	32.	Cuba	3	1	1	1	5	12
9.	Yugoslavia	25	10	5	10	45	34	33.	Belgium	9	1	1	7	12	25
10.	USSR	19	10	3	6	30	21	34.	Turkey	3	1	0	2	10	11
11.	Holland (Netherlands)	16	8	3	5	32	19	35.	Israel	3	0	2	1	1	3
12.	Poland	14	9	1	4	27	17	36.	Morocco	3	0	1	2	2	6
13.	Austria	18	9	1	8	33	36	37.	Australia	3	0	1	2	0	5
14.	Czechoslovakia	22	8	3	11	32	36	38.	Iran	3	0	1	2	2	8
15.	France	20	8	1	11	43	38	39.	Colombia	3	0	1	2	5	11
16.	Chile	18	7	3	8	23	24	40.	Norway	1	0	0	1	1	2
17.	Spain	18	7	3	8	22	25	41.	Egypt	1	0	0	1	2	4
18.	Switzerland	18	5	2	11	28	44	42.	Dutch East Indies	1	0	0	1	0	6
19.	Portugal	6	5	0	1	17	8	43.	El Salvador	3	0	0	3	0	9
20.	Mexico	24	3	4	17	21	62	44.	South Korea	2	0	0	2	0	16
21.	Peru	12	4	1	7	17	25	45.	Haiti	3	0	0	3	2	14
22.	Scotland	11	2	4	5	12	21	46.	Zaire	3	0	0	3	0	14
23.	East Germany (GDR)	6	2	2	2	5	5	47.	Bolivia	3	0	0	3	0	16
24.	Paraguay	7	2	2	3	12	19								

* including Germany 1934-1938

1930–1978 World Cup Attendances and Goals

Year	Venue	Attendances	Average	Matches	Goals	Average
1930	Uruguay	434,500	24,139	18	70	3.88
1934	Italy	395,000	23,235	17	70	4.11
1938	France	483,000	26,833	18	84	4.66
1950	Brazil	1,337,000	60,772	22	88	4.00
1954	Switzerland	943,000	36,270	26	140	5.38
1958	Sweden	868,000	24,800	35	126	3.60
1962	Chile	776,000	24,250	32	89	2.78
1966	England	1,614,677	50,458	32	89	2.78
1970	Mexico	1,673,975	52,312	32	95	2.96
1974	West Germany	1,774,022	46,685	38	97	2.55
1978	Argentina	1,610,215	42,374	38	102	2.68

World Cup
FINAL SERIES 1930–1978 (PARTICIPATING COUNTRIES & RESULTS)

	1930	1934	1938	1950	1954
ARGENTINA	France 1–0 Mexico 6–3 Chile 3–1 USA 6–1 (SF) Uruguay 2–4 (2nd)	Sweden 2–3			
AUSTRALIA					
AUSTRIA		France 3–2 Hungary 2–1 Italy 0–1 (SF) Germany 2–3 (4th)			Scotland 1–0 Czechoslovakia 5–0 Switzerland 7–5 West Germany 1–6 (SF) Uruguay 3–1 (3rd)
BELGIUM	USA 0–3 Paraguay 0–1	Germany 2–5	France 1–3		England 4–4 Italy 1–4
BOLIVIA	Yugoslavia 0–4 Brazil 0–4			Uruguay 0–8	
BRAZIL	Yugoslavia 1–2 Bolivia 4–0	Spain 1–3	Poland 6–5 Czechoslovakia 1–1 Czechoslovakia (r) 2–1 Italy 1–2 (SF) Sweden 4–2 (3rd)	Mexico 4–0 Switzerland 2–2 Yugoslavia 2–0 Sweden 7–1 Spain 6–1 Uruguay 1–2 (2nd)	Mexico 5–0 Yugoslavia 1–1 Hungary 2–4
BULGARIA					
CHILE	Mexico 3–0 France 1–0 Argentina 1–3			England 0–2 Spain 0–2 USA 5–2	
COLOMBIA					
CUBA			Rumania 3–3 Rumania (r) 2–1 Sweden 0–8		

Key : W==Winners ; 2nd==Runners up ; 3rd==Won match for third place ; 4th==Lost match for third place ; SF==Semi final ; p o==play-off ; r==replay

1958	1962	1966	1970	1974	1978	
						ARGENTINA
West Germany 1–3	Bulgaria 1–0	Spain 2–1		Poland 2–3	Hungary 2–1	
Northern Ireland 3–1	England 1–3	West Germany 0–0		Italy 1–1	France 2–1	
Czechoslovakia 1–6	Hungary 0–0	Switzerland 2–0		Haiti 4–1	Italy 0–1	
		England 0–1		Netherlands 0–4	Poland 2–0	
				Brazil 1–2	Brazil 0–0	
				East Germany 1–1	Peru 6–0	
					Netherlands 3–1 (W)	
						AUSTRALIA
				East Germany 0–2		
				West Germany 0–3		
				Chile 0–0		
						AUSTRIA
Brazil 0–3					Spain 2–1	
USSR 0–2					Sweden 1–0	
England 2–2					Brazil 0–1	
					Netherlands 1–5	
					Italy 0–1	
					West Germany 3–2	
						BELGIUM
			El Salvador 3–0			
			USSR 1–4			
			Mexico 0–1			
						BOLIVIA
						BRAZIL
Austria 3–0	Mexico 2–0	Bulgaria 2–0	Czechoslovakia 4–1	Yugoslavia 0–0	Sweden 1–1	
England 0–0	Czechoslovakia 0–0	Hungary 1–3	England 1–0	Scotland 0–0	Spain 0–0	
USSR 2–0	Spain 2–1	Portugal 1–3	Rumania 3–2	Zaire 3–0	Austria 1–0	
Wales 1–0	England 3–1		Peru 4–2	East Germany 1–0	Peru 3–0	
France 5–2	Chile 4–2		Uruguay 3–1	Argentina 2–1	Argentina 0–0	
Sweden 5–2 (W)	Czechoslovakia 3–1 (W)		Italy 4–1 (W)	Netherlands 0–2	Poland 3–1	
				Poland 0–1 (4th)	Italy 2–1 (3rd)	
						BULGARIA
	Argentina 0–1	Brazil 0–2	Peru 2–3	Sweden 0–0		
	Hungary 1–6	Portugal 0–3	West Germany 2–5	Uruguay 1–1		
	England 0–0	Hungary 1–3	Morocco 1–1	Netherlands 1–4		
						CHILE
	Switzerland 3–1	Italy 0–2		West Germany 0–1		
	Italy 2–0	North Korea 1–1		East Germany 1–1		
	West Germany 0–2	USSR 1–2		Australia 0–0		
	USSR 2–1					
	Brazil 2–4 (SF)					
	Yugoslavia 1–0 (3rd)					
						COLOMBIA
	Uruguay 1–2					
	USSR 4–4					
	Yugoslavia 0–5					
						CUBA

	1930	1934	1938	1950	1954
CZECHOSLOVAKIA		Rumania 2–1 Switzerland 3–2 Germany 3–1 Italy 1–2 (2nd)	Netherlands 3–0 Brazil 1–1 Brazil (r) 1–2		Uruguay 0–2 Austria 0–5
DUTCH EAST INDIES			Hungary 0–6		
EAST GERMANY (GDR)					
EGYPT		Hungary 2–4			
ENGLAND				Chile 2–0 USA 0–1 Spain 0–1	Belgium 4–4 Switzerland 2–0 Uruguay 2–4
EL SALVADOR					
FRANCE	Mexico 4–1 Argentina 0–1 Chile 0–1	Austria 2–3	Belgium 3–1 Italy 1–3		Yugoslavia 0–1 Mexico 3–2
GERMANY		Belgium 5–2 Sweden 2–1 Czechoslovakia 1–3 (SF) Austria 3–2 (3rd)	Switzerland 1–1 Switzerland (r) 2–4		
HAITI					
HUNGARY		Egypt 4–2 Austria 1–2	Dutch East Indies 6–0 Switzerland 2–0 Sweden 5–1 Italy 2–4		South Korea 9–0 West Germany 8–3 Brazil 4–2 Uruguay 4–2 West Germany 2–3 (2nd)
IRAN					
ISRAEL					

58	1962	1966	1970	1974	1978	
						CZECHOSLOVAKIA
orthern Ireland 0–1	Spain 1–0		Brazil 1–4			
est Germany 2–2	Brazil 0–0		Rumania 1–2			
rgentina 6–1	Mexico 1–3		England 0–1			
orth Ireland 1–2 (p-o)	Hungary 1–0					
	Yugoslavia 3–1					
	Brazil 1–3 (2nd)					
						DUTCH EAST INDIES
						EAST GERMANY (GDR)
			Australia 2–0			
			Chile 1–1			
			West Germany 1–0			
			Brazil 0–1			
			Netherlands 0–2			
			Argentina 1–1			
						EGYPT
						ENGLAND
SSR 2–2	Hungary 1–2	Uruguay 0–0	Rumania 1–0			
razil 0–0	Argentina 3–1	Mexico 2–0	Brazil 0–1			
ustria 2–2	Bulgaria 0–0	France 2–0	Czechoslovakia 1–0			
SSR 0–1 (p-o)	Brazil 1–3	Argentina 1–0	West Germany 2–3			
		Portugal 2–1				
		West Germany 4–2 (W)				
						EL SALVADOR
			Belgium 0–3			
			Mexico 0–4			
			USSR 0–2			
						FRANCE
araguay 7–3		Mexico 1–1			Italy 1–2	
ugoslavia 2–3		Uruguay 1–2			Argentina 1–2	
cotland 2–1		England 0–2			Hungary 3–1	
orthern Ireland 4–0						
razil 2–5 (SF)						
Vest Germany 6–3 (3rd)						
						GERMANY
						HAITI
			Italy 1–3			
			Poland 0–7			
			Argentina 1–4			
						HUNGARY
Vales 1–1	England 2–1	Portugal 1–3			Argentina 1–2	
weden 1–2	Bulgaria 6–1	Brazil 3–1			Italy 1–3	
lexico 4–0	Argentina 0–0	Bulgaria 3–1			France 1–3	
Vales 1–2 (p-o)	Czechoslovakia 0–1	USSR 1–2				
						IRAN
					Netherlands 0–3	
					Scotland 1–1	
					Peru 1–4	
						ISRAEL
			Uruguay 0–2			
			Sweden 1–1			
			Italy 0–0			

	1930	1934	1938	1950	1954
ITALY		USA 7–1 Spain 1–1 Spain (r) 1–0 Austria 1–0 Czechoslovakia 2–1 (W)	Norway 2–1 France 3–1 Brazil 2–1 Hungary 4–2 (W)	Sweden 2–3 Paraguay 2–0	Switzerland 1–2 Belgium 4–1 Switzerland 1–4 (p-o)
SOUTH KOREA					Hungary 0–9 Turkey 0–7
MEXICO	France 1–4 Chile 0–3 Argentina 3–6			Brazil 0–4 Yugoslavia 1–4 Switzerland 1–2	Brazil 0–5 France 2–3
MOROCCO					
NETHERLANDS (HOLLAND)		Switzerland 2–3	Czechoslovakia 0–3		
NORTHERN IRELAND					
NORTH KOREA					
NORWAY			Italy 1–2		
PARAGUAY	USA 0–3 Belgium 1–0			Sweden 2–2 Italy 0–2	
PERU	Rumania 1–3 Uruguay 0–1				
POLAND			Brazil 5–6		

1958	1962	1966	1970	1974	1978

ITALY

1958	1962	1966	1970	1974	1978
	West Germany 0–0	Chile 2–0	Sweden 1–0	Haiti 3–1	France 2–1
	Chile 0–2	USSR 0–1	Uruguay 0–0	Argentina 1–1	Hungary 3–1
	Switzerland 3–0	North Korea 0–1	Israel 0–0	Poland 1–2	Argentina 1–0
			Mexico 4–1		West Germany 0–0
			West Germany 4–3		Austria 1–0
			Brazil 1–4 (2nd)		Netherlands 1–2
					Brazil 1–2 (4th)

SOUTH KOREA

MEXICO

1958	1962	1966	1970	1974	1978
Sweden 0–3	Brazil 0–2	France 1–1	USSR 0–0		Tunisia 1–3
Wales 1–1	Spain 0–1	England 0–2	El Salvador 4–0		West Germany 0–6
Hungary 0–4	Czechoslovakia 3–1	Uruguay 0–0	Belgium 1–0		Poland 1–3
			Italy 1–4		

MOROCCO

1958	1962	1966	1970	1974	1978
			West Germany 1–2		
			Peru 0–3		
			Bulgaria 1–1		

NETHERLANDS (HOLLAND)

1958	1962	1966	1970	1974	1978
				Uruguay 2–0	Iran 3–0
				Sweden 0–0	Peru 0–0
				Bulgaria 4–1	Scotland 2–3
				Argentina 4–0	Austria 5–1
				East Germany 2–0	West Germany 2–2
				Brazil 2–0	Italy 2–1
				West Germany 1–2 (2nd)	Argentina 1–3 (2nd)

NORTHERN IRELAND

1958	1962	1966	1970	1974	1978
Czechoslovakia 1–0					
Argentina 1–3					
West Germany 2–2					
Czechoslovakia 2–1 (p-o)					
France 0–4					

NORTH KOREA

1958	1962	1966	1970	1974	1978
		USSR 0–3			
		Chile 1–1			
		Italy 1–0			
		Portugal 3–5			

NORWAY

PARAGUAY

1958	1962	1966	1970	1974	1978
France 3–7					
Scotland 3–2					
Yugoslavia 3–3					

PERU

1958	1962	1966	1970	1974	1978
			Bulgaria 3–2		Scotland 3–1
			Morocco 3–0		Netherlands 0–0
			West Germany 1–3		Iran 4–1
			Brazil 2–4		Brazil 0–3
					Poland 0–1
					Argentina 0–6

POLAND

1958	1962	1966	1970	1974	1978
				Argentina 3–2	West Germany 0–0
				Haiti 7–0	Tunisia 1–0
				Italy 2–1	Mexico 3–1
				Sweden 1–0	Argentina 0–2
				Yugoslavia 2–1	Peru 1–0
				West Germany 0–1	Brazil 1–3
				Brazil 1–0 (3rd)	

	1930	1934	1938	1950	1954
PORTUGAL					
RUMANIA	Peru 3–1 Uruguay 0–4	Czechoslovakia 1–2	Cuba 3–3 Cuba (r) 1–2		
SCOTLAND					Austria 0–1 Uruguay 0–7
SPAIN		Brazil 3–1 Italy 1–1 Italy (r) 0–1		USA 3–1 Chile 2–0 England 1–0 Uruguay 2–2 Brazil 1–6 Sweden 1–3 (4th)	
SWEDEN		Argentina 3–2 Germany 1–2	Cuba 8–0 Hungary 1–5 Brazil 2–4 (4th)	Italy 3–2 Paraguay 2–2 Brazil 1–7 Uruguay 2–3 Spain 3–1 (3rd)	
SWITZERLAND		Netherlands 3–2 Czechoslovakia 2–3	Germany 1–1 Germany (r) 4–2 Hungary 0–2	Yugoslavia 0–3 Brazil 2–2 Mexico 2–1	England 0–2 Italy 2–1 Italy 4–1 (p-o) Austria 5–7
TUNISIA					
TURKEY					West Germany 1–4 South Korea 7–0 West Germany 2–7 (p-o)
UNITED STATES of AMERICA	Belgium 3–0 Paraguay 3–0 Argentina 1–6 (SF)	Italy 1–7		Spain 1–3 England 1–0 Chile 2–5	
URUGUAY	Peru 1–0 Rumania 4–0 Yugoslavia 6–1 (SF) Argentina 4–2 (W)			Bolivia 8–0 Spain 2–2 Sweden 3–2 Brazil 2–1 (W)	Czechoslovakia 2–0 Scotland 7–0 England 4–2 Hungary 2–4 (SF) Austria 1–3 (4th)

58	1962	1966	1970	1974	1978	
						PORTUGAL
		Hungary 3–1 Bulgaria 3–0 Brazil 3–1 North Korea 5–3 England 1–2 (SF) USSR 2–1 (3rd)				
						RUMANIA
			England 0–1 Czechoslovakia 2–1 Brazil 2–3			
						SCOTLAND
goslavia 1–1 raguay 2–3 ance 1–2			Zaire 2–0 Brazil 0–0 Yugoslavia 1–1	Peru 1–3 Iran 1–1 Netherlands 3–2		
						SPAIN
	Czechoslovakia 0–1 Mexico 1–0 Brazil 1–2	Argentina 1–2 Switzerland 2–1 West Germany 1–2			Austria 1–2 Brazil 0–0 Sweden 1–0	
						SWEDEN
exico 3–0 ungary 2–1 ales 0–0 SSR 2–0 est Germany 3–1 azil 2–5 (2nd)			Italy 0–1 Israel 1–1 Uruguay 1–0	Bulgaria 0–0 Netherlands 0–0 Uruguay 3–0 Poland 0–1 West Germany 2–4 Yugoslavia 2–1	Brazil 1–1 Austria 0–1 Spain 0–1	
						SWITZERLAND
	Chile 1–3 West Germany 1–2 Italy 0–3	West Germany 0–5 Spain 1–2 Argentina 0–2				
						TUNISIA
					Mexico 3–1 Poland 0–1 West Germany 0–0	
						TURKEY
						UNITED STATES of AMERICA
						URUGUAY
	Colombia 2–1 Yugoslavia 1–3 USSR 1–2	England 0–0 France 2–1 Mexico 0–0 West Germany 0–4	Israel 2–0 Italy 0–0 Sweden 0–1 USSR 1–0 Brazil 1–3 (SF) West Germany 0–1 (4th)	Netherlands 0–2 Bulgaria 1–1 Sweden 0–3		

	1930	1934	1938	1950	1954
USSR					
WALES					
WEST GERMANY					Turkey 4–1 Hungary 3–8 Turkey 7–2 (p-o) Yugoslavia 2-0 Austria 6–1 Hungary 3–2 (W)
YUGOSLAVIA	Brazil 2–1 Bolivia 4–0 Uruguay 1–6 (SF)			Switzerland 3–0 Mexico 4–1 Brazil 0–2	France 1–0 Brazil 1–1 West Germany 0–2
ZAIRE					

58	1962	1966	1970	1974	1978	
						USSR
gland 2–2	Yugoslavia 2–0	North Korea 3–0	Mexico 0–0			
ustria 2–0	Colombia 4–4	Italy 1–0	Belgium 4–1			
azil 0–2	Uruguay 2–1	Chile 2–1	El Salvador 2–0			
gland 1–0 (p-o)	Chile 1–2	Hungary 2–1	Uruguay 0–1			
veden 0–2		West Germany 1–2 (SF)				
		Portugal 1–2 (4th)				
						WALES
ungary 1–1						
exico 1–1						
veden 0–0						
ungary 2–1 (p-o)						
azil 0–1						
						WEST GERMANY
rgentina 3–1	Italy 0–0	Switzerland 5–0	Morocco 2–1	Chile 1–0	Poland 0–0	
zechoslovakia 2–2	Switzerland 2–1	Argentina 0–0	Bulgaria 5–2	Australia 3–0	Mexico 6–0	
orthern Ireland 2–2	Chile 2–0	Spain 2–1	Peru 3–1	East Germany 0–1	Tunisia 0–0	
ugoslavia 1–0	Yugoslavia 0–1	Uruguay 4–0	England 3–2	Yugoslavia 2–0	Italy 0–0	
weden 1–3 (SF)		USSR 2–1	Italy 3–4 (SF)	Sweden 4–2	Netherlands 2–2	
ance 3–6 (4th)		England 2–4 (2nd)	Uruguay 1–0 (3rd)	Poland 1–0	Austria 2–3	
				Netherlands 2 -1 (W)		
						YUGOSLAVIA
cotland 1–1	USSR 0-2			Brazil 0–0		
ance 3–2	Uruguay 3–1			Zaire 9–0		
araguay 3–3	Colombia 5–0			Scotland 1–1		
est Germany 0–1	West Germany 1–0			West Germany 0–2		
	Czechoslovakia 1–3 (SF)			Poland 1–2		
	Chile 0–1 (4th)			Sweden 1–2		
						ZAIRE
				Scotland 0–2		
				Yugoslavia 0–9		
				Brazil 0–3		

eft: Zaire goalkeeper Kazadi in action during the 974 World Cup in West Germany. (Syndication nternational)

oberto Bettega evades the outstretched tackle of erti Vogts (white shirt) in Italy's World Cup match ith West Germany in the 1978 final tournament. yndication International)

WORLD CUP WINNERS ANALYSIS (Final tournaments)

Uruguay (1930), Italy (1938) and Brazil (1970) have been the only winners with 100% records in one final series. They are also three of the four countries who have won the competition more than once, along with West Germany who have been the highest scorers in one tournament. They scored 25 in six matches (1954) which produced the highest average of 4.16 goals per game. England had the best defensive record in 1966 with only three goals conceded in six matches.

Year	Winners	Matches				Goals		Players	Appearances (goals)
		P	W	D	L	F	A	used	
1930	Uruguay	4	4	0	0	15	3	15	Ballesteros, Nasazzi, Cea (5), Andrade (J), Fernandez, Gestido, Iriarte (2) 4 each; Dorado (2), Macsheroni, Scarone (1) 3 each; Castro (2), Anselmo (3) 2 each; Tejera, Urdinaran, Petrone 1 each.

Final : Uruguay 4 Argentina 2 90,000 Montevideo

Italy, 1934 World Cup Champions. (Popperfoto)

Year	Winners								Appearances (goals)
1934	Italy	5	4	1	0	12	3	17	Combi, Allmandi, Monti, Meazza (2), Orsi (3) 5 each; Monzeglio, Bertolini, Schiavio (4), Ferrari (2), Guaita (1) 4 each; Ferraris IV 3; Pizziolo 2; Rosetta, Guarisi, Castellazzi, Borel, Demaria 1 each.

Final : Italy 2 Czechoslovakia 1 50,000 Rome
(after extra time)

1938	Italy	4	4	0	0	11	5	14	Olivieri, Rava, Serantoni, Andreolo, Locatelli, Meazza (1), Piolo (5), Ferrari (1) 4 each; Foni, Biavati, Colaussi (4) 3 each; Monzeglio, Pasinati, Ferraris II 1 each.

Final : Italy 4 Hungary 2 45,000 Paris

1950	Uruguay	4	3	1	0	15	5	14	Gonzales (M), Tejera, Valera (1), Andrade (R), Ghiggia (4), Perez, Miguez (4), Schiaffino (5) 4 each; Maspoli, Vidal (1) 3 each; Gonzales (W), Gambetta 2 each; Paz, Moran 1 each.

Deciding match : Uruguay 2 Brazil 1 199,850 Rio de Janeiro

1954	West Germany	6	5	0	1	25	14	18	Eckel, Walter (F) (3) 6 each; Turek, Kohlmeyer, Posipal, Mai, Morlock (6), Walter (O) (4), Schafer (4) 5 each; Liebrich, Rahn (4) 4 each; Laband 3; Klodt (1), Bauer 2 each; Herrmann (1), Mebus, Kwaitowski, Pfaff (1) 1 each. (own goal 1).

Final : West Germany 3 Hungary 2 60,000 Berne

The deciding match in the 1950 World Cup finals watched by a world record crowd. Uruguay beat Brazil 2-1. (Popperfoto)

1970 World Cup Final and Carlos Alberto holds the Jules Rimet Trophy aloft after Brazil's victory over Italy. (Syndication International)

Year	Winners	Matches				Goals		Players	Appearances (Goals)
		P	W	D	L	F	A	used	
1958	**Brazil**	6	5	1	0	16	4	16	Gilmar, Nilton Santos (1), Bellini, Orlando, Didi (1), Zagalo (1), 6 each; De Sordi 5; Vava (5), Zito, Garrincha, Pele (6), 4 each; Mazzola (2) 3; Dino, Joel 2 each; Djalma Santos, Dida 1 each.

Final: Brazil 5 Sweden 2   49,737 Stockholm

Year	Winners	Matches				Goals		Players	Appearances (Goals)
1962	**Brazil**	6	5	1	0	14	5	12	Gilmar, Djalma Santos, Mauro, Zozimo, Nilton Santos, Zito (1), Didi, Garrincha (4), Vara (4), Zagalo (1), 6 each; Amarildo (3) 4; Pele (1) 2.

Final: Brazil 3 Czechoslovakia 1   68,679 Santiago

Year	Winners	Matches				Goals		Players	Appearances (Goals)
1966	**England**	6	5	1	0	11	3	15	Banks, Cohen, Wilson, Stiles, Charlton (J), Moore, Charlton (R) (3), Hunt (3), 6 each; Peters (1) 5; Ball 4; Greaves, Hurst (4) 3; Paine, Callaghan, Connelly 1 each.

Final: England 4 West Germany 2   93,802 Wembley
(after extra time)

Year	Winners	Matches				Goals		Players	Appearances (Goals)
1970	**Brazil**	6	6	0	0	19	7	15	Felix, Carlos Alberto (1), Piazza, Brito, Clodoaldo (1), Jairzinho (7), Tostao (2), Pele (4), 6 each; Everaldo, Rivelino (3) 5; Gerson (1) 4; Paulo Cesar 2+2 subs; Marco Antonio 1+1 sub; Roberto 2 subs; Fontana 1; Edu 1 sub.

Final: Brazil 4 Italy 1   107,412 Mexico City

Year	Winners	Matches				Goals		Players	Appearances (Goals)
1974	**West Germany**	7	6	0	1	13	4	18	Maier, Vogts, Breitner (3), Schwarzenbeck, Beckenbauer, Muller (4), Overath (2), 7 each; Hoeness (1) 6+1 sub; Grabowski (1) 5+1 sub; Holzenbein 4+2 subs; Bonhof (1) 4; Cullmann (1) 3; Flohe 1+2 subs; Heynckes, Herzog 2 each; Wimmer 1+1 sub; Netzer, Hottges 1 sub each.

Final: West Germany 2 Holland 1   77,833 Munich

Year	Winners	Matches				Goals		Players	Appearances (Goals)
1978	**Argentina**	7	5	1	1	15	4	17	Fillol, Luis Galvan, Olguin, Passarella (1) Tarantini (1), Gallego, Kempes (6) 7 each; Ardiles 6; Bertoni 5+1 sub; Ortiz 4+2 subs; (2) Luque (4) 5; Houseman (1) 3+3 subs; Valencia 4; Larrosa 1+1 sub; Alonso 3 subs; Villa 2 subs; Oviedo 1 sub.

Final: Argentina 3 Holland 1   77,000 Buenos Aires
(after extra time)

WORLD CUP APPEARANCES

Antonio Carbajal (Mexico) is the only player to have appeared in five World Cup final tournaments. He kept goal for Mexico in 1950, 1954, 1958, 1962 and 1966, with 11 appearances in all.

Uwe Seeler (West Germany) established a record of appearances in World Cup final tournaments by making a total of 21 appearances in 1958, 1962, 1966 and 1970 as a centre-forward.

Pele (Brazil) is the only player to have been with three World Cup winning teams, though he missed the final of the 1962 competition because of injury. He made four appearances in the 1958 final tournament, two in 1962 before injury and six in 1970. He also appeared in two matches in 1966 for a total of 14 appearances in all.

Mario Zagalo is the only man who has won a World Cup winners medal and managed a World Cup winning team. He played in the 1958 and 1962 World Cup winning teams of Brazil and was manager when they achieved their third success in 1970.

GOALSCORING

The record margin of victory in a World Cup final tournament is nine clear goals; in 1954: Hungary 9 South Korea 0 and in 1974: Yugoslavia 9 Zaire 0. The record scoreline in any World Cup match is West Germany 12 Cyprus 0 in a qualifying match on 21 May 1969.

Just Fontaine (France) scored a record 13 goals in six matches of the 1958 World Cup final tournament. **Gerd Muller** (West Germany) scored 10 goals in 1970 and four in 1974 for the highest aggregate of 14 goals. **Fontaine** and **Jairzinho** (Brazil) are the only two players to have scored in every match in a final series, as Jairzinho scored seven goals in six matches in 1970.

Including World Cup qualifying matches in the 1970 series, **Muller** scored a total of 19 goals with nine coming from six preliminary games and ten in the final stages.

Pele is the third highest scorer in World Cup final tournaments, having registered 12 goals in his four competitions.

Geoff Hurst (England) is the only player to have scored a hat-trick in a final when he registered three of his side's goals in their 4–2 win over West Germany in 1966.

The first player to score as many as four goals in any World Cup match was **Paddy Moore** who registered all the Republic of Ireland's goals in the 4–4 draw with Belgium in Dublin during a World Cup qualifying match on 25 February 1934.

Robbie Rensenbrink (Holland) scored the 1,000th goal in World Cup finals when he converted a penalty against Scotland in the 1978 tournament.

The first goal scored in the World Cup was credited to **Louis Laurent** for France against Mexico on 13 July 1930 in Montevideo. France won 4–1. With the time difference the news reached France on Bastille Day, 14 July.

The fastest goal scored in a World Cup final tournament was probably attributed to **Olle Nyberg** of Sweden against Hungary on 16 June 1938 in Paris, after approximately 30 seconds of play. **Bernard Lacombe** scored for France against Italy in 31 seconds during the 1978 tournament.

Vava (real name Edwaldo Izidio Neto) of Brazil is the only player to have scored in successive World Cup finals. He did so against Sweden in 1958 (scoring twice) and against Czechoslovakia in 1962. **Pele** is the only other to score in two finals, twice in Sweden in 1958 and once against Italy in 1970.

Leading World Cup scorers
(final tournament)

Year	Name	Country	Goals
1930	Guillermo Stabile	Argentina	8
1934	Angelo Schiavio	Italy	4
	Oldrich Nejedly	Czechoslovakia	4
	Edmund Conen	Germany	4
1938	Leonidas da Silva	Brazil	8
1950	Ademir	Brazil	7
1954	Sandor Kocsis	Hungary	11
1958	Just Fontaine	France	13
1962	Drazen Jerkovic	Yugoslavia	5
1966	Eusebio	Portugal	9
1970	Gerd Muller	West Germany	10
1974	Grzegorz Lato	Poland	7
1978	Mario Kempes	Argentina	6

The record invididual score in a World Cup final tournament is four goals, a feat which has been achieved on eight occasions:

Name	For	Against
Gustav Wetterstroem	Sweden	v Cuba 1938
Leonidas da Silva	Brazil	v Poland 1938
Ernest Willimowski	Poland	v Brazil 1938
Ademir	Brazil	v Sweden 1950

WORLD CHAMPIONSHIP
·JULES RIMET CUP

Final

ENGLAND v WEST GERMANY
SATURDAY·JULY 30·1966
EMPIRE STADIUM

SOUVENIR
PROGRAMME
WEMBLEY

PRICE
2/6

THE WORLD CUP
THE OFFICIAL PROGRAMME
LE PROGRAMME OFFICIEL
EL PROGRAMA OFICIAL
OFFIZIELLES PROGRAMM

6s
30p

FIFA

MEXICO 1970

Juan Schiaffino — Uruguay v Bolivia 1950
Sandor Kocsis — Hungary v W. Germany 1954
Just Fontaine — France v W. Germany 1958
Eusebio — Portugal v North Korea 1966

World Cup endurance

Helmut Schoen who retired as West Germany's team manager after the 1978 World Cup finals was the most successful international coach. In 1966 his team finished runners-up in the World Cup, were third in 1970 and became European Championship winners in 1972. They won the World Cup in 1974 and were runners-up in the European Championship in 1976. Schoen had been in charge for 14 years.

Making his 100th international appearance for Poland, Kazimierz Deyna had a penalty kick saved by the Argentine goalkeeper Ubaldo Fillol in the 1978 tournament.

The longest period that a goalkeeper has kept his charge intact during a World Cup final tournament is 475 minutes. Josef 'Sepp' Maier of West Germany conceded a penalty to Holland in the first minute of the 1974 World Cup Final itself and was not beaten again until Holland scored against him in the 1978 tournament.

Eusebio of Benfica and Portugal. (Syndication International)

Uruguay v. Holland in the 1974 World Cup and Johan Neeskens, the Dutch midfield player, is tackled by Uruguay's Juan Masnik *(right)*.

Johnny Rep (Holland) heads towards goal for Holland in the 1978 World Cup Final, watched by Daniel Passarella. (Syndication International)

NORTH AMERICA

Vancouver Whitecaps won the Soccer Bowl 79 for the North American Soccer League championship by beating Tampa Bay Rowdies 2–1 in the Giants Stadium in New Jersey.

A crowd of 50 699 watched the match, though another 14 144 bought tickets and were absentees presumably because the local New York Cosmos, winners in the previous two years, had not reached the final. Some 600 Whitecaps supporters made the 3000 mile journey from Vancouver to take their places. The match was televised live to 16 countries with ABC showing the game coast to coast in the United States, though in Canada, despite a Canadian team playing, it was only shown in Vancouver and Toronto.

In the League schedule itself 14 teams recorded increased attendances in the season over 1978, eight reported decreases and two teams were not operating in the same location which made any comparison impossible for them.

Cosmos were again the best supported team with an average of 46 689, though this was down on 1978 when they managed 47 856. Tampa Bay's gates went up from 18 123 to 28 546 to make them the next best in attendances and though Minnesota slumped from 30 926 to 24 579 they were still the third highest.

But nine of the 24 teams had crowds under 10 000 on average, though this was an improvement on 1978 when there had been ten.

And an innovation for the 1980 season was that none of the competing teams had moved their franchise.

The new season produced a further influx of leading international players from Europe and South America, with Rudi Krol joining Whitecaps from Ajax and Julio Cesar Romero of Olimpia, Paraguay moving to New York Cosmos (as the runner-up in the South American Footballer of the Year award) as the leading captures from both continents. The £200 000 transfer fee was a record for Paraguay.

Paul Child in his ninth season with the North American Soccer League became the third man in League history to reach the 200 point mark as he scored twice for Memphis Rogues against Atlanta Chiefs in a 4–3 win on 29 April 1980. Under the NASL system, a goal counts two points and an 'assist' one point.

Child (27), was top scorer in 1974 with 15 goals and six assists for a total of 36 points. The previous winners of the milestone were Yugoslavian

North American Soccer League—winners	
1967	Oakland Clippers (National Professional Soccer League)
1968	Atlanta Chiefs
1969	Kansas City Spurs
1970	Rochester Lancers
1971	Dallas Tornado
1972	New York Cosmos
1973	Philadelphia Atoms
1974	Los Angeles Aztecs
1975	Tampa Bay Rowdies
1976	Toronto Metro-Croatia
1977	New York Cosmos
1978	New York Cosmos
1979	Vancouver Whitecaps

NASL Attendances 1979 season
(based on 15 home matches in regular schedule)

	Total	Average
New York Cosmos	700 348	46 689
Tampa Bay Rowdies	428 197	28 546
Minnesota Kicks	368 695	24 579
Vancouver Whitecaps	344 436	22 964
Seattle Sounders	274 993	18 999
Tulsa Roughnecks	246 373	16 424
San Jose Earthquakes	226 379	15 092
Los Angeles Aztecs	215 013	14 334
Detroit Express	210 864	14 058
Fort Lauderdale Strikers	205 616	13 707
Washington Diplomats	178 610	11 907
Toronto Blizzard	177 321	11 821
San Diego Sockers	169 071	11 271
Portland Timbers	167 584	11 172
California Surf	154 956	10 330
Edmonton Drillers	148 854	9923
Dallas Tornado	139 485	9299
Rochester Lancers	130 200	8680
Chicago Sting	120 535	8035
Atlanta Chiefs	110 244	7349
Memphis Rogues	107 071	7138
New England Tea Men	98 433	6562
Houston Hurricane	93 183	6212
Philadelphia Fury	84 357	5624

Ilija Mitic who totalled 239 points in his career and Italian striker Giorgio Chinaglia with 233 up to the day English born Child achieved his total.

In the period from their 1–0 victory in the 1950 World Cup finals against England on 29 June in Belo Horizonte until beaten 6–0 in New Jersey by France on 2 May 1979, the United States of America completed 68 full international fixtures, winning only 14 of them. Their full international record from 1916 to 1979 was: Played 94, Won 22, Drawn 15 and Lost 57.

Since the establishment of the present professional league system in 1967, they have played

Two sides of the Soccer Bowl 79 with Tampa Bay 'Wowdies' entertaining the fans before the game, and supporters of the Whitecaps from Vancouver living side by side with their opposite numbers. (Bob Thomas)

47 matches winning only ten, of which only two have come in their last 25 games.

Of the players who played regularly in the 1979 NASL season there were more from England than any other country. But the total of 113 was down from the 129 who appeared in 1978. Players from the United States of America increased from 101 to 106. Canada's total dropped slightly from 33 to 30, but West Germany increased their representation dramatically from 12 to 27, while Yugoslavia's figures were reversed.

Total figures for 1979 with those for the previous season in brackets: England 113 (129); United States of America 106 (101); Canada 30 (33); West Germany 27 (12); Yugoslavia 23 (32); Scotland 24 (30); Holland 17 (4); South Africa 12 (9); Argentina 10 (4); Brazil 9 (4); Ireland 7 (11); Wales 5 (3); Denmark 4 (1); Northern Ireland 4 (6); Mexico 4 (–); Portugal 4 (2); Hungary 3 (2); Nigeria 3 (1); Channel Islands 2 (–); Bermuda 2 (4); Iran 2 (1); Peru 2 (1); Sweden 2 (–); Barbados 1 (–); Austria 1 (–); Cyprus 1 (1); Finland 1 (1); Ghana 1 (1); Haiti 1 (1); Iceland 1 (–); Mali 1 (–); Mozambique 1 (–); Trinidad 1 (2); Turkey 1 (1); Uruguay 1 (1).

Those countries not represented in this survey, but concerned in 1978 were: Spain 3, Poland 2, Angola, Costa Rica, Greece and Israel 1 each.

Comparing the total of non-United States and Canadian born players the figures for 1979 were 204 (276 in 1978).

SOUTH AMERICA

SOUTH AMERICAN DIRECTORY
up to and including 1979

Country	Championship wins
Argentina (1893–)	Boca Juniors 17; River Plate 16; Racing Club 15; Alumni 9; Independiente 9; San Lorenzo 8; Huracan 5; Lomas 5; Belgrano 3; Estudiantes de la Plata 2; Porteno 2; Estudiantil Porteno 2; Quilmes 2; Dock Sud 1; Chacarita Juniors 1; Lomas Academicals 1; English High School 1; Gimnasia y Esgrima La Plata 1; Sportivo Barracas 1; Newell's Old Boys 1. (National League 1967–): Boca Juniors 3; Independiente 3; Rosario Central 2; San Lorenzo 2; River Plate 2; Velez Sarsfield 1.
Bolivia (1914–)*	The Strongest 18; Bolivar 10; Jorge Wilsterman 6; Deportivo Municipal 4; Litoral 3; Universitario 3; Always Ready 2; Chaco Petrolero 2; Oriente Petrolero 2; Colegio Militar 1; Nimbles Sport 1; Deportivo Militar 1; Nimbles Rail 1; Ayacucho 1; Ferroviario 1; Guabira 1.
Brazil	(Rio League 1906–): Fluminense 22; Flamengo 20; Vasco de Gama 14; Botafogo 12; America 7; Bangu 2; San Christavao 1; Paysandu 1. (Sao Paulo League 1902–): Corinthians 19; *SE Palmeiras 18; Santos 13; Sao Paulo 11; Paulistano 8; SP Athletic 4; AA des Palmeiras 3; Portuguesa 3; Sao Bento 2; Germania 2; Americano 2; Internacional 1. *formerly Palestra Italia
	(National Championships 1971–): Internacional Porto Alegre 3; Palmeiras 2; Atletico Mineiro 1; Vasco da Gama 1; Sao Paulo 1; Guarani 1.
Chile (1933–)	Colo Colo 12; Universidad de Chile 7; Union Espanola 5; Magallanes 4; Audax Italiano 4; Universidad Catolica 4; Everton 3; Wanderers (Valpariso) 2; Palestino 2; Santiago Morning 1; Green Cross 1; Hauchipato 1; Union San Felipe 1
Colombia (1948–)	Millonarios 11; Independiente Santa Fe 6; Deportivo Cali 5; Independiente Medellin 2; Nacional Medellin 2; Deportes Caldas 1; Atletico Nacional 1; Atletico Quindio 1; Union Magdalena 1; Junior Barranquilla 1; America 1.
Ecuador (1957–)	Nacional 5; Emelec 5; Barcelona 4; Liga Deportiva Universitaria 3; Everest 2; Deportivo Quito 2.

Country	Championship wins
Paraguay (1906–)*	Olimpia 26; Cerro Porteno 19; Libertad 8; Guarani 7; Nacional 6; Sporting Luqueno 2; Presidente Hayes 1.
Peru (1928–)	Alianza 16; Universitario 14; Sporting Cristal 6; Sport Boys 5; Deportivo Municipal 4; Atletico Chalaco 2; Mariscal Sucre 2; Union Huaral 1; Defensor Lima 1.
Uruguay (1900–)	Penarol 35; Nacional 32; River Plate 4; Montevideo Wanderers 3; Defensor 1; Rampla Juniors 1. (Major League 1975–): Nacional 4; Penarol 2.
Venezuela (1956–)	Deportivo Italia 5; Portuguesa 5; Deportivo Portugues 3; Deportivo Galicia 3; Valencia 2; Lasalle 1; Tiquire Aragua 1; Celta Deportivo 1; Lara 1; Union Deportiva Canarias 1; Deportivo Tachira 1.

South American Cup (Libertadores Cup) Olimpia, Paraguay's oldest club, won the South American Cup to celebrate their 77th anniversary shortly before they defeated the holders Boca Juniors (Argentina) 2–0 on aggregate in July 1979. They won the first leg at home in Asuncion 2–0, then held their opponents 0–0 in Buenos Aires.

They ended the domination by Argentina (12 wins), Uruguay (4) and Brazil (3), the three countries who have between them produced the eight different clubs to have won the 19 previous tournaments. Olimpia had been the original beaten finalists losing to Penarol (Uruguay) in 1960.

Previous winners
1960	Penarol (Uruguay)
1961	Penarol
1962	Santos (Brazil)
1963	Santos
1964	Independiente (Argentina)
1965	Independiente
1966	Penarol
1967	Racing (Argentina)
1968	Estudiantes (Argentina)
1969	Estudiantes
1970	Estudiantes
1971	Nacional (Uruguay)
1972	Independiente
1973	Independiente
1974	Independiente
1975	Independiente
1976	Cruzeiro (Brazil)
1977	Boca Juniors (Argentina)
1978	Boca Juniors
1979	Olimpia (Paraguay)

SOUTH AMERICAN CHAMPIONSHIPS

The 1979 South American Championship was split into three qualifying groups with three teams in each and decided on the League system with home and away matches. The three group winners were Chile, Brazil and Paraguay who joined the holders Peru in the semi-finals. Chile beat Peru 2–1 in Lima and drew 0–0 in Santiago to reach the final, while Paraguay defeated Brazil 2–1 in Asuncion and held them to a 2–2 draw in Rio to earn the other final place. Paraguay then beat Chile 3–0 in Asuncion, but lost 1–0 in Santiago. A third match in neutral Buenos Aires ended in a goalless draw with Paraguay declared winners because of their superior goal difference.

Group tables:

Group 1
	P	W	D	L	F	A	Pts
Chile	4	2	1	1	10	2	5
Colombia	4	2	1	1	5	2	5
Venezuela	4	0	2	2	1	12	2

Group 2
	P	W	D	L	F	A	Pts
Brazil	4	2	1	1	7	5	5
Bolivia	4	2	0	2	4	7	4
Argentina	4	1	1	2	7	6	3

Group 3
	P	W	D	L	F	A	Pts
Paraguay	4	2	2	0	6	3	6
Uruguay	4	1	2	1	5	5	4
Ecuador	4	1	0	3	4	7	2

Group 4
Peru qualified as winners of the 1975 tournament.

1916
	P	W	D	L	F	A	Pts
Uruguay	3	2	1	0	6	1	5
Argentina	3	1	2	0	7	2	4
Brazil	3	0	2	1	3	4	2
Chile	3	0	1	2	2	11	1

1917
	P	W	D	L	F	A	Pts
Uruguay	3	3	0	0	9	0	6
Argentina	3	2	0	1	5	3	4
Brazil	3	1	0	2	7	8	2
Chile	3	0	0	3	0	10	0

1919
	P	W	D	L	F	A	Pts
Brazil	3	2	1	0	11	3	5
Uruguay	3	2	1	0	7	4	5
Argentina	3	1	0	2	7	7	2
Chile	3	0	0	3	1	12	0

play-off: Brazil 1   Uruguay 0

1920
	P	W	D	L	F	A	Pts
Uruguay	3	2	1	0	9	2	5
Argentina	3	1	2	0	4	2	4
Brazil	3	1	0	2	1	8	2
Chile	3	0	1	2	2	4	1

The Argentine national team against Brazil in August 1979, a mixture of World Cup 1978 survivors and newcomers.

1921	P	W	D	L	F	A	Pts
Uruguay	3	3	0	0	5	0	6
Brazil	3	1	0	2	4	3	2
Uruguay	3	1	0	2	3	4	2
Paraguay	3	1	0	2	2	7	2

1922	P	W	D	L	F	A	Pts
Brazil	4	1	3	0	4	2	5
Paraguay	4	2	1	1	5	3	5
Uruguay	4	2	1	1	3	1	5
Argentina	4	2	0	2	6	3	4
Chile	4	0	1	3	1	10	1

play-off: Brazil 3 Paraguay 1; Uruguay withdrew after losing 1–0 in their last match to Paraguay because the Brazilian referee disallowed two goals for them.

1923	P	W	D	L	F	A	Pts
Uruguay	3	3	0	0	6	1	6
Argentina	3	2	0	1	6	6	4
Paraguay	3	1	0	2	4	6	2
Brazil	3	0	0	3	2	5	0

1924	P	W	D	L	F	A	Pts
Uruguay	3	2	1	0	8	1	5
Argentina	3	1	2	0	2	0	4
Paraguay	3	1	1	1	4	4	3
Chile	3	0	0	3	1	10	0

1925	P	W	D	L	F	A	Pts
Argentina	4	3	1	0	11	4	7
Brazil	4	2	1	1	11	9	5
Paraguay	4	0	0	4	4	13	0

two legs were played (home and away)

1926	P	W	D	L	F	A	Pts
Uruguay	4	4	0	0	17	2	8
Argentina	4	2	1	1	14	3	5
Chile	4	2	1	1	14	6	5
Paraguay	4	1	0	3	8	20	2
Bolivia	4	0	0	4	2	24	0

1927	P	W	D	L	F	A	Pts
Argentina	3	3	0	0	15	4	6
Uruguay	3	2	0	1	15	3	4
Peru	3	1	0	2	4	11	2
Bolivia	3	0	0	3	3	19	0

1929	P	W	D	L	F	A	Pts
Argentina	3	3	0	0	9	1	6
Paraguay	3	2	0	1	9	4	4
Uruguay	3	1	0	2	4	6	2
Peru	3	0	0	3	1	12	0

1935	P	W	D	L	F	A	Pts
Uruguay	3	3	0	0	6	1	6
Argentina	3	2	0	1	8	5	4
Peru	3	1	0	2	2	5	2
Chile	3	0	0	3	2	7	0

1937	P	W	D	L	F	A	Pts
Argentina	5	4	0	1	12	7	8
Brazil	5	4	0	1	17	9	8
Paraguay	5	2	0	3	10	16	4
Uruguay	5	2	0	3	11	14	4
Chile	5	1	1	3	12	13	3
Peru	5	1	1	3	7	10	3

play-off: Argentina 2 Brazil 0

1939	P	W	D	L	F	A	Pts
Peru	4	4	0	0	13	4	8
Uruguay	4	3	0	1	13	5	6
Paraguay	4	2	0	2	9	8	4
Chile	4	1	0	3	8	12	2
Ecuador	4	0	0	4	4	18	0

1941	P	W	D	L	F	A	Pts
Argentina	4	4	0	0	10	2	8
Uruguay	4	3	0	1	10	1	6
Chile	4	2	0	2	6	3	4
Peru	4	1	0	3	5	5	2
Ecuador	4	0	0	4	1	21	0

1942

Uruguay	6	6	0	0	21	2	12
Argentina	6	4	1	1	11	6	9
Brazil	6	3	1	2	15	7	7
Paraguay	6	3	1	2	12	10	7
Chile	6	1	2	3	4	15	4
Peru	6	1	1	4	5	11	3
Ecuador	6	0	0	6	4	21	0

Chile withdrew before their last match.

1945

Argentina	6	5	1	0	22	5	11
Brazil	6	5	0	1	19	5	10
Chile	6	4	1	1	15	4	9
Uruguay	6	3	0	3	14	6	6
Colombia	6	1	1	4	7	25	3
Bolivia	6	0	2	4	3	16	2
Ecuador	6	0	1	5	8	27	1

1946

Argentina	5	5	0	0	17	3	10
Brazil	5	3	1	1	13	7	7
Paraguay	5	2	1	2	8	8	5
Uruguay	5	2	0	3	11	9	4
Chile	5	2	0	3	8	11	4
Bolivia	5	0	0	5	4	23	0

1947

Argentina	7	6	1	0	28	4	13
Paraguay	7	5	1	1	16	11	11
Uruguay	7	5	0	2	21	8	10
Chile	7	4	1	2	14	13	9
Peru	7	2	2	3	12	9	6
Ecuador	7	0	3	4	3	17	3
Bolivia	7	0	2	5	6	21	2
Colombia	7	0	2	5	2	19	2

1949

Brazil	7	6	0	1	39	7	12
Paraguay	7	6	0	1	21	6	12
Peru	7	5	0	2	20	13	10
Bolivia	7	4	0	3	13	24	8
Uruguay	7	2	1	4	14	20	5
Chile	7	2	1	4	10	14	5
Ecuador	7	1	0	6	7	21	2
Colombia	7	0	2	5	4	23	2

play-off: Brazil 7   Paraguay 0

1953

Paraguay	6	4	2	0	10	4	8
Brazil	6	4	0	2	15	6	8
Chile	6	3	1	2	10	10	7
Uruguay	6	3	0	3	13	5	6
Peru	6	2	2	2	4	6	6
Bolivia	6	1	1	4	6	15	3
Ecuador	6	0	2	4	1	13	2

play-off: Paraguay 3 Brazil 2 (organised by the Paraguayan Football League) after two points deducted from Paraguay for making more than permitted three substitutions v Chile.

1955

Argentina	5	4	1	0	18	6	9
Chile	5	3	1	1	19	8	7
Peru	5	2	2	1	13	11	6
Uruguay	5	2	1	2	12	12	5
Paraguay	5	1	1	3	7	14	3
Ecuador	5	0	0	5	4	22	0

1956

Uruguay	5	4	1	0	9	3	9
Brazil	5	3	2	0	7	2	8
Argentina	5	3	0	2	5	3	6
Chile	5	2	0	3	8	11	4
Paraguay	5	0	2	3	3	8	2
Peru	5	0	1	4	6	11	1

1957

Argentina	6	5	0	1	25	6	10
Brazil	6	4	0	2	23	9	8
Uruguay	6	4	0	2	15	12	8
Peru	6	4	0	2	12	9	8
Colombia	6	2	0	4	10	25	4
Chile	6	1	1	4	9	17	3
Ecuador	6	0	1	5	7	23	1

1959

Argentina	6	5	1	0	19	5	11
Brazil	6	4	2	0	17	7	10
Paraguay	6	3	0	3	12	12	6
Chile	6	2	1	3	9	14	5
Peru	6	1	3	2	10	11	5
Uruguay	6	2	0	4	15	14	4
Bolivia	6	0	1	5	4	23	1

1959

Uruguay	4	3	1	0	13	1	7
Argentina	4	2	1	1	9	9	5
Brazil	4	2	0	2	7	10	4
Ecuador	4	1	1	2	5	9	3
Paraguay	4	0	1	3	6	11	1

1963

Bolivia	6	5	1	0	19	13	11
Paraguay	6	4	1	1	13	7	9
Argentina	6	3	1	2	15	10	7
Brazil	6	2	1	3	12	13	5
Peru	6	2	1	3	8	11	5
Ecuador	6	1	2	3	14	18	4
Colombia	6	0	1	5	10	19	1

1967

Uruguay	5	4	1	0	13	2	9
Argentina	5	4	0	1	12	3	8
Chile	5	2	2	1	8	6	6
Paraguay	5	2	0	3	9	13	4
Venezuela	5	1	0	4	7	16	2
Bolivia	5	0	1	4	0	9	1

1975

Group 1

Brazil	4	4	0	0	13	1	8
Argentina	4	2	0	2	17	4	4
Venezuela	4	0	0	4	1	26	0

Group 2

Peru	4	3	1	0	8	3	7
Chile	4	1	1	2	7	6	3
Bolivia	4	1	0	3	3	9	2

Group 3

Colombia	4	4	0	0	7	1	8
Paraguay	4	1	1	2	5	5	3
Ecuador	4	0	1	3	4	10	1

Semi-finals

Colombia v Uruguay	3–0, 0–1
Brazil v Peru	1–3, 2–0
(Peru won toss)	

Final

Colombia v Peru	1–0, 0–2, 0–1 (in Caracas)

MISCELLANY

Long-serving pivots

Jack Charlton (Leeds United), Bill Foulkes (Manchester United), Joe Shaw (Sheffield United) and Bobby McKinlay (Nottingham Forest) were one-club post-war players who had at least 20 years' service with their respective teams and shared the same distinction of occupying the centre-half position. Both Charlton and Shaw appeared in 629 League games, McKinlay in 614 and Foulkes in 567.

Three in a row

On 7 March 1970 Manchester City, already holders of the FA Cup, defeated West Bromwich Albion in the Football League Cup final. On 29 April they defeated Gornik Zabrze (Poland) in the Fairs Cup final to make them temporarily at least holders of two national and one European trophy.

The team now standing . . .

In the 1959–60 season Tottenham Hotspur managed only a 2–2 draw with Crewe Alexandra in a fourth round FA Cup tie at Gresty Road. But in the replay they won 13–2 for the highest scoring match in any comparative part of the competition since Preston North End had beaten Reading 18–0 in 1894. After the match the Crewe team left Euston station from Platform 13 and arrived at Crewe on Platform 2.

Right: A 1914 charity match at Tottenham in aid of Theatrical ladies, attracting a capacity size crowd and appealing to goalkeepers' sentiments.

Below: West Bromwich Albion on a training walk soon after the turn of the century. Fourth from the right is Jesse Pennington who once held the club's record of League appearances. Anyone for tennis?

Seamus Brennan of Manchester United was pensioned off by the Old Trafford club in the nicest possible fashion. (Syndication International)

The famous four
Barnsley, Grimsby Town, Northampton Town and Portsmouth were the only clubs to have met all the other 91 in Football League matches up to the end of the 1979–80 season. Bradford City had met all but Ipswich Town; Brentford and Bury all but Wigan Athletic; Huddersfield Town all but Mansfield Town; Lincoln City all but Wimbledon; and Port Vale all but Sunderland.

London jinx
Crystal Palace beat Chelsea 2–0 on 31 March 1973 for their first win against a London team in 32 League matches since their promotion to Division One at the end of the 1968–69 season.

Foreign Legion
Former Manchester United, Brighton and Hove Albion, Cardiff City and Portsmouth defender Jack Mansell, at 52, has now fulfilled coaching appointments in six foreign countries: Holland, United States of America, Greece, Turkey, the Persian Gulf and Israel.

The great escape
On the evening of 19 February 1966, Fulham, last in Division One, were five points behind the 20th club after having taken only 15 points from their first 29 games. But they added 20 points from their remaining 13 matches and avoided relegation.

Victorian inducement
Illegally approaching players is not a new facet of the game. In the 1890–91 season Wolverhampton Wanderers induced Sam Thomson, a Preston North End player, to join them without that club's permission and they were fined £50 for their misconduct.

Escalation and demotion
Few players can claim to have been directly involved in five promotion and five relegation campaigns, but it has happened to Graham Watson with Rotherham United, Doncaster Rovers, Cambridge United and Lincoln City.

Youthful pensioner
In August 1970 Manchester United decided to pay the Republic of Ireland international Shay Brennan a pension for life, the first such case in the

Dixie Dean seen here in action during the Everton v Chelsea match on 26 March 1932, died at the Merseyside derby on 1 March 1980 at the age of 73. (PA)

history of the game. It was £15 a week from the age of 35 until his death and it was payment in lieu of a testimonial after nearly 18 years with the club.

It's not cricket

When Chesterfield visited Darlington for a Division Three (Northern) match on 29 December 1923, the frozen ground was unfit for play. But the game was completed on the adjoining cricket pitch. Referee Bert Fogg obtained both clubs' signed agreement before the match, stating that they had agreed to the switch and would stand by the result.

Late extra-final
Roger Hunt figured in three cup finals that needed extra time—with Liverpool against Leeds United at Wembley in the FA Cup in 1955, against Borussia Dortmund in the European Cup Winners Cup at Hampden Park in 1966, and with England against West Germany at Wembley in the 1966 World Cup.

Oh! Brother
Ivor Allchurch played in the Football League for 19 seasons, but younger brother Len beat him by just one season. Both scored over 100 Football

The careers of the Allchurch brothers Len and Ivor *(above)* were of a durable nature and embraced international football as well as that at League level. (Colorsport)

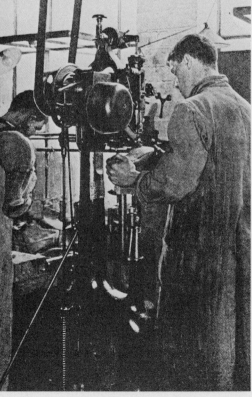

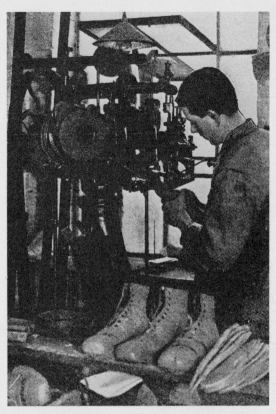

Top Left: Watch-the-birdie time at the football factory just after the turn of the century. Everything in connection with the making of a football was done by hand. Cowhide leather was used and it was said to be practically waterproof. (The author has other ideas even from a later date). The stretching of the leather was a valuable trade secret and it was well known that a ball made of badly stretched leather would quickly lose its shape.

Above: Known as 'The Wonderful American Lasting Machine' at the time it was described as a steel pair of hands. It gripped, clutched and pulled the uppers where it willed and riveted where it liked. It had the capacity to last or rivet the uppers to the soles at the rate of 1500 pairs of boots per week.

Far Left: The Stud-Making Machine was an English patent. It drove five rivets through three plates of leather and left the stud ready for fixing in one operation. A boy could use it and it turned out thirty gross of studs in one day.

Left: A Riveting Machine turned out as many as 500 pairs of football boots per day and was kept busily working throughout the football season.

League goals and each began and finished their League careers with their home club at Swansea, which they first left and then rejoined. Ivor's career spanned seasons 1949–50 to 1967–68 while Len's embraced the period from 1951–52 to 1970–71.

No! Brother
Playing for Everton in a Division One match on the ground of his former club Birmingham City, centre-forward Bob Latchford was booked for a foul on his brother David, who was keeping goal for City.

Away from it all
Tottenham Hotspur had completed their Division One programme and were on tour in Holland when they learned on 5 May 1928 that they had been relegated. A similar situation occurred for Blackpool in America on 9 May 1978 when they were relegated from Division Two.

One over the eight
Nine players scored in a Division Three match in which Bournemouth were beaten 7–3 at home by Plymouth Argyle on 11 January 1975. John Wingate, Mike Green own goal and Trevor Howard were the Bournemouth scorers, while Paul Mariner (2), Billy Rafferty, Hugh McAuley, John Delve, Colin Randell and Brian Johnson registered for Plymouth.

Doubling up
Terry Venables and Allan Harris have become the game's equivalent of Siamese twins. They were in the same schoolboy team, both progressed to England's youth international side, were players together with Chelsea and Queen's Park Rangers in turn and then came to be in further close harmony as Crystal Palace manager and second-in-command respectively.

Youth at the helm
Alan Thompson at 25 became Stockport County's manager in May 1977, and Martin Firth, only 20, was appointed Halifax Town's secretary in January 1980.

Permanent fixture
York City right-back Jack Pinder was one of the club's original players when they were elected to the Football League in 1929, and he remained in their team until the end of the 1947–48 season.

Evans the fat
The heaviest player seen in the Football League since the end of the Second World War was a Welsh goalkeeper called 'Ossie' Evans. He was an ex-Guardsman who, when signed by Fulham in January 1946, turned the scales at 17 stone 4 lb (109·75 kg).

Only foreigners need apply
Torquay United can claim to have been managed by two men born thousands of miles from the British Isles. Before the Second World War Percy Mackrill, born in East Africa, was in charge while afterwards Jack Butler, a native of Colombo, was their manager.

Hugh and I
No two brothers in the game ever kept closer together throughout their careers than Scottish forwards Frank and Hugh O'Donnell. They were pre-war associates of St Agatha's School (Fifeshire), Wellesley Juniors, Denbeath Violet, Glasgow Celtic and Preston North End and during the war with Blackpool, Heart of Midlothian and Liverpool.

Never on a Sunday
In 1909 Swindon Town and England international forward Harold Fleming was one of the first to exercise the right held by all professionals to refuse on religious grounds to figure in Sunday, Christmas Day or Good Friday matches. In January 1974 another Swindon player, Scottish-born goalkeeper Jimmy Allan, similarly refused to play on a Sunday in a match against Bolton Wanderers.

Get your colours here
Few other clubs can match, let alone surpass, either Manchester City or Bradford City for their colour schemes. Since the Second World War they have had Black, White, Green, Gray and Brown among their playing staff.

Same crowd, different place
In the Division Three meetings between Lincoln City and Wrexham in the 1976–77 season the official attendance at each club's ground was 7753.

Geographical error
Between 1937 and 1947 Mansfield Town operated in Division Three (Southern), while Crewe Alexandra were members of Division Three (Northern). But Mansfield is some 20 miles north of Crewe.

Jimmy the One
Jimmy McAlinden, an Irish international inside-forward, became the only player in history to appear in winning Irish Cup and FA Cup teams in successive seasons. He did it with Belfast Celtic in 1937–38 and Portsmouth in 1938–39.

Chelsea chairman Brian Mears with the new stand at Stamford Bridge pictured in 1975. His family have always been vitally connected with the club. (Syndication International)

Land of the giant-killers

No other county can even approach Durham's record of having had 22 non-League clubs in the FA Cup competition proper since the war, namely: Annfield Plain, Billingham Synthonia, Bishop Auckland, Blackhall Colliery Welfare, Brandon United, Consett, Crook Town, Durham City, Easington Colliery Welfare, Evenwood Town, Ferryhill Athletic, Gateshead, Horden Colliery Welfare, Ryhope, Shildon, South Shields, Spennymoor, Stanley United, Stockton, Tow Law, West Auckland and Willington.

Consistent sponge man

In the 1979–80 season Jack Wheeler, as trainer or caretaker-manager of Notts County, completed 1000 consecutive matches in that role with the club. In 1952–53, as Huddersfield Town goalkeeper, he had been one of six defenders who had been ever present for them in all 42 Division Two matches.

Years of Mears

No club in the Football League can match Chelsea's record in having had a Mears in control ever since their 1905 formation. Current chairman Brian Mears' grandfather and great-uncle founded the club, and father Joe was chairman for many years himself.

Women's Lib

In February 1979 Mrs Millie Allen became the first woman to join a Football League club's board of directors. Her husband, Bill Allen who had died a month earlier, had been Bury's chairman for seven years.

No substitute for youth

Kevan Broadhurst, at $17\frac{1}{2}$ years of age, became the youngest player to score the winning goal as a Football League substitute on his debut when he did so in Birmingham City's 3–2 win over Norwich City on 2 February 1977.

David Johnson who specialised in scoring goals on his debut also finished as leading scorer for Liverpool in the 1979–80 season with 21 League goals alone. (Colorsport)

Horse sense

In February 1969 Her Majesty the Queen named one of her racehorses Charlton after Jack and Bobby Charlton. The Queen's racing manager, Mr Richard Shelley, commented: 'Her Majesty was present at Wembley when England won the World Cup and she thought the name Charlton for her two-year-old bay colt would be a good link.'

Two ageing Rams

In 1947 Derby County had two players in Sammy Crooks and Jack Nicholas who had both been in professional service with the club for more than 20 years.

Debutant's delight
David Johnson scored on his debut for Everton at all these levels: Central League, Football League, FA Cup, European Cup, Football League Cup and Merseyside derby v Liverpool (his current club), and while with Ipswich Town he did so at full England international level as well.

All in a week's play
Former Welsh international and Arsenal inside-forward Leslie Jones played for three clubs in four days in 1940 when he turned out for Fulham on a Monday, West Ham United on a Wednesday, and Southampton on the Thursday.

Lest we forget
When 24-year-old Peter Eastaway of Litherland near Liverpool became the father of a boy in August 1966 he christened the infant Peter Derrick Banks Cohen Stiles Charlton Moore Ball Hurst

Keep in touch
In February 1959 Bobby Tambling and Barry Bridges made their Football League debuts on the same day as Chelsea 17-year-olds against West Ham United. Both scored in the first half, became full England internationals, and both later played for clubs in the Republic of Ireland.

Above: **Bobby Tambling was a colleague of Barry Bridges on both sides of the Irish Sea. (Colorsport)**

Right: **Barry Bridges celebrating a goal for Queen's Park Rangers against Middlesbrough in 1969, later found his shooting boots had not deserted him in the Emerald Isle.**

Hunt Peters Ramsey Eastaway to commemorate the triumph of the England team which had just won the World Cup.

'A' for effort
Up to the end of the 1979–80 season Arsenal had maintained membership of Division One for 54 seasons. The record was established by Sunderland who completed 57 seasons in succession from 1890–91 to 1957–58 inclusive.

Spreading his talent
Inside-forward Bill Horton's first three appearances in first class football were made in three different national competitions with Aldershot in the FA Cup in 1961–62 and the Football League Cup and the Football League in that order in 1962–63.

Never a dull moment (1)
Phil Ashworth left Nelson for Blackburn Rovers in January 1975, and his new club became Division Three champions that season. He was with Workington when they were voted out of the Football League in 1977, with Southport when they suffered a similar fate a year later, and with Rochdale when they were re-elected in 1979. He moved to Portsmouth in September 1979, but they just gained promotion to Division Three. He had made his Football League debut with Bournemouth after leaving Blackburn, and in the season of Southport's demise he had scored in each of their first seven League matches.

Expensive errors
England winger Peter Taylor was a teenager trialist with Southend United, Crystal Palace and Tottenham Hotspur. He later signed for Southend, who in turn transferred him to Palace for a six-figure transfer fee, who themselves received £200 000 from Spurs for him in September 1976.

Tortoise and the hare
Manchester United achieved 32 points from their first 20 Division One matches in the 1971–72 season, but their next eleven games brought just four points and they ended the season ten points behind the champions Derby County.

Teenager sees Red
Mark Halsey became the youngest player to be dismissed in his Football League debut match when playing for Norwich City against Newcastle United on 26 April 1978. He was 18 years old at the time and it happened before the lowest attendance at a Division One match since the 1960s when the crowd was returned as 7600.

Union Jack keepers
In the 1979–80 season Swansea City had goalkeepers on their books from England, Wales and Scotland with respectively Geoff Crudgington, Glan Letheran and David Stewart filling such birthplace requirements.

Whatever happened?
The first two seasons of the Football League Cup in 1960–61 and 1961–62 were successful ones for Rochdale who won seven ties in the competition. The last 18 seasons since then have produced only another seven wins for them.

Keeping it down
When Stewart McCallum played for Wrexham against Crewe Alexandra on 7 April 1951 he was under doctor's orders not to head the ball. Concussion sustained in a previous match was the reason for the strictness of this medical advice.

Flannelled fouls?
The lengthy ranks of County Cricketers who have also made Football League appearances were added to in the 1979–80 season when Ian Botham made his debut for Scunthorpe United after several games with the club's reserve side. Botham, a Test player and more recently England captain, is not the first to have coupled these roles. Wally Hammond, once a Bristol Rovers inside-right, and Brian Close, formerly an Arsenal and Leeds United centre-forward, rank as the only two who have skippered England in Test match cricket and also become Football League professionals.

On the move
Three Football League clubs have changed their headquarters since the Second World War: Queen's Park Rangers, Southend United and Port Vale.

Bracing in the south
Carlisle United are the only club situated in the north to have risen to Division One since the Second World War without previously having done so, but the south can claim eleven such cases: Fulham, Luton Town, Ipswich Town, Orient, Southampton, Northampton Town, Coventry City, Queen's Park Rangers, Crystal Palace, Norwich City and Brighton and Hove Albion.

The Clarke family relegation
If Wayne Clarke—youngest of the five brothers, all of them forwards, who have reached Football League status—should find himself relegated with Wolverhampton Wanderers, his present club or any

other, he would complete a unique family relegation situation. Allan Clarke went down with Fulham in 1967–68 and Leicester City a year later, Frank with Carlisle United in 1974–75, Derek with Oxford United in 1975–76 and Kelvin with Walsall in 1978–79.

Oh! Lord
When Hereford United manager Frank Lord was a Rochdale centre-forward he was the victim of an unusual coincidence. He broke his leg on the ground in August 1954, and it happened again on the identical spot exactly three years later.

Double take
In a Division Three (Northern) match against Wrexham on 26 August 1950, Jimmy Rudd, a Rotherham United outside-left, became the only player who ever scored direct from a corner twice in one Football League match.

League and Cup double
Crystal Palace and Chelsea rank as the only clubs to have played home League games on the same grounds used as a venue for the FA Cup final. Palace did so before the First World War, and Chelsea during the first three seasons after it.

How the mighty . . .
Since the Second World War Nottingham Forest, Derby County, Middlesbrough, Aston Villa, Preston North End, Blackburn Rovers, Bolton Wanderers, Blackpool, Huddersfield Town, Burnley and both Sheffield United and Wednesday have experienced relegation to Division Three for the first time in their history.

Relatively speaking
During the last two seasons these pairs of brothers have played together in the same League club teams: Jimmy and Brian Greenhoff (Manchester United), Eddie and Frank Gray (Leeds United), Paul and Ron Futcher (Manchester City), Ray and Graham Wilkins (Chelsea), Neville and Mark Chamberlain (Port Vale), Mike and Gary Saxby (Mansfield Town) and Kevin and David Moore (Grimsby Town). Transfers of Brian Greenhoff to Leeds, Frank Gray to Nottingham Forest, Ray Wilkins to Manchester United and Mike Saxby to Luton Town then ended some of these family associations.

Ten-up Norman
During his service with Leeds United, Norman Hunter appeared in ten cup finals excluding replays in eleven seasons. They read: FA Cup 1964–65, 1969–70, 1971–72 and 1972–73; Football League

Norman Hunter, after playing in the top flight with Leeds United and Bristol City, was still in action for Barnsley in Division Three during the 1979–80 season. (Colorsport)

Cup 1967–68; European Cup 1974–75; Fairs or UEFA Cup 1966–67, 1967–68 and 1970–71 and Cup Winners Cup 1972–73.

Beginners luck
During the 1977–78 season, his first in the Football League, Kenny Dalglish of Liverpool played at Wembley three times and without being on the losing side, once in the FA Charity Shield, then in the Football League Cup and European Cup finals.

Anglo-Scottish solo
Only one Englishman has figured in both FA Cup and Scottish Cup winning teams. He was left-back James Welford who did so with Aston Villa in 1895 and Celtic in 1899.

The Italian job
Only once have two Football League clubs in the same town or city been knocked out of the same European cup competition in the same season by the same opposition. In the 1966–67 UEFA Cup, Manchester City were beaten in the first round and Manchester United in the second by Juventus on each occasion.

Kenny Dalglish of Liverpool and Scotland whose experiences of Wembley were of an encouraging nature. (Syndication International)

Have boots, will travel

Though Sir Stanley Matthews was associated with only two different Football League clubs in his peacetime career, Stoke City and Blackpool, he turned out for clubs in all four countries in the British Isles as a war-time guest player with Wrexham (Wales), Airdrieonians (Scotland) and Cork United (Republic of Ireland) among other clubs.

Two weeks with honour

Sam Weaver won his first honour playing for England against Scotland at Wembley in April 1932. His second was when he was in Newcastle United's FA Cup winning team against Arsenal in the same arena a fortnight later.

Many are called . . .

Cyril Webster was an Everton professional inside-forward from May 1929 until the end of the 1938–39 season, but he was never selected for first team football. Similarly, Norman Young was an Aston Villa professional centre-half for ten years before the Second World War without being given a solitary League outing.

Stanley Matthews played in 86 FA Cup ties an impressive statistic among the many honours which came his way during a lengthy career.

Only the best

Three international players who had at least 12 years of Football League service to their credit and were still active in the 1979–80 season had never appeared in any other than Division One. They were Emlyn Hughes (Wolverhampton Wanderers) who made his debut in May 1966, Eddie Gray (Leeds United) in January 1966 and Brian Kidd (Everton) in August 1967.

Left: **Emlyn Hughes can claim to have spent his Football League career in just one division. (Syndication International)**

Above: **Eddie Gray, another of the players with lengthy service in one division and in his case, all spent with Leeds United. (Syndication International)**

Sam Weaver was famous for several accomplishments, not the least of them being one of the longest-throwing wing-halves in his day. (Colorsport)

Dying art

Many goalkeepers took penalty kicks in former days, but less do so now except in penalty competitions to decide the outcome of cup-ties.

The last time a goalkeeper converted from the 12-yard spot in a League game was during a match between Crewe Alexandra and York City on 3 May 1980. Crewe were leading 1–0 when their goalkeeper Bruce Grobbelaar, celebrating his election as the club's Player of the Year and made captain for the day, successfully scored from the penalty spot to complete a 2–0 win. The previous occasion was when Alan Starling did so for Northampton Town two minutes after the start of a home game against Hartlepools in April 1976.

Almost cup-tied

In April 1977 Alex Cropley played in Aston Villa's Football League Cup winning team against Everton at Old Trafford in the second round replay, after he had received a bonus through being Arsenal's substitute, though not called upon, in a second round tie against Carlisle United in the previous August.

Flighty young thing!
Mark Nightingale, a Salisbury-born midfield player, had been with clubs in all four grades while still only 19 years old in spells with Bournemouth (Division Three in 1974–75 and Four in 1975–76) and then with Crystal Palace (Division Two) and Norwich City (Division One).

Four for No. 4
In the 1937–38 season West Ham United had three brothers all of whom filled the same right-half position. They were the Scottish born trio of David, Jim and Bob Corbett while a fourth brother, Norman, was right-half for Heart of Midlothian.

Family alliance
In the 1946–47 season Joe Edelston was Reading's manager, daughter Kathleen was the club's secretary and her brother Maurice was a regular member of the first team forward line.

Honourable positions
The role of Football Association secretary and also that of England team manager has often led to inclusion in a Royal Honours List. Frederick Wall, Stanley Rous and Denis Follows were knighted, as were managers Walter Winterbottom and Alf Ramsey, while Don Revie received an OBE.

Unpaid but ubiquitous
In the 1922–23 season Arsenal included three amateurs in their Divison One team: Stanley Earle, Reginald Boreham and Dr James Paterson. In the 1946–47 season they again had three: Bernard Joy, Dr Kevin O'Flanagan and Albert Gudmundsson.

O'Flanagan played for Ireland against France at rugby on 27 January 1946 in Dublin, for Ireland v Scotland at soccer the following week in Dublin and was chosen for Ireland v England at rugby again seven days later. But his train was late at Liverpool, he missed the boat to Dublin and unable to travel by air he missed a unique hat-trick. His brother, Michael, played centre-forward with Kevin at outside-right for the Republic of Ireland against England in Dublin on 30 September 1946.

Kevin, who played rugby for London Irish, was first capped for the Republic of Ireland in pre-war days while playing for Bohemians, his brother's club.

Will ye no come back?
Full-back Steve Ritchie is the only player in recent years to have come into the Football League three times from Scotland. Bristol City first recruited him, then he returned to play for Greenock Morton. He came back to Hereford United, moved north to Aberdeen and returned to join Torquay United where he played during the 1979–80 season.

Dr Kevin O'Flanagan being presented to the President of Eire, His Excellency Sean T. O'Kelly, before the international rugby match between Ireland and France in Dublin on 28 January 1946. (Keystone)

Regionalisation

The Football Association has never had a secretary who was born in the north, and the Football League have never had one who came from the south.

Unbalancing

With York City in the 1971–72 and 1972–73 seasons, Brian Pollard missed relegation to Division Four on goal average. He went up with the same club to Division Two in 1973–74, went back down to Division Three in 1975–76 and Division Four in 1976–77. With Watford he won promotion from Division Four in 1977–78, and came up from Three to Division Two in 1978–79. With Mansfield Town in 1979–80 he went down to Division Four.

That sinking feeling

Geoff Hutt was with Huddersfield Town when they were Division Two winners in the 1969–70 season, when they were relegated from Division One in 1971–72, Two in 1972–73 and Three in 1974–75; with York City when they went down from Division Three in 1976–77 and was with Halifax Town when they were re-elected in 1978–79.

Injury starts career

Frank Moss became the manager of Heart of Midlothian at the age of 27 in March 1937. A famous English international goalkeeper, his career had been terminated prematurely with Arsenal after injury. He had played four times for England.

The lire lure

In November 1951 Norwich City paid Brescia, the Italian club, 7 million lire, the equivalent of £4000, which the selling club insisted upon receiving instead of English currency, for the signature of Walter Sloan, the former Manchester United, Arsenal, Sheffield United and Irish international inside-forward.

Oh! Danny boy

Scottish-born centre-half Danny Malloy played six seasons in the Football League for Cardiff City and then Doncaster Rovers from 1956–57 to 1961–62, and put through his own goal on 14 occasions during that period.

He's a knock-out

Former international referee Arthur Ellis of Halifax was the only member of the Pools Panel (which assesses results of postponed matches) when it first sat on 26 January 1963, and who was still functioning on it in the 1979–80 season.

Now brothers

The first attempt to form a Players Union was made in October 1893 when Wolverhampton Wanderers goalkeeper W C Rose sent letters to all the captains of clubs in Division One, proposing the formation of a Union 'to protect professional interests'.

Old becomes new

Manchester United became one of only a few clubs to have moved headquarters during an actual playing season when they left Bank Street, Clayton (described as the worst ground on which English first class football was ever played) for Old Trafford, where they played their first match on 19 February 1910 against Liverpool.

Mistaken identity

On 22 March 1958 Walsall centre-forward Tony Richards missed a penalty kick in a League match at Swindon. Later in the game he took over in goal from the injured John Savage and saved a penalty.

Arthur Ellis, the Halifax referee, before his days with the It's a Knock-out team on BBC television. (Colorsport)

David Peach *(right)* **on the receiving end of a possibly friendly hug from Manchester United's Joe Jordan, established a penalty taking milestone with Southampton. (Syndication International)**

Sixty glorious goals
When David Peach converted a penalty kick for Southampton against Everton on 17 February 1979, he became the first full-back to score 60 Football League goals.

Jones the book
Norwich City's Welsh international centre-half David Jones did not kick a ball in a first class match throughout the 1978–79 season after sustaining a serious knee injury, yet he was cautioned by a referee. It happened when referee Malcolm Sinclair booked him at a match against Ipswich Town because of comments he made as a spectator on the bench.

Heavy weather
At one time or another since the formation of the Football League names of players who have appeared in the competition have included Blizzard, Snow, Frost, Gale, Hale, Howling, Tempest, Fogg, Blew, Breeze and Raine.

Double vision
Bradford City used to have two players called Johnny Millar on their playing staff at the same time. They often mistakenly picked up each other's wage packet. Grimsby Town had two Charlie Wilsons, and West Bromwich Albion two Bill Richardsons. There were two Billy Owens at Newport County as well at one time. In the 1979–80 season Stoke City had two players named Paul Johnson, and Sheffield Wednesday had a

Mark Smith as did their neighbours Sheffield United.

Family tradition
There have been two instances since the First World War of father and son both winning Division One championship medals: Alec Herd (Manchester City in 1936–37) and David Herd (Manchester United in 1964–65 and 1966–67), and Jack Aston (Manchester United in 1951–52) and John Aston (also United in 1966–67).

Nut-crackers
Barcelona have eliminated more Football League teams from one European cup competition or another than any other Continental club. They defeated Birmingham City and Wolverhampton Wanderers in 1959–60, Sheffield Wednesday in 1961–62, Chelsea 1965–66, Aston Villa and Ipswich Town 1977–78, and Ipswich again in 1978–79.

The March of time
On 9 March 1978, the deadline transfer day, 30 players changed clubs, 21 in cash deals and nine on loan. The nearest to missing such a deadline occurred on 16 March 1967, when inside-forward Bill Atkins was transferred from Halifax Town to Stockport County four seconds before midnight.

Oh! no John
When substitutes were introduced in the Football League in 1965 Plymouth Argyle were technically the first of the 92 clubs to use one. John Newman, now Derby County's assistant manager, was taken ill before the match and substituted by John Hore against Portsmouth.

Willow winners
Six members of FA Cup winning teams since the Second World War also played in first-class cricket: Raich Carter (Derby County 1946) with Derbyshire, Leslie and Denis Compton (Arsenal 1950) with Middlesex, Jack Dyson (Manchester City 1956) with Lancashire, and Jim Standen and Geoff Hurst (West Ham United 1964) with Worcestershire and Essex respectively.

Died with his boots on
Andy Ducat who played for England at soccer and cricket had a longer career simultaneously in the Football League and first-class cricket than any other player in history. As an Arsenal, Aston Villa and Fulham half-back and Surrey batsman he was an all-the-year-round non-stop performer from 1906 to 1924. He died at Lord's in 1942 while batting in a Home Guard representative match.

Show business star Elton John *(top)* has combined his musical talents with rocking the chair at Watford, while Jasper Carrott *(above)* has tuned into the Birmingham City Boardroom. (Syndication International)

Ancient mariners
Robert Walker was a Grimsby Town director for 51 years from 1919 to 1970. Former trawler skipper Jack Evans retired as a director of the club in 1980 after 30 years. He was 82 and had joined the club as a boot and tea boy 70 years previously.

There's no business . . .
Show business personalities are much in evidence

in the game today. Elton John (Watford), Dickie Attenborough (Chelsea), Jasper Carrott (Birmingham City), Eric Sykes (Oldham Athletic) and Charlie Williams (Barnsley) have become directors of League clubs as Tommy Trinder (Fulham), Eric Morecambe (Luton Town) and Norman Wisdom (Brighton and Hove Albion) used to be.

Seven clear itch

Walsall established a post-war record in the 1972–73 season by using seven goalkeepers in Football League matches. Bob Wesson appeared in 23 Division Three games, Dennis Peacock in ten, Glen Johnson, John Osborne and Ian Turner three each and Keith Bell and Jimmy Inger two each.

Preferential treatment

During the last 12 seasons Norwich City have won just three FA Cup ties, but over the same

Bruce Rioch can claim to have had different experiences in different divisions . . . (Colorsport)

Below: The 91st Sheffield derby between Wednesday and United was notable for many reasons, not the least of them that no arrests were made among the almost 50 000 crowd. (Sheffield Newspapers Ltd)

Oxford put pressure on their Light Blue opponents from Cambridge in the 1910 University match. In the 1979 version Maurice Cox produced the fastest goal ever scored at Wembley in 20 seconds.

period in the League Cup they have achieved 26 wins.

Three-quarter movement
English-born at Aldershot but Scottish international midfield player Bruce Rioch has figured in championship-winning teams in three of the four divisions of the Football League. He achieved the first of these honours with Luton Town in Division Four in 1967–68 then with Aston Villa in Division Three in 1971–72 and Derby County in Division One in 1974–75.

The Good Old Days
During the north-east derby between Newcastle United and Sunderland in 1901, fighting broke out between rival supporters in a 50 000 crowd. The corner flags and goal-posts were torn down, the pitch was turned into a ploughed field, and the match was abandoned without a start being made. It happened on Good Friday.

On Boxing Day 1979 a crowd of 49 309 broke the record for a match in Division Three at Hillsborough for the Sheffield derby between Wednesday and United. The police reported neither arrests nor trouble.

Eighteen-year-old 'veteran'
John Sissons was 18 years 214 days old when he played for West Ham United against Preston North End in the 1964 FA Cup Final at Wembley. But it was already the fourth time he had appeared there. His first visit had been as a member of the England schoolboys against Wales, and the next two occasions had been for England youth teams against Ireland and the Rest of Europe.

Blue flash
The fastest goal recorded at Wembley was in the University match on 5 December 1979 when Maurice Cox scored for Cambridge against Oxford 20 seconds after the kick-off. Oxford eventually won 3–1.

Cox was the only player on the field with Football League experience, having made his debut for Torquay United as a non-contract player in April 1979 when he scored against Scunthorpe United. He turned professional with them in January 1980.

The famous five
On 21 November 1923 Millwall were reported to have offered £50 000 for the Raith Rovers forward line of Bell, Miller, Jennings, James and Archibald. Another version was that Raith wanted £50 000 and it was too high a price for Millwall, considering the record fee at the time was £5500. In the 1925–26 season Alex James was transferred himself to Preston North End for £3250, and Raith were relegated at the end of the season.

The Callender brothers Tom *(above)* **and Jack were truly men for all seasons . . .**

Men for all seasons

Two of the most consistent players for Gateshead in the early post-war years were the Callender brothers Tom and Jack. Jack was chiefly a right-half and joined the club in 1942, and had made 470 Football League appearances up to 1957–58. Tom had made his debut in the League for Lincoln City in 1938–39, making 23 appearances. He joined Gateshead in 1945 and captained them from centre-half. In one period of eight years he missed only two Leagues games. A penalty expert, he scored ten in one season in 1949–50. He made 439 League appearances for them up to 1956–57.

United Nations XI

Charlton Athletic are the first club to have had players from a full team of foreign countries. At one time or another they have had recruits born in Mexico, Jamaica, Singapore, India, New Zealand, South Africa, Nigeria, Italy, Denmark, Sweden and Holland.

Max the first

Until the First World War Max Seeburg, a Tottenham Hotspur inside-forward, was the only German to have played in the Football League. Since the Second World War these German-born players have all appeared in the competition: Alec Eisentrager (Bristol City), Bert Trautmann (Manchester City), Dietmar Bruck and Wilf Smith (both Coventry City), Ray Tunks (Preston North End), George Berry (Wolverhampton Wanderers), and Ian MacDonald (Carlisle United).

Seeburg, an inside-forward or outside-left, had

appeared in Division Two as early as 1908–09. Born in Leipzig he had a spell with Cheshunt before joining Chelsea. He made his Division Two debut with Spurs, and in the following season 1909–10 he joined Leyton. He returned to the Football League with Burnley in 1910–11, making 17 appearances, and added 20 more with Grimsby Town the next season. He finished with Reading in the Southern League in 1912–13, making eight appearances. Seeburg was probably the first foreigner to play in the Football League.

Handy Andy

Andy Davidson holds the record for the longest spell any Scot had on the pay-roll of a Football League club in the period since the Second World War. As a player originally, and then on the administrative staff, he was with Hull City from 1947 to 1980.

Born in Douglas Water, he came from a foot-balling family. His elder brother, David Davidson, was also a Hull City outside-left, and his cousin Jimmy played for Partick Thistle and Scotland.

Andy Davidson came to Boothferry Park, Hull, in February 1947, and after one trial match was taken on the ground staff. But in the public practice match he broke his right leg at the age of 16 and was out of the game for nine months. At 18 he was called up for national service in the Royal Air Force, but eventually played his first League game at centre-forward against Blackburn Rovers in the 1952–53 season, though he had previously played as a wing-half. Within a month of his demobilisation he was the first team centre-half, but broke his left leg at Swansea in January 1953 and was out of action again for a further nine months; at one time Davidson seemed likely to have to retire completely.

In November 1953 he came back in the 'A' side and broke his leg in the same place. He was 20. One year later he turned out for the reserves and was back in first team action before the end of the season. But in the 1955–56 season he established himself as a regular choice, and in 1967 had completed a club record 511 League appearances.

Fancy seeing you

In the Football League Cup Final in 1966 Martin Peters was a member of the West Ham United team which defeated West Bromwich Albion. In the Albion team was Tony Brown, and he was also in their side in a fourth round tie against Norwich City for whom Peters was playing in 1979–80.

Pies high and dry

The smallest crowd at any FA Cup Final in this century was 20 470 at a Bolton replay between Sheffield United and Tottenham Hotspur in 1901. Thousands of spectators stayed away because of fear of the crush, leaving hundreds of meat pies left unsold and given away.

One in three

Ambrose Fogarty, a Dublin-born inside-forward, was sent off in all three national competitions. He was dismissed playing for Sunderland in the FA Cup against Everton in January 1958, and with Hartlepools United against Barnsley in Division Four in October 1965, and against Bradford Park Avenue in the Football League Cup in August 1966.

Seven-month itch

Jim Smith, Newcastle United's Scottish inter-national forward, was sent off twice in home matches in the same year. On both occasions it was in a cup tie. The first dismissal occurred against Torino in the Anglo–Italian tournament on 2 May 1973, and the second in a Texaco Cup match with Birmingham City on 5 December.

Slow Burns

Swindon Town defeated Newcastle United in the FA Cup in the 1928–29 season and Ipswich Town in the same competition in 1947–48. In both matches the opposing goalkeeper was the same Mick Burns.

Cup tradition

Starting with a game against Luton Town in the 1938–39 season, Liverpool won all the 16 FA Cup ties they played at Anfield before being beaten there by Huddersfield Town in 1954–55.

Two times four

Tranmere Rovers are the only club to figure in ties that needed four meetings in both the FA Cup and Football League Cup. They defeated Blyth Spartans in the second round in 1951–52 at the fourth attempt and had a similar experience against Chester in the second round of the 1968–69 League Cup.

Quick bouncer

Alan Ball scored in the first minute in different Football League matches against the same team on the same ground. Playing for Arsenal against West Ham United at Highbury on 29 August 1972, he scored in 40 seconds and then after 55 seconds on 20 March 1976.

He also claims to have been in four winning teams in League games against Liverpool at

Alan Ball *(above)* became Blackpool's manager in 1979–80, though he was still a Southampton colleague of Charlie George earlier in the season. (Syndication International)

Anfield, with Everton in March 1970 and Arsenal in February 1973, April 1974 and November 1974.

Never a dull moment (2)
Charlie George was sent off on the first and last days of the 1976–77 season, at Newcastle on 21 August and at home to Ipswich on 14 May. In an away match at Middlesbrough on 15 January 1977, also playing for Derby County, he had a penalty given against him for shirt-pulling on David Mills, was booked for a foul, and then conceded an own goal in attempting to clear a centre from David Armstrong.

Treble red
Phil Boyer was sent off in three League Cup ties, with Norwich City v Sheffield United in November 1974, and with Southampton v Crystal Palace in August 1977 and Leeds United in January 1979.

Never looked back
George Hardwick put through his own goal on his debut for Middlesbrough against Bolton Wanderers in December 1937. But ten years later he made his

George Hardwick began by putting through his own goal as a full-back and finished it by scoring goals for his own side as a centre-forward. (Syndication International)

Quick off the mark
Five players achieved hat-tricks on their League debuts during the 1946–47 season: Jesse Pye (Wolverhampton Wanderers), George Robledo (Barnsley), Melvyn Daniel (Luton Town), Dennis Thompson (Hull City), and Maurice Owen (Swindon Town)

Jesse Pye *(left)* was a hat-trickster on his debut as was Maurice Owen, a wartime member of the famous Chindits. (Colorsport)

international debut and went on to captain England and complete 13 appearances. He finished his League career as a forward with Oldham Athletic.

Oldest inhabitant
Jim Langley, born in February 1929, became the oldest player seen in a Football League Cup final when he appeared at left-back in the Queen's Park Rangers side which defeated West Bromwich Albion at Wembley on 4 March 1967. He also became the oldest in an FA Challenge Trophy final when he turned out for Hillingdon Borough against Telford United on 1 May 1971.

Wembley dismissals
Only four players have been sent off in first-class matches at Wembley: Antonio Rattin (Argentina) against England in July 1966, Gilbert Dresch (Luxembourg) in March 1977 also against England, and Billy Bremner (Leeds United) and Kevin Keegan (Liverpool) in an FA Charity Shield match in August 1974.

Yugoslavian invasion
The influx of players from Yugoslavia into the Football League during the past three years has included: Bosco Jankovic (Middlesbrough), Ivan Golac (Southampton), Petar Borota (Chelsea), Ivan Katalinic (Southampton), Dragoslav Stepa-

novic (Manchester City), Nikolai Jovanovic (Manchester United) and Radojka Avramovic (Notts County).

Giant-killers supreme
Yeovil Town have reached the third round of the FA Cup on nine occasions: 1934–35, 1937–38, 1938–39, 1948–49, 1949–50, 1956–57, 1963–64, 1970–71 and 1979–80. Since the Second World War they have eliminated Football League clubs including Bury, Sunderland, Gillingham, Walsall, Southend United, Crystal Palace, Bournemouth and Brentford. But Peterborough United, before they entered the League in 1960, claimed eight victims: Torquay United, Aldershot, Bradford Park Avenue, Lincoln City, Ipswich Town (twice), Shrewsbury Town and Walsall.

It's a knock-out racket
World heavy-weight boxing champion Joe Louis once signed for Liverpool, tennis champion Fred Perry for Arsenal and comedian George Robey for Millwall.

Forecasting
The 1947–48 and 1962–63 seasons provided the post-war extremes in postponements due to adverse weather conditions. There were only six in the former season, but 307 in the other.

The stopper
Herbert John Emery, a Welshman, saved nine out of ten penalty kicks he faced in Rotherham United first and reserve team matches in the 1929–30 season.

Home disadvantage
No other club has played Football League home matches as far afield as Crystal Palace and Millwall have done due to their grounds being under suspension. In November 1920 Palace met Exeter City at Southampton, and in April 1978 Millwall's 'Home' game against Bristol Rovers was played at Portsmouth.

Trekking north
Of all FA Cup ties since the Second World War before the third round, the one involving the longest single journey was a second round match in the 1954-55 season. Torquay United had to travel from Devon to Northumberland to fulfil the fixture with Blyth Spartans.

Three in one
Three ties in the FA Cup first round were played simultaneously in the Essex town of Leyton on 22 November 1952: Leyton Orient v Bristol Rovers, Leyton v Hereford United and Leytonstone v Watford.

Moore, Moore and Moore
Bobby Moore was involved in cup winning teams at Wembley in three successive seasons: with West Ham United in the 1963–64 FA Cup, and Cup Winners Cup in 1964–65, and England in the 1966 World Cup.

Discrimination
Since the Second World War England have played five full international matches, and Northern Ireland two others at Everton's Goodison Park. But during this period the ground has never been chosen for an FA Cup semi-final apart from replays.

Not you again!
Halifax Town met Hartlepools United in three successive seasons in the FA Cup on the same ground in 1933–34, 1934–35 and 1935–36, and drew 1–1 at home on each occasion. Leeds United were beaten 2–1 at home by Cardiff City in the same competition in seasons 1955–56, 1956–57 and 1957–58.

Consistent
Sheffield Wednesday played 32 consecutive times at Hillsborough in the FA Cup without defeat.

After losing to Everton in the 1920–21 season they won 20 and drew 12 other games before being beaten by Preston North End in the 1946–47 season.

Final debutants
When Bill Whittaker (Charlton Athletic 1947), Johnny Crosland (Blackpool 1948), and Sam Ellis (Sheffield Wednesday 1966) figured in FA Cup final teams none of them had previously appeared in the competition in any match.

Not at home
Shrewsbury Town were drawn away in all the first five rounds of the FA Cup proper in the 1964–65 season against King's Lynn, Exeter City, Manchester City, Millwall and Leeds United.

Never to return?
Relegation from Division One has to date meant no return since the Second World War for Brentford who descended in 1947, Grimsby Town in 1948, Charlton Athletic in 1957, Portsmouth in 1959, Preston North End in 1961, Cardiff City in 1962, and Orient in 1963.

Short, not sweet
More than 200 different non-league clubs have figured in the FA Cup since the Second World War. The one with the shortest name, Ware (Hertfordshire) were beaten 6–1 by Luton Town in the first round of the 1968–69 competition.

The half Nelson
Arsenal full-back Sammy Nelson had already played in eight full international matches for Northern Ireland by the time he had made six League appearances for his club.

Haven't we met?
Everton and Sheffield Wednesday have been drawn together more times in the FA Cup than any other pair of clubs in history. They have clashed in eleven ties in 1892–93, 1894–95, 1895–96, 1905–06, 1906–07, 1920–21, 1936–37, 1946–47, 1953–54, 1964–65 and 1965–66, when they met in the final.

Left foot forward
Among the left-footed goalkeepers operating in the Football League during the 1979–80 season were: Ray Clemence (Liverpool), Paul Bradshaw (Wolverhampton Wanderers), Paul Cooper and Laurie Sivell (both Ipswich Town), Kevin Keelan (Norwich City), Mark Wallington (Leicester City), Geoff Crudgington (Swansea City) and David Lawson (Stockport County).

We have ways

Swindon Town's ground was once surrounded with barbed wire to keep people from getting out. During the Second World War it was used as a prisoner-of-war camp until May 1945.

The lights that failed

Football League clubs who have been compelled to postpone or abandon matches because of electric power failure in their floodlighting systems are Tottenham Hotspur, Ipswich Town, Middlesbrough, Chelsea, Orient, Watford, Mansfield Town, Aldershot and Shrewsbury Town.

Two into four

The Nicholl brothers are arguably the only pair who each figured in all four divisions of the Football League. Chris served Halifax Town, Luton Town, Aston Villa, and was still with Southampton in 1979–80 while Terry, his younger brother, played for Crewe Alexandra, Sheffield United, Southend United, and was with Gillingham in 1979–80.

Anfield aristocrats

In the last 15 seasons up to the end of the 1979–80 season Liverpool have never been lower than fifth in Division One, an unequalled record for the Football League.

Kevin Keelan, the Norwich City goalkeeper, who came close to reaching the record of League appearances for the club during the 1979–80 season when he took his total to 571. (Colorsport)

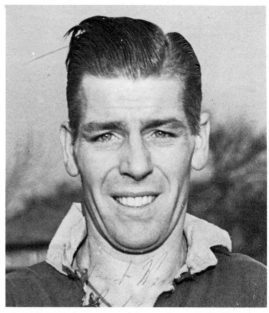

Jack Connor was something of a latecomer to the business of scoring goals in the Football League, but was quick to make his presence felt among opposing defences.

Never too old

Jack Connor did not emerge as a first-class centre-forward until the latter part of the Second World War when he was already in his middle 20s; and when after five seasons with Stockport County he had scored a club record 132 League goals, he was 36 years old.

Though born in Lancashire he became a professional with Ipswich Town, and in 1945–46 during war service he made guest appearances for Carlisle United. Transferred to Carlisle in December 1946 he spent two seasons there before moving to the Irish League club Ards. But in December 1948 he linked up with Rochdale when aged 29, and in the next nine seasons took his total of League goals to 201 with Bradford City and finally Crewe Alexandra, after leaving Stockport in September 1956.

Down among the Z men

One of the most unusually named players to have appeared in the Football League was Zechariah G March, an outside-left who was 5ft 6½in (1·69m) tall and was generally known as Zill or Zachy. Born in Bosham, Sussex, he joined Brighton and Hove Albion in 1913 during their Southern League days. He made two appearances that season and was still with them when they entered the Football League in 1920–21. He was transferred to Portsmouth in 1922.

Index

OTHER GUINNESS SUPERLATIVES TITLES

Facts and Feats Series

Air Facts and Feats, *3rd ed.*
John W R Taylor, Michael J H
Taylor and David Mondey
Rail Facts and Feats, *3rd ed.*
John Marshall
Tank Facts and Feats, *3rd ed.*
Kenneth Macksey
Car Facts and Feats, *3rd ed.*
edited by Anthony Harding
Yachting Facts and Feats
Peter Johnson
Motorboating Facts and Feats
Kevin Desmond
Motorcycling Facts and Feats
L J K Setright

Film Facts and Feats
Patrick Robertson
Golf Facts and Feats
Donald Steel
Business World
Henry Button and Andrew
Lampert
Music Facts and Feats
Robert and Celia Dearling with
Brian Rust
Art Facts and Feats
John FitzMaurice Mills
The Guinness Book of Antiques
John FitzMaurice Mills

Animal Facts and Feats, *2nd ed.*
Gerald L Wood FZS
**Mountains and Mountaineering
Facts and Feats**
Edward Pyatt
Plant Facts and Feats
William G Duncalf
**Structures – Bridges, Towers,
Tunnels, Dams . . .**
John H Stephens
Weather Facts and Feats
Ingrid Holford
Astronomy Facts and Feats
Patrick Moore

Guide Series

French Country Cooking
Christian Roland Délu

Game Fishing
Dr William Currie

Freshwater Angling
Brian Harris and Paul Boyer

Saltwater Angling
Brian Harris

Field Sports
Wilson Stephens

Equestrianism
Dorian Williams

Grand Prix Motor Racing
Eric Dymock

Motorcycling
Peter Carrick

Bicycling
J Durry and J B Wadley
Waterways of Western Europe
Hugh McKnight
Water Skiing
David Nations OBE and
Kevin Desmond
Steeplechasing
Richard Pitman and
Gerry Cranham

Other Titles

Guinness Book of Answers,
3rd ed.
edited by Norris D McWhirter
The Guinness Book of Records
edited by Norris D McWhirter
The Guinness Book of 1952
Kenneth Macksey
The Guinness Book of 1953
Kenneth Macksey
The Guinness Book of 1954
Kenneth Macksey
Kings, Rulers and Statesmen
Clive Carpenter
Derby 200
Michael Seth-Smith
and Roger Mortimer

History of Land Warfare
Kenneth Macksey
History of Sea Warfare
Lt-Cmdr Gervis Frere-Cook
and Kenneth Macksey
History of Air Warfare
David Brown, Christopher
Shores and Kenneth Macksey
English Furniture 1760–1900
Geoffrey Wills
English Pottery and Porcelain
Geoffrey Wills
Antique Firearms
Frederick Wilkinson
AAA Centenary '
Peter Lovesey

The Guinness Book of Names
Leslie Dunkling
100 Years of Wimbledon
Lance Tingay
**The Guinness Book of British
Hit Singles,** *2nd ed.*
edited by Tim and Jo Rice, Paul
Gambaccini and Mike Read
Hits of the 70s
Tim and Jo Rice, Paul
Gambaccini and Mike Read
**The Guinness Book of World
Autographs**
Ray Rawlins
**The Guinness Book of
Winners and Champions**
Chris Cook

Britain's Natural Heritage

Wild Flowers
Mary Briggs, FPS, FLS

Woodland Birds
Michael Everett

EUROPEAN SURVEY 1979/80

	Champions Matches	Points	Clubs in division	Most wins	Fewest defeats	Most goals
Italy	Internazionale 30	41	16	Juventus 16	Internazionale 3	Internazionale 44
Liechtenstein	(No national league competition. Clubs play in Swiss Regional leagues.					
Luxembourg	Jeunesse d'Esch 22	33	12	Jeunesse d'Esch 16	Progres Niedercorn 3	Progres Niedercorn 58
Malta	Valletta 18	31	10	Valletta 14	Valletta 1	Valletta 59
Netherlands	Ajax 34	50	18	Ajax 22	Ajax, Feyenoord 6	Ajax, AZ 67 77
Norway	Viking Stavanger 22	32	12	Viking Stavanger 13	Viking Stavanger 3	Moss 41
Poland	Szombierki Bytom 30	39	16	Szombierki Bytom 16	Szombierki Bytom, Widzew Lodz 7	Wisla Krakow 58
Portugal	Sporting Lisbon 30	52	16	Sporting Lisbon 24	Sporting Lisbon, Porto 2	Benfica 79
Rumania	Uni. Craiova 34	44	18	Baia Mare 18	Uni. Craiova, Steaua 7	Steaua 74
Scotland	Aberdeen 36	48	10	Aberdeen 19	Aberdeen, Celtic 7	Aberdeen 68
Spain	Real Madrid 34	53	18	Real Madrid 22	Real Sociedad 1	Real Madrid 70
Sweden	Halmstad 26	36	14	Elfsborg Boras 14	Halmstad 2	Hammarby 46
Switzerland	Basle* 36	33	14	(No comparison feasible, see footnote)		
Turkey	Trabzonspor 30	39	16	Rizespor 14	Trabzonspor 3	Rizespor 37
USSR	Spartak Moscow 34	50	18	Spartak Moscow, Dynamo Kiev 21	Spartak Moscow, Dynamo Tbilisi 3	Spartak Moscow 66
Wales	No national league competition					
Yugoslavia	Red Star Belgrade 34	48	18	Red Star Belgrade 19	Red Star Belgrade 5	Sarajevo 55

* Basle's record after 26 matches in qualifying table and 10 more in top 6 clubs play-offs in which half of their qualifying points total are added to those gained in the play-offs, hence only 33 points achieved.